St. Michael the Archangel Parish

Dear Friends,

The book you now hold chronicles the history of the Archdiocese of Baltimore, which includes the story of the establishment of the Roman Catholic Church in the United States. St. Michael the Archangel is a part of that broader history and this volume shows how our parish community fits into the larger picture of the Church in the Archdiocese of Baltimore.

The history of St. Michael the Archangel parish dates to April 14, 1913 when property was purchased in Overlea for a new Catholic church. In the fall of 1914, Bishop Owen Corrigan presided at the blessing and laying of the cornerstone for the church with Fr. John J. Dillon, the first pastor. In 1926 the present upper church was completed and dedicated to accommodate the growing community. That same year, St. Michael's opened its school, staffed by the Ursuline sisters, in the lower church building. There were 140 students initially enrolled. Fr. Gilbert MacDonald was pastor.

Msgr. William Sauer oversaw a period of great expansion. During his pastorate, the new school building, convent and rectory were completed in 1950. The Daughters of Charity arrived to staff the parish school.

In 1958 the parish acquired several residential properties and in 1959 ground was broken for St. Catherine Labouré Hall, which opened the following fall.

The main church was renovated in 1968 during the pastorate of Msgr. John Dunn. In 1981, during the pastorate of Fr. Robert Armstrong, the church underwent a major restoration and was rededicated by Archbishop William D. Borders. On May 20, 2006 Cardinal William H. Keeler rededicated the sanctuary which was reconfigured and redecorated.

Our historic church building is a house of God and the house of God's people. St. Michael the Archangel's mission is to "joyfully proclaim the presence of Jesus to the total community," a mission that dates back to the 1980's and remains a central focus in the many ministries and outreaches of our parish. St. Michael's remains an anchor in the Overlea-Fullerton community and a visible testimony to a faith that is alive and strong.

May God love and bless you,

Fr. James Proffitt
Pastor

First &
Forever

THE ARCHDIOCESE OF BALTIMORE

A People's History

by Rafael Alvarez

In memory

of my Catholic grandmothers

Frances Prato Alvarez

of Our Lady of Pompei & Holy Redeemer Chapel

and

Anna Potter Jones

a lifelong parishioner of St. Casimir

Foreword

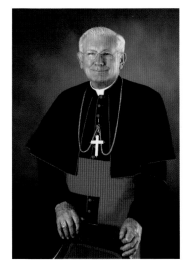

Dear Friends,

It gives me great pleasure to present First and Forever, a book that reveals the rich history of the Catholic Church in Baltimore, as told by the many people whose lives have been uniquely shaped by the Church in this historic Archdiocese.

While scholarly works such as Thomas Spalding's, The Premier See, provide a great deal of historical detail about the founding and development of the Archdiocese of Baltimore, First and Forever blends a unique contrast of historical account and compelling narrative to reveal the colorful history of our Church through the stories of those who lived it.

Author Rafael Alvarez, who some years ago accepted the challenge of capturing this history, writes with great sensitivity and depth, as he takes readers on a nostalgic journey through the pages of this book. Timeless photographs provide a vivid complement to the many touching accounts, guiding the reader through the historic times of Archhbishop John Carroll, Cardinal James Gibbons and Archbishop Michael Curley, while stopping to witness what it was like "growing up Catholic" in the Archdiocese of Baltimore.

I am grateful to the many people who labored in producing this book and pray that it will instill in all those who read it, a sense of the proud history of our Church and a connection with the many people, past and present, whose lives so richly impacted the history of the Archdiocese of Baltimore.

Sincerely yours in Christ,

Archbishop of Baltimore

Published by
Éditions du Signe
B.P. 94 – 67038 Strasbourg – Cedex 2 – France
Tel (+33) 388 789 191
Fax (+33) 388 789 199
info@editionsdusigne.fr

▪ ▪ ▪

Publishing Director
Christian Riehl

Director of Publication
Joëlle Bernhard

Publishing Assistant
Marc de Jong

▪ ▪ ▪

Design and Layout
Sylvie Tusinski

Photographers
Frantizek Zvardon
John Glover

▪ ▪ ▪

Photoengraving
Atelier du Signe - 104362

▪ ▪ ▪

Copyright Text
Archdiocese of Baltimore

1958 St. Patrick's Day Parade,
Baltimore; (l to r): Gov. Theodore
McKeldin, Edward J. Morris, and
Abp. Keough.
Credit: © 1958, reprinted with the
permission of *The Baltimore Sun*

Table of contents

CHAPTER
1
The Colony of Maryland

*"Growing up in Baltimore,
I thought everybody was Catholic..."*

Marguerite Patricia Gilner

It began as a nation unto itself.

Founded in 1789 to encompass the original 13 states, the Diocese of Baltimore grew along with the infant United States of America. By the time the Louisiana purchase was complete in 1804, parishes under the authority of the Premier See in Baltimore stretched west from both shores of the Chesapeake Bay to the edge of Idaho and zigzagged down from the Canadian border to the parishes of New Orleans.

The reach of the first archbishop, John Carroll, descended from the Catholic elite of Maryland's founders, nearly extended from the islands of Maine to the islands of the Caribbean.

In total: some 800,000 square miles.

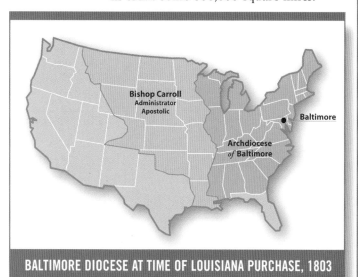

BALTIMORE DIOCESE AT TIME OF LOUISIANA PURCHASE, 1803

This is how the current archbishop, Cardinal William H. Keeler, number 14 in a direct line from John Carroll, tells the story.

"On November 6, 1790, life began to change dramatically for a priest named John Carroll of Maryland. Called by Pope Pius VI to be the first Bishop of Baltimore, [Carroll] found himself with a diocese embracing the 13 original States and the Northwest Territory, including most of what we call the Midwest today. By 1804, the Louisiana Purchase had been negotiated, and the Diocese of New Orleans was added to his responsibilities. The Catholic people living in what today are 36 of the United States looked to Bishop Carroll as their shepherd in the Lord. In his early decisions we find a legacy that still guides and inspires us in service to Church and Nation."

Like St. Clement's Island in the Potomac River, where the first settlers landed with Leonard Calvert and his family's dream of government prosperity and religious freedom, the physical size of the diocese has shrunk considerably in the 213 years since its creation.

Since 1634, when Calvert led some 150 settlers to Maryland, St. Clement's Island has eroded from 400 acres to a mere 40 today. From 1789, when Pope Pius VI made John Carroll the first bishop in the United States, the expanse of the original diocese centered in Baltimore has been whittled down to the city for which it is named and nine surrounding counties.

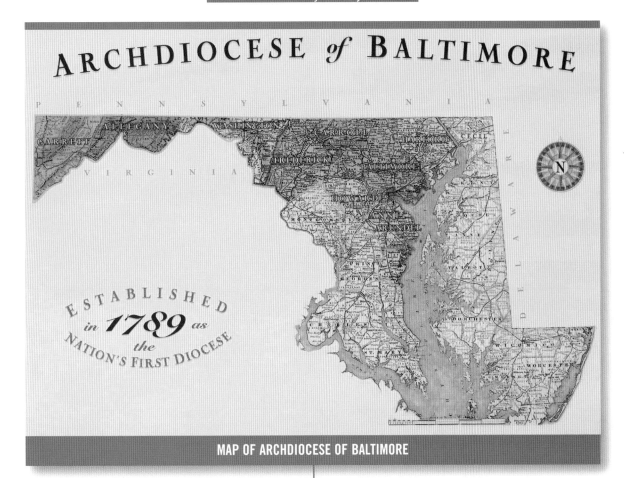

MAP OF ARCHDIOCESE OF BALTIMORE

Honored as the nation's Premier See, second only in the New World to the Primatial See of Santo Domingo, the Archdiocese of Baltimore now numbers 162 parishes and missions, serving a total Catholic population of over 500,000 people.

"We are called to believe," says Sister Irene Mary Pryle, SSND, principal of Our Lady of Hope/St. Luke School in Dundalk, "but our faith in God and other people must be nurtured."

The local story of this nurturing begins in late 1633 about 14 years after the landing of the Pilgrims at Plymouth Rock, a time when persecution by the Church of England kept the Catholic minority throughout Britain and its empire from practicing their faith openly.

George Calvert, the first Lord Baltimore, sought a land charter along the Chesapeake - a paradise compared to his original charter in Newfoundland - from King James I.

George reached the coast of Virginia while researching possible sites along the Chesapeake but, in what would prove symbolic of the struggles to come, refused to take the required loyalty oath and did not get off the ship.

Permission to settle in Maryland was granted two months after George's death in 1632.

Upon his passing, the title Lord Baltimore and responsibility to finish negotiating the charter passed to his eldest son Cecil, who organized 17 Catholic investors to launch the colony.

The second Lord Baltimore was kept so busy defending his family's plans from repeated attacks in England; he never made it to Maryland.

CECIL CALVERT, SECOND LORD BALTIMORE

Credit: portrait by Florence Mackubin Courtesy of Enoch Pratt Free Library

In the summer of 2001, art conservators from the Yale Center for British Art took a portrait of Cecil Calvert to New Haven, Connecticut for a show called: *Great British Paintings from American Collections: Holbein to Hockney.*

According to Tom Chalkley, who wrote about the portraits of the six Lords Baltimore that hang in the lobby of the Enoch Pratt Free Library on Cathedral Street, the painting of Cecil by Gerard Soest "really is a great painting."

Soest, according to Chalkley, "captured a rugged face, tight lips, and a sharp glance to one side; the nobleman looks tough and wary, but tired. Under a long velvety coat, he wears what we might call a dress, with gold embroidery rendered in great detail and authentic light. Unlike the other five portraits, Soest's masterpiece features two smaller figures that give the picture both balance and interest. Stepping in from the left, a black servant gazes down at a small child, who gestures at a map of Maryland."

The charter gave Lord Baltimore sovereign authority over the new colony with the most important power being the right to enact laws. In the spirit of his father, Cecil used this right to establish religious toleration, to start a colony where it was not only safe to be Catholic, it was safe to do so side-by-side with those who were not.

The charter also allowed the Calverts to appoint all officials; control the courts, militia, feudal manors, trade, taxes and custom duties; and own all lands.

Leonard Calvert [1610-to-1647], George's second son, was chosen to implement this "pious enterprise," and left the Isle of Wight in late 1633 with some 150 English settlers. Setting out in ships christened the Ark and the Dove, they sailed for a land they called "The Wished-For Country."

Leonard sailed with strict conditions for the new colony laid out by his brother Cecil, guidelines on topics ranging from the planting of corn to trading with the natives to the conduct of worship services.

Catholics were cautioned against public displays of their faith or discussing religion with Protestants, who outnumbered the Catholics nearly 5-to-1.

Be good to the non-Catholics, Cecil counseled his brother, and do not try to evangelize them.

Among the Catholic minority were three Jesuits --Father Andrew White, Father John Altham, and a lay brother, Thomas Gervase-- none of whom boarded the Ark until the ship's pilot had gotten off after guiding the ship through the Thames.

After stops in Barbados and Old Point Comfort, Va., the former warship Ark and the much smaller Dove sailed into the Chesapeake Bay and some 25 miles up the Potomac River.

On March 25, 1634, the ships were in sight of three islands near the mainland shore of what would become Maryland. Anchors were dropped at the largest island, which was promptly named for Saint Clement, the patron saint of sailors on whose feast day the settlers had departed the previous November.

THE PLANTING OF THE COLONY OF MARYLAND
Credit: portrait by Francis Blackwell Mayer.

GEORGE CALVERT

First Lord Baltimore [1580 (ca.) - 1632]

The great ideal of George Calvert's life --community based on religious tolerance-- grew out of his weariness for a century of European wars in the name of God.

A favorite of King James I of England, George was born in Kiplin, the first son of an obscure family from North Riding, Yorkshire. George came of age during a time when the Spanish Armada was defeated, and Shakespeare triumphed.

His family seems to have abandoned Catholicism around 1590, which enabled George to attend Trinity College, Oxford, where he gained status through education and soon added political savvy to his resume.

George gained the notice of Sir Robert Cecil, minister to King James I, and began working for Cecil as a secretary. Through hard work and shrewdness, George won the favor of the King and was knighted in 1617.

Two years later he was appointed principal secretary of state. He was also a member of Parliament, representing his native Yorkshire in 1621 and Oxford in 1624.

George's knowledge and integrity won him wide respect and the reward of substantial grants - both in money and land - from King James and, after him, King Charles I.

In 1621, King James granted George 2,300 acres in County Longford, Ireland, on one condition, a stipulation that rubbed George the wrong way, a thorn that would influence the history of North America.

All settlers on the Calvert estate, James decreed: "Should be conformable in point of religion."

In 1624, George re-embraced the Catholicism of his forebears. At the time, anti-Catholic legislation was underway in Parliament, and George responded by surrendering his Irish manor and resigning from the secretaryship of England.

But George was too good to lose. So fond of Calvert was James that the king returned the manor, minus the religious clause; retained him in the Privy Council and, in 1625, elevated him to Baron Baltimore in County Longford.

Several years earlier, in 1620, Lord Baltimore bought a plantation in Newfoundland, named it Avalon, and ruled with near-royal authority. Visiting his holdings in 1627 in the company of two priests, George hoped to establish a colony where all might enjoy the freedom to worship as they chose.

He returned the following spring with his family, including Lady Baltimore, his second wife, and some 40 colonists, including a Catholic priest. Sometime in this year, 1628, Calvert requested a new grant in a less harsh climate. Before the King decided, George traveled to Virginia and, as a Roman Catholic, was rudely received.

He returned to England and at first received from King Charles I a grant of land south of the James River. Not wanting to fight and endure anti-Catholic persecution from the Virginians, who would later bedevil his heirs for the same reasons, George won from the court vast and unprecedented powers to govern broad holdings on both sides of the Chesapeake Bay.

Before the charter was sealed, however, George Calvert died.

When finally approved on June 20, 1632, it became the means of translating into reality the first Lord Baltimore's dream of American colonization.

In the Calvert charter, the name of Maryland, "Terra Mariae" appeared for the first time and leadership passed to his son Cecil Calvert, the Second Lord Baltimore.

Not only was it the first day of spring, but also the Feast of the Annunciation of the Blessed Virgin, good signs for the voyagers, who had survived 123 days at sea.

Leonard claimed the land in "solemn possession of the Country for our Savior and for our Sovereign Lord the King of England" and declared it a "sanctuary."

Mass was celebrated that same day when Father White ordered the construction of a cross from trees on the island. In the shadow of that rough cross took place the first sacrifice of the Mass in the Original Thirteen English Colonies.

Some 60 years earlier, Spanish explorers had also settled near the Chesapeake and no doubt consecrated the Eucharist to praise the Creator for such a bounty.

But the Spaniards were annihilated by natives. However, these same tribes, notably the Piscataways, received Father White and his fellow Englishmen with friendship and grace.

Leonard Calvert, a forceful man whose governorship was just short of a monarchy, was especially interested in the support and regulation of trade with the Indians. In the summer of 1634 he dispatched the Dove, loaded with corn, to Boston to trade for fish and other stores.

Much of the good will between the colonists and the Indians can be attributed to Father White.

Remembered as a patient man, Father White worked for ten years with the natives, preparing a grammar/dictionary and Catechism in their native tongue, the first Englishman to distill an Indian language into grammatical form.

In the Lauinger Memorial Library at Georgetown University in Washington are several pages of prayers in the Piscataway language in Father White's hand. The manuscript arrived at the university's archives in 1953 from the Jesuit residence in Leonardtown.

FATHER WHITE CELEBRATES MASS ON ST. CLEMENT'S ISLAND.

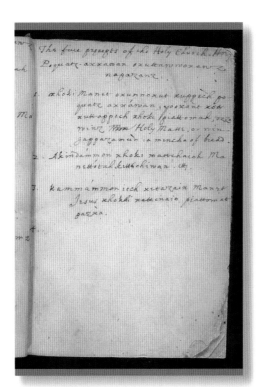

PRAYERS IN PISCATAWAY

Credit: Lauinger Library, Georgetown University.

Several pages of Catholic prayer translated into the Piscataway language in the original manuscript by the Rev. Andrew White.

CATHOLIC AMERICAN FIRSTS IN BALTIMORE

■ First Roman Catholic Diocese in the United States. The Rev. John Carroll named the nation's first bishop. **1789.**

■ First seminary in the nation for the training of priests, St. Mary's, established in downtown Baltimore by the Sulpicians. **1791.**

■ In **1793**, worshippers coming together in the name of St. Francis Xavier become first African-American Catholic Eucharistic community in the U.S., evolving into the nation's first black Catholic parish in **1863**.

■ Cornerstone for the first Catholic cathedral in the United States, the Basilica of the Assumption of the Blessed Virgin Mary, is set in place by Bishop John Carroll on July 7, **1806**.

■ Elizabeth Ann Seton, the first native-born American to be canonized a saint **(1975)**, laid the foundations in Baltimore for Catholic parochial education in the U.S. in the first decade of the 19th century.

■ St. Frances Academy, still in operation, becomes the first Catholic school for African-American children. **1828.**

■ The Oblate Sisters of Providence become the first community of Roman Catholic nuns of African descent. **1829**.

■ At St. James the Less Church on Aisquith Street, future bishop John Neumann becomes the first Redemptorist to take the vows of a priest in the United States. **1842**. Neumann became the first American bishop to be canonized a saint. **1977**.

■ Charles Uncles becomes the first African-American priest ordained in the United States. Father Uncles takes his vows at the Basilica before Cardinal James Gibbons. **1891**.

■ The College of Notre Dame of Maryland on North Charles Street becomes the first Roman Catholic college for women officially chartered in the United States. **1896**.

■ Prior to the Second Vatican Council, Baltimore was the site of the first Commission for Christian Unity in the U.S. **1961**.

REV. CHARLES RANDOLPH UNCLES

Charles Uncles became the first African-American ordained in the United States and was one of five priests who founded the Josephite Fathers, who had been given the ministry of Negro missions in the U.S. by Pope Pius IX.

In his yearly *"Account of the Colony of the Lord Baron of Baltimore,"* penned as much as an advertisement for potential settlers as an official record of life in Maryland, Father White wrote of his accomplishments amongst the various tribes to whom he brought the Gospel.

In the wake of Father White's successes, and the excitement they engendered, Jesuits throughout Europe began clamoring for permission to do missionary work in the New World.

In fact, by 1763 there were six large Jesuit estates in the Maryland area: Bohemia near the Cecil County/Delaware line where John Carroll was schooled; St. Thomas Manor in Charles County; St. Francis Xavier at Newtown, recently restored to its 18th century appearance; St. Inigoes in St. Mary's County; White Marsh in Prince George's County; and Priest Neale's Mass House at Deer Creek in Harford County. In all, Jesuit holdings in Maryland were 12,000 acres.

Founded in 1641, St. Ignatius is one of the oldest Catholic parishes in continuous service in the U.S. Fr. Andrew White settled among the Indians at Chapel Point, learned to speak their language, and soon baptized their Chief. After the American Revolution, the current church was built in 1798 and was blessed by fellow Jesuit, John Carroll. Though suppressed worldwide in 1773, the Society of Jesus was restored in America by those who took their vows in this church in 1805. Saddle priests rode from Inigoes to serve all of Charles County, as well as parts of Prince George's and Calvert Counties.

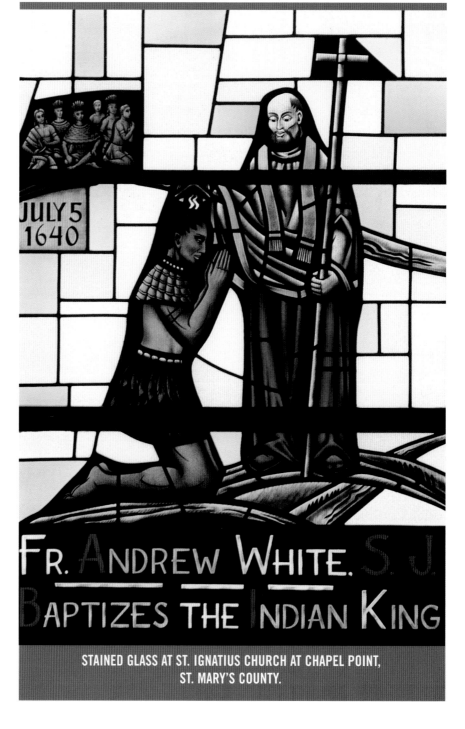

JULY 5 1640

FR. ANDREW WHITE, S.J.
BAPTIZES THE INDIAN KING

STAINED GLASS AT ST. IGNATIUS CHURCH AT CHAPEL POINT, ST. MARY'S COUNTY.

Father White worked with the natives along the Potomac and Patuxent Rivers and carried Scripture to the Anacostans near the swamps of what became the District of Columbia. On July 5, 1640, with Governor Leonard Calvert present, he converted and baptized Chitomachon, the "Emperor of Piscataway."

At the ceremony, the emperor, called Tayac, and his wife, took the Christian names of Lord and Lady Baltimore.

To this day, Southern Maryland descendants of native Americans converted by Father White remain largely Catholic. The Piscataways sold the English land and married their daughters to colonists. Relations were generally harmonious as the village of St. Mary's began to take shape.

The site of the provincial government, St. Mary's City encompassed about 10 residences, a forge, a mill, and a Catholic chapel. Maryland's capital from the time the Ark and the Dove landed until 1695, the settlement's original state house was built in the 1660s.

The colony was at risk both from the proximity of other English settlements that did not share the Calverts' vision of religious tolerance nor appreciate the bounty granted the Lords Baltimore by the throne.

Things got bad and then they got worse during the mid-1600s.

In 1637 a Jesuit named Fr. Thomas Copley arrived to advance the spiritual and economic interests of the Society of Jesus. Copley was intent upon missionary work in Protestant Virginia, which only brought trouble to the Marylanders, and in time the Jesuits were demanding that canon law be recognized in the colony.

In February 1638, Leonard Calvert and a small militia forced a trading post on Kent Island, established by William Claiborne in 1631, to comply with his rule as the island came within the bounds of his charter.

By the 1640s, Puritans, buoyed by the election of a Puritan parliament in London, seized the Calvert government, and the Protestant settlers on Kent Island took up arms to re-take their land from the Marylanders.

In 1643, Leonard sailed to England to discuss disputed policies in the colony with Cecil, leaving the affairs of Maryland to an acting governor. By 1644, Claiborne and Richard Ingle, the captain of a vessel named the *"Reformation,"* roused the Protestants to attack the Catholics. St. Mary's City was captured, forcing Leonard to flee to Virginia.

During the plundering time of the 1640s, the property of Catholics, disparaged as "papists and malignants," was seized and many colonists, including Governor Calvert, fled to Virginia. The Catholic chapel was destroyed and the two leading Jesuits, Father White and Father Copley, were arrested and transported to England for trial.

About the same time, King Charles I, a strong supporter of the Calverts, lost all political power to the Puritan Parliament. Thus followed two years of occupation referred to by the Marylanders as "plundering time."

During the three rebellions that took place in the Maryland colony during the mid-17th century, Catholic churches were burned, they were stripped of their rights, and their clergy, namely the Jesuits, were deported in chains.

In short, the Catholics were despised.

In her doctoral thesis on the Catholic Community of St. Mary's County during the colonial period, Dr. Tricia Pyne, director of the Associated Archives of St. Mary's Seminary and University in Roland Park, questioned the idea that Catholic colonists uniformly upheld the Calverts' order to worship as quietly as possible.

"From the public celebration of Mass on St. Clement's Island in 1634 to the building of the Great Brick Chapel in St. Mary's City in the 1670's, Catholics were openly practicing their faith in the colony," Dr. Pyne said.

In 1646, Leonard re-took St. Mary's City, whose palisade had been fortified with light cannon, one of which now guards Georgetown University.

At the time of Father White's expulsion, it was a criminal charge for a priest to land on English soil. At his trial for treason, the evidence against Father White was the fact of his priesthood. Acquitted on the argument that he had been brought to England by force, Father White spent the rest of his life in very low profile missionary activities and tried in vain to make it back to Maryland.

Catholic households in Maryland were looted and vandalized in on-going persecution that continued until late 1646, when Leonard raised a force of Virginians and exiled Marylanders to re-take the colony. Restored to rule, Leonard offered a pardon to all citizens willing to take an oath of fidelity. In June of 1647, he died in office in Maryland.

The rise of Oliver Cromwell in 1649 caused more problems for Maryland. Now governed by Thomas Greene, the colony acknowledged the new government of England while Virginia stayed loyal to King Charles II, who ascended upon the beheading of Charles I.

The act reads: "Whereas the enforcing of the conscience in matters of religion hath frequently fallen out to be of dangerous consequence in those commonwealths where it hath been practiced, and for the more quiet and peaceable government of the province and the better to preserve mutual love and amity amongst the inhabitants thereof: Be it therefore enacted that no person or persons whatsoever within this province... professing to believe in Jesus Christ, shall henceforth be in any way troubled, molested or discountenanced for or in respect of his or her religion or in the free exercise thereof within this province nor in anything compelled to the belief or exercise of any other religion against his or her consent."

Author: Cecil Calvert

STATUE OF CECIL CALVERT
Credit: Kirsten Beckerman

That same year, the General Assembly of Maryland passed "An Act Concerning Religion," widely known and celebrated as the Toleration Act. The act codified what had been the rule and practice of the provincial government from the founding of the colony: religious freedom.

Statue of Cecil Calvert, son of the first Lord Baltimore – George Calvert – who conceived the Maryland colony for the Catholic faithful – stands outside of the Clarence Mitchell Jr. courthouse on St. Paul Street in downtown Baltimore.

This was the first law in history to make religious freedom the foundation of a state. It was passed unanimously by the Assembly, in which Catholics were the majority.

By 1650, some 300 Puritans had settled near what is now Annapolis. Their harassed brethren in Virginia were offered refuge in Maryland and were guaranteed not only their property rights but freedom of worship. Four years later, the Puritans thanked their protectors by seizing the Maryland government and re-instituting religious and political persecution in the colony.

On and on it went like this, tit-for-tat, back and forth as the Lords Baltimore attempted to hold on to their charter and their dreams and when they could not, re-take them.

After a direct appeal to Oliver Cromwell, freedom of religion was restored in Maryland and held for nearly 30 years until the Glorious Revolution of 1688, when the Catholic King James II was deposed by his Protestant daughter Mary and her husband, William of Orange.

Using allegiance to the new monarchs and complaints about Catholic dominance in the Maryland government and political appointments as a pretext, Protestants gathered an army, mounted a revolt and seized the government at St. Mary's City.

The new government was comprised of Protestants only. Catholics were removed from all official positions. In 1689, Maryland ceased to be a proprietary colony and became a royal colony.

A new governor, charged with reporting directly to the crown, was dispatched to Maryland in 1692. With this, the rule of Lord Baltimore ended along with a guiding policy of religious freedom. The Church of England and no other became the established church.

Yet, the "pious enterprise" of freedom of worship managed to prevail through many subsequent battles and became a founding principle of the American republic, guaranteed throughout the United States, with the drafting of the Constitution.

Ultimately, the Maryland colony was "successful, even though things changed for the worse in England with the so-called Glorious Revolution, in establishing religious tolerance," according to the Rev. Michael Roach, pastor of St. Bartholomew's in Manchester and an instructor of Church history at Mount St. Mary's Seminary in Emmitsburg.

"Mass was celebrated quietly, discreetly, often in the back woods, but it continued and was not suppressed," said Father Roach. "All of the legislation passed to [persecute Catholics] was often winked at and though they had to stay out of the mainstream for some time, their dream survived and endured."

The seeds of separation between church and state were planted on St. Clement's, a philosophy now protected by the United States Constitution.

FREEDOM OF CONSCIENCE STATUE
St. Mary's County, Maryland

First & *Forever*

THE ARCHDIOCESE OF BALTIMORE

CHAPTER 2

Turmoil

The Rise of John Carroll and The American Revolution

"As a minority, Catholics in Maryland were conscious of developing peaceful relationships with Protestants...
but 50 years after the Act of Religious Toleration this was severely challenged by the Protestant ascendancy.
By the early 18th century, Catholicism was proscribed..."

Christopher Kauffman,
historian and parishioner, Corpus Christi

Political and religious battles in Maryland, us against them, topplings and seizings, outright hatred, did not subside with the advent of the 18th century, more than six decades after the landing of the Ark and the Dove.

In those 60-odd years, however, the St. Mary's settlement recorded the first vote cast in the English colonies by a man of African descent, Matthias de Sousa, the first request by a woman for the right to vote, Margaret Brett, and the first printing press in the colonial South.

By 1669, Catholics in Maryland numbered some 2,000 people with much of their civil strife traced directly to Mother England. Back in Britain, anti-papist furor endured on waves of war with Catholic France and Catholic Spain. Seemingly endless, these wars propelled George Calvert

to seek something better in North America, where the loyalty of Catholics to the Crown was in constant question.

During the Protestant Revolution in England, the reign of William and Mary took political control in Maryland. Though his property and revenues were left intact, the third Lord Baltimore, Charles Calvert, grandson of George, lost the power to govern.

Charles (1637-1715) was born during a period when the Calvert family was straining to maintain and strengthen a young colony of some 10 million acres.

The only son of Cecil Calvert and Anne Arundell, the daughter of a powerful Catholic nobleman and the woman for whom the county just south of Baltimore is named, Charles was bred to assume the responsibilities and privileges of a future governor.

CHARLES CALVERT, THE THIRD LORD BALTIMORE
Credit: Enoch Pratt Free Library

By the time Charles realized his birth-right, arriving in Maryland at age 24 in 1661 and laying claim to his family's holdings upon the death of his father Cecil in 1675, there was nothing but trouble.

Protestants outnumbered Catholics 10-to-1 in a colony whose population also included a growing number of convicts and indentured servants dispatched from Britain.

While Charles worked hard at his many problems, he was less than diplomatic, a trait which contributed to his being married four times. His second wife, Jane, gave birth to Benedict Leonard Calvert, who would become the fourth Lord Baltimore.

ANNE ARUNDELL, WIFE OF CECIL CALVERT, MOTHER OF CHARLES.

When William Penn was given his land grant in 1681, Charles now had a northern boundary to defend. Penn won most of the political battles before the royal court, leaving Charles to argue in vain about precedents established in the Calverts' favor by regimes long gone.

A new and radical spirit of representative government had taken hold of Englishmen on both sides of the Atlantic. Before long it would be outright revolution in the colonies, and this combined with a loss of royal support to undercut Charles' authority.

In 1692, England dispatched the first royal governor, Lionel Copley, to Maryland. The seat of government moved from St. Mary's City to Annapolis, and the Church of England became the colony's official religion with all residents forced to pay taxes supporting the church.

REPLICA OF THE *DOVE*, which arrived with the Ark at St. Clement's Island on March 25, 1634.

In short time, St. Mary's was a city in name only and Charles was reduced to a wealthy landowner, spending the rest of his life trying to restore his family's authority.

Upon his death on February 21, 1715, his son Benedict assumed his title and the colony's charter.

The lag between the overthrow of Charles Calvert in 1689 and the enactment of the first "Anti-Popery" laws in 1704, legislation which closed all Catholic churches and schools and forced Mass underground, was due to the political clout maintained by Catholics and the lingering protection of King William.

In 1704, the Catholic Chapel in St. Mary's, of which no original drawings have survived, was closed. The Jesuits dismantled the building and used the bricks to construct a larger chapel on their farm located outside of St. Mary's City, St. Inigoes.

CHARLES CALVERT, THE FIFTH LORD BALTIMORE
Credit: Enoch Pratt Free Library

The 1708 census commissioned by Governor Seymour counted more than 500 Catholic families scattered throughout Delmarva.

In 1715, which saw the deaths of the third and fourth Lords of Baltimore, father Charles and son Benedict, Maryland again broke free of the crown.

The colony was ruled by Benedict's 16-year-old son, Charles. The fifth Lord Baltimore, Charles was guided by a guardian appointed by the Crown until he reached the age of majority.

By 1718, Catholics had lost the right to vote. This disenfranchisement, for virtually all non-Anglicans, would last until the whole of the American landscape was re-made by revolution.

Despite oppression, Catholic missionary work in Maryland continued, and in 1731 a new chapel was built at Newtown to replace the original 17th century sanctuary. Named for St. Francis Xavier, the church was Spartan in design to keep from attracting attention to its purpose.

Charles, twice a member of the Parliament and remembered as honest and good-natured but lacking the will needed to rule, got off to a bad start by dealing arrogantly with the Maryland General Assembly.

The first of the proprietors to visit the colony in half-a-century, Charles arrived in Maryland in 1732 to continue his family's boundary disputes, this time over the accuracy of a map that gave away Cape Henlopen, with the heirs of William Penn.

Once the Maryland-Pennsylvania boundary dispute was finally settled in 1767 by the surveyors Mason and Dixon, it became clear that thousands of square miles once in Maryland became part of Delaware and Pennsylvania.

After Charles, only two more family members would attempt to run the Calvert colony on the Chesapeake: Frederick, the sixth and last Lord Baltimore (1731-1771) and Henry Harford, Frederick's illegitimate son.

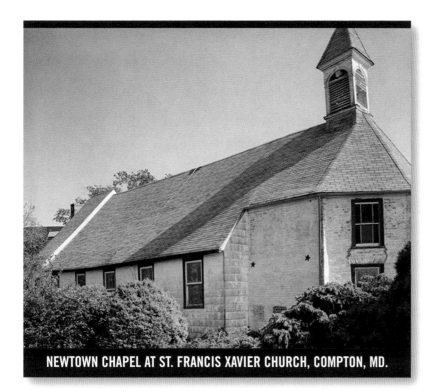

NEWTOWN CHAPEL AT ST. FRANCIS XAVIER CHURCH, COMPTON, MD.

Known as "Newtown Neck," during colonial days, the Newtown mission was launched about 1638. Jesuit priests lived there and lived off of the crops they raised. Originally built to look like a tobacco barn to fool Protestant authorities, it was only when George Calvert's ideal of religious tolerance became the norm – more than a century after the first charter for Maryland was granted - that a vestibule and choir loft were added. It was a working plantation and the profits were used to support the Jesuits' missionary efforts.

Frederick Calvert never set foot in Maryland. His regal attitudes and arrogant policies were responsible for much of the colony's anti-imperial sentiment in the years leading to the American Revolution.

In an 1967 edition of *American Heritage* magazine quoted by Tom Chalkley in his essay on the Lord Baltimore portraits, historian William Wilson described Frederick as "weak, querulous ...something of a fool... And vicious as well."

He died at age 40, bequeathing colonial Maryland to Henry, then age 9. The inheritance was contested in England before he was eventually recognized as the rightful heir by the Maryland Assembly. After the Revolution, the new American government paid Henry $50,000 for his land claim. Active ties between Maryland and the Calvert bloodline had ended.

Henry, of whom images are rare, left his name to one of Maryland's 23 counties and a fabled artery that runs through northeast Baltimore to Pennsylvania.

Today, three active parishes are located on Harford Road: St. Francis of Assisi in Mayfield, St. Dominic in Hamilton, and St. Ursula in Parkville.

As the Calvert family's influence on Maryland began to subside, that of John Carroll rose.

Born in Upper Marlboro in 1735, Carroll was a Jesuit educator destined to become the first bishop of a nation that would not even exist until he reached middle-age.

Through John Carroll the infant country and the ancient Church grew together on a principle of mutual benefit to both institutions: freedom of worship.

"John Carroll could travel in any circle within the colonies," said Father Michael Roach. "He was a nationally recognized religious leader who served on a revolutionary committee with Benjamin Franklin."

"Carroll was very cosmopolitan," said Christopher Kauffman. "He served on boards of colleges and charities with Protestant ministers, and he was known for his loyalty to the American republic. He was particularly pleased with separation of church and state which allowed Catholics the freedom of religion. As a supporter of religious liberty, he represents enlightened Catholicism."

In the course of his career, a spectacular span during which he emerged as the First Father of Catholic America, John Carroll founded Georgetown University, engaged the Sulpicians to establish St. Mary's Seminary in Baltimore, and encouraged a young widow, Elizabeth Ann Seton to open a school and form a community of women religious.

BISHOP JOHN CARROLL STAMP

John Carroll, first bishop of Baltimore on Vatican stamp honoring the bi-centennial of the founding of the Archdiocese of Baltimore. Among his many accomplishments, Carroll established Georgetown University and invited the French Sulpician Fathers to establish St. Mary's Seminary in Baltimore. Both were among the many Catholic-American firsts in Baltimore.

He also served as chairman of the Board of Trustees of Washington College in Chestertown.

In 1745, when he was ten-years-old, John and his cousin Charles Carroll of Carrollton were enrolled in a Jesuit school for boys in the Old Bohemia area near Delaware. John and Charles continued their Jesuit education at St. Omer in Flanders.

Charles Carroll, believed to be the wealthiest man in the country during his life, was the only Catholic signer of the Declaration of Independence. Carroll risked his fortune on the American Revolution and became president of the Maryland Senate after victory over the British secured independence. When he died in 1832, he was the last surviving signer of the Declaration and was buried from the Basilica with many honors. The day of his funeral the federal government closed its offices.

Ordained at age 34 in 1761, John Carroll returned to America as a missionary in 1773, three years before the signing of the Declaration of Independence.

BUST OF BISHOP JOHN CARROLL IN THE BALTIMORE BASILICA

By the early 1770s, Pope Clement XIV, bowing to political pressure from European royalty, suppressed the Jesuits and John Carroll began building a mission church at his mother's house in the Rock Creek area of Montgomery County that would serve area Catholics and those from nearby Virginia. St. John's, Forest Glen, is successor to this chapel Carroll built on the family estate.

In 1776 Carroll accompanied a group that included Benjamin Franklin, whose friendship would prove valuable in the rise of the future bishop on a mission of the Continental Congress to Quebec. Carroll's cousin Charles was also on the venture.

A decade-and-a-half earlier, Canada had become a British colony. The mission to Quebec intended to persuade French-Catholic Canada to join the American Revolution against Britain.

Although Carroll had little hope for the mission that ultimately failed, the effort did result in securing Canada's neutrality during the war. In 1774, the British Parliament passed the Quebec Act, which, among other things, gave freedom of worship to Canadian Catholics, allowed priests to collect tithes from their parishioners, and maintained the supremacy of the Crown.

Until the American Revolution, Catholics in the British colonies were subjects of the Vicar Apostolic of London, at times either a fugitive in England or an exile in France.

The American victory severed virtually every formal tie, both religious and political, that the fledgling United States had to the Old World and its prejudices. A Catholic hierarchy needed to be established, and in 1784 John Carroll was appointed Prefect-Apostolic, "Superior of the Mission of the Thirteen United State," by Pope Pius VI.

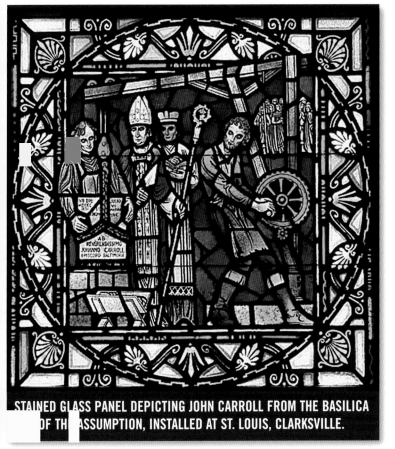

STAINED GLASS PANEL DEPICTING JOHN CARROLL FROM THE BASILICA OF THE ASSUMPTION, INSTALLED AT ST. LOUIS, CLARKSVILLE.

Stained glass like this depiction of John Carroll was removed during the restoration of the Basilica to the original design by Benjamin Henry Latrobe.

Changes that "seriously compromise" Latrobe's design and aesthetic intent, the closing of the main dome skylights and the installation of stained glass windows were specifically cited, "need to be reversed if the building is to regain its original aesthetic and historical integrity," according to architects involved in the project.

When the building first opened, light filtered in through 24 skylights built as part of the great dome. But the source of the light was not readily apparent to the worshipers below, resulting in a sublime luminosity that evoked the heavens, the perfect ambiance for a basilica.

The light pattern changed significantly when the skylights were taken out in 1946, after becoming a maintenance problem. Under the restoration plan replicas of the originals will be installed to bring back that original "mysterious" quality of light.

■ Ed Gunts, Baltimore Sun, Dec. 2000

His responsibility: guiding the Church in the infant republic.

To this end, in 1784, Carroll wrote an "Address to the Roman Catholics of the United States of North America" in reply to attacks by non-Catholics. Published in Annapolis, the essay is the first work published by an American Catholic in the United States.

■ ■ ■

A significant pilgrimage was launched from Maryland in 1785 when a "league" of families, about 60 in all, pledged to establish Catholic settlements in Kentucky.

Banding together, their aim was to protect themselves against Indian assaults while creating a parish. In the first year, two dozen families arrived in what is now Bardstown.

By the early 19th century, when the vast expanse of the Diocese of Baltimore was first divided, Bardstown, now the Archdiocese of Louisville, became one of the original spin-off dioceses along with Boston, New York, and Philadelphia.

In 1786, Carroll set up residence in Baltimore, where he became a popular and influential cleric.

Three years later, Carroll was named bishop of the newly created Diocese of Baltimore, which encompassed the entire United States and much of its territories. He would direct the Church in America for the next 25 years and see the population of Catholics grow from 25,000 in 1789 to approximately 160,000 in 1820.

With the election of George Washington as the nation's first President and the adoption of the Bill of Rights in 1791, American Catholics were euphoric over their hard-won freedom.

It was with the foundation of these guarantees that Bishop Carroll opened the first Catholic synod in the United States in 1791 at St. Peter's pro-Cathedral.

Here in 1800, the Rev. Leonard Neale, a Maryland native and a cousin of John Carroll, became the first bishop consecrated in America and joined Carroll as coadjutor bishop of Baltimore.

Without question, Baltimore reigned as the center of Catholic life in the United States.

Growing up Catholic

Baltimore Becomes an Archdiocese and The death of John Carroll

Here in the fabled Archdiocese of Baltimore, where Archbishop John Carroll blended ancient faith with America's revolutionary ideal of religious tolerance, you don't need a book to figure out what it means to be Catholic.

"In this city, people have the history of the church at their fingertips," said Sr. Helen Fish, a School Sister of Notre Dame who was led to the convent, in part, by the kindness of her grade school nuns after the sudden death of her mother on Christmas Eve, 1942.

From Cresaptown to Catonsville, ask just about anyone who passes by.

Even if people aren't Catholic, it's inevitable that they can lead you to someone who is: someone they grew up with or went to school with or who married into their family.

And that Catholic - whether devout,

"It is very hard for me to separate being Catholic and being from Baltimore. In what other city do you ask someone where they live and they tell you what church they go to? In what other city do you stroll down the street and see the Blessed Mother, the Pope and the Sacred Heart of Jesus hanging in the front window?"

Suzanne Griffin,
indelibly Catholic, Griffin believes true faith expresses itself in not judging others

"I am not Catholic but I have noted the tendency of our Catholic population to identify areas as being in such and such a parish. When I would tell people where I lived, I was often asked whether I knew Father so and so..."

John Schmidt,
grandson of an early 20th-century milkman whose route ran through "Schwamp Pudel," the village of Czechs and Bohemians near St. Wenceslaus in East Baltimore.

non-practicing, convert or from the cradle - will lead you to the next steamer trunk of memories which will deliver you to the next.

Michael Anthony Cronin, 56: "When I was growing up in the Sixties, I thought Govans was the cultural center of the universe and I was certain that St. Mary's was its great cathedral."

Tom Kilchenstein, 62: "My great-grandfather was John Adam Kilchenstein and he owned a grocery store at Harford Road and

Taylor Avenue and put so much money into building St. Dominic's that the first four pews on the right hand side had our name on it."

Kathryn "Kit" Lathroum, Mercy High School, Class of 1970: "I still remember how the concept of God was handled. I had teachers who encouraged us to seek a personal involvement with God that would transcend dogma. They were trying to give us a basis for a life-long involvement with a spiritual life. And it worked, at least for me."

MEMORIES OF NO MEAT ON FRIDAYS IN GLYNDON

Like thousands of Maryland Catholics still getting used to the changes of the Second Vatican Council in the 1960s and early 1970s, Suzanne Griffin's family did not eat meat on Friday.

"It was shrimp Creole every Friday night," remembers Griffin. "I'd skip in from soccer practice and open the back door to 'the smell' of the shrimp being steamed. Whatever joy I had in my heart was stamped out. I would slowly go up to my bedroom praying for a breath of fresh air somewhere in the house. Just talking about it makes me want to gag. My mother would call, 'DINNER!' proud to serve such a great meal and I'd sit at the table holding my nose.

"And let's not forget the BIG bay leaves you had to pick your way around because they may choke you! Welcome to Friday night at the Griffin's!"

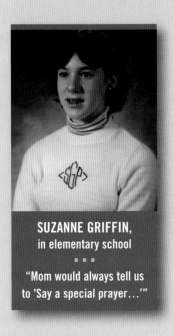

SUZANNE GRIFFIN,
in elementary school

▪ ▪ ▪

"Mom would always tell us
to 'Say a special prayer...'"

Shrimp Creole

*   1 green pepper, chopped
*   1/2 cups diced celery
*   2 Tablespoons oil
*   1 1/2 cups water
*   1 bay leaf
*   1/8 tsp. pepper
*   1/2 cup onion, chopped
*   1 garlic clove, minced
*   1 - 6 oz. can tomato paste
*   1 Tablespoon salt
*   1/4 tsp. thyme
*   2 cups cooked shrimp

Cook all vegetables in oil under tender. Add paste, water, and seasonings. Simmer 15 minutes, stirring occasionally. Add shrimp and heat. Serve to grateful family with hot rice if desired.

▪ ▪ ▪

These are some of the indelible Catholic memories of Suzanne Griffin, whose Confirmation name is Neumann because her grandmother "loved Bishop John Neumann," a Redemptorist born in Bohemia and associated with Baltimore's St. James parish in the early 1840s.

[Czech émigrés would found St. Wenceslaus parish near Johns Hopkins Hospital in 1872.]

**BISHOP AND SAINT:
JOHN NEUMANN**

Neumann, a shepherd for mid-19th century immigrants like himself, later served as rector of the St. Alphonsus congregation at Park Ave. and Saratoga St. downtown.

Neumann is regarded by the School Sisters of Notre Dame as their "father in America," because in 1847, when he was superior of the Redemptorist Order in the U.S., he welcomed the teaching sisters from their native Munich.

The future bishop found the School Sisters a home in Baltimore. Their current residence sits dramatically at the corner of North Charles Street and Bellona Avenue. He gave them teaching assignments in Redemptorist parish schools from Baltimore to Buffalo.

In return, they never failed to spread the legend of his graciousness.

Neumann became an American citizen on Feb. 10, 1848, renouncing his allegiance to the Emperor of Austria. On his 41st birthday in 1852, he was consecrated bishop of Philadelphia by Baltimore Archbishop Francis Kenrick at St. Alphonsus.

Griffin, an independent film producer, grew up in a strong Catholic family at Glyndon's Sacred Heart parish and will never forget her grandmother, Margaret Potthaust of the famous Baltimore furniture company, taking her to Rome in 1977 for a private audience with Pope Paul VI during John Neumann's canonization.

There, she remembers touring the Spanish Steps and the Sistine Chapel. From her walks along the narrow streets of South Baltimore, she remembers row houses decorated with Catholic patrons.

"I am not so certain that this happens everywhere," she said of local window decorating.

Griffin especially remembers that her mother would call on many of these patrons for strength when the kids were driving her up the wall with stunts like turning up their nose at a home cooked meal.

"It still makes me laugh, the way Mom would ask for help," says Griffin.

"Jesus, Mary, and Joseph give me strength!"

"Mother Mary, pray for me!"

"Mother of God, help me!"

All requested, laughs Griffin, while wielding a wooden spoon!

The connection between Catholicism and the City of Baltimore says Griffin, is one of "pride and tradition... every day was a memorial to something," she says.

"Mom would tell us to 'Say a special prayer for your grandfather, it's the anniversary of his birth, today.' Or just as likely: 'Say a special prayer for your grandfather; it's the anniversary of his death today'".

"The traditions just slipped in and became a part of you," she says. "I live in Harpers Ferry now, not so close to Baltimore. But when I repeat a tradition which I learned in my childhood, I slip back home in my heart."

This history of the archdiocese is a Catholic family album, a decidedly parochial view which may have overlooked an essential fact or moment of historical significance.

As such, I erred on the side of reminiscence over scholarship. Academic work on the history of Britain's first Catholic colony in the New World, anchored by *"The Premier See,"* by Brother Thomas W. Spalding, would easily fill a small library.

Volumes and essays on Saint Elizabeth Ann Seton alone take up several long shelves, with the first – *"Life of Mrs. Eliza A. Seton"* - published in 1853 by the Rev. Charles I. White, pastor of St. Charles, Pikesville.

While relying on previously published histories as a foundation for this book, the ornaments were collected with a simple question.

"Did you grow up Catholic?"

SR. GWYNETTE PROCTOR, SND

photo credit: Mark Champion

Sr. Gwynette Proctor, a Sister of Notre Dame de Namur, sits before a statue of the order's foundress, Saint Julie Billiart, 1751-1816, at the order's Provincial Center on Cable Street in Roland Park.

Saint Julie often told her sisters - who teach and serve on five continents - that they should have "hearts as wide as the world."

"I grew up in the immense history of Catholicism in Baltimore," said Sr. Gwynette Proctor, SND, the former director of Our Daily Bread whose African-American family was among the first to integrate Blessed Sacrament parish in Govans.

The history of local Catholicism carried with it problems of the greater American culture that left strong marks on young Gwynette.

"When I was growing up, our Catholic schools were struggling with integration, we actually lived closer to St. Matthews and St. Mary's [Govans] but my parents found a place for us at Blessed Sacrament," she said. "I never went on a school trip because they always went to a segregated amusement park, so I know first-hand the influence the church had on me and the influence the civil rights movement had on the church.

THOMAS W. SPALDING

Brother Thomas W. Spalding, virtually without peer, is the acknowledged historian of the Archdiocese of Baltimore.

In January of 2003, Spalding, 78, died at his home in Louisville, Kentucky, native state of his relative, Martin John Spalding, 7th Archbishop of Baltimore [1864-to-1872], whose life he also chronicled.

His work includes the long story of the St. Vincent de Paul parish on Front Street near the Baltimore Shot Tower, which he co-authored in 1995 as *"St. Vincent de Paul of Baltimore: the Story of a People and their Home."*

Spalding joined the congregation of the Brothers of St. Francis Xavier in 1942, took a master's from Fordham University and earned his doctorate in history from the Catholic University of America.

Among his many books, Spalding's great work is "The Premier See: A History of the Archdiocese of Baltimore, 1789-1994"

A quarter-century ago, he was commissioned to write a history of the Archdiocese of Baltimore by the late Cardinal Lawrence Shehan. The result – the finely detailed *"Premier See"* - took two years of full-time work plus a dozen subsequent summers before it was complete.

One of Spalding's great heroes was Archbishop Michael J. Curley, the Irish-born priest who served Baltimore from 1921 to 1947. Spalding was especially respectful of Curley for the popular archbishop's strong stand on racial harmony and his decision to live in poverty.

Of *"The Premier See,"* which in 1990 won the Maryland Historical Society History Book Prize, Spalding said: "I was given full freedom to tell the story... as I saw it."

Brother Spalding considered Baltimore his second home.

"My grandfather, a laborer named Orlando Jones, helped build St. Pius V and he was relegated to the balcony," said Sr. Gwynette. "On her death bed, my grandmother read of Bishop [John] Ricard's appointment and that began her stories of the old days. She had lived through the days in Baltimore when black Catholics were relegated to the balcony to the moment when a black man had been appointed a bishop in Baltimore and she was ecstatic."

The daughter of a mailman, Gwynette Proctor grew up in Baltimore's Original Northwood community in the 1950s.

BISHOP JOHN H. RICARD, S.S.J., appointed by Pope John Paul II as Bishop of the Diocese of Pensacola-Tallahassee in early 1997. Bishop Ricard served as auxiliary Bishop in the Archdiocese of Baltimore - where he was responsible for the parishes in Baltimore City - from the time of his Episcopal ordination in 1984 to his appointment in Florida.

Her mother, Yolanda Proctor, was taught by the Oblate Sisters of Providence at St. Frances Academy on Chase Street.

Her parents were active in Blessed Sacrament when Gwynette attended school there, her father coaching her basketball team and her mom, a city school teacher, coaching her sister's team.

They were her example of "Good Catholic men and women who wanted to give something back. When I was an adult, I knew it was time to give something back."

Credit: St. Joseph Society of the Sacred Heart

MOTHER LANGE THE OBLATE SISTERS OF PROVIDENCE AND THE ST. FRANCES ACADEMY

MOTHER MARY LANGE
CREDIT: CNS

Born Elizabeth Clarisse Lange to a family of means in Haiti, Lange fled the chronically troubled Caribbean island in 1817 and landed in Baltimore.

Using an inheritance from her father, Lange established a school in her home on Bank Street near the Fells Point wharves and began educating black children.

St. Frances Academy traces it's founding to this effort, using the year 1828 as the official date.

On July 2, 1829, Lange made history when - with the help of the Father James Joubert and the blessing of Archbishop James Whitfield – she and three others women of African descent color took formal vows of poverty, chastity and obedience in the lower chapel of St. Mary's Seminary, founding the Oblate Sisters of Providence.

The other original members were Mary Rosine Boegues and Mary Frances Balas, both of Haiti, and Mary Theresa Duchemin, a Baltimorean.

Earlier vows were taken in Lange's residence on George Street. A born leader, she took her religious name in honor of the Blessed Virgin Mary and was elected the order's first superior.

Mother Lange, who died in 1882, defined the order thus: "...a religious society of Colored Women [who] renounce the world to consecrate themselves to God, and to the Christian education of young girls of color."

The Oblate Sisters of Providence did their pioneering work in early 19th-century, slave holding Maryland, known as the Free State for its history of religious tolerance.

It was a time when white nuns in Baltimore balked at educating black children, the Church tried to relegate the Oblates to domestic servants for white priests, and certain Catholic theologians argued in Rome that black people were born without souls.

What Mother Lange achieved in the face of this, the founding of St. Frances Academy some 40 years before the Civil War as well as the manifold good works by first order of black Catholic nuns in the New World, are miracles in themselves.

Thus, Cardinal William H. Keeler put the full weight of the Archdiocese of Baltimore behind the campaign to have her canonized.

Said the Cardinal: "After hearing so much about her, I asked 'What do we need to do?' to promote her sainthood."

The effort has taken more than 15 years of research, including reports from scholars dispatched to Haiti and Cuba to learn of Lange's early life.

That phase of the work was closed by Cardinal Keeler in 2005 with the pertinent documents – six, thick binders in all – delivered to the Vatican's Congregation for Causes of Saints.

If the candidacy approved, the next step would be for the Oblate founder to be declared "venerable," a process that could take up to two years.

A documented miracle would then be necessary for her to be among the come "blessed" and a second miracle recognized by the Vatican for Lange to achieve sainthood.

The documents describe Mother Lange's faith as "heroic" and "indomitable." Even these superlatives - based on diaries kept by two Sulpician superiors who worked with her among other sources - are somewhat understated.

According to Monsignor Jeremiah Kenney, presiding judge of the Archdiocese of Baltimore's inquiry into her canonization, Mother Lange defied racial prejudice and challenged laws against educating black children with a "spectacular courage."

"People would spit at her when she walked down the street," he said. "They pushed [Oblate] sisters off the sidewalks because they thought though black women shouldn't be nuns."

In 1831, Pope Gregory XVI – who eight years later would officially condemn the slave trade - gave his approval to the Oblates.

In 1834, with the death of her patron, Archbishop Whitfield, Mother Lange found herself in conflict with Whitfield's successor, Archbishop Eccleston. The son of a Maryland slave-holding family, the new archbishop ordered the Oblates to disband and become servants.

Neither occurred, although the sisters did take in sewing and laundry to support their cause; persevering through at least two episodes when angry mobs stormed Lange's home.

While the work of the Oblates began with service to large numbers of black refugees from Haiti - including ministering to victims of the 1832 cholera epidemic - it soon focused on education.

After the surrender of the Confederacy, the order established an orphanage for black children whose parents were lost in the war. Soon, the

Oblates were operating a widow's home; a Bible school; vocational training; a night school where blacks could learn to read and write after a hard day of work.

Eventually, Oblate communities developed in New Orleans, St. Louis, Philadelphia, Lange's native Caribbean - including four houses in Cuba - and Central America.

But it is in their birthplace of Baltimore that the order flourished. As the unofficial capital of both American Catholicism and free black America prior to the Civil War, the port city of the Patapsco offered the Oblate Sisters of Providence their strongest base of support.

Among the books which detail the work of the Oblates are "Persons of Color and Religious at the Same Time: The Oblate Sisters of Providence, 1828-1860," by Diane Batts Morrow; and a memoir published in 1914 by Oblate Sister Mary Petra Boston titled "Blossoms Gathered from the Lower Branches."

REV. JOUBERT

The son of an attorney, the Rev. James Hector Nicholas Joubert de la Muraille, S.S was born to French nobility in 1777, educated in a military school and worked in a tax office before sailing in 1800 for the French money-maker known as Haiti. Three years later, massacres by former slaves in Santa Domingo forced Joubert to seek refuge in Cuba and then the United States. For the priesthood at St. Mary's Seminary on Paca Street and in 1810 was ordained through the Society of Saint Sulpice. It was at St. Mary's — where he taught French and geography - that Fr. Joubert met Elizabeth Lange. Both refugees from the same turmoil in the Caribbean, they shared a cultural heritage that harkened back to France, a devotion to the Catholic Church and an enduring commitment to the education of black children.

Their partnership turned out to be one of the most historic in American Catholicism.

St. Frances Academy - the nation's oldest school for African-American children still in operation - is located in Baltimore's Johnston Square neighborhood, a rough area near Green Mount Cemetery.

The impoverished neighborhood has housed a variety of jails and prisons since 1799. In this bleak atmosphere, St. Frances has struggled, endured and thrived.

The Oblate Sisters of Providence gathered around
Archbishop Michael Curley on the portico
of the Basilica upon the occasion of
the 100th anniversary of their founding.
"Oblate" is interpreted by the sisters as meaning:
"to make an offering of your life to God."

More than 70 percent of the students live below the poverty line. Tuition is $4,700, although the true cost to educate each child was $6,300 in 2005.

Because of the sacrifices of its staff and a range of benefactors, including the Archdiocese of Baltimore, more than half of the students only pay a portion of the tuition or none at all.

"We have to believe that God is at work within them" Sister John Francis Schilling, principal of St. Frances told the New York Times in May of 2005.

"So many of them come here down on themselves. I think that the hope that we give them is, first of all, hope in themselves. I see this as my ministry."

The struggles and success of the institution was widely celebrated in 2003 when St. Frances marked its 175th anniversary.

The entire jubilee year was spent publicizing the good works done over the past two centuries. It was an opportunity to enlist help for future challenges while reflecting on past indignities suffered and overcome.

It included a high-profile visit – and severe, well-publicized quotes - by Camille Cosby, wife of entertainer Bill Cosby.

"The Church did not consider slavery a sin," said Mrs. Cosby, who was educated by the Oblates in the District of Columbia. "The archdiocese in Baltimore, at least once, sought the cooperation of the Maryland chapter of the American Colonization Society, a political group that sought to rid the country of all free blacks, who were perceived to be dangerous."

Mrs. Cosby made her comments while receiving a Mother Lange Award. The same year, she contributed $2 million to St. Frances Academy, the largest single gift in the school's history.

"I know what these nuns do," said Mrs. Cosby said in the New York Times. "I know how much time they put into educating their students. They're not buying into the repetitive messages about hopelessness. They're not buying into the message that you can't do it."

ST. FRANCES ACADEMY

Named for St. Frances of Rome, a 15th-century mystic, the fabled school stands with dignity in one of the poorest sections of Baltimore, a city where half of those who start public high school never finish. The current St. Frances building was built in 1871. A new gymnasium, planned for 60 years, opened in 2002. An all-girls institution until 1974, St. Frances uses college-level texts and requires students to take algebra, a foreign language, African-American studies and either chemistry or forensics. While home to many students who have excelled for years, St. Frances is the last opportunity for others to get a high school education. Many students enter St. Frances at a sixth-grade reading level. Within three years, however, most have made it to a 12th grade level. Upon earning a St. Frances diploma, 90 percent go on to college.

History teacher David Bowles teaches a class at St. Frances Academy in October 2003.

John Bowen grew up in Baltimore during the Great Depression and attended Mass at a handful of parishes before landing at St. Gregory the Great, named for the sixth-century pope.

There, young Bowen did well enough to earn a half-scholarship to Mount St. Joseph High School. He wasn't long with the Xaverians before he won a full scholarship to the St. Charles Seminary in Catonsville, enrolling for his sophomore year at age 15.

"At that time, people had large families. It was taken for granted that one or more than one would enter religious life," said Bowen, who desired the priesthood at an early age. "The minor seminary was a place for people to see if they really wanted the religious life."

Only 20 percent of his class at St. Charles became priests, said Bowen, ordained after graduating from St. Mary's Seminary. The rest sought success in other professions.

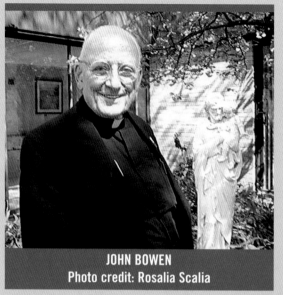

JOHN BOWEN
Photo credit: Rosalia Scalia

Today, Bowen lives in a retirement community near the old St. Charles seminary campus where he taught for 13 years and next door to the Little Sisters of the Poor. In 2003, his mother died at the age of 102.

"My friends tell me that I have 22 more years to go," he laughed.

The Rev. John Bowen turned 81 in 2005 having spent 56 years as Sulpician father. He taught at the old St. Charles seminary in Catonsville and also in Seattle before returning to Baltimore.

Father Bowen's other duties have included archival work for the Sulpicians and various parish duties at St. Mark's in Catonsville. For the past 25 years in Baltimore, he has served as chaplain for the Oblate order.

One morning after Mass, the sisters approached him about working to advance the cause for the canonization of Mother Lange. He asked for time to think about it. Before Bowen could decide, he was called to a meeting with Cardinal Keeler and the mother superior of the Oblates. His decision had been made.

As postulator for the cause, Bowen - aided by researchers dispatched to Haiti, Cuba and France - gathered six volumes of information regarding Mother Lange's life and accomplishments.

Gwynette Proctor graduated from Mercy High School in 1970 and went on to Frostburg State, where she was good enough at basketball to try-out for the 1972 U.S. Olympic team. Eight years later, now 28, she took her vows with the Sisters of Notre Dame de Namur. Three of her cousins grew up to be Oblate Sisters.

"It wasn't a question of whether I could respond to a vocation. That was already a reality in my family," she says. "It was seeing the sisters at Mercy come and go - getting in their cars and having their own lives - that intrigued me."

As a physical education teacher in Baltimore public schools before she entered the convent, Gwynette became involved in youth ministries at St. Ambrose parish on Park Heights Avenue because the "teaching wasn't enough to fulfill me. With this combination of youth ministry and teaching, the seed was planted" for her vocation.

In 1979, Gwynette attended a weekend retreat at Ilchester in Howard County and met women who had joined the Sisters of Notre Dame de Namur. Her course was set.

She has directed Christopher's Place Employment Academy for men working to put their lives back together and the Our Daily Bread soup kitchen, where Pope John Paul II broke bread with the poor in 1995.

The youngest member of the Order's local province, the median age is about 60, Sr. Gwynette serves as consultant to Associated Catholic Charities, headquartered in Baltimore. Her specialty is helping formerly homeless men, particularly ex-offenders, find work.

"There was always the feeling that I could be part of something bigger than just me," she said. "Since then, I have invited other women [to religious life] and they have come. It's a good life. I will continue to invite them until the day I die. "Old-school Baltimoreans

POPE JOHN PAUL II AT OUR DAILY BREAD.

"Feed the hungry..."

AGNES PAVLICK

photo credit: Mark Champion

Agnes Cavanaugh Pavlick, Seton High School, Class of 1957.

"The thing that has changed most about my Catholicism over the years is going to confession. As a kid, we went every week. Somewhere along the line, it seems they changed the intention of confession; that you didn't have to go unless you had committed a mortal sin. To me, the only mortal sin was turning away completely from God, so gradually I stopped going except maybe once or twice a year. Lately I've been thinking I will start going more regularly because penance is a sacrament... This is not just to forgive sins, but to receive grace..."

identify city neighborhoods not by proper name or cross streets but by the Catholic parish which anchors the community. For many years, when houses were advertised for sale, newspaper ads identified the property as being "in the Little Flower area" or the "St. Elizabeth neighborhood."

■ ■ ■

"I've been going to St. Philip Neri for more than 30 years, but St. Rose in Brooklyn will always be my home," said Agnes Cavanaugh Pavlick, who lives down the street from the Linthicum church, a circular, post-Vatican II sanctuary that was a local marvel when it was dedicated in 1965.

Agnes Pavlick has worked as a part-time teacher at St. Philip Neri grade school for many years. While all four of the children she has raised with her husband Richard, a retired Westinghouse engineer, attended the school near Baltimore-Washington International Airport, Pavlick's heart will always lie just over the county line.

"I was baptized at St. Rose of Lima," she said. "I made my first Communion there, my Confirmation and I was married there."

CONFESSIONAL

In 1983, American bishops estimated that Confession in the United States had dropped off as much as 70 percent since the late 1960s. Roman Catholics had abandoned the sacrament at least once before - between the 6th and 9th centuries - when the Sacrament was changed from public confession and penance to the private one-on-one system used today.

Agnes Pavlick has attended Mass every Sunday of her life and made regular Miraculous Medal novenas as a young woman.

Her sister Mary Cavanaugh Nicoli attends Mass every morning at St. Athanasius in Curtis Bay. Mary and her husband, Eddie, say the rosary together each evening and attend Sunday Mass at the St. Jude Shrine near the Lexington Market on Paca Street.

A second sister, Pat Cavanaugh Davis, worships at St. John's in Westminster.

Clearly, faith is the rock of these women's lives.

On February 3, 1956, the Cavanaugh girls lost their widowed mother, the former Stella Neff, in a parish oyster roast fire at Arundel Hall. The fire took 11 lives.

"St. Rose had a lot of tragedies," said Agnes, whose nephew, Patrick Nicoli, was an altar boy when St. Rose's roof collapsed under heavy snowfall in 1967. Although no one died in the accident, about 35 people were injured.

"I was 16 when my mother died and I was very angry," Agnes said. "It was a time when I questioned whether there really was a loving God.

"My sisters and I were all angry. I remember praying hard but it was whistling in the dark. That's not what prayer is," said Agnes, who went to live with her grandmother on 9th Street in Brooklyn after the tragedy.

"I get up in the morning and pray at my desk, certain prayers that are meaningful to me," said Agnes. "Some days I feel more connected than others," she said. "But I never let it stop me. Every aspect of my life is governed by what I believe."

■ ■ ■

Out of the blue one day, a few months into the research for this book, I got a call from a woman named Peggy Wellein. Peggy had grown up in Highlandtown, the old immigrant neighborhood on the east side of town.

There, in 1929, my father's parents were married at Our Lady of Pompei and throughout the 1960s, I would walk my Italian grandmother through the alleys to attend Mass at Holy Redeemer Chapel on Oldham Street.

In 2002, the Archdiocese closed Holy Redeemer, along with its nearby twin, St. Gerard Chapel in O'Donnell Heights, citing lack of attendance.

Wellein lives in Linthicum now, "where my parents have lived since the summer the Orioles won their first pennant in 1966." In the waiting room of a Linthicum doctor's office, Peggy noticed one of my books about Baltimore amidst the magazines of movie stars and sport fishing.

She wanted to talk about her childhood, about the Highlandtown she had once known.

"Are you Catholic?" I asked.

"Not me," she said. "But my husband was an altar boy...the whole nine yards."

And before you can say "St. Mary's Industrial School," I was sitting in a Hammonds Ferry Road living room with a devout Catholic so devoted to St. Clement parish in Lansdowne that they named a service award in his honor.

Clement Wellein, Peggy's 81-year-old father-in-law, is the inspiration for the "Clement F. Wellein Spiritual Award," established in 1989 for "outstanding contributions in the promotion and practice of the faith."

CLEMENT AND CATHERINE WELLEIN, 2002.
Young sweethearts from Baltimore City's old St. James parish, Clem Wellein (left) and the former Catherine Eichelman, have been married for more than 50 years.

Both Mr. Wellein and his wife Catherine were baptized at the old St. James parish at Aisquith and Eager Streets and educated there. Their parents knew each other from the neighborhood around Hope and Eager Streets.

Most folks think that Clem was named for Pope St. Clement, the first-century martyr for whom St. Clement in Lansdowne is named. But he was christened in honor of St. Clement Mary Hofbauer, for whom the Chesaco Avenue parish in Rosedale was dedicated. The Rosedale church honors the Clement who was an outstanding Redemptorist in the 18th century. He is also known as "the apostle of Vienna."

Clem goes back to the days of Coolidge when the St. James choir sang in Latin and the parish had its own fife and drum and bugle corps. He graduated from the parish's business school and was drafted into the service after Pearl Harbor.

"Our drum corps was so good that it was invited to play at FDR's first inaugural parade," said Clem, whose brother William became a monsignor in the Diocese of Raleigh, N.C. "I wanted to be in that band but my mother said, 'No, you're going to be an altar server.'"

Catherine was born on Hope Street near a long-gone piano factory. She and Clem met in the St. James drama club. After their marriage, Catherine gave her wedding gown away to be made into vestments for a priest in India.

"I had to think about it," said Catherine. "And I couldn't think of a better use for it…"

Until his health slowed him down recently, Clem Wellein attended Mass every day at St. Clement Church in Lansdowne for more than 40 years. He has put together most of the church bulletins in that time and has been present at nearly every funeral held there.

Of his faith, he says: "I am a member of the true church of God, the one founded by Jesus Christ when he told Peter, 'You are the rock and I shall build my Church upon you.'"

Without question, Baltimoreans from all backgrounds have influenced the life of the Church here.

From the women who laundered altar linens to teenage boys cutting parish lawns to Cardinals Gibbons and Shehan growing up to head their hometown's archdiocese, the Baltimoreans who make up the mystical Body of Christ have long been many and varied.

Gary Brown, for instance, spent much of his life supporting the Sacred Heart of Mary parish in Dundalk in the traditional ways of the laity: helping out at the annual carnival and chaperoning CYO dances.

Today, Brown's ministry is more direct, more grounded in the gospels as he directs outreach ministries for the sick and poor through Immaculate Heart of Mary in Baynesville.

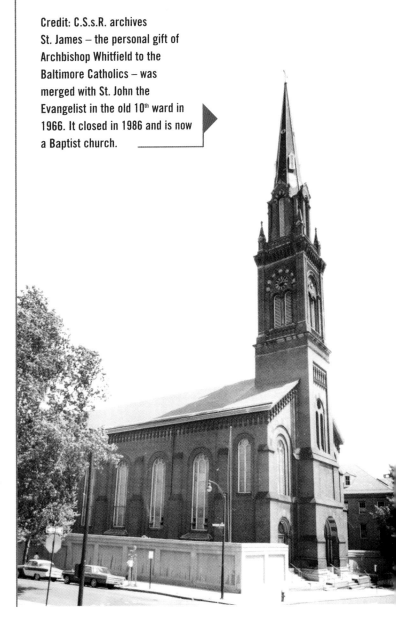

Credit: C.S.s.R. archives
St. James – the personal gift of Archbishop Whitfield to the Baltimore Catholics – was merged with St. John the Evangelist in the old 10th ward in 1966. It closed in 1986 and is now a Baptist church.

"It's hard when you see people who are hurting and you know you can only do so much for them," said Mr. Brown. "But at the same time, it's rewarding to bring a bit of companionship to their lives. They look forward to seeing you."

"An annual fundraiser from my childhood that I remember distinctly is the Father's Club dance. Three times a year, the grown-ups would organize a dance attended by themselves and their friends from outside the parish. Featuring a deejay or bands such as Ashton Golt or Gazze, these were community events that raised money for school improvements. They also set an example for the students at Our Lady of Hope. Both my sister and I grew up with this service mentality. Whether it was helping set up booths for the school carnival or checking coats at the Fathers' Club dances, community service at the church or school was just something we did."

Just as significant is the role that the Church played in shaping the general culture along the shores of the Chesapeake Bay.

"I would say its greatest influence was through Catholic hospitals and immigration," said author Christopher J. Kauffman, a member of the Corpus Christi parish in Bolton Hill and a historian of U.S. Catholicism at the Catholic University of America in Washington.

"The Church assimilated the immigrants into American life. Well before Ellis Island, Baltimore was the principal (east coast) port of entry into America.

"Those immigrants who were Catholic were brought into American mainstream through educational and voluntary Catholic societies in the United States," said Kauffman, who holds the Catholic Daughters of the Americas chair at Catholic University of America in Washington, D.C.

As immigrants swelled Baltimore's neighborhoods, new parishes popped up across the city and so increased the ranks of local priests. Eighty seminarians were ordained at the original St. Mary's Seminary in downtown Baltimore between 1849 and 1860.

GARRETT BROWN AND HIS FATHER GARY AT THE IMMACULATE HEART OF MARY OUTREACH OFFICE IN BAYNESVILLE.

"There were Irish and German before the Civil War and then Italians and Poles and then the Asians," said retired Archbishop William D. Borders, author of "Spiritual Living in a Secular Society," published in 1996 by the Cathedral Foundation Press of Baltimore.

In a foreword to the book, Cardinal Keeler wrote: "Of special note are the ways in which [Archbishop Borders] draws upon major themes of the Second Vatican Council and, at the same time, stresses very down-to-earth themes such as our need to practice the virtue of humility and to be aware and open to the power of God's grace."

At age 93, Archbishop Borders continues to write about issues important to his ministry and maintains office hours at Catholic Center headquarters on Cathedral Street.

■ ■ ■

"In colonial days, the church in Maryland represented people who'd been persecuted... They were well-educated people who not only wanted to practice their faith but to influence the general culture and they did," said Archbishop Borders. "In the 19th century, the church gave immigrants security in their process of becoming attuned to the culture of the United States and they leaned on their parishes for this.

"It began with the Irish of St. Patrick's in Fells Point and then the Germans on Butcher's Hill and Highlandtown and later the Italians at St. Leo's on up to today where we have a Korean parish in Woodlawn and a Vietnamese church in the Dundalk area..."

He concludes, "immigrants can keep the faith and take advantage of the new culture while gradually being absorbed into the American scene."

A native of St. Louis, like Baltimore, a city of churches steeped in the American Catholic tradition, Christopher Kauffman migrated to Baltimore to research and write *"Tradition and Transformation in Catholic Culture: The Priests of Saint Sulpice in the United States from 1791 to Present"* for MacMillan publishers.

"I was already aware of the richness of [Catholic] Baltimore and Maryland and when I studied the Sulpicians, I became immersed in it," said Kauffman, who wrote his doctoral thesis on the anti-defamation mission of the Knights of Columbus, founded in Connecticut in 1882.

"Of course, I wanted to see the Basilica and Fells Point where the [black Catholics] from Haiti arrived in 1793. St. Patrick's was the parish closest to the wharves, but the Haitians were escaping revolution and felt more comfortable with the French-speaking Sulpicians" who protected them.

CHRISTOPHER J. KAUFFMAN

Christopher J. Kauffman, author of several Catholic histories, including *"Ministry and Meaning: A Religious History of Catholic Health Care in the United States."*
In 1823, notes Kauffman, the first hospital in the state, Maryland Hospital in downtown Baltimore, was staffed by Sisters of Charity. "The nuns held the keys," said Kauffman, "and the interns had to be in bed by lights out."

In 1791, the same year the Sulpicians founded St. Mary's Seminary in what is now known as the Seton Hill section of Baltimore, Bishop John Carroll convened the first diocesan synod in the United States at St. Peter's pro-Cathedral at Saratoga and Little Sharp Streets.

Opened in 1770 for all Catholics regardless of nationality, before the coming century in which Baltimore would be divided into ethnic villages, St. Peter's was closed in 1841. Its records are part of the archives of the Basilica of the Assumption, which replaced it.

In 1800, the Rev. Leonard Neale, a native of Port Tobacco, Maryland, became the first bishop consecrated in America as well as co-adjutor bishop of Baltimore.

Neale replaced John Carroll upon the original bishop's death in 1815.

Without doubt, the burgeoning ship-building city on the Patapsco was the epi-center of Catholic life in the New World at the end of the 18th century.

In 1792, the first Mass was said for the Irish of lower Broadway when the Rev. Anthony Garnier, a Sulpician, celebrated the Eucharist near the corner of Fleet and Bond Streets.

Those gathered would become the congregation of St. Patrick's, which began in a boxlike building on Apple Alley, a narrow waterfront lane that was home to laborers of all races.

The alley sanctuary was dedicated by Bishop John Carroll in 1797, and since 1806 several churches in honor of St. Patrick have stood at the northeast corner of South Broadway and Bank Street.

At one time, a steeple there housed a clock, installed with the help of municipal funds in 1853, that was officially known as the Town Clock of East Baltimore.

In 1995, St. Patrick's was "twinned" with its nearby neighbor, the old German parish of St. Michael at Wolfe and Lombard Streets, founded in 1852, as city congregations dwindled and priests became scarce.

"At first we didn't like it," said Richard Novak, 70, and a deacon of the church he grew up in. "But now we see it as a good thing. We didn't want to admit it, but we knew we were dying and the twinning, along with an influx of Hispanic Catholics in the neighborhood, helped turned things around."

ST. JOHN THE EVANGELIST / FREDERICK

The history of St. John's in Frederick- 116 East Second Street - is synonymous with the history of the Catholic Church in central Maryland. Its beginnings go back to 1750 when Charles Carroll of Carrollton persuaded English, German and Irish Catholics to settle there.

Jesuits from Southern Maryland and Pennsylvania served these families. The Rev. John Dubois, founder of Mt. St. Mary's University, served the parish in the closing days of the 18th century and named the church for his personal patron.

The Jesuits had their American novitiate here until 1902 when Fr. William Kane became the first non-Jesuit pastor. Following Kane were a long line of pastors trained in the Archdiocese of Baltimore.

The current pastor is The Rev. Wayne G. Funk and the 1837 church on the grounds is one of the most beautiful in the Archdiocese, with some 3800 families enrolled.

St. John's sponsors 31 different outreach programs, including a service in American sign language that attracts hearing-impaired Catholics from nearby communities.

ST. PATRICK / BALTIMORE

MEMBERS OF ST. PATRICK'S PARISH

Members of St. Patrick's parish at Bank Street and Broadway include, clockwise, from left: Deacon Michael Flamini, Deacon Richard Novak, the Rev. James Gilmour C.Ss.R, former Pastor, Frank Rehling and Jeanne Velez.

The first bishop of the Diocese of Bardstown in Kentucky was ordained at St. Patrick's in Fells Point in 1810.

"I grew up in St. Patrick's – graduated from 8th grade there and was married there," said Tunia O'Dea Piaskowski.

"We'd walk over from our house on Shakespeare Street. But for the past 35 years, I've been with Sacred Heart of Mary in Dundalk. But I still try to get back for Mass on St. Patrick's Day. Sometimes it makes me feel sad."

ST. MARY'S HAGERSTOWN

The current sanctuary at St. Mary's sits on the site of the original log house and chapel in which Jesuit missionaries celebrated Mass in the mid-18th century. Construction on the present church began in 1826.

ST. MARY / ANNAPOLIS

Pioneering Catholics in the Hagerstown area began attending Mass, performed by Jesuit "circuit riders" on horseback, as early as 1758, when the Eucharist was celebrated in private homes. Later, Mass was held in a mission chapel across the state line from Pennsylvania. The St. Mary's parish of today was formally founded in 1790.

The faithful endured religious persecution in the early years, going underground at times to attend Mass when the activity was illegal and referring to priests as "Mister" on the street to keep their identities secret. Prominent figures associated with St. Mary's in Hagerstown include the Calvert family - both George and his son Cecil – as well as St. John Neumann, who celebrated Mass there.

The current pastor of the 1,200 family congregation is the Rev. George Limmer, who grew up in the St. Ursula parish in Parkville.

According to Father Limmer, parishioners continue a long tradition of outreach to the needy in the Hagerstown area through contributions to the St. Vincent de Paul Society as well as helping neighbors pay utility bills, rent and other needs that arise in a crisis.

He pointed to the parish "rummage sale" as a way for congregants to clean out their basements of stuff they no longer want. Donated items are then sold to folks who need them at a low price.

"We make a lot of money off of people's castoffs and in turn, that money supports the church and church activities," he said, noting that the most recent sale brought in about $12,000, some of which went to keep the parish school running.

Paula Bowers, the church secretary, began working at St. Mary's about 30 years ago when her children began school there. Today her grandchildren are members of the parish as well. Part of the beauty, she said, is the feeling people get at St. Mary's of belonging to a large, extended family.

"It's very peaceful," said Bowers, who noted that people still kneel when they receive Communion at St. Mary's. "We know so many people and they are very kind to one another."

THOMAS PANGBORN
Credit: Catholic Review

Thomas Pangborn was an especially generous member of St. Mary's, an industrialist and philanthropist who made a fortune in sand blasting and gave much of it away to various Catholic causes in Hagerstown and across the nation.

Among the buildings established by his gifts are the Pangborn School of Science and Engineering at Catholic University in Washington, D.C.; Pangborn Hall at the University of Notre Dame in South Bend, Ind.; and a hall, also named for him, at Mount St. Mary's in Emmitsburg.

At the National Shrine Grotto of Lourdes in Emmitsburg, Mr. Pangborn is responsible for a 95-foot bell tower that features a large, bronze statue of the Blessed Mother sparkling with gold leaf.

At Mr. Pangborn's funeral in 1967, Lawrence Cardinal Shehan said, "He looked on all he was and all he had as a gift from God to be used for the good of his fellow men and for Christ's church... he was ever conscious that he would be held accountable for the use he made of his gifts."

JOE THOMAS, HUMBLE SERVANT

JOE THOMAS

photo credit: Kirsten Beckerman

Joe Thomas, a devoted member of St. Michael parish at Wolfe
and Lombard Streets in East Baltimore, is a regular volunteer
at the Beans and Bread soup kitchen, 402 South Bond Street,
just above Fells Point. Founded by Sister Mary Louise Zollar,
a Daughter of Charity, Beans and Bread is an outreach of
the St. Vincent DePaul Society.

Joe Thomas was born in Baltimore on July 26, 1923 and was baptized that same year at St. Michael parish at Wolfe and Lombard Streets in East Baltimore.

For 42 years, he worked in administration for the Bethlehem Steel shipyard.

A veteran of several East Baltimore parishes, Joe served as a lector at Our Lady of Pompei Church from 1964 to 1983. After many years at the Sacred Heart of Jesus parish in Highlandtown, Joe returned to St. Michael in the late 1970s when the parish's Legion of Mary was given a row house on South Chester Street to use as a headquarters and needed someone to look after it.

For a quarter-of-a-century, Thomas has showed up at the Maryland State Fair in Timonium to give away Legion of Mary prayer cards and instructions for praying the rosary.

"One of the things we faced in this area [around South Broadway] was evangelization," said Joe. "We saw a lot of potential to bring [the faith] to children. I think it did a lot of good; it brought a sense of spirituality to the neighborhood.

"On Sunday afternoons, a few of us would go down to Broadway and leave church bulletins in all the stores and restaurants. We'd talk to people in the street and invite them to come to church. We brought in a lot of Spanish-speaking people that way."

Originally a parish of Germans and German-Americans, St. Michael celebrated its 150th anniversary in 2002 and has been reinvigorated by an influx of Spanish-speaking Catholics, whom Joe Thomas tries to reach.

"We offer Hispanics a little bit of their country," said Sr. Sonia Marie Fernandez, a Mission Helper of the Sacred Heart who arrived at St. Michael in 1994 to work with the Hispanic community.

"We celebrate patron saints from 20 different countries that are represented in the neighborhood," said Sr. Sonia. "Not just Our Lady of Guadalupe."

Recent renovations at the church included restoring the clock, re-covering the steeple in copper, and fixing the bells, which had not been rung in more than a decade. The largest of the five St. Michael bells measures 58.5 inches in diameter and weighs about 4,000 pounds. The smallest weighs 700 pounds.

Joe Thomas weighs considerably less than that-- he is a gentle, sprightly man with a twinkle in his eye-- but his life's work on behalf of the church and its people rings as loud as any clock tower bell.

The same year that St. Patrick's began welcoming worshippers, the regular celebration of Mass was started at a chapel in the Harford County hamlet of Hickory. The sanctuary was dedicated in honor of St. Ignatius.

In 1803, the United States Senate ratified the Louisiana Purchase, greatly increasing the acreage and population under Bishop John Carroll's responsibility. That same year, architect Maximillan Godefroy completed his commission-- "Chapel of Our Lady of the Presentation"-- alongside of St. Mary's Seminary in the historic Seton Hill neighborhood.

St. Ignatius is the oldest continuously-active parish in the Archdiocese of Baltimore. "It's a real family atmosphere. Everybody participates," said parishioner Gail Ann Driscoll Hopkins. "Each year, everybody volunteers to make Christmas wreaths."

ST. MARY'S CHAPEL

Along with his fabled Battle Monument at the intersection of Calvert and Fayette Streets downtown — the most enduring symbol of municipal Baltimore and the centerpiece of the city's flag — Godefroy's chapel is one of the oldest examples of Gothic Revival architecture in America. The interior of the chapel was designed, in part, by Benjamin Henry Latrobe, architect of the U.S. Capitol building and the Baltimore Basilica.

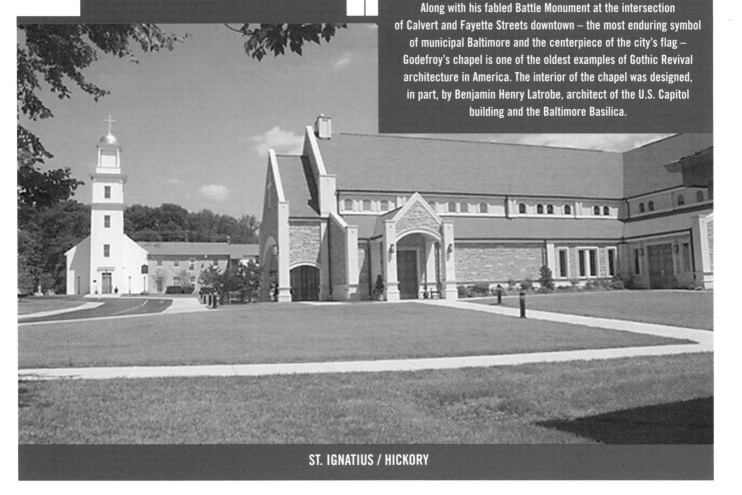

ST. IGNATIUS / HICKORY

In the spring of 1804, explorers Lewis and Clark, with a keelboat, two large canoes and not quite 50 men, began pushing up the Missouri in the first official exploration of unknown spaces by the fledgling United States.

In 1805, the Sulpicians received the charter from the state to establish St. Mary's College on the grounds of their seminary, opening it to all for enrollment, including religious and lay, Catholic and non-Catholic. It lasted until 1852, when Loyola College opened.

In 1806 Bishop John Carroll set in place the cornerstone for the first Roman Catholic Cathedral in the United States: the Basilica of the Assumption of the Blessed Virgin Mary on Cathedral Street in Baltimore.

■ ■ ■

Mount St. Mary's University resides in Emmitsburg, near the graves of Saint Elizabeth Seton and her nephew, James Roosevelt Bayley, the 8th archbishop of Baltimore [1872-1877].

Both Seton and Bayley were converts to the faith. The Rev. John DuBois, the founder of the college, was Mother Seton's confessor.

■ ■ ■

In 1808, John Carroll and Baltimore were together raised when Pope Pius VII elevated the diocese to an archdiocese. On April 8 of that year, on the recommendation of Bishop Carroll, Rome created the following dioceses: Boston, New York, Philadelphia, and the heavily-Catholic community of Bardstown, Kentucky.

These dioceses did not begin to function until 1810, when the first bishops of Philadelphia, Boston and Bardstown were ordained in Baltimore.

According to *"The Premier See,"* by Spalding, prohibitions included "theater going, dancing and the reading of books harmful to faith and morals, especially novels."

Mount Saint Mary's University and Seminary, founded by Father John DuBois in Emmitsburg in 1808, is the oldest private independent Catholic college in the United States. The University is co-ed with approximately 1400 undergraduate students, most of who live on campus. The seminary is the second oldest in the country. It has more than 150 seminarians and offers a M.A. in theology and a Masters of Divinity.

MOUNT ST. MARY'S UNIVERSITY / EMMITSBURG.

THE BASILICA OF THE NATIONAL SHRINE OF THE ASSUMPTION OF THE BLESSED VIRGIN MARY MOTHER CHURCH OF ROMAN CATHOLICISM IN THE UNITED STATES

"...erect a church in the form of a Cathedral,
in as much as time and circumstances allow...

from papal decree of 1789 establishing the Diocese of Baltimore.

In 1806, on land owned by General John Eager Howard, Revolutionary War hero and Maryland's fifth governor, ground was broken on a hill overlooking Baltimore harbor for a spectacular Catholic cathedral.

Howard's estate, Belvedere, covered much of what is now midtown Baltimore, and the property was sold to the Archdiocese in 1803 for $20,000, then considered a lot of money.

The architect selected for the new Cathedral was Benjamin Henry Latrobe, American's first professionally trained architect, and the architect of the United States Capitol under President Thomas Jefferson. Latrobe was at work on the U.S. Capitol when Bishop John Carroll's plans for a grand cathedral became known. Latrobe, a Protestant, immediately offered to design the proposed Cathedral for free.

The massive church would be the first Catholic cathedral in America, the first great house of worship built after the adoption of the Bill of Rights and its Constitutional guarantee of religious freedom sought over a century before by the Calvert family. It became a symbol of the nation's hard-earned religious freedom.

BENJAMIN HENRY LATROBE
by Thomas Sully

Scholars have established that Jefferson had some influence on the design of the Basilica, particularly its great dome and 24 skylights. Jefferson, who was close to Latrobe, insisted on a dome and skylights for the House of Representatives in the U.S. Capitol and wrote to Latrobe suggesting similar adornments for the Basilica."

The Basilica embodies Latrobe's evolving architectural ideas and represents the pinnacle of his architectural maturity. Once finished, it rivaled the Capitol in size, scale, and sophistication.

It also bears the astute political insights of the architecturally literate Bishop John Carroll who understood that if the Catholic Church was to be accepted in the new republic, it needed to have a definitively American symbol.

Construction of the Basilica occurred over two campaigns: 1806 to 1810 and 1817 to 1821, when it was completed and dedicated by Archbishop Maréchal.

Known as the "St. Peter's of North America" throughout the 19th century, the Cathedral hosted a series of Provincial and Plenary Councils, which guided the Church as the nation pushed westward and the Catholic population of the country, particularly in eastern cities like Baltimore, increased dramatically.

While Latrobe described the relationship between the Cathedral's two domes as "a feather upon the back of an elephant," the combination made for a spectacular view.

The outer dome was perforated with skylights, while the inner dome created a chamber to capture direct sunlight, the diffusion of which passed through the inner dome's 22-foot oculus to the marble floor below.

This original luminescence was described by early visitors as mystical, thus the term, *"lumiere mysterieuse."*

In 1906, Cardinal James Gibbons said of the Basilica, "what Mecca is to the Mohammedan, what the temple of Jerusalem is to the Israelite, and what St. Peter's Basilica is to the faithful of the Church Universal" that is what Baltimore's cathedral is to the church in America.

Around the world, Benjamin Latrobe's Basilica is studied as a work of genius. It is, said the scholar Nikolaus Pevsner, "North America's most beautiful church."

In 1937, acknowledging the church's importance and beauty, Pope Pius XI raised the Cathedral to the rank of Minor Basilica.

The Holy Father visited the Cathedral in 1969 as the Cardinal-Archbishop of Krakow and in 1995 as Pope.

Also in 1995, the Basilica was declared a National Shrine. The following year Mother Teresa, along with over 1,000 pilgrims, prayed in the church.

In 1999, the Basilica of the Historic Trust, Inc., whose mission is to preserve and maintain the Cathedral, launched a $32 million campaign to restore and repair the church. Necessary and long delayed repairs of the infrastructure are the primary goals of the restoration, along with return to the original Latrobe design.

In October 2001, Cardinal Keeler led members of the Basilica Historic Trust to the Vatican to present restoration plans for the Basilica to Pope John Paul II and to give the pontiff a framed rendering of the completed church, which the Pope described as the "architectural worldwide symbol of religious freedom."

Exterior work includes replacing the dilapidated century-old roof with a new roof that is true to the original design, installing new copper sheeting around the dome, repairing the sandstone columns of the portico, as well as stucco repair and the pointing of the Basilica's exterior stone.

One group that has been particularly helpful to the Basilica of the Historic Trust in helping them reach their fundraising target has been the Knights of Columbus, both nationally and locally, who spent several months in 2002 and 2003 selling raffle tickets to benefit the Basilica restoration.

"We'd like to contribute $50,000," said Romeo Gauthier, past state deputy of the Knights of Columbus, Maryland Council. "That was our pledge to the project."

A member of St. Bartholomew's parish, home to Knights of Columbus Council No. 9127, Gauthier said the Knights have done a good job of recruiting new members in an age where similar groups are struggling.

"We're one of the few fraternal organizations that are growing," said Gauthier. "I'm sure it is because of our very close ties to the Catholic Church. Our five areas of activity are church, community, the council, family, and youth."

Mr. Gauthier has been a frequent visitor to the Basilica in the time of its restoration. He particularly enjoyed a Mass celebrated there by Cardinal Keeler on the anniversary of the ordination of the Rev. Michael J. McGivney, founder of the Knights of Columbus.

Father McGivney was ordained at the Basilica by Cardinal Gibbons and his life's work is commemorated there.

Completion of the restoration project is set for the cathedral's bi-centennial in 2006.

The Basilica is co-Cathedral of the Archdiocese of Baltimore with the Cathedral of Mary Our Queen, which was dedicated in 1959.

ROMEO GAUTHIER

Knights of Columbus Past State Deputy and member of St. Bartholomew's parish in Manchester. Nationally, the Knights of Columbus have donated $1,000,000 to the restoration of the Basilica.

Credit: Basilica Historic Trust

An artist's rendering of the restored Basilica, scheduled to be re-dedicated in November 2006.

ST. ANTHONY SHRINE

Today, parishioners of the St. Anthony Shrine, about 370 families, participate in a range of ministries. They work as Eucharistic ministers, make regular visits to the sick, adopt needy families in the Emmitsburg/Thurmont area and prepare luncheon receptions for funerals.

The St. Anthony Shrine is part of an ecumenical committee in Frederick County that reaches out to the local poor and performs much of this work in conjunction with its neighbors at the Our Lady of Mt. Carmel parish, also in Emmitsburg.

Part of the ecumenical committee's mission, said St. Anthony parish secretary Diane Decker, is to help the poor maintain their dignity in asking for help without a lot of red tape.

When the needy arrive at the Seton Center screening and outreach office, supported by St. Anthony and other area churches, they only have to tell their story once instead of going, hat in hand, from door-to-door for help.

The pastoral life director at the St. Anthony Shrine is Sr. Joan Maenner, O.S.F.; John Hawkins served as permanent deacon and Sr. Valenta Rusin, F.S.S.J. is director of religious education.

Named for Saint Anthony of Padua, the Shrine parish near Emmitsburg harkens to Colonial days when Catholic families from Southern Maryland moved to Frederick County to farm. Legend holds that a conch shell was brought from the shores of Southern Maryland to call Catholic settlers of the valley to Mass said by traveling Jesuits. A chapel in the house of the Elder family was used for the first Eucharistic celebration, possibly as early as 1734. St. Anthony mission was established in 1805 and the St. Anthony sanctuary was consecrated in the late 1800s.

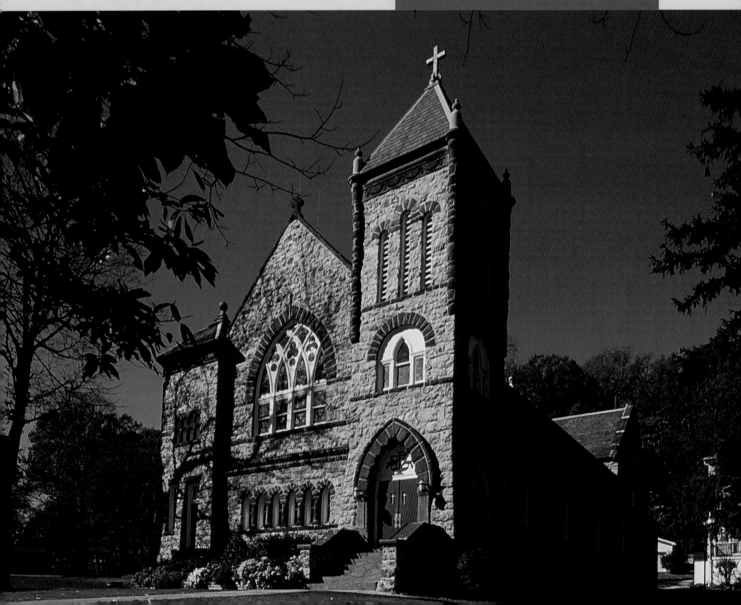

Catholics had been living in the Frostburg area of Western Maryland as early as 1812, the year in which Michael Frost, founder of the city, built a home on East Main Street.

Father John J. Chanche, later the Bishop of Natchez, Mississippi, offered the first Mass in Eckhart, a small mining town. Both Frostburg and Eckhart were missions of Mount Savage.

The first Catholic mission in what is now Garrett County was St. Mary's at Blooming Rose. Once a small settlement, Blooming Rose exists only in name today as an area a few miles west of Friendsville.

■ ■ ■

On Dec. 3, 1815, at age 79 John Carroll's extraordinary journey in this world came to an end on the feast day of the legendary Jesuit missionary, St. Francis Xavier.

The Baltimore *Telegraph* reported that the archbishop's funeral: "brought together a greater crowd than we have ever witnessed... the great and the rich, the poor and the lowly..."

CRYPT OF JOHN CARROLL AT THE BASILICA

John Carroll will be remembered as a patriot, religious pioneer and advocate for the education of all. Said Cardinal Keeler: "His writings show an early appreciation of using English in the liturgy..."

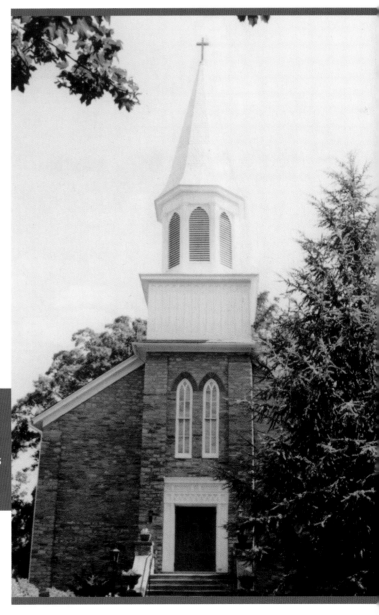

ST. JOSEPH-ON-CARROLTON MANOR / BUCKEYSTOWN

Established in 1811, the first church was constructed in 1820 under the direction of a Jesuit priest from Belgium, Fr. Francis Maleve, S.J. on land donated by the Carroll Family.

MOTHER ELIZABETH ANN SETON, AMERICA'S FIRST SAINT

*"Faith lifts the staggering soul on one side, hope supports it on the other.
Experience says it must be and love says let it be."*

- from letter written by Mother Seton in 1810

Saint Elizabeth Ann Seton was a convert to Roman Catholicism who founded the first order of sisters borne in the United States.

So many roles had Mother Seton in her brief 46 years: wife, mother, widow, single parent, educator, social minister, and spiritual leader. Elizabeth Bayley Seton was the first person born in the United States to be canonized a saint, bestowed upon her on Sept. 14, 1975.

Born in New York City two years before the United States declared independence from Britain, Seton came from a prominent Anglican family in Manhattan.

Elizabeth – who'd fallen into a severe depression when her father and stepmother separated – was disposed to contemplation, finding contentment in nature, poetry and music. She was especially fond of the piano and made frequent diary entries that spoke of religious calling.

She married in 1794 to Willam Magee Seton. Samuel Provoost, first Episcopal bishop of New York, presided over the wedding vows. The marriage to the merchant Seton thrust Elizabeth into social prominence.

ST. JOSEPH / EMMITSBURG

The beginnings of the St. Joseph parish go back to Catholic settlers who arrived as early as 1730. Samuel Emmit, an immigrant from Ireland, arrived in 1757, acquired 2,250 acres and gave his name to the area.

In 1793, the Rev. Matthew Ryan arrived from Frederick to be the first resident pastor of the St. Joseph parish. The first church was built that same year and lasted until it was razed for the present sanctuary. He was followed by the Rev. Samuel Cooper in 1818. A former sea captain, Cooper graduated from St. Mary's Seminary in Baltimore and gave the money used to buy property for Mother Elizabeth Ann Seton and her Sisters of Charity.

In 1841, Father John McCaffrey arrived as pastor and built a new church, which stands today. McCaffrey also served as president of Mount St. Mary's College.

At the end of World War II, Father Francis Stauble became pastor of St. Joseph's. The Daughters of Charity donated land on which Stauble was able to create a new parish cemetery on South Seton Avenue.

In 1976, the year after Mother Seton was canonized, the chapel and altar in honor of the saint were dedicated in the chapel of the St. Joseph's Provincial House and future basilica.

Seton's "Stone House" was named to the National Register of Historic places as well.

In 2001, the Rev. James O. Kiernan, C.M., took office as pastor. Kiernan was most recently at work on a Stewardship Program for the parish, coordinating the effort wth the Archdiocese of Baltimore.

He also hired Sister Eileen Healey, a Daughter of Charity, to supervise religious education programs.

ANNE THERESA O'NEILL

Diagnosed with acute, lymphatic leukemia as a child, O'Neill was a student at Seton High School on North Charles Street when her patron was under consideration for sainthood in the early 1960s.
At that time, O'Neill and her family traveled to Rome to testify to Seton's intercession in the girl's recovery.
Because Elizabeth Seton considered her first vocation to her children – and then to the young women entrusted to her order – mothers in need often turn to her for help.
Such was the case of Anne O'Neill's mother in 1952 when the then-four-year-old lay dying.
While Mrs. O'Neill made a Novena to Mother Seton, medical science was failing her daughter and when the child came down with an acute case of chicken pox in addition to leukemia, doctors gave the family no hope.
It was then that Sister of Charity Mary Alice Fowler instructed her Order and the children in all of the Order's schools to join Mrs. O'Neill in her Novena.
Eighteen days later, Anne came home from the hospital, her cancer in remission.

STATUE OF MOTHER SETON
photo credit: Michael Carter

Emmittsburg statue of the foundress and First Superior of the Sisters of Charity in the United States.
Seton and her Sisters of Charity cared for orphans, widows, and poor families with special attention to those oppressed by poverty in all its forms as well as children who lacked education and instruction in the faith.
In time, the Sisters of Charity as a community multiplied into six independent new communities across North America.

Elizabeth, however, was drawn to acts of corporal mercy and – with her sister-in-law and closest friend, Rebecca Mary Seton – tended to the sick and dying among family, friends and neighbors in need.

She helped to found the Society for the Relief of Poor Widows with Small Children in 1797 and served as the group treasurer. Along the way, she and her husband had five children.

Bad luck, however, began to hound the Setons: three of their children would die early and when William's father died in 1798, Elizabeth and her husband were forced to take over the family business, which ultimately failed and cost them their home.

As William's health began to falter from the onset of tuberculosis, the family sailed to Italy in the hope that a warmer climate would restore him.

Instead, he died in Pisa, leaving Elizabeth – a woman who had written her beloved marvelous love letters, whose passion for him was only equaled by her later vocation - a widow at the age of 29 with five children under the age of eight.

The experience – combined with the hospitality of their Italian hosts - changed Elizabeth and her oldest child forever. And forever changed the history of Catholicism in the United States.

Having been introduced to Roman Catholicism in Italy, Elizabeth found a text of the Memorare after her return to the United States in June of 1804 and began to look into the faith.

She wanted to know about the Sacred Liturgy, the Real Presence in the Eucharist, and the Church's direct unbroken link with Christ and the apostles.

In a memoir written for her sister-in-law Rebecca Seton, Elizabeth reveals the intimate details of her journey to conversion. Her Protestant friends and relatives were not supportive. Indeed, they were hostile.

The death of Rebecca, combined with financial stress that forced her to move the family into ever less expensive housing, deepened Elizabeth's anguish.

In the midst of trying to discern God's will – consulting with various clergy and pursuing prayer - the Blessed Mother became a focus of her faith.

She became a Catholic on March 14, 1805 at St. Peter's Church in lower Manhattan. Two weeks later she made her First Communion and on Pentecost Sunday of 1806, she was confirmed by Bishop John Carroll and took Mary as her confirmation name.

Thereafter, she was Mary Elizabeth Ann Seton.

Early attempts at establishing herself as a teacher failed, and she continued to struggle to support her children.

In 1806, she happened to meet the Sulpician priest Louis William Dubourg when he visited New York. For a good ten years, Dubourg had wanted an order of religious women to teach girls in Baltimore.

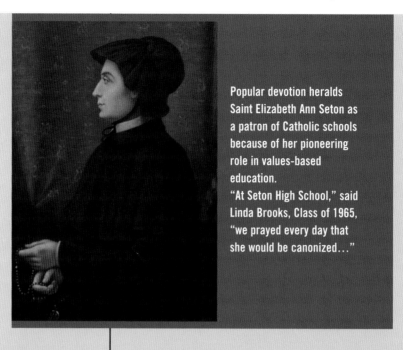

Popular devotion heralds Saint Elizabeth Ann Seton as a patron of Catholic schools because of her pioneering role in values-based education.
"At Seton High School," said Linda Brooks, Class of 1965, "we prayed every day that she would be canonized..."

Along with John Carroll, whom Elizabeth had long considered her spiritual father, she was invited to the Premier See Baltimore to fulfill Dubourg's wish of beginning a small school and developing a sisterhood modeled on the Daughters of charity of Paris.

Elizabeth arrived on the banks of the Patapsco River on June 16, 1808 on the ship Shepherdess, for whom the Seton High School yearbook was named.

She taught school for the next year as the Sulpicians recruited candidates for the new order. On March 25, 1809, Elizabeth took a vow of chastity and obedience to John Carroll for one year in Godefroy's chapel at Saint Mary's Seminary on Paca Street.

The archbishop gave her the title "Mother Seton" and in June, for the first time, the sisters appeared in uniform habits: a black dress, cape and bonnet patterned after the widows of Italy that Elizabeth had met there.

A wealthy seminarian and convert, Samuel Sutherland Cooper, bought 269 acres near Emmitsburg for the order. Cooper wanted to build an institution for female education rooted in Catholic values and faith. There would also be programs for the poor and the elderly. Cooper wanted Mother Seton to run the educational program.

William Emmit – for whom the mountain town is named - was a witness to the purchase of the Fleming property for Mother Seton by Samuel Cooper.

Elizabeth arrived in Emmitsburg with her sisters in June of 1809. The Rev. John Dubois, the Sulpician

who founded Mount Saint Mary's University and Seminary in Emmitsburg offered the women his cabin on Saint Mary's Mountain until their lodging in the nearby valley was ready.

In February of 1810, Elizabeth opened Saint Joseph's Free School, educating local girls in need for free, the first Catholic school of its kind in the nation.

All subsequent works sponsored by the Daughters of Charity followed the original charter granted by the State of Maryland in 1817 for the care of the sick, the elderly, the needy and general education.

Saint Joseph's Academy began May 14, 1810, with boarding students who paid tuition, allowing the Sisters of Charity to finance their free school. This, along with the work of the Georgetown Visitation nuns at the end of the 18th century, was the genesis of Catholic education in the United States.

Though carving out a community was not easy, nearly 100 women turned up in Emmitsburg in Seton's decades of work there, with 86 of them taking vows as Sisters of Charity.

Of these, some 70 percent remained Sisters of Charity for life. For many it was a short life and Mother Seton buried 18 of her fellow sisters at Emmitsburg, in additon to two of her daughters – Annina, her oldest and Rebecca – as well as sisters-in-law Harriet and Cecelia Seton.

Elected by the community to be the first Mother of the Sisters of Charity, Elizabeth Seton was reelected to the top spot until her death on January 4, 1821 at age 46.

To the last, her spiritual director was the Rev. Simon Gabriel Bruté, a Sulpician assigned to Mount Saint Mary's who also served as chaplain for the Sisters of Charity.

Bruté advised Elizabeth to read and translate the lives and spiritual writings of of Louise de Marillac and The Life of the Venerable Servant of God Vincent de Paul, whose rule of community was adopted by the Sisters of Charity.

Dominant themes in Elizabeth's writing include a single-hearted pursuit of God's Divine Will, nourishment from the Eucharist and Scripture – confidence in God's Will as revealed through Providence and service to Jesus Christ through the poor.

Her work has been published in Elizabeth Bayley Seton Collected Writings (New City Press) and exists in the early documents of the Sisters of Charity of Saint Joseph's.

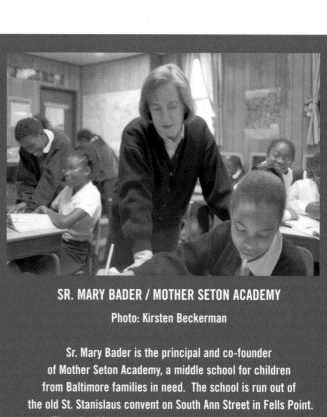

SR. MARY BADER / MOTHER SETON ACADEMY

Photo: Kirsten Beckerman

Sr. Mary Bader is the principal and co-founder of Mother Seton Academy, a middle school for children from Baltimore families in need. The school is run out of the old St. Stanislaus convent on South Ann Street in Fells Point. The school began at the old St. Patrick parish school on Broadway in 1993. The next year it moved to St. Stan's. "Baltimore feels like a very Catholic city compared to other cities, particularly those in the South," said Bader. "The Catholic presence is very much noted in the number of religious here, the many Catholic institutions and strong social outreach – Catholic Charities and Catholic Relief Services. "And the Church is very alive and present in the city. Partners in Excellence provides scholarships for low-income children to receive a Catholic education and the Cardinal's Lenten appeal has raised $10 million to support these programs as well." Continued Bader: "I see Catholic urban education as a means of evangelization. Most urban students aren't Catholic. Yet their families want them to receive a strong Christian education which teaches solid values and morals. Though many folks have left the city - both Catholics and non-Catholics - the Church's mission to serve the poor remains the same."

MOTHER SETON

Cardinal James Gibbons initiated Mother Seton's case for canonization in 1882. It was officially introduced at the Vatican in 1940 and moved ahead steadily. Blessed John XXIII declared Elizabeth venerable December 18, 1959, beatifying her on March 17, 1963.

Pope Paul VI canonized Saint Elizabeth Ann Seton on September 14, 1975, the Catholic Church's International Year of the Woman.

Three miracles were accepted by the Holy See as occurring through Mother Seton's intercession. In addition to the recovery of the Baltimorean Anne O'Neill, from leukemia, other cures included St. Louis Daughter of Charity Gertrude Korzendorfer of cancer and New Yorker Carl Kalin from a rare form of encephalitis.

City of Baltimore on the Rise

The Ethnic Urban Village and Civil War

"To be a real Baltimorean, three of your grandparents have to be born here. The church grew throughout the city through our ethnic grandparents and great-grandparents... people wanted a place to worship where they could speak their own language. Of course the Mass was in Latin, but what about the sermon and the bingo and the men's club?"

The Rev. Richard Lawrence

real Baltimorean and pastor
St. Vincent de Paul, Front Street

With the death of Archbishop John Carroll, a giant by any standard, the task of filling the void fell to the Rev. Leonard Neale. A Maryland native from a well-established Port Tobacco family, Neale was one of five siblings enter religious life.

Prior to succeeding Carroll, Neale served as president of Georgetown University, a seven-year stretch during which he reinvented the small school for men into a college of genuine prestige.

After leaving his position at Georgetown, Neale was consecrated a bishop by Carroll, the

ARCHBISHOP LEONARD NEALE

The second bishop of Baltimore, Archbishop Neale was the first bishop consecrated within the boundaries of the United States.

first ceremony of its kind in the United States, in 1800.

Some 15 years later – within months of Pope Pius VII's restoration of the Jesuits as a world order, Neale succeeded Carroll as bishop of Baltimore.

Archbishop Neale, buried in the crypt beneath the Visitation convent in Georgetown, served as Ordinary of Baltimore for less than two years before his death in 1817.

In that time, he seldom stayed in Baltimore and traveled to the seat of his archdiocese only when absolutely necessary, preferring to stay in Georgetown where he could be close to the

Visitation Sisters, whom he favored. In 1817, having the community officially recognized by Rome and affiliated with the Order of the Visitation, he succeeded in raising the Order to a monastery with the blessings of Pope Pius VII.

The primary contribution of the Visitation Sisters to Catholic life in Baltimore was the founding in 1852 of the Mount de Sales Academy just over the city line near St. Agnes parish and Catonsville.

Over the years, Mount de Sales has educated young women among them Mary Pinkney Hardy, the mother of General Douglas MacArthur, and Estelle Wetzler, the first woman from the Western world to ascend Mount Fuji.

Wetzler, who died near Baltimore in 1999 at age 85, joined an expedition trudging up Mount Everest when she was 71-years-old. She reached 16,000 feet before turning back.

Mount de Sales ceased to be a boarding school in 1933, and in 1979 the Visitation nuns decided to leave Baltimore. The school was purchased by the Board of Trustees and is now administered by the Dominican Sisters of Nashville.

Mount de Sales was the first private school in Baltimore County to offer education to young women of all religious backgrounds. At the beginning of the 21st century, enrollment at the college preparatory school was about 450 students. The girls are identified by uniforms featuring a large insignia of the Miraculous Medal.

In celebration of the academy's 150th Anniversary in 2002, Mount de Sales published a hard-cover history titled: *"An Academy of Every Virtue."*

■ ■ ■

With the death of Archbishop Neale in 1817 came the French-born Sulpician Ambrose Maréchal to take over the archdiocese in 1817. Maréchal was consecrated

MOUNT DE SALES ACADEMY

More than 95 percent of all Mount de Sales graduates go on to college. Graduates are also entering the convent, with more than a half-dozen vocations coming from the school in the past 20 years.

INSTITUTE OF NOTRE DAME, 901 AISQUITH STREET

third Archbishop of Baltimore at St. Peter's in Baltimore on December 14, 1817 and received the Sacred Pallium two years later.

Serving as archbishop until his death in 1828, Maréchal oversaw the completion of the Basilica of the Assumption.

At the time of Maréchal's appointment, the Premier See comprised parishes in Maryland, Virginia, the Carolinas, Georgia, and the territory west of the Peach State to the Mississippi. According to the archbishop's estimate, there were 100,000 Catholics throughout those lands.

Some 10,000 Catholics lived in or near the City of Baltimore at the time, a significant increase from the 800 or so counted when the diocese was founded in 1789.

Maréchal's former students back in Marseilles presented him with a marble altar at the time of his rise to prominence in Baltimore that is still used in the Basilica.

Further evidence of French influence can be seen in the founding of the School Sisters of Notre Dame--from the Congregation of Notre-Dame founded by St. Peter Fourier in France in the late 16th century.

"I did not sense the importance of IND while I was there... There were many girls who went there because their mothers and grandmothers had gone there. I chose IND because my best friend was going. I remember the 'old side' where some of the nuns lived – original statues and stained glass – it was quite awesome, even for a self-involved 16-year-old who wasn't really aware of the history of her surroundings..."
Lindley Corcoran, class of 1983

Six sisters arrived in Baltimore from Elk County, Pennsylvania via Germany in early August of 1847, establishing their first Motherhouse on Aisquith Street near Central Avenue where they would open the Institute of Notre Dame and Notre Dame College of Maryland.

Founded in East Baltimore more than 150 years ago, IND is one of the most fabled Catholic institutions in Baltimore, the result of the School Sisters' finding space in a Redemptorist compound at St. James Church.

Used for many IND functions, such as the first Mass of the new school year and the crowning of the Blessed Mother on May Day, St. James was sold by the Redemptorists in 1990 and is now the Urban Baptist Fellowship.

So great was German immigration by the mid-to-late 19th century that by the turn of the century, one-third of Baltimore's population spoke German and newspapers claimed that a fellow could walk from one end of Baltimore to the other and never hear English.

Clipper ships built along the harbor ferried tobacco to Bremen and brought back immigrants.

The census of 1850 reported that the Catholic Church, swelled by the newly landed Germans, more than 30 percent of whom were Catholic, ranked No. 3 in size for Maryland denominations with 65 churches seating 31,000 people.

By 1870, a generation after the School Sisters landed on Aisquith Street, more than half the immigrant population of Baltimore was German.

Among the hundreds of thousands arriving from the Fatherland, a greater number pouring into Baltimore at times than New York City, were butchers, silversmiths, brewers, harness-makers, innkeepers, priests, and nuns.

■ ■ ■

Like all Catholic high schools in metropolitan Baltimore, be it Archbishop Curley or Seton Keough, the Institute of Notre Dame benefits from the affection and loyalty of generations of alumnae. Few are more devoted than Sarah "Sally" Murphy, tireless volunteer from the class of 1951.

A three-day-a-week volunteer in IND's development office, Murphy helps with the school's annual auction and fund drive, its 5K run, various class reunions, and, mostly, every little thing.

A true Catholic of Baltimore, Sally Murphy is the daughter of Jerome Murphy,

SALLY MURPHY, IND CLASS OF 1951

"Being a Catholic means putting into effect everything you've learned through the years at home and at school, to practice your faith. Traditional values are a way of life. It's the satisfaction of completing something and knowing that we were put on Earth to serve one another..."

a pharmacist born near IND on Eager Street in 1897, and the former Sarah Tumbleson, whose father owned a drug store opposite the old Carmelite convent near Valley and Eden Streets.

"My mother was born in 1899, she was one of eight children," said Sally Murphy. "In the summer, they'd carry cold drinks over to the sisters."

Jerome, a graduate of Loyola High School, and Sarah, a medical secretary who completed a commercial course for girls in the old St. Paul's parish, were married in 1922 in the sanctuary of St. Ann's at Greenmount Ave. and 22nd Street.

"Dad was a downtown pharmacist at Charles and Chase Streets for Hynson, Westcott and Dunning, the pharmaceutical company which developed the antiseptic mercurochrome.

"I was born in 1933 and they called me Sally from the start. We lived in the 2200 block of Cecil Avenue with a lot of other Irish families when I was born and I went to St. Ann's grade school."

She was particularly keen on the musicals and operettas the adult drama club put on at St. Ann's, but by the time she was old enough to join, the group had disbanded.

"They'd do dress rehearsals for the kids in the school," she said. "From my house on Cecil Avenue to IND was about a half-hour walk. To get here by 7:30 a.m., I took two streetcars, the No. 13 at North Avenue and Cecil and then I transferred to the No. 19 at North and Harford Road.

"I came so much for glee club practice," she said. "That my father said we had more rehearsals than the Vatican choir."

From an early age, Sally was aware of the school's history, the 2nd, 3rd, and 4th generations of young women who enrolled, how "many families didn't even look anywhere else" to send their daughters.

Former Baltimore mayor, "Young Tommy" D'Alessandro III, is on the school's Board of Directors.

In the lat 1980s, the former mayor went in person to the Redemptorist provincial on behalf of IND to inquire about acquiring St. James Church, which historically had been used for many school functions such as the first Mass of the new school year and the annual awarding of class rings.

"You can see that steeple from almost any part of Baltimore," said D'Alessandro, a graduate of Loyola High School and Loyola College whose mother and sister graduated from IND. "When I was a kid they [St. James] had one of the best fife and drum corps in the country."

Other IND alumnae included Mary Gail Hare, Class of 1964, and veteran *Baltimore Sun* reporter.

ROUTE 66 TV STARS

Mary Gail Hare: "Sr. Leone, the newspaper moderator, let a group of freshman go where they were filming an episode of the Route 66 television show in Baltimore. We had been promised interviews with the stars. We had to wear our IND uniforms, blue plaid skirts, four-inches below the bend of the knee, blazers and white starched blouses, and our miraculous medals around our necks. Sister told us we could talk to them, but only outside, not anywhere near a motel room."

[Note: The episode Hare refers to is "The Mud Nest," which aired in November, 1961. While cruising through a small Maryland town, Buzz Murdock-- played by the good-looking George Maharis-- meets people who resemble him, leading to a search for his long-lost mother. Along the way, there are early Sixties scenes of Mount Vernon, East Baltimore and Johns Hopkins Hospital.]

MARY GAIL HARE AND HUSBAND DAVID, 1998 AT WEDDING OF THEIR DAUGHTER, MARY CONSTANCE HARE, AT ST. MARY'S IN GOVANS.

"IND imprints itself on your soul. It was the blue-collar school and when I went back recently to give a talk on journalism, it was like nothing had changed, there were still walls of windows looking out over the City. The wealthier girls went to Notre Dame Prep... I think we tried harder to be better than them."

In Sally Murphy's senior year of IND, when tuition, now more than $7,000 a year, was about $100, Murphy's mother passed away. After graduation, she stayed home to keep house for her father and brother Joseph, who was two years Sally's junior and died in 1987.

"We sold the Cecil Avenue house for somewhere between $8,000 and $10,000 in

SR. DOLORES BAUMGARTNER, SSND

Dolores Baumgartner was born in Philadelphia in 1920 and entered the School Sisters of Notre Dame in 1936. Some 67 years later, she is one of the few nuns in the United States who still wears a veil.

"I'll be out in a restaurant and someone will come up to me and say 'thank you,' for being willing to still look like a nun," she said. "I think we owe that to people, to be a symbol of what we profess. I believe in it."

SSND MOTHER HOUSE
North Charles Street and Bellona Avenue.

SR. DOLORES BAUMGARTNER, SSND

"I haven't had a sorrowful life... it's been exceptionally good..."

Soon after entering the convent during the Great Depression, Sr. Dolores was assigned to the teaching order's provincial mother house on Aisquith Street in East Baltimore.

An entire section of the original mother house has been renovated as a center to help women in the impoverished East Baltimore neighborhood around IND prepare for and pass the state high school equivalency exam. It is called Caroline Center.

"It's a practical thing," said Sr. Dolores, once the principal of Blessed Sacrament parish school. "Education enables people to reach their full development."

"They learn how to present themselves for employment. The same way we taught our girls [in the old days] when any bank or business would seek out our students because of their accuracy."

Of Catholic Baltimore, in which she has spent so much of her life, Sr. Dolores said: "There are so many famous stories... like Mr. [Thomas J.] O'Neill who promised to build a Cathedral if his department store was protected from the Great Fire of 1904. Well the wind changed, the fire went the other way and he was true to his word."

Although most are not as dramatic in their gratitude as the department store king, Sr. Dolores believes that "Baltimore Catholics are very generous with their time and their means."

Certainly, Dolores Baumgartner has been generous with her life. Over the years, she has worked with the sick and the elderly, helped battered children get a kindergarten education in a safe environment, and helped young women find their way to religious vocations.

From 1961 to 1968, she served as postulant directress of SSND, guiding women through the preparatory stage of becoming a School Sister of Notre Dame.

"After Vatican II there was a big exodus and the last year it was very lean," she said. "There were just about 18 girls" who stayed on to take final vows.

The scarcity of interested candidates, after peak years in the 1950s and early 1960s that saw many hundreds of girls come forward troubles the aging nun.

"We were so large when I was directress that we had to split the province," she said. "We have one postulant now in our entire province, a woman in her 30s. What can we do if the girls aren't entering?

"We were founded to be educators and our schools are closing after all those years when we flourished," she said. "We're not getting new recruits and the sisters are dying."

Near the end of her own life, in the midst of a once flourishing movement struggling to find a new way in a new century, Sr. Dolores prayed to her God for guidance.

"I was praying to find out what the Lord wanted me to do and a sister came to ask if I'd be interested in coming to the mother house and make visits to the infirmary," she said. "So now I'm a traveling companion for sisters who have to go to the doctor and other things.

"It's not a chore; it's a privilege. Life isn't long enough to spread that message, that we're all one."

1954 and moved to Argonne Drive, where we joined Blessed Sacrament parish," she said.

At Blessed Sacrament, Sally helped with Cardinal Shehan's annual campaign and in 1971, the family moved to the St. Pius X parish in Rodgers Forge, where she still lives.

The education and discipline, a truer sense of discipline than the cliché of a ruler on the knuckles, that Murphy received at IND prepared her for a long career with the City of Baltimore.

"After graduation, I decided I wanted to enter the business world but did not want to be a secretary," she said. "The head of the sanitation department in the City was a classmate of my father's at St. John's and they bumped into each other and were talking one day about their kids and the man told my father to come down. I was hired.

"At first I kept track of things like tonnages [of garbage] collected by the trucks every day," said Murphy. "But I was able to finish that job by 10 a.m. and couldn't sit and do nothing. I kept asking if they had anything else for me to do. The department had a PR lady at the time – Dorothy Shipley Granger – and she had a weekly radio show. She'd been a product of Catholic schools and when she found out I had graduated from IND she took a great interest in me."

Nearly half-a-century later, with only her IND diploma, old school savvy mixed with moxie, and her Catholic values as a compass, Murphy would retire from city government as a public works administrator in charge of a multi-million dollar budget.

"All through my education, values were part of the curriculum," she said. "No matter what the subject, no matter what the task, 100 percent effort was always given. You know what's expected and you don't twiddle your thumbs. From that, you get a sense of satisfaction."

The Basilica – an immense project launched by Archbishop Carroll in 1806 – was completed under Maréchal and consecrated on May 31, 1821. In the same year, St. Peter opened in Libertytown, Frederick County.

ST. PETER THE APOSTLE / LIBERTYTOWN

St. Peter the Apostle stands about ten miles east
of Frederick on Route 26.
"I've been around Baltimore 45 years, since I came
to Baltimore with the U.S. Coast and Geodetic survey,"
said deacon Mike Misulia, an 85-year-old native of Manhattan.
"My first church, when I was just married
during World War II, was Blessed Sacrament,
but I wanted to live in the country
and have Catholic education for my sons
and lo and behold, I found Libertytown
with St. John's schools nearby. I've been in every Catholic
organization in Libertytown and finally I became a deacon.
"We have 850 families now. When I arrived a half-century ago,
it was only 200. It's grown as a bedroom community for
Washington." The church was destroyed by fire on June 3,
2004 and plans for a new church are underway.
See chapter nine for full story
on the blaze and campaign to rebuild.

56

MIKE MISULIA OUTSIDE ST. PETER'S

"I'm a convert from Russian orthodoxy
and as far as I can tell, the only difference
is the primacy of the Pope."
Deacon Mike Misulia

"The Carmelites have long been a prayer presence in Baltimore and have always had close relationships with the people and with other religious communities as they were founded or came to the area," said Sr. Connie FitzGerald, who has been directing a major renovation of the Carmelite's residence at 1318 Dulaney Valley Road, where they have been in residence for more than 40 years.

"From the beginnings of the Archdiocese, John Carroll and the first [Baltimore] bishops who went out to other new dioceses, visited the nuns and relied on their prayer support and friendship. This has taken many forms through 213 years."

"Culturally, our sisters, like the Jesuits – and unlike other religious communities in the area - were Americans from some of the oldest families in Maryland, women who had gone to monasteries in Europe beginning in the middle of the 18th century and returned in 1790 to found the first community of women religious in the thirteen original colonies," said FitzGerald.

Well-known to many older Baltimoreans was the Carmelite monastery at Caroline and Biddle Streets, razed by the City of Baltimore after the order left in 1961 and now the site of a public elementary school.

**CARMELITE MONASTERY
1318 DULANEY VALLEY ROAD
TOWSON, MARYLAND**

"We especially give thanks to God
for our Carmel in Baltimore
celebrating its 200 years
in the Archdiocese of Baltimore,
Maryland 1790-July 21, 1990."
From the preface to
"Carmel in America."
The sisters moved from Port Tobacco
to the City of Baltimore in 1831
and in 1961 left the Biddle Street
cloisters for Dulaney Valley.

SAINT THERESA & ELEANOR STEIN

"Our first daughter died five days after her birth and I prayed to St. Gerard to become pregnant," said Eleanor Stein. "Our second daughter was born Feb. 19, 1960, but after the second day, she started to have problems feeding and began losing weight."

After a month, the infant continued to throw up everything she was fed and doctors wanted to do exploratory surgery. The Steins refused and when a nun working as a nurse at Mercy asked the baby's name, she was told: "Theresa Gerard."

"St. Therese will storm the gates of heaven," said the nun of the Carmelite saint, [1873-1897].

The next day, the infant was found to have gained a half-pound and was keeping down her food. Soon, she was gaining weight daily and came home from the hospital on March 25, 1960.

"The pediatrician told us that he did not do anything to cause her to stop vomiting and gain weight, but that someone very powerful put their hands on her," said Mrs. Stein of the baby who is now 45 and a mother of her own.

"Of course, we attribute this to the Little Flower storming the gates of heaven."

Eleanor Cucco Stein and family.
A lifelong parishioner of St. Leo the Great in Little Italy,
Mrs. Stein credits prayers to St. Gerard
and St. Therese of Lisieux.
The "Little Flower" of Jesus through
the Carmelite Sisters,
for the survival of her daughter, Theresa.

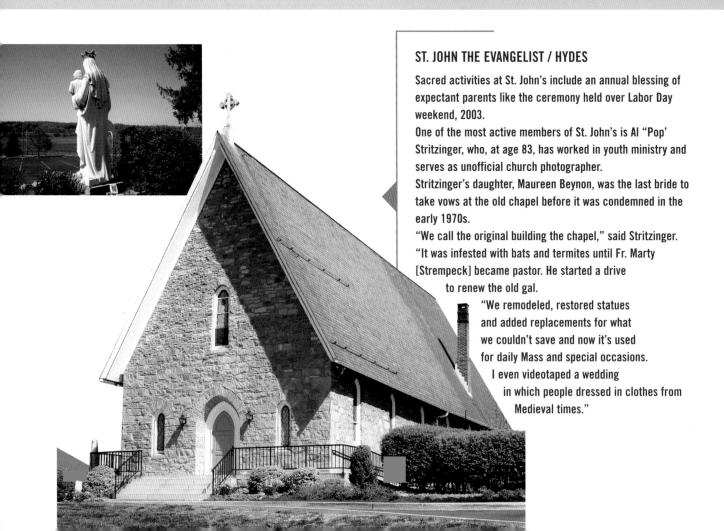

ST. JOHN THE EVANGELIST / HYDES

Sacred activities at St. John's include an annual blessing of expectant parents like the ceremony held over Labor Day weekend, 2003.

One of the most active members of St. John's is Al "Pop' Stritzinger, who, at age 83, has worked in youth ministry and serves as unofficial church photographer.

Stritzinger's daughter, Maureen Beynon, was the last bride to take vows at the old chapel before it was condemned in the early 1970s.

"We call the original building the chapel," said Stritzinger. "It was infested with bats and termites until Fr. Marty [Strempeck] became pastor. He started a drive to renew the old gal.

"We remodeled, restored statues and added replacements for what we couldn't save and now it's used for daily Mass and special occasions. I even videotaped a wedding in which people dressed in clothes from Medieval times."

AL "POP" STRITZINGER, 83, WITH WIFE BARBARA

"I came to Maryland from Pennsylvania in 1936 and went to Sacred Heart of Jesus when we lived at 2937 Eastern Avenue. I was married in 1943 at Sacred Heart and my wife and I [the former Barbara Vasold, a graduate of St. Michael's business school] moved to Middle River in 1944 and went to Our Lady of Mount Carmel.

"We had an Italian priest there and he had a strong accent. One Sunday the sermon was about alcohol and he said, 'A little glass of wine now and then doesn't hurt anybody…'

"Then in 1945 we moved to Parkville and I attended St. Ursula's and then back to Highlandtown until 1948 when we moved to Govans and attended Mass at St. Mary's until 1960 when we moved out here to Long Green. We've been at St. John's [Hydes] ever since.

"Being a part of all those parishes has been a blessing," said Stritzinger, who retired from a career in furniture and appliance refinishing, working at one time on the Rosa Ponselle estate.

"We got to meet so many different people from so many cultures. It was broadening."

The Stritzingers have been married for 60 years and were blessed with seven children.

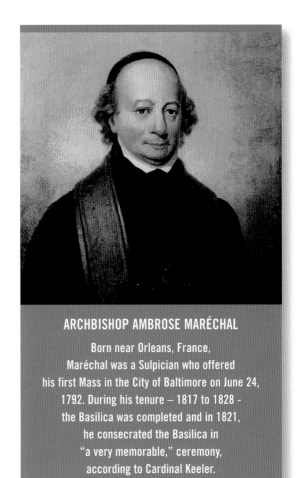

ARCHBISHOP AMBROSE MARÉCHAL

Born near Orleans, France, Maréchal was a Sulpician who offered his first Mass in the City of Baltimore on June 24, 1792. During his tenure – 1817 to 1828 - the Basilica was completed and in 1821, he consecrated the Basilica in "a very memorable," ceremony, according to Cardinal Keeler.

In 1826, he visited Emmitsburg and became ill with a chest infection, spending much of the next year in recuperation. One of his prominent legacies was improved relations between the Archdiocese of Baltimore and the Vatican.

Upon Maréchal's death on January 29, 1828, he was succeeded by the Liverpudlian, James Whitfield.

ARCHBISHOP WHITFIELD

The fourth Archbishop of Baltimore, James Whitfield served from 1828 until his death in 1834. Said Cardinal Keeler of Whitfield: "Archbishop Whitfield gave approval to the Oblate Sisters, the first nuns of African descent in the New World."

In the early 1820s, Archbishop Maréchal "moved with ease in most circles" of society in and around Maryland, enjoying not only society gatherings but young people, farmers, tradesmen, and tavern keepers, according to Spalding's history, *The Premier See.*

An unpretentious Frenchman, he wasn't averse to dropping a fishing line now and then with Catholic anglers.

Baltimore's fourth archbishop was consecrated on May 25, 1828 at the Basilica, the first sanctified in the city's new Cathedral. In the autumn of the following year, Whitfield convened the First Provincial Council of Baltimore. It was followed two years later by a synod of 35 priests charged with carrying out the decrees of the council.

By now, there were 80,000 Catholics in Maryland out of a total population of 407,000.

■ ■ ■

A future Archbishop of Baltimore, Martin John Spalding, was born in Bardstown, Kentucky in 1810. A graduate of St. Thomas Seminary in Bardstown, he headed for Rome in 1830, where he entered the Urban College of the Propaganda. At the end of his second year of study, was awarded the Gold Medal. He took the doctorate with distinction and publicly defended 256 propositions ranging from theology to canon law.

He was ordained a priest in Rome on August 13, 1834 and celebrated his first Mass in the crypt of St. Peter over the tomb of the Apostle upon whom Christ built His Church.

■ ■ ■

The cornerstone of St. Charles College, the minor seminary of the Archdiocese of Baltimore, was blessed by Archbishop Whitfield in July of 1831.

According to author Thomas Spalding, St. Charles began with the generosity of Charles Carroll, the sole Catholic signer of the Declaration of Independence.

Carroll, a cousin of the first Archbishop of Baltimore, donated 254 acres near his home at Doughoregan Manor along with 50 shares of bank stock for the funding of a college to educate "pious young men...for the ministry of the gospel."

By 1833, the construction was near complete. When Carroll died, however, so did sufficient funding and construction was stalled. It finally opened in 1848 with four students and two faculty members.

By 1865, the college had 45 students from the Archdiocese of Baltimore in addition to students from other dioceses. By 1876, the number of students grew so large that Archbishop Bayley encouraged the Sulpician community to expand it.

In 1911, St. Charles was destroyed by fire and the school was reborn in Catonsville, with a cornerstone of the new seminary set in place in June of 1912.

Archbishop Curley donated most of the $200,000 he received during the silver jubilee of ordination to finish an administration building at the seminary.

In 1960 ground was broken for an $800,000 dormitory and classroom building. The high school at St. Charles College was discontinued in 1969, and the seminarians studying philosophy on Paca Street downtown were moved to the Catonsville campus.

The Paca Street building was demolished in 1975. St. Charles ceased educating seminarians in 1977, and in 1983 was reborn as the Charlestown Retirement Community.

THE REV. LEO J. LARRIVEE, S.S., PASTOR.
Photo credit: Kirsten Beckerman

"You still find people in Catonsville who have no idea that this college was back here," said Father Larrivee, a native of Northern Virginia who was one of 400 students at the seminary in 1969.

"From 1979 to 1983 this property was not used much and the chapel fell into disrepair before being heavily renovated in 1996. St. Mary's and the Sulpicians owned St. Charles and they sold all of the property for the retirement community except for the chapel and the cemetery."

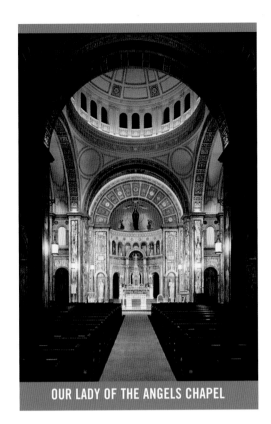

OUR LADY OF THE ANGELS CHAPEL

"This is yet another gift of the Jenkins family... Robert and Elizabeth Jenkins built it in honor of their parents Alfred and Elizabeth Jenkins. All four are buried in crypts here.

"We have about twice as many Protestants living here as Catholic and a small number of Jewish people. Cardinal Keeler is very big on building ecumenical relationships and people talk about it all the time but it rarely happens. Here it happens."
- Father Leo Larrivee, S.S.

CHARLESTOWN RETIREMENT COMMUNITY

Archbishop Samuel Eccleston is recognized as the second founder of St. Charles College, which opened in 1848. Through the next century and a half it educated many future bishops and archbishops of the U.S. Church.

The Charlestown Retirement Community opened on the grounds of the former minor seminary in Catonsville in December of 1983.

More than 2,300 seniors live at Charlestown, some 800 of them Roman Catholics from nearly every parish in the Archdiocese of Baltimore.

Many of the Catholics at the idyllic village off of Maiden Choice Lane relocated to Charlestown because of the beauty, convenience and aura of Our Lady of the Angels chapel.

"I serve a generation of deep faith," said the Rev. Leo J. Larrivee, S.S., pastor of Our Lady of the Angels, where confession is offered every Wednesday afternoon. "I do a lot of funerals but it's not depressing because these people have lived a good long life and they fully believe that they are going to heaven."

MR. JOSEPH VELENOVSKY

A retired chemist, Mr. Velenovsky was born in 1914 and baptized at St. Wenceslaus, the old Bohemian parish still serving East Baltimore. He has lived at Charlestown since 1990.

"My family moved when I was two or three to Northwest Baltimore and we attended All Saints Church until about 1948," said Mr. Velenovsky, who looks forward to visits to Charlestown by the All Saints choir. "All Saints was a little parish with no school so the Sisters of St. Joseph came in on Saturdays to give us catechism instruction. They really liked to have processions. It seems like I was always having to go to practice for a procession.

"I was married at All Saints and then we moved to St Rose of Lima in Brooklyn before switching over to St. Philip Neri when it was built in Linthicum."

MRS. GERTRUDE BUXBAUM PARLETT, RETIRED ACCOUNTANT, NATIONAL BUSINESS MACHINES.

A retired accountant for National Business Machines, Mrs. Parlett was born into St. Peter the Apostle near the Hollins Street Market in 1921 and baptized at St. Joseph Monastery in Irvington. She was a member of St. Benedict's parish from the age of three until her marriage in 1946. She has strong childhood memories of seeing her mother and aunts donate their jewelry to the Church to be transformed into chalices. Mrs. Parlett has resided at Charlestown since 1996.

"Being Catholic made me very confident," said Mrs. Parlett. "When you talked to the nuns or the priests, they always gave you a push in the right direction. I could go to Mass any place in the world and be at home."

SR. VICTORIA KESSLER, SSND, CHARLESTOWN RETIREMENT COMMUNITY.

"I've been assigned in and out of the Baltimore area since 1953. I taught first grade for 38 years, some at St. Benedict's on Wilkens Avenue and before that - from 1956-to-1966 – at St. Augustine in Elkridge." Sr. Victoria's role at Charlestown is to do visitations and welcome new members, to minister to the homebound, but mostly, she says: "Just to be."

photos credit: Kirsten Beckerman

MR. LOUIS LEILICH

Mr. Leilich was born 1914 into the St. Martin's parish, where he made his First Communion. He worked for the Swift meat packing company in Camden Yards long before there was a ballpark there. A 16-year resident of Charlestown, he attends Mass there daily at Our Lady of the Angels chapel. He credits the beauty and convenience of the chapel for persuading many seniors to resettle at Charlestown.

"I stayed at St. Martin's until 1939 when I was married and then we attended St. William of York on the Westside," said Mr. Leilich. "Growing up Catholic at the time that we did, you learned respect for your elders and authority. You took situations that maybe you couldn't ask your parents about to the brothers. I think that the lack of vocations today is connected to the demise of religious education in our Catholic schools.

"Years ago, we had Mass every morning and once a week benediction and the Stations of the Cross during Lent."

MRS. MARY HECKWOLF

Mrs. Heckwolf was born into the St. Mary's Star of the Sea parish in South Baltimore in 1915. A daily communicant at Our Lady of the Angels chapel, she has lived at Charlestown for more than 14 years.

"The blue star on top of St. Mary's was to guide sailors in from the sea," said Mrs. Heckwolf, who retired as an executive secretary at the McCormick Co. spice factory when it was located downtown on Light Street.

"I was baptized, made my First Communion and graduated from grade school at St. Mary's Star of the Sea. I graduated from Seton in 1933 when I think tuition was about $60 a year. In 1954, I moved to St. Bernard's in Waverly."

Heckwolf had an uncle – Leonard J. Ripple – who served as an archdiocesan priest at St. Rose of Lima in the 1920s. She also had an aunt who entered the convent and their dedication to the faith made young Mary think about a vocation.

"I was very seriously considering the Sisters of St. Joseph or Mother Seton's Sisters of Charity, but I prayed about it and changed my mind.

"I think Catholic faith and education nurtured my conscience. I got a good feeling of right and wrong which helped me solve a lot of problems over the years.

"I remember a lot of anti-Catholic feelings when I was young and it made me angry. It seemed to die out after a while."

MRS. HELEN O'CONNELL BOARMAN

Mrs. Boarman was also born in the St. Martin's parish at Fulton Avenue and Fayette Street and baptized there in 1912. She graduated from the St. Martin's Academy in 1931 and remembers using a slate and chalk to do schoolwork at her desk. She has lived at Charlestown for the past decade.

"We lived on Hollins Streets and went to 14 Holy Martyrs back when it was all German – it seemed like we were the only Irish family around – and they used to have German festivals with the streets closed off and dancing and bakery tables," said Mrs. Boarman. "When World War II broke out, they all stopped speaking German.

"H.L. Mencken lived a block from us and all of the children were told not to make any noise because Mr. Mencken didn't like noise and he didn't like children."

The same care and compassion so easily found at Charlestown were also hallmarks of both the Oblates and the Sisters of Charity, who took care of the sick and dying during the cholera epidemic of 1832.

"They were right there when many others would not dare to go," said Christopher Kauffman, a church historian. "It hit everywhere, but the sisters were fearless in their willingness to help."

In 1833, the Maryland Province of the Society of Jesus was formally established. That same year, in October, Archbishop Whitfield convened the Second Provincial Council at the Basilica.

In 1834, out of his private fortune, Archbishop Whitfield built St. James Church at the corner of Eager and Aisquith Streets. The St. James convent was later purchased from the Redemptorists by the School Sisters of Notre Dame for their motherhouse.

nomic. Until the late 1600s, the land on which the parish would locate was known only to the Susquehannocks who encamped about a thousand feet above what was then the shoreline of the Northwest Branch of the Patapsco River on a tributary that would be called the Jones Falls. As early as 1606, however, Capt. James Smith of Virginia, in search of new sources of wealth, sailed into the Patapsco. He called it the Bolus, Latin for bole, a reddish clay rich in iron ore. Among the partners who would establish a successful ironworks in the area 125 years later was Charles Carroll, Esquire, of Annapolis."

■ ■ ■

In September of 1834, Archbishop Whitfield consecrated the Rev. Samuel Eccleston, a Sulpician, as his coadjutor. Whitfield died the following month and Eccleston, just 33-years-old, succeeded him.

ARCHIBSHOP SAMUEL ECCLESTON

Born in Chestertown, Maryland, Eccleston served as the fifth Archbishop of Baltimore from 1834 to 1851. The son of an Episcopal minister, he was first introduced to Catholicism when his widowed mother married a Catholic. Eccleston began his conversion while studying at St. Mary's College in Baltimore. He was ordained in 1825 by Archbishop Maréchal. Two years later, he became vice president and faculty member at St. Mary's. In 1829, he became president of St. Mary's College and held the post until 1834 when he was appointed coadjutor of Baltimore by Pope Gregory XVI. Archbishop Eccleston presided over the Third (1837), Fourth (1840), Fifth (1843), Sixth (1846) and Seventh (1849) Provincial Councils of Baltimore. Said Cardinal Keeler of Archbishop Eccleston: "He presided over a number of provincial councils of Baltimore, including the sixth, at which Our Lady of the Immaculate Conception was named the patroness of the Church in the United States."

St. James was first used by English-speaking Catholics, and soon it became too small for the growing congregation. Church leaders envisioned a parish closer to the old waterfront village of Jonestown and built St. Vincent de Paul on Front Street, just north of the Shot Tower and Little Italy.

According to Thomas Spalding's 1995 book, *The Story of a People and Their Home,* written with Kathryn Kuranda, "The community on Front Street that called itself St. Vincent de Paul Parish was the product of a number of forces that came together toward the end of the 1830s. The oldest was eco-

In 1834, the Archdiocese encompassed all of Maryland, Virginia, and the District of Columbia and included 70 churches and nearly as many priests. It was the year that St. Peter opened in the Washington County village of Hancock.

In 1836, a priest assigned to St. Patrick's in Cumberland began a mission in the McKenzie family settlement of Garrett County and soon, Christian Garlitz was adding a large room to his log cabin in Walnut Hill as a sanctuary for Catholics scattered along the far reaches of Western Maryland.

ST. PETER / HANCOCK

"As workers came west to build the C&O canal and the railroad, they built churches along the way... a lot of them have a very strong Irish influence. We still have a number of parishioners who are descended from them," said the Rev. Joseph Cosgrove, pastor of St. Peter's, which serves about 200 families.

"A civil war battle was partially fought on our grounds and the church was occupied by Union troops with Stonewall Jackson on the other side of the Potomac. We have our ups and downs but it's beautiful here," said Cosgrove. "We're in the foothills of Appalachia... used to be the apple growing center of the United States."

Between the town's Canal Apple Days, held each year in mid-September and the apple butter festival in nearby Berkeley Springs, St. Peter typically sells some 9,000 apple dumplings to folks who come looking for the autumn treat.

The recipe is so closely guarded — a mixture of sugar, cinnamon, and margarine in dough shaped like a cross - that even Father Joe can't pry it loose.

The congregation of St. Ann, Avilton, evolved from the folks who celebrated Mass in the log cabin. The current church stands in the Grantsville section of Garrett County.

ST. ANN / GRANTSVILLE

St. Ann's Church was dedicated in August of 1874. It is said to have cost about $2,000 and is nestled in a pine grove at 2,770 feet. A well-kept cemetery stands behind the church. The Avilton sanctuary was designated a shrine in 1977.

In 1976, it merged with St. Stephen in Grantsville, which had been established in Garrett County in 1894.

ST. ANN'S CEMETERY

A well-kept cemetery stands behind the church. The Avilton sanctuary was designated a shrine in 1977. In 1976,the shrine merged with St. Stephen in Grantsville, which had been established in Garrett County in 1894, with the new congregation known as St. Ann's.

In 1837, the Third Provincial Council of Baltimore was held at the Basilica. Among other business, the council – presided over by Archbishop Eccleston and attended by eight bishops – decided that ecclesiastical property is to be secured by the best means of civil law affords and that priests would be prohibited from raising funds outside of their own parish. Pastors were also warned about permitting unsuitable music at Mass.

The following year, St. Paul the Apostle was established in Ellicott City.

Most people only see the sanctuary of St. Vincent de Paul while speeding up and down the Jones Falls Expressway, noticing the whitewashed church tower hard against Baltimore's main post office, the spire competing for attention with the Shot Tower.

It's a shame that the front steps of the church open onto a cramped side street, but it's not the sacrilege avoided when the City shifted the route of the expressway back in the early 1960s to spare the third oldest Catholic church building in Baltimore.

ST. PAUL THE APOSTLE / ELLICOTT CITY

St. Paul the Apostle opened in the mill town of Ellicott City in 1838. The parish operates the Resurrection parochial school. On October 17, 1914 – just a kid not long out of St. Mary's Industrial School and two years before pitching the Boston Red Sox to a World Series championship – the great Babe Ruth was married here to Helen Woodford (at St. Paul's, 3755 St. Paul Street in Howard County). The incorrigible Babe would separate from Helen, but because they were Catholic in a more stringent age they did not divorce. In April of 1929, Helen Woodford Ruth died in a house fire, leaving the Babe free to marry his longtime mistress, the actress and model Claire Hodgson. Hodgson and Ruth remained married until the magnificent slugger's death in 1948.

ST. VINCENT DE PAUL, FRONT STREET

"When I was growing up, this was one of the great old churches that parents took their kids to see... we make our buildings and then they make us..."
The Rev. Richard Lawrence, pastor

FATHER LAWRENCE SHOVELS SNOW OFF OF FRONT STREET

St. Vincent de Paul parish is roughly bounded by Little Italy, the downtown area near City Hall, and the Fallsway.

It is part of the historic Jonestown community, once an independent village during the colonial development of the harbor. In 1840, the cornerstone was laid on Front Street.

On Nov. 7, 1841, the church was dedicated by Bishop John Chanche, the bishop of Natchez, Mississippi, a native of Baltimore, and one-time president of St. Mary's College in Baltimore. The parish is committed to the overall quality of life in the neighborhood. In 2001, Father Lawrence served as chair of the Jonestown Planning Council.

"The Archbishop [Whitfield] attended, vested in cope," reads the diary of the Rev. Louis Regis Deluol, superior of the Sulpicians in Baltimore.

"I grew up in the St. Charles Borromeo parish in Pikesville... the earliest we know about our family history is that my mother's great- grandfather- Richard G. Moran - was a captain on the steamboat packets that used to run from Baltimore to Norfolk."

"There were ten priests and twelve seminarians and eight altar boys. [The Rev. Patrick] Moriarty [superior of the Augustinians of Philadelphia] preached for an hour and 20 minutes, poorly." The crowd, wrote Deluol, was large.

The next day, pews were sold at auction and seating was awarded according to class and purse.

"This began as a very structured church in a very structured society," said Lawrence. "There were 'pew rents' and of course the wealthier families got the best seats.

"In the center aisle on the floor was the English gentry - the Catons and the Carrolls. Then you had your lace curtain Irish, also in the center, and the side aisles for the shanty or railroad Irish who didn't have a penny... there were three free pews and the [balcony] was for the slaves of parishioners or free blacks."

Father Lawrence paused to puff his trademark pipe and consider the co-existence of Christianity and slavery under the same sanctified roof.

In the first years of the 21st century – as Little Italy becomes gentrified and townhouses have gone up on the site of old high-rise projects on Fayette Street, the St. Vincent congregation is 80 percent white, 15 percent black, and five percent "other."

According to church records, at least half of the worshippers come in from the suburbs, and the rest reside in the city.

Many of the faithful are well educated. Others are nearly destitute. St. Vincent welcomes them all and endures as one of the most vibrant parishes in the archdiocese.

"These books represent my inheritance," said Father Lawrence, but the 13th pastor in St. Vincent's long history.

He is standing on the altar of the church, holding large volumes of the Old Testament and the New Testament.

The books are bound in buffalo calfskin, a rare and expensive hide, and were paid for with Lawrence's share of his family's estate upon the death of his parents.

"This Bible represents half of the house I grew up in," he says with a grin.

The sacred texts, believes Lawrence, represent the word and the Word Made Flesh, the bringing together of three great traditions too long separated: not just the beliefs of the children of Israel with the children of the Messiah, but the traditions of the One Holy and Apostolic Church of Rome with those of the more text-based Protestant movement.

One of the great Baltimore traditions is the "Printers' Mass" of St. Vincent de Paul. It began in the early 1920s when the city had numerous daily newspapers and Catholic printers would work late Saturday night into the next morning to get out the Sunday paper.

St. Vincent's was near all of the great publishing plants, including the old News-Post on the Pratt Street waterfront and The Sun just across the Jones Falls on Calvert Street.

Instead of struggling to get up in a few hours for morning Mass, the printers, and soon folks who had been out on the town for a good time, would attend one of four late night Masses at St. Vincent: 12:15 a.m. in the sanctuary; 12:30 a.m. in the downstairs chapel; 2:15 a.m. upstairs and 2:30 a.m. downstairs.

There were even showers for the printers to clean the cheap ink off themselves before fulfilling their Sunday obligation in the days before Saturday evening Mass.

The pastor at the time, the Rev. Phil McGuire, received permission from Rome for the unorthodox Mass schedule, according to Lawrence.

"There were a lot of young Italian immigrants from pious families nearby," said Lawrence, while sitting on a fire escape that looks west toward downtown.

"We used to have 1400 people for the printers' Mass. You could take your best girl to a dance, drink until 1 a.m., make 2:15 a.m. Mass and get her home at a quarter to dawn with the Mass bulletin and when you said you'd just come from Mass, her old man would let you live."

Not only does Saturday evening Mass now fulfill the Sunday obligation but there is only one daily newspaper left in town, The Sun, and its printing is done in Port

Covington. The last remnant of the printers' Mass is the weekly 12:15 a.m. service, which still draws a good crowd.

"This church has changed every fifty years or so as Baltimore has changed," said Fr. Lawrence. "In 1890, the skylight went in and the slave balcony came down. By now, the English and the Irish have a few dollars to move away from downtown and the Italians are at the bottom of the heap. The Irish were giving them a hard time here at St. Vincent's so they started St. Leo's."

■ ■ ■

St. Peter the Apostle in southwest Baltimore, now part of a tri-parish community that includes St. Jerome and St. Martin, opened in a then-Irish neighborhood near the Hollins Street Market in 1842.

PAST AND PRESENT PARISH LEADERS AT ST. PETER THE APOSTLE

photo credit: Kirsten Beckerman

Father John Harvey, O.F.M. Cap. on the steps of the church with (clockwise) Odette Smith-Fort, Sr. Mary Kenneth McGuire, Mary Cronin and Brother John Mahoney.

ST. PETER'S THE APOSTLE / W. BALTIMORE

Originally known as the Pro-Cathedral—St. Peter's was established in 1770 as the first Roman Catholic church in Baltimore and served as the Cathedral for the emerging Catholic community under the newly-installed Bishop John Carroll in 1790. After the construction of the Cathedral of the Assumption in 1821, daily Mass and large events continued at nearby St. Peter's until 1843, when a new church was built in West Baltimore to accommodate the influx of Irish railroad workers. Baltimore Architect Robert Carey Long designed the new St. Peter the Apostle church to resemble the famous Grecian temple, Theseus, with classic Doric and Corinthian constructions, outside and inside respectively. When the cornerstone was laid on May 23, 1843 at Poppleton and Hollins Streets, all of Baltimore's Roman Catholic churches had been located east of the Basilica, earning the new church the nickname, "Mother of the West." St. Peter's was organized for the Irish of West Baltimore by the Rev. Edward McColgan, who arrived from Piscataway to take the job. Baltimore Architect Robert Carey Long designed St. Peter the Apostle to resemble the famous Grecian temple, Theseus, with classic Doric and Corinthian constructions, outside and inside respectively. The first Roman Catholic church in Baltimore, it was once known as the "Mother of the West."

ST. PETER'S PRO-CATHEDRAL

69

Old School Discipline
and Wisenheimers

David Klein's father was a Jewish man named IRC who booked talent on the Block in the days of burlesque. Klein's mother was Catholic, and he grew up in his Catholic grandmother's house near Hollins Street Market. He graduated from St. Peter the Apostle grade school in 1958.

DAVID KLEIN
St. Peter the Apostle, Class of 1958

Klein remembers many things about his Catholic school days-- making Confession, learning his catechism-- but the story that endures most vividly involves a pellet gun and a diminutive principal named Sister Mary Elaine of the Sisters of Mercy.

"A kid named Henry Sullivan and I got caught shooting windows out of the school from my grandmother's backyard," remembers Klein, who said the St. Peter's school was near a broom factory about 50 yards away from his grandmother's house.

The 7th grader, who earned his pocket money by selling shopping bags at the Hollins Market, had just been given a pellet gun by one of his uncles. A maker of mischief by nature, the young Klein wondered if the gun was strong enough to reach the windows of St. Peter's school.

He and Henry soon discovered the perverse thrill of hearing windows shatter and commenced to break as many as possible.

"Dummy me, I'm shooting the windows out of my own classroom," says Klein, a

wayward youth who found some stability in cabinet-making. "The next thing we know, a window flies up and it's Sister Mary Elaine screaming at us: 'Klein! Sullivan! Get up here, right now!'"

Sister Mary Elaine put the fear of God into Klein and his father put the sting of a leather belt into his backside, making the boy turn over a month's worth of nickel profits from his shopping bag sales to pay for the windows.

"That," says Klein, "was the end of the pellet gun."

It was also the end of a Catholic education for Klein, who resisted enrolling at Calvert Hall High School in favor of the then brand-new Edmondson High School.

■ ■ ■

The Fifth Provincial Council was held at the Basilica in May of 1843. The council reported 90,000 Catholics and 70 priests in Maryland out of a population of nearly 470,000.

In 1844, the year that Samuel F.B. Morse demonstrates the telegraph by sending the message "What hath God wrought?" from Washington to Baltimore, St. Augustine opened in a hamlet between the two cities: Elkridge in Howard County.

■ ■ ■

St. Alphonsus Church was dedicated in 1845 at the corner of Park Avenue and Saratoga Streets, just west of the Basilica downtown.

St. Alphonsus houses an astonishingly grand and ornate sanctuary, like something out of Baum's Land of Oz. It is a "perpendicular style" Gothic church designed by the Romantic period architect Robert Cary Long, Jr., who made his name with Greek revival designs.

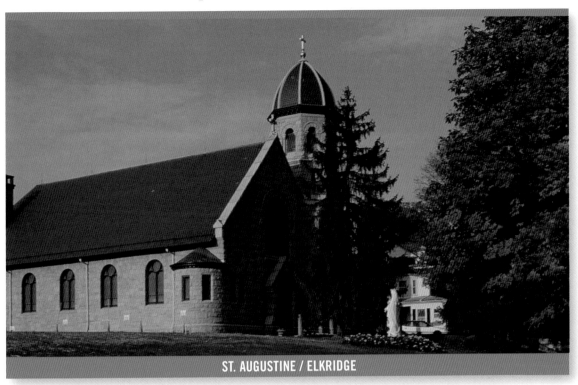

ST. AUGUSTINE / ELKRIDGE

Some 20 years before the end of the Civil War, St. Augustine Church was ministering to the people of
Elk Ridge Landing from high on a hill along the Old Washington Road, then the main pike between
Baltimore and the nation's Capitol. Between 1849 and 1851, the Rev. John Neumann – canonized in 1977 -
served as pastor. The area now known as Elkridge was once a busy port on the Patapsco River and
attracted ships from around the world, trading tobacco for a variety of goods.
In early years Mass was celebrated by circuit riders and missionary priests in the homes of local residents,
usually the more successful farmers and wealthy merchants. The laying of the St. Augustine
cornerstone was October 22, 1844, two years after Archbishop Eccleston asked
the Redemptorists to serve the parish. For twenty years they would travel to St. Augustine's from
St. Alphonsus in downtown Baltimore. Now a key location in the Baltimore-Washington transportation
corridor – close to both BWI airport and Interstate-95 - Elkridge is again thriving. In 1985, St. Augustine
had approximately 535 families; and by 2003 there were 1,143 families registered in the parish.

CRUCIFIX AT
ST. ALPHONSUS CHURCH

photo credit: Kirsten Beckerman

St. Alphonsus was dedicated as
a shrine in 1995, 150 years after
opening. Mass is celebrated in
Lithuanian, in honor of the church's
heritage, as well as Latin in
a Tridentine service faithful to
pre-Vatican II rituals. It is also
the home of a Perpetual Novena
in honor of Our Lady of
the Miraculous Medal.

71

Long used the then popular structural material of cast-iron for St. Alphonsus, which was originally built to serve German Catholics before it was designated a Lithuanian parish in 1917 by Cardinal Gibbons.

According to *"The Baltimore Rowhouse,"* [Princeton Architectural Press, 1999], cast-iron was used as a structural support in the St. Alphonsus nave, "allowing a higher and lighter interior... [as well as an] elaborate sixty-foot spire."

That spire is one of the great landmarks of downtown Baltimore and was a beacon to the family of Francis "Gene" Donnelly, the longtime publicist for the Diocese of Wilmington after serving in a similar position with the Church in Baltimore.

GENE DONNELLY

Gene Donnelly served as public relations director for the youth department of the Archdiocese of Baltimore in 1962 and 1963. From 1970 through 2000, he was director of communications for the Diocese of Wilmington.

"My parents were having trouble having a family so my father and mother went religiously to the weekly Miraculous Medal novena at St. Alphonsus to pray for a child," remembers Donnelly. "And then I was born on Nov. 27, the feast of the Miraculous Medal. Because of that, that's where I grew up worshipping. Every Sunday we'd get on the No. 8 streetcar from Rodgers Forge and go down to Saratoga Street for Mass."

These days, St. Alphonsus also offers a weekly novena - each Thursday after the 12:10 p.m. Mass - to St. Peregrine, patron saint of those suffering from cancer, HIV and AIDS as well as all other chronic diseases.

The Peregrine novena, during which the faithful are reminded "it matters not what has been taken away but what [is done] with what is left," is made in the presence of the Blessed Sacrament.

Attending a recent Peregrine novena service was a woman from Kenya named Martha who came to the United States two years ago, arriving with a searing memory of a Catholic priest from Chicago who visited Kenya in 1995 on a healing mission.

While attending a service at the St. Jude Shrine on Paca Street, Martha saw a medal in honor of St. Peregrine.

"I didn't know who he was," said Martha. "So I asked the Lord in the Blessed Sacrament, 'I want to know who this saint is.' It is like you are being pushed into something that you don't know anything about. I came to Mass here and saw the relic and saw it was the saint I had been looking for and to me it was the flowering of a seed that had been planted in Kenya in 1995. I am not looking for a particular healing of body but of spirit, to do His will and have the Lord with me at all times. I want him above me and behind me and in front of me, to go before me and direct me..."

■ ■ ■

In 1845, Claudius Ash invented the first modern pair of dentures in America when he mounted porcelain teeth on steel springs. It was also the year that the de la Salle Christian Brothers established Calvert Hall College on the current site of Archdiocesan headquarters at Cathedral and Mulberry Streets.

Now a four-year college preparatory school on a 30-acre campus in Towson, Calvert Hall was the first permanent foundation of the Christian Brothers in the United States.

An extensive campus renewal project was recently completed, including the construction of a new sports stadium.

Long before Norman Knoerlein was born, Walt Benewicz was taking the No. 2 bus from Locust Point to attend Calvert Hall uptown, walking up the steep hill of Cathedral Street to get there.

Walt, a waterfront kid who grew up to be a leader in the local International Long-shoremen's Association – played basketball and soccer his first two years of high school but had to quit when his father – a former boxer named Tom "Flash" Benewicz - was killed in an accident on the docks.

"When my dad died, a whole bus of my

NORMAN KNOERLEIN, WRITER

"To think back on my experience at Calvert Hall, does not remind me of any specific events or times in particular, but the overwhelming comfort I still feel in all the relationships I cultivated at The Hall...
many a day was spent in the Math resource room listening to advice and kind words of patience..."
- Norman Knoerlein, Class of 1997

WALT BENEWICZ, CALVERT HALL CLASS OF 1961

"I think tuition was $280 a year when I went. I played in the school jazz band and was the first class to graduate from the new school in Towson. My grandmother was big on Catholic education and saved the money from a little grocery store my family had on Hull and Marriott Streets."

classmates came to the graveyard and I saw how caring the brothers were for me and my family," said Benewicz. "For the next two semesters the only homework I had was to take care of my mother."

Walt's sons – Ron and Matt – were recruited to play soccer at Mt. St. Joseph in Irvington, an easier distance from the family's home in Anne Arundel county than Walt's alma mater.

"I would have liked to see them go to the Hall," said Benewicz. "But it was most important that they go to Catholic school."

The year of the 1852 synod, the

ST. PATRICK / HAVRE DE GRACE

Established in 1847, St. Patrick stands at Congress Avenue and Stokes Street in the Susquehanna port city of Harford County. It replaced an earlier church built in 1844. More than 900 families belong to St. Patrick's. Currently housed in its third sanctuary-- one built of Port Deposit granite, much of it cut by then pastor Fr. James Fitz-Gerald, it had sandstone trimmings and 19 stained glass windows donated by parishioners. The church participates in two major outreach programs. One is Our Daily Bread, a favorite of parishes throughout the archdiocese. It has also joined with other area denominations in hosting lunch for the homeless in a program called Grace Place.

SS. PETER & PAUL / CUMBERLAND

Located at 109 North Smallwood Street in Cumberland,
SS. Peter & Paul began as a congregation in 1848.
Archbishop Eccleston designated the Redemptorist order
to shepherd the German-Catholics of the archdiocese
and in the mid-19th century, whenever a Redemptorist
would make it out to Cumberland, upward of 200 Catholics
from the Fatherland would walk scores of miles to attend Mass.
In 1847, it was decided that a permanent church would
be built and the cornerstone of Saints Peter & Paul was laid
at the site of an old fort on Independence Day, 1848.
The church was completed by September of 1849
and dedicated by the Redemptorist order.

FRANCIS P. KENRICK

The sixth Archbishop of Baltimore, Francis Patrick Kenrick was born in Dublin at the end of the 18th century. His younger brother went on to become an Archbishop of St. Louis.

In 1829, while teaching theology at St. Thomas Seminary in Bardstown, Ky., Kenrick attended the First Provincial Council of Baltimore as a theologian and in 1842 was named a bishop of Philadelphia. Pope Pius IX promoted him to the metropolitan See of Baltimore on August 3, 1851. He presided over the First Plenary Council of Baltimore in 1852. This council sought uniformity of Church discipline throughout the United States. Archbishop Kenrick convened the archdiocesan synods for priests of Baltimore in 1853, 1857 and 1862. He also presided over the Eighth and Ninth Provincial Councils of Baltimore in 1854 and 1858.

He polled American bishops' opinions on the promulgation of the dogma of the Immaculate Conception and was present at it proclamation in Rome on December 8, 1854. Fluent in a half dozen languages, he contributed to the American Church what was considered an excellent dogmatic and moral theology, although his pro-slavery stance has tarnished some of this. He also translated a new English version of the Bible. He died on July 6, 1863 at age of 65.

Redemptorists dedicated St. Michael the Archangel at the corner of Wolfe and Lombard Streets in Baltimore.

When the first Polish immigrants settled around the southeast Baltimore waterfront around 1860s, they attended St. Michael's.

The majority of the Poles had emigrated from provinces under Prussian domination and could speak and understand some German. In 1872, they and the Czech worshippers at St. Michael joined together to form the Slavic congregation known as St. Wenceslaus, which remains open at Collington and Ashland Avenues near Johns Hopkins Hospital.

Once friction caused a split between the Czechs and Poles, some of the Polish believers returned to St. Michael's until the city's first Polish parish, St. Stanislaus Kostka, was launched at the corner of Ann and Aliceanna Streets in 1879.

St. Stan's, which served generations of Baltimore Poles who made their living on and around the waterfront, was closed in 2002.

Back at St. Michael, several blocks to the north, the ceaseless re-invention of the city through immigration has revitalized the parish with an influx of Hispanic Catholics that have settled around lower Broadway.

"We are creating a new reality here at

St. Michael's with the Hispanic community," said former pastor Father James Gilmour, called "Santiago" by his Spanish parishioners. "This is true both culturally and religiously. We honor each culture, whether it's Mexico or Panama."

Father Gilmour sees evangelizing as St. Michael's greatest challenge.

"Not just more priests," he said, "but lay people taking on the role of evangelizers to build their communities from here to White Marsh."

PAST AND PRESENT MEMBERS OF ST. MICHAEL'S PARISH

The leaders of St. Michael's include (front row from left):
Joseph Thomas, Rev. Andrew Carr, C.Ss.R,
and Rev. James Gilmour, C.SS.R (former pastor),
Back Left: Ms. Olga Diaz, S.F.O.,
and Sr. Sonia-Marie Fernandez.

The year 1855 brought the Eighth Provincial Council to Baltimore's Basilica. Eight American Sees were represented during a council that set regulations for pew rents and collections.

In 1856, Catholics in Baltimore numbered about 81,000 with 13 churches in the city proper. In the diocese as a whole - Maryland and the District of Columbia – some 99 churches and chapels, attended by 130 priests, served a Catholic population of 120,000.

In 1858, the Ninth Provincial Council was held in Baltimore, establishing the devotion of the 40 Hours.

At the Council's request the Holy See granted to the Archbishop of Baltimore the precedence in councils and meetings held by the prelates of the United States, even if he were not senior archbishop present.

■ ■ ■

ST. MICHAEL THE ARCHANGEL / LOMBARD AND WOLFE STREETS

Used in the filming of the Disney motion picture "Ladder 49," in 2003, the sanctuary was the setting for a funeral, a baptism and a midnight Mass service on Christmas Eve. Deacon Richard Novak was on the altar for the Baptism scene. "They shot that scene so many times that I thought the baby was going to be old enough to vote before they were done." St. Michael celebrated its 150th anniversary in 2002.

LOYOLA COLLEGE IN MARYLAND

The second-oldest chartered college in Baltimore, founded in 1852, Loyola College celebrated its 150th anniversary with a year long celebration that began in October of 2001 with the traditional Mass of the Holy Spirit. During the sesquicentennial anniversary, the annual Sr. Cleophas Costello Lecture focused on the poor – and how they should be served – in a speech by author Barbara Ehrenreich. In April of 2002, the anniversary party moved downtown to the site of Loyola's first campus in Baltimore on Calvert Street, concluding with a Mass at St. Ignatius Church.

In the twelve years of Archbishop Kenrick's service, St. John the Evangelist rose at the corner of Eager and Valley streets in 1853 and the next year Canton saw St. Brigid open on Hudson Street.

In 1856, St. Ignatius Loyola appeared on Calvert Street downtown and its first pastor, the Rev. John Early, S.J., founded Loyola College - now at Charles Street and Cold Spring Lane - alongside it.

ST. JOHN THE EVANGELIST / 10TH WARD
photo credit: Jim Burger

In 1966, after years of decline as the children and grandchildren of early parishioners moved out of the city, St. John's was combined with St. James Church about a mile away near the Institute of Notre Dame. St. John's closed for good that same year, engendering societies and reunions to perpetuate its memory and spirit.

The devotees continue to march under the St. John's banner in Baltimore's annual St. Patrick's Day Parade.

NEAL "REDS" DRISCOLL AND MEMORIES OF ST. JOHN THE EVANGELIST
CAPITAL OF BALTIMORE'S OLD 10TH WARD

CAROL SWEENEY REILLY WITH PAINTING OF ST. JOHN THE EVANGELIST CHURCH AT EAGER AND VALLEY STREETS.

Carol Sweeney Reilly poses with a landscape of St. John the Evangelist Church at Angelina's restaurant in Hamilton. A parishioner at the Immaculate Heart of Mary in Towson, Reilly bought Angelina's —known far and wide for its crab cakes — in 1969 with her late husband, Bob. She sold the restaurant in 1987 but still works there.

On a wall of the restaurant's basement saloon hangs the picture of St. John's, painted in the midst of its early 20th century glory days by George Chelton.

"I've been at the Immaculate Heart for more than 30 years but I grew up in the Little Flower parish, was baptized there, went to grade school there, was married there," said Reilly. "I can't imagine being anything else but Catholic. I couldn't stay away, not even during the [recent] scandal. If I didn't have my faith, then just shoot me..."

Like St. Stan's in Fells Point and St. Adalbert in the demolished neighborhood of Wagner's Point, St. John the Evangelist no longer exists as a parish.

A pity to see, the decaying church building remains at Valley and Eager streets in Baltimore's old 10th ward colony of Irish Catholics and its memory remains one of the most cherished in the history of the Archdiocese of Baltimore.

Reds Driscoll knew it well, from the time he was born at 719 Mura Street in 1928 until he moved in 1959 to become part of the St. Mary's parish in Govans.

REDS DRISCOLL

photo credit: Kirsten Beckerman

The ninth of 10 children born to a silversmith named Daniel Driscoll and his wife, Margaret, a homemaker. "I got married at St. John's," said Reds. "Every one of my sisters got married at St. John's and many an Irish wedding reception was held at the old Plumbers Union Hall at Biddle and Asquith Streets."

"My father would go to St. John's every morning during Lent – get up at 5:30 a.m. and go to Mass, come home, eat his breakfast and go to work at Stieff," said Driscoll.

"The 4th or 5th rows on the right hand side of St. John's were the Driscoll's; they had a little name plate on the pews and every Sunday, that's where you sat with your family...

"Once ,when we were kids playing in the street, the neighborhood ladies counted 52 kids living in the 700 block of Mura Street, all of us six and seven and eight years old...

"There were 38 houses in that block, 19 on each side with a grocery store at one end and Brown's Bar on the other.... this was off of Greenmount and Preston, that was the hub of that part of the city," remembered Driscoll. "You had the Musket shoe company and other businesses around there and at 5 p.m., all these streetcars stopped to let people off and pick people up-- the No. 27, the No. 8 to Catonsville, the No. 8 to Towson, all those streetcars crossed that corner, it was Times Square in Baltimore from 4 to 6 p.m.

"The neighborhood was built on a hill that ran down and looked onto the train tracks coming out of Penn Station and I remember going to watch the train go by with FDR's body on it... they had all the windows lit and you could see into the baggage car where they had his coffin and everybody in the neighborhood came out to stand on this big dirt hill to look as it went by."

Funerals, said Reds, were a big deal in the neighborhood.

"Viewings and wakes were in the houses back then and when my grandmother died, the couch came out, the wreath went up on the door and the coffin up against the wall with a big candle on each end. Anybody could walk in to visit.

"On the dining room table you had a ham, in the kitchen a half-keg of beer," laughed Driscoll. "And a priest was always there, no matter what time of the day, a priest was there and you had to get a coffin sitter to sit and greet any one who showed up. And then it was an all day thing to follow the coffin in a horse and wagon to New Cathedral Cemetery down past Irvington."

In 1945 – a little more than 16-years-old and too young for military service - Reds left school and got a job at the Continental Can Company on the East Baltimore waterfront.

"I didn't go back to school in September, I stepped right into the world," he remembered. "Right into the big world."

The world got bigger in 1953 when Reds married Mary Lou McCloskey, a Govans girl. They bought 729 Mura Street – on the same block where he had grown up – for $4,500. When they left for McCloskey's old neighborhood in 1959, they got $2,300 for the Mura Street house. In 1963, the Driscolls left Govans for Northeast Baltimore.

The couple had five children and their daughters attended Seton High School. Mrs. Driscoll died in 1988.

"For the May Procession, we used to walk up Valley Street to the Little Sisters of the Poor at Valley and Biddle," remembered Driscoll. "All the poor people lived inside the walls on a single block... The May procession was students from the first to the eighth grade with everybody dressed in white and a girl in the 8th grade was elected the queen and we'd all sing on the way up and all the old people would sit outside in rocking chairs and watch.

"The girl who was the May queen would crown the Blessed Mother and then we'd go inside the church hall and they'd give us ice cream and cake."

NEW CATHEDRAL CEMETERY
photo credit: Adrianna Amari
The only cemetery operated by the Archdiocese of Baltimore, New Cathedral opened in 1871 in the 4300 block of Old Frederick Road.
It replaced Cathedral Cemetery (1816-1887) on Fremont Avenue.
Gates are open every day of the year from 8:30 a.m. to 4 p.m.
Among the dead buried at New Cathedral are four members of the Baseball Hall of Fame: John McGraw, Wilbert Robinson, Joe Kelley and Ned Hanlon, all members of the National League's 19th century Orioles.
The cemetery has printed a map for fans to find the graves of these long-gone heroes as well as the graves of three bishops.

SISTERS OF CHARITY IN FULL HABIT
"We were taught by the Sisters of Charity with those sailboat hats.
If you went home and said you'd been hit by a nun in school, your parents wanted to know what you'd done to deserve it."
Reds Driscoll

There are numerous churches named for St. Charles Borromeo, the 16th century Archbishop of Milan who was vital to the Catholic counter-Reformation, worked with victims of the plague, and is credited with inventing the confessional.

Baltimore's memorial to St. Charles opened in Pikesville in 1849.

ST. CHARLES BORROMEO

Detail from painting by
Stella Hazard for the
parish sesquicentennial.

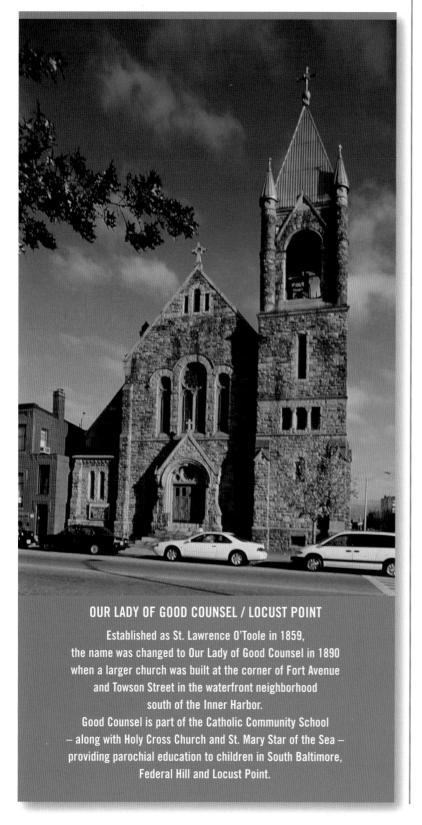

OUR LADY OF GOOD COUNSEL / LOCUST POINT

Established as St. Lawrence O'Toole in 1859,
the name was changed to Our Lady of Good Counsel in 1890
when a larger church was built at the corner of Fort Avenue
and Towson Street in the waterfront neighborhood
south of the Inner Harbor.
Good Counsel is part of the Catholic Community School
— along with Holy Cross Church and St. Mary Star of the Sea —
providing parochial education to children in South Baltimore,
Federal Hill and Locust Point.

ST. CHARLES BORROMEO / PIKESVILLE

The members of St. Charles began
celebrating their 150th anniversary
as a parish at noon Mass on Sunday, Sept.
13, 1998. Retired Archbishop William D.
Borders celebrated Mass with assistance
from Father Joseph Cote and the late
Monsignor Martin Schwalenberg,
pastor emeritus among others.
At the reception afterward, lifelong
parishioner Phil McCusker and three of
his children entertained with live music.

PHILIP AND MARY PATRICIA MCCUSKER

Photo credit: Kirsten Beckerman

Philip and the former Mary Patricia Coughlin were married in St. Cecilia parish at the corner of Windsor Avenue and Hilton Street in 1946. St. Charles Borromeo has been the McCuskers' home parish for several generations. Also pictured is Bridget O'Connor McCusker, one of their six children.

Philip McCusker, a retired attorney, was born in 1922.

His mother's father, a small contractor named James White, helped build the St. Charles Borromeo Church in Pikesville.

Although baptized at St. Ambrose-- his mother was living in Pimlico at the time of his birth-- McCusker has been associated with St. Charles parish all his life.

"My grandfather had teams of horses and he helped transport blocks of Port Deposit granite from the Western Maryland railroad spur up to where they were building the church," said McCusker, who still has the Boy Scout axe he bought from Sam Goldstein, who owned the local hardware store.

"I knew my mother's father, but not too well. I was five when he died. He was also one of the founding members of the Pikesville volunteer fire department."

McCusker's mother and father – who met at St. Ambrose during Sunday services and were married there in 1915 – moved to Walker Avenue in Pikesville when young Philip was a year old.

"St. Charles is the only parish I know," said McCusker, "and my faith is the home port of my life. It's like St. Peter said to Christ: 'To whom shall we turn?'

"As the prayer says, our faith is our refuge and our strength... and Catholicism has been my family's grounding in civilization," said McCusker. "Then again, I look at all of it through Catholic eyes. It's all I know."

Bridget McCusker attended the Institute of Notre Dame for two years in the early 1970s and then – for a variety of adolescent reasons - left for public school, a decision she regrets today.

"Transportation was a problem, getting down there from Pikesville, but I would have gotten a better education," said Bridget, a social worker in the field of mental health. "IND was not an easy place to play around like I wanted to do back then."

A non-practicing Catholic, Bridget joined St. John the Evangelist parish in Columbia several years ago and took a course called "Remembering," for those who had been away from the Church.

"I liked it; we met every week for about 12 weeks and went through the history of the Church and the Church today. It helped me remember the good stuff," said Bridget. "Then I joined the social ministry at St. John's and went to Haiti with them for five days. They're trying to establish links between the Archdiocese of Baltimore and parishes in Haiti.

Of Haitians, Bridget said: "They're so poor, they need everything and in spite of all its problems, the Catholic Church does a good job of helping the needy."

■ ■ ■

80

Administered by the Vincentians since its founding and established in 1850, Immaculate Conception was dedicated on September 21, 1851 to the Blessed Mother. At first a two-story brick building with a "well lighted basement" on Mosher Street, it is the first parish in the United States to bear the title of "Immaculate Conception."

At the time of its construction on Mosher and Ross Streets, now Druid Hill Park, the area was considered rural, and with the exception of St. Mary's Chapel on Paca Street, it was the only Catholic Church in Northwest Baltimore. By 1854 then-pastor Rev. Joseph Guistinianni realized the church's need to expand and in June the corner stone for the second church structure was laid. Three years later, Archbishop Kenrick consecrated the new, larger church were Father Guistinianni served for 32 years.

Father Guistinianni's church was once "the finest example of Tuscan Baroque

CHURCH OF THE IMMACULATE CONCEPTION / BALTIMORE

[architecture] in the city," according to "Lost Baltimore Landmarks," by Carleton Jones.

"In 1973 it was simply another marooned ecclesiastical masterpiece… impeccable inside and sweepingly moving without," wrote Jones, and was torn down to make way for the current structure. Immaculate Conception was "twinned" with St. Cecilia in 1995 and remains vibrant, operating a variety of community outreach programs that serve the needy, ex-offenders, and recovering addicts.

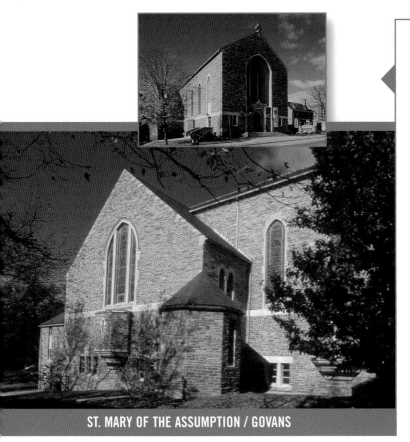

ST. MARY OF THE ASSUMPTION / GOVANS

Located in the 5500 block of York Road since 1942, the first church was dedicated on September 23, 1850 with the cornerstone of the old church laid in the village of Govans in 1849.

One of the great parishes of the archdiocese, St. Mary's is often referred to as "The Mother Church of North Baltimore" and for years stood as the only Catholic church in all of North Baltimore and the surrounding countryside.

At the time, the population of the United States was a little more than 23 million and immigrants arrived almost daily in Fells Point, many fleeing the starvation in Ireland.

Father James Dolan greeted the new arrivals at St. Patrick's on South Broadway and was key in purchasing land near Govanstown where he opened the "Orphans' Home" for boys who had lost their families.

By 1918, Govanstown had been absorbed into the City of Baltimore and after the Great War, the area began to boom as Homeland was developed and a larger church was needed. At the time of its dedication in the fall of 1942, the new church could seat 850 people comfortably, but with the advent of the post-World War II baby boom – the generation of Michael Cronin – folks sometimes wound up standing outside of the church during Mass.

Michael Cronin and St. Mary's

As a kid growing up in North Baltimore, Michael Cronin thought that Govans "was the cultural center of the universe and St. Mary's was its great Cathedral."

"Both of my parents were serious Catholics, although Dad, who had three brothers that became priests and a sister who was a nun was more serious than Mom," said Cronin. "They liked to tell a story about when I was three-years-old and saw a couple of priests walking down the road and I said: 'Look at the uncles!'

"My earliest memories of practicing my faith are centered around getting ready for First Communion, which was taken very seriously indeed," said Cronin.

"And I remember being petrified by the thought of going to Confession for the first time. Communion was scary, too, because we were expected to follow certain procedures to the T... with the implication that severe punishment would follow on the heels of any departure from it."

As in all other Catholic churches in Baltimore the early 1960s, May Day was "very big" at St. Mary's and Cronin remembers "all the boys in their little light blue suits and all the girls in their white dresses parading up York Road to a statue of the Virgin Mary to pray the rosary..."

Cronin, who as a boy believed that the Orioles and Colts were religions unto themselves, sometimes complained that the May Day celebration "interfered with listening to the Orioles on the radio when the team was always in the early weeks of a new season full of hope and excitement."

In his years at St. Mary's school – only seven because he was skipped past the second grade – Mike Cronin never had a lay teacher.

There was Sr. Carolina in the first grade and Sr. Jean, "a pretty novice, I didn't know nuns were allowed to be pretty back then," in the third grade.

Sr. Mona presided over the fifth grade and then he faced his adversary, Sr. Ethelreda, in both the seventh and eighth grades, a twist that each of them considered somewhat cruel.

"I was never officially an altar boy because I was basically a scared kid and I figured I would screw it up," laughs Cronin. "But I did learn how to be one so my older brother and I could serve at the 25th anniversary of my Uncle John [Cronin] who had done some work for Richard Nixon in the 1950s and

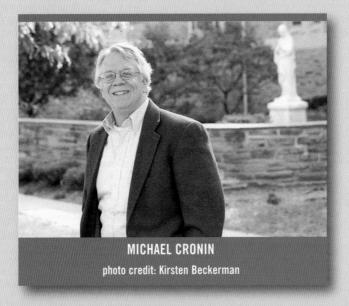

MICHAEL CRONIN
photo credit: Kirsten Beckerman

Cronin stands on the grounds of St. Mary of the Assumption in Govans, the place where his faith – and much of his attitudes about life – were formed.
"I hated wearing a uniform to school each day," said Cronin. "We were the butt of many jokes from the non-Catholics in the neighborhood and though I envied them wearing anything they wanted to school, I was certain that those poor unfortunates were destined for a fiery afterlife!"

there Tricky Dick was in the [Washington, D.C.] church with his wife and daughters."

With all of his fear and anxiety over the strictures of the faith, Cronin knew "from the time I was about 8 or 9 that I wanted to be a priest… just like my Uncle Jimmy [John Cronin's brother], the great hero of my youth and now retired but active at St. Joseph in Fullerton."

Cronin pauses for a moment before confessing.

"In truth, Brooks Robinson and John Unitas were the great heroes of my youth, but I knew I could never be like them."

Now and then, Cronin's love for sports and his Catholic faith would come together in wonderful ways.

"The Orioles would hold inter-faith night at the stadium and we'd all go as a family. I always felt like the mingling of religions was a good thing and there was usually a good crowd. Back in the 60's, inter-faith night usually held the record for the Orioles' biggest walk-up crowd.

"Then there was Section 39 in the upper deck for Colts games when virtually all of the people around us were from St. Ursula's where Uncle Jimmy was stationed… we were even able to park sometimes at some Catholic institution near the stadium and walk to the game."

Faith in something greater than the home team became a more serious thing for Cronin in high school when "everyone knew I was going to be a priest so I was treated with a certain amount of deference… add to that, I was younger than everyone else because I had skipped a grade and had a late birthday so my social life was just about nil, which contributed to my keeping a pledge to enter the St. Charles Seminary in Catonsville."

Alas, recalled Cronin, "it was not to be.

"I only lasted 6 weeks, primarily the result of a suffocating homesickness that was fed by the sound of cars on the Beltway whizzing their way to freedom,"

said Cronin, who nevertheless went on to graduate from Biscayne College, a Catholic school in Miami now known as St. Thomas University.

His graduate degree was also earned at a Catholic institution, the University of Detroit.

"Looking back," said Cronin, "I think my Catholic upbringing had good parts and bad. On the good side, it provided a sense of community and a moral framework on which to place the values I learned from my parents, who were good people, though not without their demons.

"On the bad side, the God I learned about in my grade school youth was an angry God of retribution. Maybe this is not what the nuns were trying to teach me but it's what came through and I found it hard to reconcile this with my knowledge of my uncles who were priests, especially Uncle Jimmy, who were human and fun loving and wonderful people.

"But I was a kid… what did I know?"

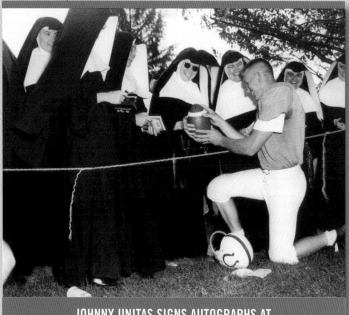

JOHNNY UNITAS SIGNS AUTOGRAPHS AT COLTS TRAINING CAMP

Unitas, arguably the most admired athlete in the history of Baltimore sports, attended St. Joseph Catholic Church in Texas, Md. He died at age 69 on Sept. 11, 2002 and was bid farewell with a Mass of Christian burial from the Cathedral of Mary Our Queen.

St. Peter's, Immaculate Conception Chapel in the mining town of Kitzmiller—until recently a mission placed under the care of St. Peter's, and St. Peter of the Lake, a mobile congregation working to build their own sanctuary, minister to residents and vacationers to Deep Creek Lake and other mountain areas.

ST. JOSEPH / FULLERTON

In the early 19th century, 24 German immigrant families were settling in the Perry Hall/Fullerton area, traveling many miles to attend Mass. A request was granted for a church of their own and a log cabin chapel was erected on Buck's Schoolhouse Road, launching St. Joseph parish in November 1850.

For the next 100 years or so, St. Joseph remained a little country church on the hill.

Today it is a modern sanctuary serving some 4500 families and if you look up at the ceiling during Mass you may see planets and stars lighting the faithful below.

Of the ten stained glass windows in the nave, only two are easily identifiable as religious, such as the "Creation Window" on the north side. The rest deal with the way we live and work.

The most celebrated of the windows shows the gift known as water and all that it provides us: a white marlin off the coast of Ocean City, the 7-mile lighthouse on the Chesapeake, the fabled Blue Crab so closely identified with the state and then the boats and trucks and trains used to ship the water's harvest to the world.

The bottom panel shows an oyster boat on the Chesapeake.

Completed in 1971, the windows of St. Joseph are the work of Roy A. Calligan, a child of St. Joseph, Fullerton now retired to Florida.

For more than 150 years, St. Peter the Apostle in Oakland, the southern arm of Garrett County, has served the area's Catholics and was the first church of any denomination within Oakland city limits when it was dedicated in June of 1852.

In 1901 work began on the stone structure with its impressive steeple that comprises the current church. Today, the church remains the linchpin to the Roman Catholic community of southern Garrett County.

ST. PETER THE APOSTLE / OAKLAND

In an area with few Catholics,
St. Peter's is the face of Catholicism
for the greater community.
The current pastor is Father Donald Parson.

From 1975 through 1993, the church was pastored by the much beloved Father Martin Feild, who helped to celebrate the anniversary Mass.

"It's unique," said Father Marty of his old church.

"Because the resort is so close to Deep Creek Lake, you meet all types of people. There have been outdoor Masses for tourists in the summer and Masses at the Wisp ski area in winter."

Asked what it means to be Catholic while enjoying eggs and sausage after the anniversary Mass, parishioner Jane Nolan got straight to the point.

"Enjoying the presence of the Blessed Sacrament and not letting my religion get in the way of my faith," said Nolan. "From the cradle to the grave, no matter what happens, I'm here to stay."

ST. PETER / WESTERNPORT

Established in 1852 in Allegany County, St. Peter is located in a community of some 2,000 people just south of Frostburg along Route 135.

In 1852, the parish of St. Joseph was established in an area of Northern Baltimore County known as Texas.

St. Joseph, known today as St. Joseph, Cockeysville, served the Irish working in the limestone and marble quarries that provided much of the material for Baltimore's famous white marble steps.

ST. JOSEPH / COCKEYSVILLE

St. Joseph began on land donated in the mid-19th century by John Clarke. Father Philip O'Reilly became St. Joseph's first permanent pastor in 1850 and the dedication of the new church on October 31, 1852 was witnessed by more than a thousand of the faithful. When St. Joseph parish celebrated its centennial, it was a rural parish extending from Seminary Avenue to the Pennsylvania Line. Parishioners numbered about 1,000.

In 1959, St. Joseph Parish opened a new school with nearly 500 students. In 1966, Mass was celebrated in the enlarged and renovated church, which seats about 1,000.

Monsignor Paul Cook, pastor since 1977, made the first addition to a rectory that was built to house one priest.

St. Joseph now serves about 3,500 families: 10,000 parishioners, 450 school students and close to 800 Religious Education students.

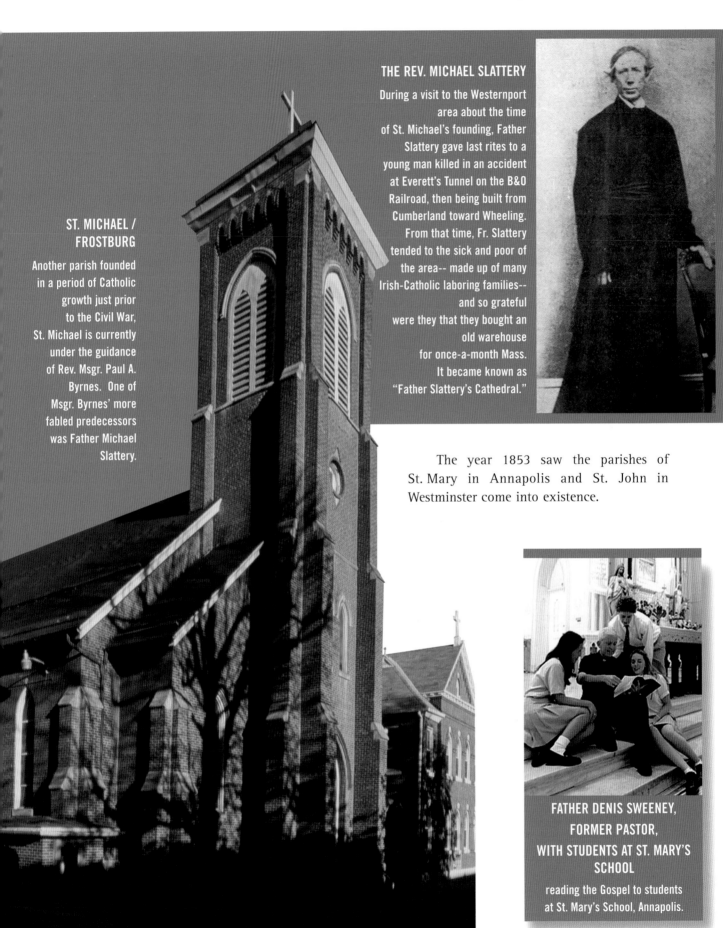

THE REV. MICHAEL SLATTERY

During a visit to the Westernport area about the time of St. Michael's founding, Father Slattery gave last rites to a young man killed in an accident at Everett's Tunnel on the B&O Railroad, then being built from Cumberland toward Wheeling. From that time, Fr. Slattery tended to the sick and poor of the area-- made up of many Irish-Catholic laboring families-- and so grateful were they that they bought an old warehouse for once-a-month Mass. It became known as "Father Slattery's Cathedral."

ST. MICHAEL / FROSTBURG

Another parish founded in a period of Catholic growth just prior to the Civil War, St. Michael is currently under the guidance of Rev. Msgr. Paul A. Byrnes. One of Msgr. Byrnes' more fabled predecessors was Father Michael Slattery.

The year 1853 saw the parishes of St. Mary in Annapolis and St. John in Westminster come into existence.

FATHER DENIS SWEENEY, FORMER PASTOR, WITH STUDENTS AT ST. MARY'S SCHOOL

reading the Gospel to students at St. Mary's School, Annapolis.

ST. MARY / ANNAPOLIS

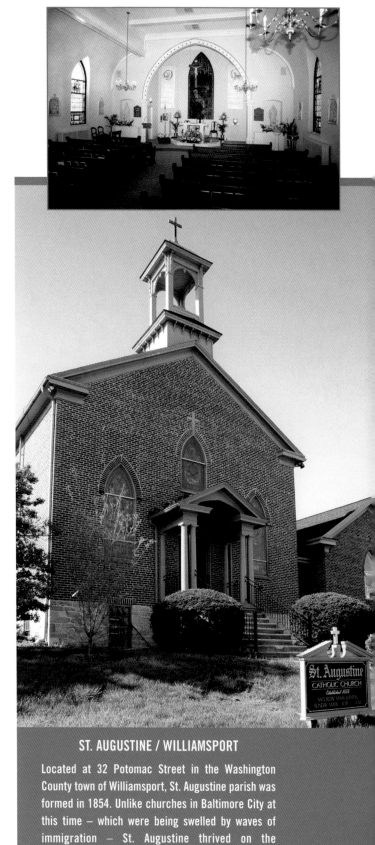

ST. AUGUSTINE / WILLIAMSPORT

The Gothic church of St. Mary stands in the Historic District of Annapolis and is served by the Redemptorists and School Sisters of Notre Dame.

A former choirmaster — Professor Charles Adams Zimmerman of the nearby Naval Academy — composed "Anchors Aweigh."

And a former pastor — Father Francis Xavier Seelos - was recently beatified by late Pope John Paul II. He joins St. John Neumann as part of our rich heritage.

St. John Neumann, for whom St. Mary's current mission church is named, visited Annapolis in 1858 to lay the cornerstone of the current church building and to bless one of the four bells in the church steeple.

St. Mary's has had a number of missions over its history and is recognized to be the "Mother Church" for this region of the state.

Located at 32 Potomac Street in the Washington County town of Williamsport, St. Augustine parish was formed in 1854. Unlike churches in Baltimore City at this time — which were being swelled by waves of immigration — St. Augustine thrived on the multiplication of local families.

The year 1854 also saw St. Brigid erected at Ellwood Avenue and Hudson Street in Canton to serve the Irish that lived among the Germans and native born.

In 1855, the Church of St. Louis the King took root in the Clarksville area of Howard County with a small church that still stands on Dayton Road near the church cemetery.

In 1878, St. Louis began its annual parish picnic, which continues to this day and remains the major single source of revenue for the parish. What is now known as the chapel was finished in 1889 and dedicated the following year by Cardinal Gibbons.

Every Monday evening, the small church is used for a Novena to the Blessed Mother.

ST. BRIGID'S CARNIVAL

photo credit: Kirsten Beckerman

Father Joe Bochenet, pastor of St. Brigid, and Baltimore writer Michele Wojciechowski – Loyola College, Class of 1990 - at the annual spring carnival on the St. Brigid playground in 2001. Wojciechowski, whose roots go back to Sacred Heart of Jesus on Conkling Street, volunteered for several years to organize the carnival.

ST. BRIGID / CANTON

Among the many pastors of St. Brigid was Cardinal James Gibbons, who was assigned to the parish. He visited Fort McHenry from St. Brigid's to minister to the Union and Confederate soldiers during the Civil War.

ST. LOUIS / CLARKSVILLE

St. Louis remained a small country parish until the 1970s when — with the advent of Columbia and an explosion in Howard County's housing market — it boomed along with the rest of the county. There are about 4,000 families today. The original church building still stands on Dayton Road and traces its origins to a small chapel in Doughoregan Manor, the home of Charles Carroll of Carrollton, one of the signers of the Declaration of Independence. To finance construction of its new school several years ago, the parish established the League of St. Louis—now the League of the Little Flower—which provided financial aid to rural parochial schools throughout Maryland. Activities at the church include monthly food collections, a picnic committee and a quilting group.

ST. MARY OF THE ASSUMPTION / PYLESVILLE

St. Mary of the Assumption in Pylesville also began offering Mass in 1855.
"Our church is not just a sacred place, but it is an assembly of believing parishioners," said Fr. Henry Kunkel, pastor.
"By praying and working together for the Lord, we embody the spirit of what it means to be church."

ANNE HADDAD AND THE SANCTUARY OF ST. IGNATIUS CHURCH

Several years ago, Michigan native and Baltimore transplant Anne Haddad read a humorous flyer that said the Catholic Church had "built a reputation for teaching children and letting the adults play."

Her first thought?

"Bingo!"

In her 42 years as a lifelong Catholic, Haddad has lived in the Midwest, New England and now Baltimore. In that time, she has found just a few churches willing and able to "educate the grown-ups as earnestly as they provide schools for the children.

"God knows we need it," she says. "Our questions are harder and our stakes are higher. "

At St. Ignatius in downtown Baltimore, from the priests to the parishioners, she found a congregation "with the collective will and intellectual resources to keep learning together.

"I need someone to challenge me to look inward and outward to answer, continually, this complex question: 'What does it mean to be Catholic?'

"Without this church, I would be in the grips of complacency," she said. "There's no complacency at St. Ignatius. There is a commitment to educating the poor and to social service -- helping homeless and addicted men who are not easy to love but who need it all the more."

When Haddad happened upon St. Ignatius in 1994 during her time as a reporter for *The Baltimore Sun* just down the block, it was a relatively small congregation.

"Here was a church where the priest called on people during the homily now and then -- as if it was a college seminar," she said. "We were always relieved that we had an answer. The Sunday evening Mass might have as few as 30 people. I signed up for the 'Renew' program, and got to know a circle of people better than I had at any other church since my childhood.

photo credit: Jeff Bill
Anne Haddad stands inside the St. Ignatius sanctuary with her daughter Daisy and son Evan.

"For the first time, I had peers to talk to about how to pray and why to do it. We talked about humility, and charity and forgiveness and what those things mean in our real lives. We talked about where our faith fits into our professional lives. That core of devoted parishioners is still there every Sunday, and more join us each week."

Now, said Haddad, she and the good people she met at St. Ignatius are working to educate their children.

"I used to be able to count on my two hands -- and sometimes on one -- all the children at any given Mass," she said. "But a lot of families have joined this church and we have a fledgling Sunday school with about 40 children enrolled -- including mine. They fidget during the homilies that absorb their parents. But this is a church they can grow up in."

In the meantime, her daughter, Daisy Hart, thinks that church is boring.

"That doesn't worry me much, because I saw her face last Thanksgiving, when we helped deliver meals prepared by St. Ignatius parishioners," said Haddad. "An elderly woman who had nothing else to do on this family holiday but sit in an empty apartment greeted us and pulled Daisy in for a big hug."

Daisy, said her mother, was stunned at her power to make a difference.

And some day may use the experience as an answer to that complicated question.

"What does it mean to be Catholic?"

ST. IGNATIUS / BALTIMORE

photo credit: Jeff Bill

Founded on Calvert Street in 1856 by the Jesuits as part of what was then Loyola College, St. Ignatius Church was considered an architectural marvel in the middle of the 19th century. The church interior consisted of a lofty ceiling—sans pillars—detailed plaster cornices, a marble high altar and sanctuary flooring by master artisan Hugo Sisson.

Today, 150 years later, St. Ignatius serves about 500 families, many from outside of the city while continuing to serve the needy from the downtown area.

Its Loaves and Fishes program is a weekly mobile outreach bringing sandwiches, soup, and desserts to Baltimore's homeless each Sunday. St. Ignatius Loyola Academy, an independent, tuition-free, middle and lower school, educates boys from lower-income families.

The church is also the home of the Radio Mass of Baltimore, broadcast live every Sunday at 9:30 a.m. on WBAL reaching homebound, nursing home populations, prisoners, and others unable to attend Mass.

OUR LADY OF MOUNT CARMEL / THURMONT

The earliest known record of Our Lady
of Mount Carmel Church appears in an 1859
edition of The Metropolitan Catholic Almanac as
"Mechanics' Town, Church building – attended
from Mt. St. Mary's College."
Mechanics' Town has been called Thurmont
since the end of the 19th century.
The university has an 1828 manuscript
by a priest who suggested that as
Mt. St. Mary's University grew, its priests might
take care of nearby congregations.
Land was purchased for a church in early 1857.
The present Gothic-styled church was
dedicated, Sunday, June 5, 1859.

HOLY CROSS / FEDERAL HILL

Originally established as a mission of
St. Alphonsus for the Germans of
South Baltimore, Holy Cross began
with a schoolhouse in 1855.
A church was built three years later.
With the continued influx of German
immigrants Holy Cross was enlarged
in 1885, the year that National
Bohemian beer was first brewed
in Baltimore.
The old church school – closed in
the early 1970s due to declining
enrollment – was being renovated
for luxury harbor condominiums
in early 2004.

During the American Civil War, Archbishop Kenrick, a Unionist, did not fly the American flag over the Basilica, as many of his fellow archbishops did atop their cathedrals.

Most of the bishops reporting to Kenrick were sympathetic to the Confederacy, although he was successful in persuading a Sulpician Vicar Apostolic in St. Augustine, Florida, to suppress a pro-slavery pamphlet.

"All men are by the law of nature equal, no one is by nature master of another," wrote Archbishop Kenrick. "Yet by the law of nations not only the dominion of jurisdiction, but also the dominion of property is granted to man over man; and this the old law ratified."

The slave trade had been condemned by Pope Gregory XVI in 1839, although Jesuits in Maryland owned slaves who worked on their plantations, they sold their slaves in 1838. Sulpicians were not large landowners and thus owned only a few slaves.

In 1862, with the Civil War in full swing, the Baltimore Province comprised the cities of Philadelphia, Pittsburgh, Charleston, Savannah, Richmond, Wheeling, Erie, and the Vicariate Apostolic of Florida.

The Diocese of Baltimore included 124 churches and chapels, 170 priests, 36 schools, 35 institutions devoted to charity and a population of Catholics numbered at about 150,000.

ST. PATRICK / LITTLE ORLEANS

Opened in Little Orleans – also known as 15 Mile Creek – in 1860 as a mission of St. Peter in Hancock. The church was built near the boundary of Allegany and Washington counties on land donated by Lady Stafford, one of the Caton sisters.

That year, St. Gabriel parish was organized in the Allegany County town of Barton.

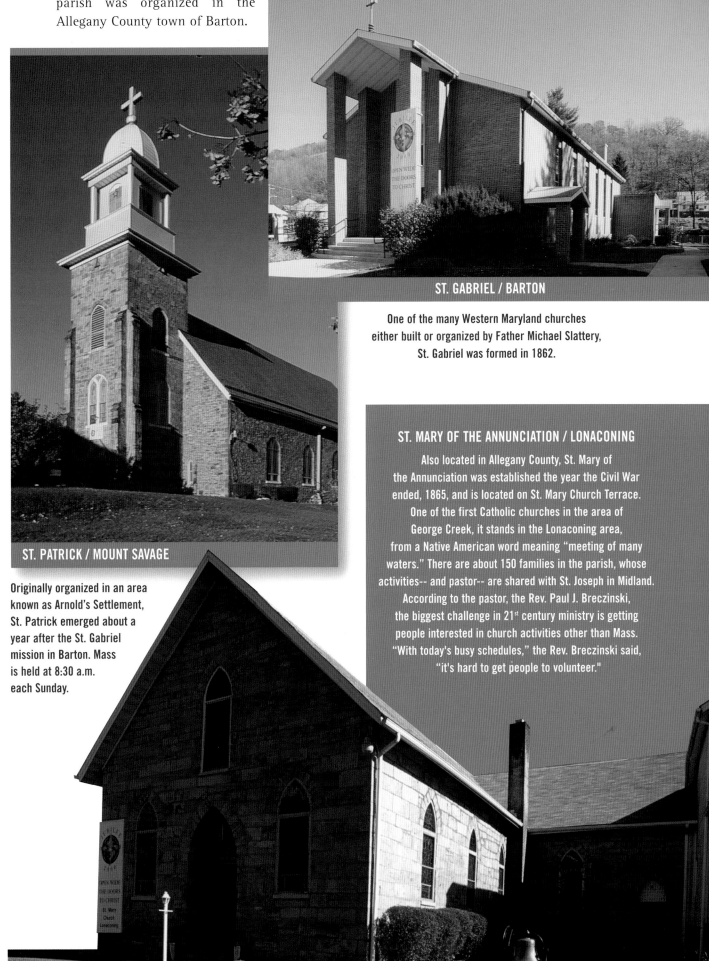

ST. GABRIEL / BARTON

One of the many Western Maryland churches
either built or organized by Father Michael Slattery,
St. Gabriel was formed in 1862.

ST. MARY OF THE ANNUNCIATION / LONACONING

Also located in Allegany County, St. Mary of
the Annunciation was established the year the Civil War
ended, 1865, and is located on St. Mary Church Terrace.
One of the first Catholic churches in the area of
George Creek, it stands in the Lonaconing area,
from a Native American word meaning "meeting of many
waters." There are about 150 families in the parish, whose
activities-- and pastor-- are shared with St. Joseph in Midland.
According to the pastor, the Rev. Paul J. Breczinski,
the biggest challenge in 21ˢᵗ century ministry is getting
people interested in church activities other than Mass.
"With today's busy schedules," the Rev. Breczinski said,
"it's hard to get people to volunteer."

ST. PATRICK / MOUNT SAVAGE

Originally organized in an area
known as Arnold's Settlement,
St. Patrick emerged about a
year after the St. Gabriel
mission in Barton. Mass
is held at 8:30 a.m.
each Sunday.

On July 4, 1863, less than a week before 100 Union and Confederate soldiers died in a clash on South Mountain in Boonsboro, Rev. Louis Regis Deluol raised the Union flag over St. Mary's Seminary for the first time since the war began.

Not to do so, he argued, would be "a sign of disloyalty" to the nation which granted Catholics freedom of worship.

On July 6, Archbishop Kenrick passed away.

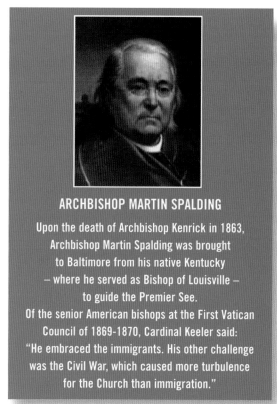

ARCHBISHOP MARTIN SPALDING

Upon the death of Archbishop Kenrick in 1863, Archbishop Martin Spalding was brought to Baltimore from his native Kentucky – where he served as Bishop of Louisville – to guide the Premier See.
Of the senior American bishops at the First Vatican Council of 1869-1870, Cardinal Keeler said:
"He embraced the immigrants. His other challenge was the Civil War, which caused more turbulence for the Church than immigration."

In February of 1864, a new church for St. Francis Xavier Church – a parish devoted to the needs of African-American Catholics since the community had been formed in 1793 – was dedicated on East Oliver Street in Baltimore.

At the time of the Emancipation, some 16,000 black Catholics lived in Maryland.

From St. Francis Xavier would evolve congregations known as St. Monica's, St. Peter Claver and – in 1907 – St. Barnabas, all parish-designated African-American.

As the Civil War was coming to an end in the early spring of 1865, a Jesuit priest, Father John Gaffney, arrived at

ST. STEPHEN / BRADSHAW

St. Stephen's dates to 1841 but wasn't a formal parish until 1863 when a wooden building and an acre of land on the north side of Bradshaw Road were deeded to the Archdiocese of Baltimore by trustees of the Gunpowder Division of the Sons of Temperance for $500.
On June 28, 1864, Father W. J. Clarke, S.J., of Saint Ignatius, Baltimore, dedicated the two-story building – an upper room for church and a lower one for school.
In late spring of 1869, the cornerstone of the present church – often referred to as "The Little Cathedral" - was put in place.
It was completed and dedicated in 1890.
On December 13, 1931, Archbishop Curley blessed St. Stephen's school, dedicated a convent built for the Franciscan Sisters, and confirmed sixty-five young Catholics.
Eventually the parish high school was closed and the old school building was demolished when the John Carroll School opened in Harford County. In December of 1973, the church was heavily damaged by an electrical fire. Only 13 years later, a second fire, also caused by a short circuit in wiring, hit the church.
Once again, it was restored and a Mass of Dedication, celebrated by Archbishop William Borders, was held on January 18, 1987.
Today, St. Stephen's boasts membership of nearly 2,000 families.

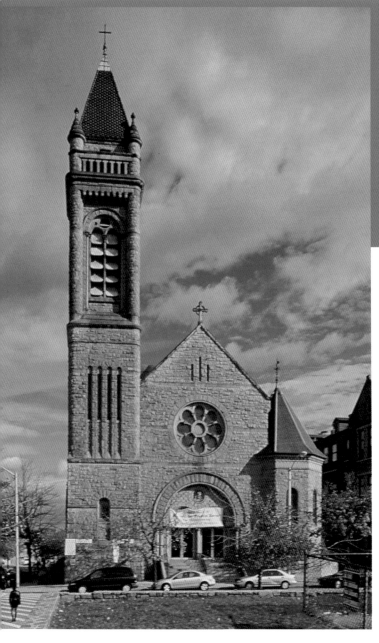

ST. FRANCIS XAVIER / BALTIMORE

Black Catholics in Baltimore began receiving the Eucharist in the basement of St. Mary's Seminary when it was downtown. From there, they were welcomed into the basement chapel of St. Ignatius on Calvert Street. In 1863, the Jesuits bought a building at Calvert and Pleasant Streets. It was dedicated as St. Francis Xavier on February 21, 1864.
In 1932, the congregation moved to Eager and Caroline Streets and in 1968 settled in its current location at Caroline and East Oliver Streets.

St. Joseph-on-Carrollton Manor in Buckeystown to celebrate Mass.

In time, Gaffney would become responsible for parishes in Libertytown,

Petersville and Middletown, making his ecclesiastical rounds on a pony named Harry.

The thriving Catholic community of Urbana, built around St. Ignatius in nearby Ijamsville near Frederick, was especially grateful to the priest and his pony.

The end of the Civil War also saw the emergence of the St. Bartholomew parish in the Carroll County town of Manchester.

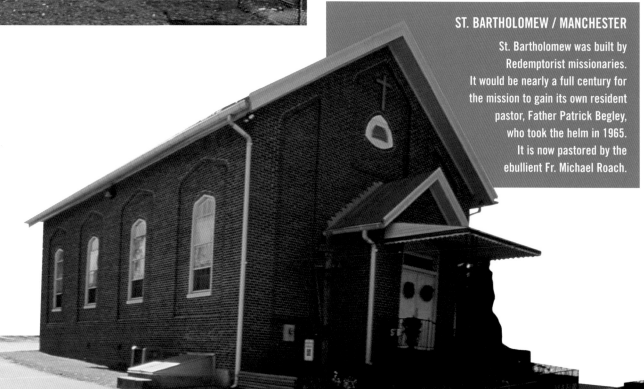

ST. BARTHOLOMEW / MANCHESTER

St. Bartholomew was built by Redemptorist missionaries. It would be nearly a full century for the mission to gain its own resident pastor, Father Patrick Begley, who took the helm in 1965. It is now pastored by the ebullient Fr. Michael Roach.

FRIENDSHIP AND GENEROSITY

Jeff Rudacille, a Dundalk born truck driver in his early 40s, has leaned on his faith throughout a variety of personal struggles.

He has seen to it that each of his three daughters-- Jessica, Victoria and Angela-- have made their First Holy Communion and often visits the old church at St. Ignatius in Hickory to meditate and honor the presence of Christ in the Holy Eucharist.

Rudacille, a product of Our Lady of Hope, with oldest daughter Jessica at her First Holy Communion. St. Clement Mary Hofbauer, 1996. "We had to learn the 10 commandments and make a big banner that said my name and had pictures of the Eucharist on it," said Jessica. "The banners were on the wall when we walked in to make Communion." "I think," she said, "that I'll always be Catholic."

In 1972, Rudacille was a fifth grade altar boy at Our Lady of Hope in Dundalk and Father Michael Roach was a rookie priest already going bald.

"I served Mass with my cousin, Bruce Herman, and once we laughed through the whole service. Once we started, we couldn't stop. After Mass, Fr. Roach really reamed us out. We'd never heard a priest talk like that. After that we sort of straightened up."

When it was time for the adolescent boys at Our Lady of Hope to get the sex education talk, Father Roach was the guy who got the assignment.

"You could tell he was uncomfortable, because all we knew were all these slang terms and he was being serious," said Rudacille. "But it was an open discussion and he did a good job."

Rudacille went on to attend public high school in Dundalk, get married, have kids, get divorced and work every day to keep his family afloat.

After Our Lady of Hope, Father Roach began a tour through various parishes in the archdiocese, including a memorable tenure at St. Peter the Apostle, while earning a reputation as a keen scholar of church history.

Through the years, as Rudacille struggled with life on life's terms, he remembered the earnest young priest who'd yelled at him for goofing off on the altar. And he'd remember that Father Roach was a good guy that he always liked and respected.

"I hadn't seen him for a lot of years when I decided to go to him for some help and the first thing he did was call me the same name he used to when I was a kid: Ruda-Bird," laughed Rudacille. "He gave me a blessing and then I didn't seem him again until 2002 when my marriage was breaking up. I called Our Lady of Hope, and they told me where he was."

Fr. Michael J. Roach, pastor of St. Bartholomew in Manchester, teaches Church history at Mount St. Mary's Seminary in Emmitsburg. An expert in American Church history, Irish Americans and the history of the Archdiocese of Baltimore, Father Roach graduated from Loyola College in Maryland and holds a master's degree from the Catholic University of America.

"I went out to Manchester and he was the same guy I'd known when I was little," said Rudacille. "With all the things priests have gone through lately, Father Roach fits the old school tradition that's important to me: a very compassionate, very loving, good and decent man.

"He listened and told me I was going to make it, that I'd gone through adversity before and I'd get through this one."

The time that Rudacille sought out his old friend happened to coincide with the sex scandal that hounded the Church at the beginning of the 21st century.

"He gave me another blessing when I left and then he stopped me for a moment and said: 'You know Jeff, we could use some prayers these days too...' "

ST. MARTIN / W. BALTIMORE

Named for the patron saint of Archbishop Spalding, St. Martin's parish laid its cornerstone
on July 9, 1865 with a crowd of 20,000 people and a parade some two miles long.
Originally serving a largely Irish membership and a sizable German population as well, the church was dedicated in 1867. In
1920, it was the third largest parish in the archdiocese with some 7,300 members.
An anchor for African-American Catholics on the Westside since the early 1960s, St. Martin stands at the corner
of Fulton Avenue and Fayette Street and is part of a tri –parish community that includes St. Jerome and St. Peter the Apostle,
Along with its sibling parishes, St. Martin is involved in the Christmas Basket outreach, which coordinates community
clean-up with the distribution of holiday food and gifts. The parish has liturgical dance ministers
and altar linen cleaning volunteers as well as a cadre of programs geared toward teens and pre-teens.
St. Martin, St. Jerome and St. Peter the Apostle parishes joined together
to form the Transfiguration Catholic Community in 2004.

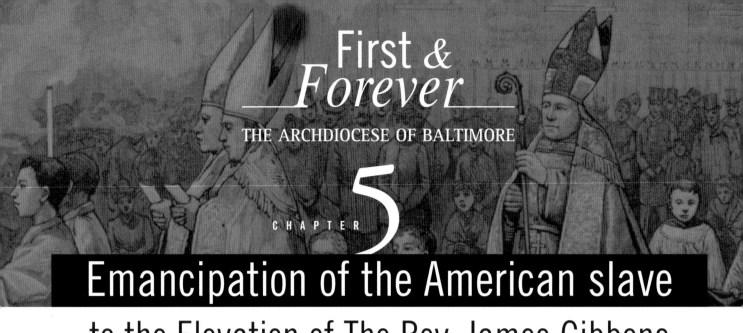

First & *Forever*

CHAPTER 5

Emancipation of the American slave
to the Elevation of The Rev. James Gibbons as Archbishop of Baltimore

On Sunday, August 16, 1868, Father James Gibbons became the youngest bishop in the American Church after his consecration as Vicar Apostolic of North Carolina at the Cathedral of the Assumption in Baltimore.

In this same year, St. Lawrence the Martyr opened for worship on the Anne Arundel County line in Jessup. Also in the first year after the end of the Civil War, the village of Owensville welcomed Our Lady of Sorrows in West River, St. Michael opened in the Clear Spring area of Washington County and St. Francis de Sales was established as a mission in the Abingdon section of Harford County.

Nearly a full century later, in 1964, St. Francis de Sales would become an independent parish.

ST. LAWRENCE / JESSUP

St. Lawrence was organized in 1866 at Jessup's Cut to serve the growth of the Catholic population in Anne Arundel County.

OUR LADY OF SORROWS / OWENSVILLE

In 1866, the first church was a simple wood frame that was restored and enlarged until being razed in 1951.

The name of the parish honors the Seven Sorrows endured by the Blessed Virgin Mary: The Prophecy of Simeon, The Flight into Egypt, The Loss of Her Son for Three Days, Mary Meets Jesus on the Via Dolorosa, the Crucifixion, Jesus is Taken from the Cross, and the Burial of Jesus.

In 1951 the current Georgian colonial style church was begun and dedicated in 1953 as a new diocesan church.

Fr. Mark J. Logue, pastor since August 1996, tackled the job of enlarging church seating from 150 to more than 400 without disturbing the Georgian architectural style.

The first Mass in the "new" church was Easter 2001.

ST. FRANCIS DE SALES / ABINGDON
St. Francis de Sales, located at 1450 Abingdon Road, offers a Sunday Mass in Spanish and a Byzantine service each Sunday

In 1866, under the direction of Archbishop Spalding, St. Mary's Industrial School for Boys was built on the southwest side of town with 70 boarders and Xaverian Brothers from Belgium in charge.

ST. MARY'S INDUSTRIAL SCHOOL

Built on the southwest edge of the city near the parish of St. Agnes in the late 19th century, the orphanage and reform school – surrounded by a wall with guards on duty - has remained known long after it ceased because of it's most famous ward: an incorrigible kid from the waterfront streets named George Herman Ruth.
"The Babe" would go on to say that the most important man in his life, by far, was Brother Mathias, the school disciplinarian who taught him the finer points of the game of baseball.

ST. MICHAEL / CLEAR SPRING

Mission of St. Mary in Hagerstown. Established in 1866 in the area of Clear Spring-Williamsport.

Proudly calling itself "the Heart of Mount Washington Since 1867," the Shrine stands at the corner of Smith and Greeley avenues. "We are a Roman Catholic community with a commitment to worshiping well, living our faith by reaching out beyond our boundaries, and strengthening each other in our faith journey by building our bonds of community," says the Rev. Msgr. Richard Cramblitt, pastor. "You are welcome to join us for prayer and for the life of our parish."

SHRINE OF THE SACRED HEART / MT. WASHINGTON

JAY TINKER

photo credit: Kirsten Beckerman

Jay Tinker, of St. Thomas Aquinas parish in Hampden, shown in the chapel of the S.S. John W. Brown Liberty Ship docked on South Clinton Street in Baltimore. Tinker is a volunteer seaman on the World War II vessel.

The ship's non-denominational chapel features a pivoting, three-sided altar. With the push of a button the table rotates, enabling the Catholic, Protestant, or Jewish face of the altar to turn toward the congregation.

"Being Catholic means a lot to me," said Jay Tinker. "It is neat to hear someone say, 'Oh, you're one of those Catholic boys!'"

Like many Catholics, Tinker does not agree with everything the Church asks its members to believe, but argues: "Does everyone agree with what their mayor, governor or president believes is best for us? I hold my faith and the faith of my Church very high and wouldn't want any other faith."

Tinker was asked if he felt closer to his Creator while at sea.

"When I'm at sea, all I can see is the colors that God gave us," he said. "The blues and grays of the sky, the greens and browns of the land, the blues and greens of the water. I can see God everywhere I look. Up, down, or around, He's there... you can see it in the way the water moves."

ST. THOMAS AQUINAS / HAMPDEN

St. Thomas Aquinas is located at 1008 West 37th Street in Hampden. The parish prayer group meets weekly in the Church. Father James Farmer, pastor, leads the prayers for local and personal intentions as well as the good of the world.

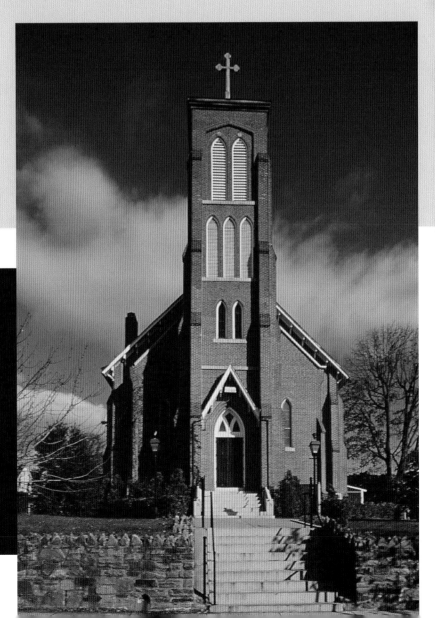

First & Forever
THE ARCHDIOCESE OF BALTIMORE

CAROL "SUE" ABROMAITIS

Dr. Abromaitis in the sanctuary of her beloved
St. Thomas of Aquinas in Hampden. The former Sue Nevin
graduated from St. Thomas grade school in 1952.

"My memories of the parish are intermingled with memories of the school that was staffed completely by the School Sisters of Notre Dame," remembers Sue Abromaitis, veteran professor of English literature at Loyola College.

"First Communion was a glorious parish event, occurring on the first Sunday in May at the Children's Mass... in my year Pat Smith, now Sister Patricia Smith, R.S.M., was the May Queen. Graduation from the grade school occurred on Sunday with a special Mass followed that evening by a special CYO graduation dance."

Our Christian Youth Organization, "started by one of the assistants, Father Hannan [later archbishop of New Orleans] was one of the first CYOs in the United States. An important part of our social life was the dance on Thursday nights; former members still have reunions every few years.

"My earliest memories include annual 'missions' the women, one week, men, the other; these would be given by order priests-- Passionist Fathers, Redemptorists, and Jesuits.

"Where the [church] parking lot is now was the old school building, decrepit but roomy. Other than storage, the only time I saw it used was as the site for the sale of religious goods."

There was, she remembers, the annual parish picnic, summer fairs to benefit the Saint Vincent de Paul Society, weekly Confession, May Processions, Lenten Stations, Forty Hours, Benediction, Novenas, Midnight Mass, Tenebrae.

[For those of you who don't know or have forgotten: **ten·e·brae**. from the Medieval Latin meaning darkness. Used with a singular or plural verb, Tenebrae is the office of matins and lauds sung on the last three days of Holy Week with a ceremony of candles. These hymns commemorate the sufferings and death of Christ.]

"All of these," she remembers, "were markers in the life of the parish."

And still more: "The children's choir and the adult choir provided the music for weekly Masses and special events. The Holy Name Society flourished with monthly Masses, meetings, and a yearly retreat, usually at Manresa. In the Sodality the women of the parish had similar activities.

"Sunday School for children not in the parish school prepared them for the sacraments. That evolved into the C.C.D. program that, in turn, grew and expanded until it included religious instruction for adults as well and discussion clubs where women would meet weekly and talk about religious texts that they had read for the meeting.

And the names of the religious the children looked up to are indelible.

"Fr. McGraw, Fr. Wolfe, Fr. Whelan, Fr. Scannell, Fr. Gribbin are just a few of the wonderful priests who served in my youth," said Abromaitis. "Pictures and words, learning and laughter, recall many of the nuns including Sisters Philip Neri, Humiliana, Adelaide, Ruzena, Christina, Ethelreda, and Ada.

"In its witness to what was one of the few Protestant working-class neighborhoods in Baltimore, Saint Thomas Aquinas was an inspiring presence for those of us who were part of it."

ST. JAMES / BOONSBORO

Organized in 1868, St. James stands at the corner of Ford and Main streets in Boonsboro, Washington Country. It is a mission parish of St. Augustine Church in Williamsport. "We seek to imitate Jesus Christ in our daily lives through our collective works and prayers... We follow the traditions Christ gave the Church through his Apostles and the teaching authority of the Church..."

ST. JOSEPH / SYKESVILLE

The beginnings of St. Joseph in the Sykesville area go back to 1852 when several hundred Catholic families were served by Jesuits riding in on horseback from Frederick, and Sulpicians who founded St. Charles College about eight miles away. From that start, the parish now serves some 2,600 families.

In September of 1865 Dr. and Mrs. Orrelana H. Owings donated the ground for the church building to the archdiocese. In August 1867, the cornerstone of the first Sykesville church was laid.

The building was used for services even before the roof was in place. The rear wall collapsed before completion and wasn't replaced until five years later. Finally, in 1873, construction of the Sykesville church building was completed. More than 100 years later, construction began on the present church. The sanctuary, which includes a chapel to the Blessed Sacrament, is connected to the structure built in 1965. It was dedicated on October 9, 1998.

ST. JOSEPH PASSIONIST MONASTERY / IRVINGTON

Organized in 1868, the Monastery parish was one of the first to form a parish council in the days before the Second Vatican Council. The grand sanctuary was begun shortly before the Great Depression and is one of the last built in Baltimore with such magnificence.

THE NEVILLE FAMILY OF AUGUSTA AVENUE

The Rev. Michael Murphy, chaplain at Mount St. Joseph High School, comes from a long line of Irish and German Catholics with roots in Irvington.

When it finally came time to sell the old family house on Augusta Avenue – his great-grandparents' house, a house in which 15 children had been raised, two of which went on to become nuns – Father Mike celebrated a goodbye Mass there.

An altar was set up in the living room – the room where the large family once ate dinner in two shifts - and they adorned the Eucharistic table with photos of Frederick and Ella Neville and their many descendents.

"We sang all the old hymns," said Ella "Sissy" Neville Machlinski, born in 1917. "Some of us broke down, some laughed and some joked."

That's what happens with bittersweet memories that are bigger than any house can hold, even the big house at the corner of Augusta and Massachusetts Avenue.

"Our love made it a home," said Father Mike. "Celebrating Mass there, I could feel the spirit of so many who had passed through there."

The Nevilles settled there in the first decade of the 20th century, when it was still something of a rural hamlet on the outskirts of Baltimore, home to slaughter-houses and Victorian houses with big wrap-around porches.

The Catholic anchors of the neighborhood were the St. Joseph Passionist Monastery on Morley Street and, just a half-mile or so further west on Frederick Avenue, Mt. St. Joseph High School.

"Our mother [Ella Neville] was raised in the Monastery parish and we grew up there, all of us," said Sr. Gemma Neville, who took her name from the late 19th century Italian saint, Gemma Galgani.

Most of the Neville boys attended Mt. St. Joe. Five of the daughters attended Seton High School. Two became nuns of the Bon Secours order – Sr. Gemma and Sr. Angela – and credit the inspiration to Sr. Malachy, a legendary Bon Secours nun who helped their mother through a touch-and-go convalescence after childbirth.

"Our mother almost died when Angela was born [at home] and the doctor and the priest took her to Bon Secours," said Sissy. "Mom said that when they wheeled her through the hospital, she looked up and saw these nuns trimming a Christmas tree, all in white, and she thought, 'Oh my God,' worrying about the 12 children back at home.

"I remember my father sitting on the piano stool and when my uncle came by and asked how Mom was, my father started to cry. But she pulled through. The doctor said she couldn't have anymore children but she delivered three more at Bon Secours."

So involved were the religious in the day-to-day life of the Neville family that the sisters of Bon Secours made Sr. Gemma's First Communion gown, complete with tiny pearls.

"It was hard leaving home for the convent. I left on a Sunday in 1943 and I can still see all of us in the hallway when I said goodbye," said Sr. Gemma.

"When I received my habit - the Bon Secours dressed in the French style, a full black habit like a peasant dress with a medal on a black ribbon - most of my brothers were home on leave from World War II.

"We dressed as brides when we took our vows and when we began the procession I could hear my brother Joe say, to our mother 'Here's she comes Mom, here she comes...'"

"Such a closeness," said Sissy.

"It's a depth of faith," said Sr. Gemma.

"It's special that Michael is a priest," said Father Murphy's mother, Carol Berg, a 1960 graduate of Seton High School. "But my mother is the one who instilled the faith in us. I feel my faith and it has made me strong. I have often prayed for that strength."

"I pray for vocations in the family," said Sissy, who remembers when the parking lot at Bon Secours hospital on West Baltimore Street was a convent and more vividly remembers when her sister Mary Jo left home to become Sr. Gemma, followed by Angela.

"We took it hard, we missed each other and cried when when they went away to convent," said Sissy. "But we rejoiced too because we knew it was something good."

Sr. Angela took her first vows in 1950 and retired in 2001, although as both she and Gemma know, once a religious, always a religious.

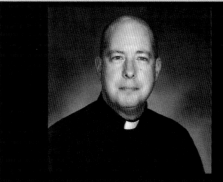

FR. MICHAEL MURPHY

"I'm an Archdiocesan priest and I move around a lot to help out in different parishes. My first assignment was to Saint Patrick's in Cumberland. I was there for three years and I often go back for weddings and baptisms.

I also learned a lot from the three Franciscans who staffed a parish in Midland, a small community a little further out from Cumberland. They helped shape my priesthood in so many ways - through example and suggesting books to read. From there I went to Saint John's in Columbia. I was there only a year before coming to the Mount as chaplain. Columbia was challenging in that it was a more liberal community from Cumberland. But again, the folks were terrific."

"Every part of it has been good," said Sr. Angela. "I've worked with the chemically dependent, helped [addicts] through the 12 steps to take an inventory of their whole life."

Today, a large part of the old Monastery campus near the old house on Augusta Avenue is a detox center. The congregation of addicts and recovering addicts in Baltimore seems to grow faster than the faith itself.

"All the addicts I worked with had a higher power," said Sr. Angela. "For some it was God, for others it was nature."

Sr. Gemma has a doctorate in ministry and a masters in Divinity. She studied at the Berkley School of Theology under the Jesuits and has trained people for spiritual direction. She retired from active service in 2002 after 58 years.

"The most important times [of my ministry] was when I served the sick and dying," said Sr. Gemma. "We'd set the Communion table up for them and one woman I'll never forget.

"She really wanted to get something off her mind and told me her whole life story. When the priest came in, he gave her absolution without her having to repeat it."

BON SECOURS HOSPITAL

Founded in 1881, the hospital was blessed by Cardinal Gibbons in 1918. It was a gift of Mr. and Mrs. George C. Jenkins.

The Tenth Provincial Council opened at Baltimore's Basilica on April 25, 1869. There, Archbishop Spalding was able to persuade the council to establish special missions for black Catholics as well as special collections to aid them if possible.

He also encouraged the Oblate sisters to extend their ministries to black communities in other dioceses.

That same year, St. Alphonsus Rodriguez was established on Old Court Road in Woodstock.

ST. MARY, STAR OF THE SEA / FEDERAL HILL

Organized in by the Irish in the waterfront community of South Baltimore in 1868, St. Mary's at Riverside Avenue and Gittings Street is known to seafarers and landlubbers alike for the blue star atop its steeple.

ST. ALPHONSUS RODRIGUEZ / WOODSTOCK.
St. Alphonsus is located on Old Court Road in Woodstock. During the 2003 holiday season, the congregation pitched in to help its brothers and sisters at St. Gregory the Great parish in Baltimore and received this reply from Fr. Damien Nalepa:

"Thank You, Thank You, Thank You… on behalf of the many needy people you have 'blessed' with a beautiful Thanksgiving. These people would not have been able to have a Thanksgiving Dinner if it wasn't for your love and concern for others. Your love and devotion to share with others brings to mind when Scripture says, 'For I rescued the poor who cried out for help, the orphans and the unassisted.' [Job 29:12]; 'Tell them to do good, to be rich in good works, to be generous, ready to share.' [1st Timothy 6:18].

"Truly you have lived up to what these readings from the bible, the word of God…"

101 SOUTH MOUNT STREET
FOURTEEN HOLY MARTYRS / SOUTH MOUNT
AND LOMBARD STREETS / LAST MASS SAID THERE
OCT. 18, 1964

In the summer of 1872, Archbishop Spalding died and was replaced by the Rev. James Roosevelt Bayley, a 57-year-old native of Rye, New York, and nephew of Mother Elizabeth Ann Seton.

■ ■ ■

The eighth archbishop of Baltimore, James Roosevelt Bayley was a convert to the faith.

After resigning his position as rector of St. Peter's Episcopal Church in Harlem, New York, he went to Rome in 1841. He was baptized there in 1842 and ordained two years later.

In 1853 he published, *"A Brief Sketch of the Early History of the Catholic Church on the Island of New York."* That same year, when the Diocese of Newark, New Jersey, was established, Bayley was named its first bishop.

Said Cardinal Keeler of Archbishop Bayley: "His admiration for his aunt [Mother Seton] showed all through his life."

ARCHBISHOP JAMES R. BAYLEY

During his five years as head of the Archdiocese of Baltimore, Archbishop Bayley presided over the dedication of several churches, including two on the east side of Baltimore: St. Wenceslaus near Johns Hopkins Hospital and Sacred Heart of Jesus in Highlandtown.

ST. WENCESLAUS / E. BALTIMORE

Located at 2111 Ashland Avenue at the corner of North Collington Avenue in an old Bohemian neighborhood. St. Wenceslaus was organized in 1872 and continues today as a neighborhood parish for African-Americans and old-timers who return to the parish of their youth.

The first black students began enrolling at St. Wenceslaus in the late 1960s. Prior to that, a student had to have at least one parent of Bohemian descent to attend. "There were Irish kids on our block who couldn't go," remembers Frank Lidinsky.

It is at St. Wenceslaus that Mother Teresa, canonized by Pope John Paul II, established an AIDS hospice-- the Gift of Hope-- through her Missionaries of Charity. She was present when the hospice was dedicated and at the time of her death in 1997, Cardinal Keeler said: "We give thanks to God for the wonderful memories Mother Teresa leaves us: her commitment to daily prayer, her building up of a worldwide network of religious sisters, brothers and priests who offer direct care to the suffering poor and homeless."

Referencing the Gift of Hope residence at St. Wenceslaus, the Cardinal added: "In a special way, we in Baltimore are grateful..."

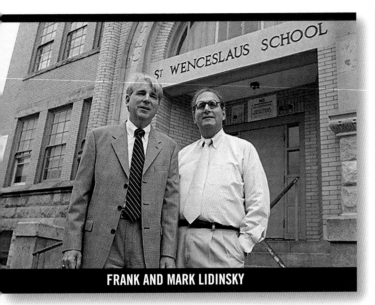

FRANK AND MARK LIDINSKY

The Lidinsky brothers – Frank (left) and Mark stand
in front of the old St. Wenceslaus School which
they attended as children growing up at 921
North Linwood Avenue. Richard A. Lidinsky was also
survived by his son, Richard, Jr. and a daughter,
Mary Angela Mahoney.
"I can remember," said Frank, "people from
the neighborhood waiting on our porch for my father
to come home from work so they could ask him
for help finding a job or something."

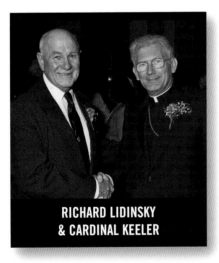

**RICHARD LIDINSKY
& CARDINAL KEELER**

Richard Lidinsky poses with Cardinal Keeler
at a civic function.
A Mass of Christian burial for Mr. Lidinsky,
who served eight Baltimore mayors
as deputy comptroller for Baltimore, was held Dec. 15,
2003 at the Cathedral of Mary Our Queen.
"Dad lived by the famous quote of St. Thomas More,"
said Mark Lidinsky in his eulogy,
"I serve my King
– in his case the City of Baltimore – but God first.'"

Frank Lidinsky, an attorney who graduated from Mount St. Mary's in Emmitsburg, believes that his father's faith came from his parents and his East Baltimore neighborhood near St. Wenceslaus.

"Dad grew up in a time when people depended on their church for spiritual, social, educational, and recreational activity," said Lidinsky. "Nobody had a car, most people still walked and the church was the center of all activity. He connected on that spiritual level at such an early age, going to daily Mass every day as a kid, vespers and benediction, and it grew through his entire life."

A tailor's son and one of ten children, Richard Lidinsky was born above his father's shop, the Comet Tailor Shop, at Linwood Avenue and McElderry Street near the Northeast Market. All his life he would shop there for meats and cheese and other delicacies.

Young Richard contemplated going to seminary until about 1940 when he met Angela Miller, a girl from the St. Elizabeth parish who worked for the Bocek Bros. Electrical Co.

"In those days if you were from St. Wenceslaus and you married someone from St. Elizabeth's, that was considered a mixed-marriage," said Lidinsky.

Richard Lidinsky was especially devoted to the Mother of Perpetual Help and asked that the portrait of the Virgin and Child that hung in his City Hall office be displayed on the altar at his funeral.

"When they remodeled City Hall back in the 1970s they appointed some kind of art commission and you had to get approval from them before you could hang anything on the walls," remembers Frank Lidinsky.

"Of course my father hung his picture of the Mother of Perpetual Help and when someone came around from the design commission they said it didn't fit and he'd have to take it down."

To which the mild mannered Mr. Lidinsky, a man who tipped his hat to women he recognized on the street, replied: "I'll leave before it comes down."

SR. KATHLEEN FEELEY, SSND AND THE COLLEGE OF NOTRE DAME IN MARYLAND

SR. FEELEY

A veteran professor of English literature at the College of Notre Dame on North Charles Street, Sr. Kathleen Feeley, SSND, holds a doctorate from Rutgers University and is a noted scholar of the Catholic writer Flannery O'Connor.

On Oct. 17, 1962, O'Connor gave a lecture to a small group of students at Notre Dame's LeClerc Hall. Most of the young women attended on assignment but Sr. Kathleen, who had not known of O'Connor previously, said the frail but powerful writer "took the top of my head off when she spoke."

In 1972, Sr. Kathleen published *Flannery O'Connor: Voice of the Peacock*. "O'Connor writes about those who know they are redeemed," said Sr. Kathleen. "And those who don't, she calls us to know."

Born in 1929 near Fulton Avenue and West Fayette Street, Sr. Kathleen spent her early years at St. Martin parish and took her final vows at age 20. In 2003, she returned to St. Martin for a visit after being away for nearly 50 years.

"It's still a grand church," she said. "Today, it's missionary territory like a lot of Baltimore. Several of the orders of sisters are looking to create parish-based Catholic schools that have no parish boundaries, particularly for girls who show potential. To be Catholic in Baltimore, said Sr. Kathleen, "Is to know a sense of solidarity. There's a Catholic world here…"

Founded as a high school in 1873 by the School Sisters of Notre Dame (SSND), the College of Notre Dame of Maryland was the first Catholic college for women to award a four year baccalaureate degree, which they did in 1895. Located in the Homeland neighborhood of North Baltimore, Notre Dame's dedication to young women continues, although classes for working adults are open to men and women. Campus tours are available throughout the year.

ST. ELIZABETH OF HUNGARY / EAST BALTIMORE

St. Elizabeth of Hungary parish faces Patterson Park on East Baltimore Street at the corner of Belnord Avenue. It was organized in 1895 and has received national recognition for the soccer teams it has sponsored. The pastor is Rev. Robert Sisk, T.O.R.

COLLEGE OF NOTRE DAME OF MARYLAND
photo credit: Shawn Baron

SACRED HEART / GLYNDON

The historic Sacred Heart church was built in 1873 and dedicated four years later as a mission of St. Charles in Pikesville. Many dedicated families worked and prayed for the independent parish church that was established in 1946, with Fr. Francis J. Egan as its first pastor.

The parish school as we know it today was dedicated November 4, 1956, under the direction of the Daughters of Charity who staffed the school until 1984. Sacred Heart School currently has an enrollment of 640 students from pre-school through 8th grade.

The parish now serves more than 3,300 families from a new sanctuary dedicated in 1993.

On September 7, 1873, Archbishop Bayley set in place the cornerstone of Sacred Heart of Jesus-- planned for the Germans of southeast Baltimore, soon to be known as Highlandtown, and presided over by the Redemptorists.

MARY BEVERLY BROOKS WOJCIECHOWSKI HANAN

The former Mary Beverly Brooks is shown on the evening of her Catholic High School Senior Prom.

"In all my years at Sacred Heart, I don't ever remember drinking a carton of cold or even cool milk since it was delivered before school started and sat in a case on the floor until recess... Sister Godrica would paste stickers on the pages of the student whose handwriting was acceptable. I'd write 'back-handed' because my friend Frannie wrote that way and I thought it looked cool. Sister Godrica said I'd never get a sticker if I continued to write like that..."

During Lent, remembers Mary Beverly Hanan, each student at Sacred Heart of Jesus received a "mite box" to fill with coins saved from whatever was given up for Lent.

"When it got close to the time the mite boxes were to be returned, I'd find as many pennies as I could to fill it up," said Hanan, whose eighth grade class was so large it was divided into four home rooms. "The money collected was used to buy "pagan babies"... we never did learn what a pagan baby was.

SACRED HEART OF JESUS / HIGHLANDTOWN

Built for the Germans who had claimed what were then the suburbs over the East Avenue city line at Canton, Sacred Heart of Jesus was once the great cathedral of Highlandtown when the area was a Catholic stronghold.

"Each desk had an ink well, but I don't remember if they were filled with ink. We were only allowed to use Script's Blue ink. Once, while living on the edge, I bought a bottle of Script's Peacock blue at Yenni & Block on Highland Avenue, and Sister gave me detention.

"All books had to be covered with a paper book cover, handed out by the nuns. At the end of the school year, we'd have to go through each book, page by page and erase any marks, etc., then we'd have to sandpaper the edges of the books."

■ ■ ■

Linda Brooks, Mary Beverly Hanan's sister-in-law, had a very similar Highland-town childhood.

Brooks' great memory of being a little kid at Sacred Heart was Sr. Pamphelia, who taught generations of kindergarten students and kept a green parrot in her class.

"What a fine woman she was," said Brooks. "I don't know how she was able to work with 55 children all at once, but she did. I remember learning the alphabet and learning numbers, but most of all the special projects she did with us.

"She taught us all how to knit using a used wooden spool of thread that had four nails driven into the top upon which the wool was wound. We created knitted hot pads to give to our Mom's for Mother's Day. Even the boys liked this project."

In 1873, a sea captain named William Kennedy provided the money to build a church on Greenmount Avenue near 22nd street. Nine months before his death, Captain Kennedy released $55,000 for the church, to be built on his summer estate on York Road.

A captain of the fabled Baltimore Clipper ships, Kennedy provided great anchor that sits outside of the sanctuary.

"I played on that anchor growing up," said Father Thomas Polk, pastor of St. Francis of Assisi in Baltimore. "I was only 10 when I left St. Ann's. It was predominantly Irish

then and priests were always visible. I went back as a priest in 1967 and stayed through 1976. There were some very difficult times, but we tried."

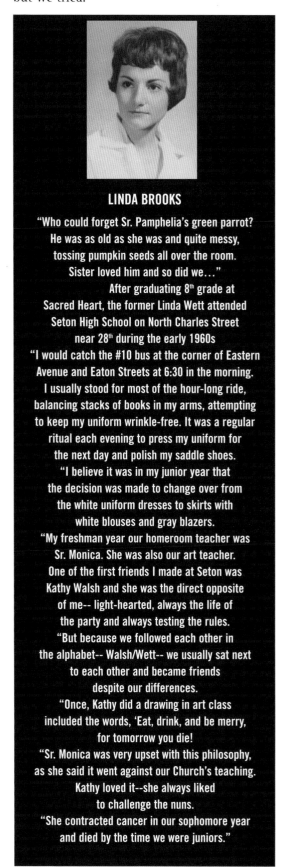

LINDA BROOKS

"Who could forget Sr. Pamphelia's green parrot? He was as old as she was and quite messy, tossing pumpkin seeds all over the room. Sister loved him and so did we..."
After graduating 8th grade at Sacred Heart, the former Linda Wett attended Seton High School on North Charles Street near 28th during the early 1960s
"I would catch the #10 bus at the corner of Eastern Avenue and Eaton Streets at 6:30 in the morning. I usually stood for most of the hour-long ride, balancing stacks of books in my arms, attempting to keep my uniform wrinkle-free. It was a regular ritual each evening to press my uniform for the next day and polish my saddle shoes.
"I believe it was in my junior year that the decision was made to change over from the white uniform dresses to skirts with white blouses and gray blazers.
"My freshman year our homeroom teacher was Sr. Monica. She was also our art teacher. One of the first friends I made at Seton was Kathy Walsh and she was the direct opposite of me-- light-hearted, always the life of the party and always testing the rules.
"But because we followed each other in the alphabet-- Walsh/Wett-- we usually sat next to each other and became friends despite our differences.
"Once, Kathy did a drawing in art class included the words, 'Eat, drink, and be merry, for tomorrow you die!
"Sr. Monica was very upset with this philosophy, as she said it went against our Church's teaching. Kathy loved it--she always liked to challenge the nuns.
"She contracted cancer in our sophomore year and died by the time we were juniors."

In 1876, General George Armstrong Custer and his cavalry were massacred by the Sioux at Little Big Horn in Montana, Archbishop Bayley consecrated the Basilica in Baltimore – now free from its debt – Holy Family parish took shape in Randallstown and Mt. St. Joseph College began taking in boarders on Frederick Road in Irvington.

Gordon England, Secretary of the Navy under President George W. Bush, graduated from St. Joe in 1955.

He earned his tuition by selling peanuts and ice cream at Bugle Field, home of the Baltimore Elite Giants of the Negro Baseball League.

England walked to school from his home on Mulberry Street in West Baltimore and belonged to St. Bernardine's parish in his youth.

"As soon as I was old enough, my father began to take me with my older brother and sister every Sunday to the 7 o'clock Mass at St. Ann's while my mother would remain home with our younger brother to prepare breakfast for us on our return ...she would go off to a later Mass alone..."
- Cardinal
Lawrence Shehan

ST. ANN / GREENMOUNT AVENUE

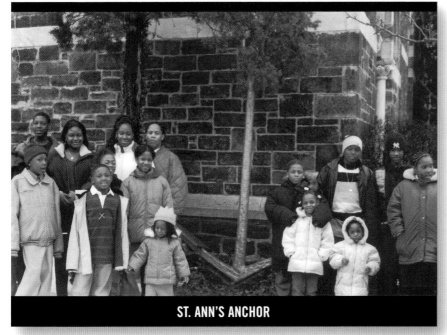

ST. ANN'S ANCHOR

photo credit: Thomas Wilde
The children of the St. Ann community with the fabled Captain Kennedy anchor.

The church plays a crucial role in its under-served and often un-churched neighborhood with services provided to parishioners and the neighborhood at large.

In addition to Sunday school and the youth group, there is the "Jubilee Women" senior group and St. Ann's Outreach Center. The outreach program was recently moved to the old rectory, renovated for its new use.

The old school now houses an emergency shelter and a transitional and convalescent care unit for men in recovery. The former convent is a neighborhood youth center sponsored by the Sisters of St. Francis of Assisi.

Holy Family is located at 9535 Liberty Road. The parish staff includes Rev. Andrew S. Mohl, pastor; Patricia DiLeonardi, youth minister; the Rev. Walter J. McGovern, Senior Priest and Susan Nitsch, school principal.

HOLY FAMILY CHURCH / RANDALLSTOWN

ST. IGNATIUS / IJAMSVILLE

In 1876, a Jesuit named Father John Gaffney bought an acre of land in Urbana near Ijamsville for $130 and founded the mission of St. Ignatius of Loyola. Gaffney, along with a black man named Ignatius Toodle and other Catholics both black and white, raised enough money to build a church on the property. Early estimates put the number of parishioners at about 400. It remained a mission of St. Joseph of Carrollton Manor for a century and did not become an independent parish until 1986.

ARCHBISHOP BAYLEY TOMB

photo credit: Michael Carter
The Bayley era came to an end on October 3, 1877, when he passed in his old room at the Diocese of Newark, N.J. Archbishop Bayley is interred in this building on the grounds of the cemetery of the Sisters of Charity at St. Joseph in Emmittburg. For a time, at the archbishop's request, Bayley was buried alongside of his aunt, Saint Elizabeth Ann Seton. Mother Seton was later moved to the Shrine at Emmittsburg.

ST. JOHN / WESTMINSTER

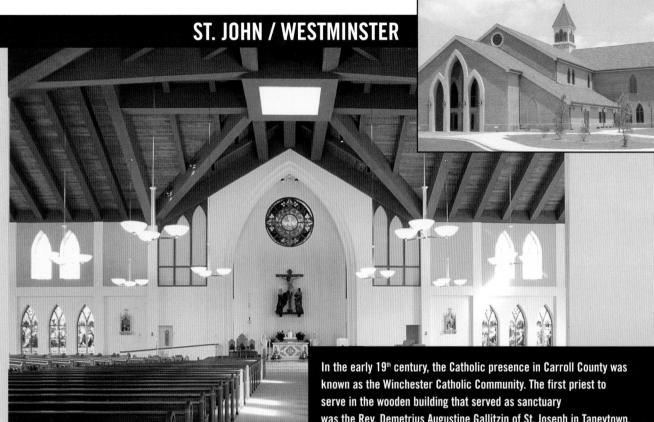

In the early 19th century, the Catholic presence in Carroll County was known as the Winchester Catholic Community. The first priest to serve in the wooden building that served as sanctuary was the Rev. Demetrius Augustine Gallitzin of St. Joseph in Taneytown. In 1853, the Rev. Thomas O'Neil became the first pastor of St. John Catholic Community in Westminster when the mission was made a parish by Archbishop Francis P. Kenrick. The current pastor is Msgr. Arthur Valenzano.

The bricks that were used to build the third Catholic sanctuary in Westminster – about a half-million of them – were donated by a man named Orendorff. They were brought to Main Street by mule teams from the Orendorff' farm on Old Bachmann Valley Road.

On April 18, 1865, the day before Abraham Lincoln's funeral procession made its way down Pennsylvania Avenue in Washington, the cornerstone for St. John's was set in place. In attendance were Archbishop Martin Spalding and Maryland governor Augustus Bradford. On November 22 of the following year, the Gothic-styled church that would be used for the next century - affectionately known as "No. 3" - was dedicated.

During a June thunderstorm in 1952, the St. John's steeple crashed through the church roof and adjoining rectory. The church was back in use by the end of the year. The steeple was not replaced.

In 1967, it was noted that the walls of the church were beginning to bow from the pressure of a heavy slate roof and a century of passing freight trains rattling the foundation. The last Mass at the third church was celebrated on February 4, 1968.

Three years later, on Memorial Day weekend in 1971, ground was broken for the fourth St. John's on 30 nearby acres. A Mass to dedicate the new church was held on April 23, 1972. This sanctuary held 800 people and was used through 2003.

In the time that the fourth church was used, Carroll County and its Catholic population continued to grow the way Parkville and Glen Burnie had swelled their churches at the beginning of Archbishop Keough's tenure in the early 1950s.

By 1995, under the leadership of the Msgr. Valenzano, the parish decided to built yet another St. John's – No. 5.

Opened during the 150th anniversary year, the new church holds 1,400, and serves 4,300 families with more than 1,000 children enrolled in the parish school and other religious education.

St John's has a health care ministry that reaches out to the elderly, the infirmed, the lonely and the homebound as well as a prison ministry. A Mass in Spanish is held each Sunday.

The Winning Smile

The Extraordinary Reign of Cardinal James Gibbons 1877-1921

"From the Third Plenary Council of 1884 until his death in 1921, Cardinal Gibbons would be the unchallenged spokesman of the Catholic Church in the United States..."

- Thomas W. Spalding

FATHER JAMES GIBBONS
by G.P.A. Healy, 1881

James Gibbons, the son of a merchant, was born on July 23, 1834 in the city he would serve for nearly all his life. From the second floor of his early home on Gay Street, young James could see the dome of the Basilica, in whose rectory the priest would live for more than half of his life.

Cardinal James Gibbons served as Archbishop of Baltimore for 44 years, from just before the Civil War to just after the First World War.

It was during his era that the great bulk of European immigration took place in Baltimore and with it the rise of ethnic neighborhoods built around the local parish.

Upon his elevation to Archbishop, he is reported to have rejoiced: "Thy will be done! In Thy hands is my fate!"

In an overview of how much America and the Catholic Church within it had evolved since the early days of the republic, Gibbons said: "The morning of Bishop Carroll's consecration in 1790 brings us back to the dawn of our American history which followed the dark and eventful night of our American Revolution.

"...the United States as then constituted had a population short of 4 million; the City of Baltimore, which now rejoices in its hundreds of thousands of souls, had only 13,500 while the Catholic population of the United States at that time may be estimated at 25,000 souls, or less than one-fourth of the present Catholic population of Baltimore."

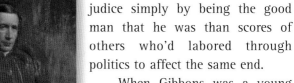

PORTRAIT OF CARDINAL GIBBONS
by G.P.A. Healy, 1887

As the Catholic labor movement sought better wages and working conditions - without a sharp turn toward socialism, which had been condemned by Rome – Cardinal Gibbons played an important role in getting permission from the Vatican for American Catholics to join labor unions. Maryland, after all, was the state which he often lauded as "the land of the sanctuary and the asylum of civil and religious liberty…" The Third Plenary Council of 1884, hosted and directed by Cardinal Gibbons, was the largest held outside of the Vatican since the Council of Trent and the impetus for the building of Catholic schools across a nation that had still not completely accepted the faith as "American." Said Cardinal Keeler, "He was a conciliator by nature. He was outstanding in helping Americans appreciate that Catholics could be supporters of America."

"Bishop Carroll did not wish to see the Church vegetate as a delicate exotic plant," wrote Cardinal Gibbons of the stewardship he inherited. "He wished it to become a sturdy tree... to bloom with the development of the country."

The long tenure of Cardinal Gibbons – who as a young priest served as a volunteer Army chaplain at Fort McHenry - is considered the most important period in Baltimore Catholicism since the pioneering work of John Carroll.

A man whose charm and character won him friends from every walk of life, James Gibbons dispelled more anti-Catholic prejudice simply by being the good man that he was than scores of others who'd labored through politics to affect the same end.

When Gibbons was a young boy, his father Thomas became ill, gathered his wife and children and returned to his native Ireland where he died. His widow, Bridget, returned to America with the children.

When the family landed in New Orleans, James was 13. The teenager worked in a grocery store to help his mother make ends meet and was quickly recognized as a natural in business – quick, savvy and honest. A successful future as a merchant seemed his for the taking.

But in 1854, now 19, Gibbons heard a sermon which called him to the priesthood. James left the grocery store, and his dismayed employer, for St. Charles College in Ellicott City.

He next entered St. Mary's Seminary and was ordained on June 30, 1861, at the beginning of the worst civil strife in the young nation's history.

During the Civil War, he served as chaplain at Fort McHenry and pastor of St. Brigid at Hudson Street and East Avenue in Canton. From the southeast waterfront, he regularly rowed a boat across the harbor to celebrate Mass at the Catholic mission of St. Lawrence O'Toole, now Our Lady of Good Counsel.

Cardinal Gibbons and former President Theodore Roosevelt, September 29, 1918

Serving as advisor to several presidents on Catholic issues, James Cardinal Gibbons not only showed – but personified – how Roman Catholicism was a natural part of American life. This he accomplished in an increasingly diverse society that was still marked by anti-Catholicism from Protestants who believed that one could not be loyal to the Vatican and to the U.S. Constitution as well.

Cardinal Gibbons helped generations of Catholic immigrants join American society, wisely seeing the neighborhood parish as the safe haven where newcomers could maintain their heritage while moving toward the mainstream.

He defended the poor, preached morality, and championed the rights of labor, winning admiration from all sides.

President William H. Taft praised Gibbons for his "single-minded patriotism and love of country on the one hand and… sincere devotion to his Church and God, on the other."

More ebullient was Theodore Roosevelt. To Gibbons, the old Rough Rider said: "I think you now occupy the position of being the most respected and venerated and useful citizen of our country."

At St. Brigid, his passion for the faith and the faithful, along with strong, lively sermons, brought the young priest to the attention of Archbishop Spalding who named Fr. Gibbons his secretary in 1865. With that job came much of the work in preparing Baltimore for the Second Plenary Council held the following year.

There, Fr. Gibbons impressed the assembled bishops at the Council and was nominated to head the newly created vicariate of North Carolina. At 36, he was responsible for 700 Catholics spread over 50,000 square miles of the freshly defeated Confederate South.

He met his flock – and those happy to see a preacher of any kind – on horseback, riding through pastures and forests and winning friends among believers and non-believers.

These experiences led him to write the book: "Faith of Our Fathers."

In 1872, the young priest was named bishop of Richmond; five years later, he became coadjutor of Baltimore, taking over full responsibility as archbishop with the death of James Bayley in 1877.

During Cardinal Gibbons' long tenure more than 30 new parishes were established in the archdiocese, most of them still active. The first was St. Pius V in 1878, the same year that the new seminary building was completed at St. Mary's.

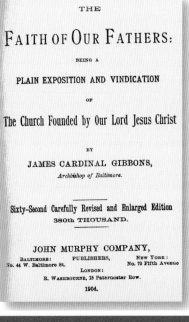

First published in 1867 – the 7th edition is shown here – "The Faith of Our Fathers" is a plain-spoken vindication of the Church. It has sold more than 1.4 million copies.

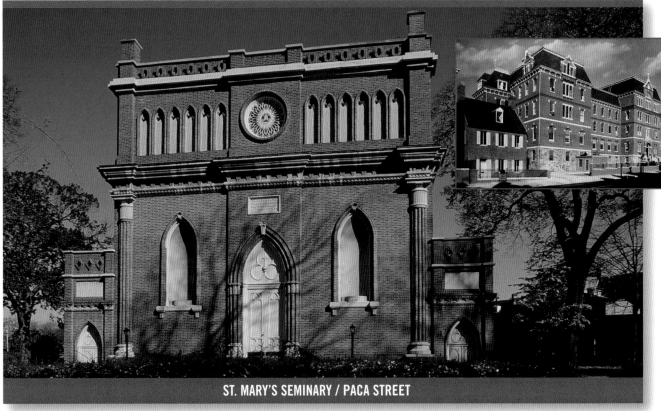

ST. MARY'S SEMINARY / PACA STREET

Designed by E.F. Baldwin – architect of Baltimore's fabled Rennert Hotel at Saratoga and Liberty Streets just west of the Basilica – the original St. Mary's was completed in 1878. The largest Gothic structure of its kind in Baltimore, it stood at the corner of Paca Street and Druid Hill Avenue until it met the same fate as the Rennert and was razed in 1975. The site is now a park.

ST. PIUS V / W. BALTIMORE

One of many historic African-American parishes in Baltimore
City, St. Pius V was erected between 1878 and 1879,
absorbing the congregation of St. Barnabas in 1931.
Under the care of the Josephite Fathers,
St. Pius V – located at the corner of Schroeder Street
and Edmondson Avenue - has worked closely with
parishioners at nearby St. Peter Claver, another Josephite
parish, on a variety of social challenges in the community.

In 2004 – the year that the people of the
Archdiocese of Baltimore sent 20,000 pounds
of clothing and school supplies to the storm-
battered Diocese of Gonaives in Haiti –
St. Edward's parish was home to some
300 families.

Sunday Mass was celebrated along the
lines of traditional African-American worship
and can last more than two hours, fueled by a
gospel choir accompanied by drums, trumpets,
and guitars.

Outreach at St. Edward's extends the
finger of God far and wide.

Led by the Lillian Humphries, parishioners
have served breakfast and lunch more than

75,000 times since the beginning of the new
millennium.

In 2004 alone they served some 45,000
meals.

Forty-five thousand!

Ms. Humphries, who demurred when
asked her age, is assisted by such solid
parishioners as Louise Parker, Mary Saxon,
Jane Frazier and Anna Eveline, each of them
80-years-old or more.

Three days a week, the crew shops, preps
and cooks the meals, three days each and
every week without fail. Every Thanksgiving,
more than 600 people attend the church's
holiday dinner. Parishioners can also be found
running a clothing bank and keeping the
school hall open for a variety of programs for
young people seven nights a week.

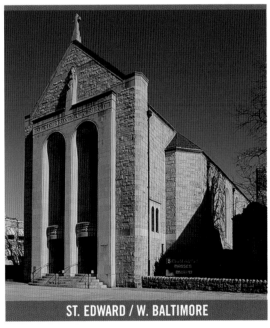

ST. EDWARD / W. BALTIMORE

Launched in 1878 as a mission of nearby St. Peter the Apostle,
St. Edward began just outside of what was then the western boundary
of Baltimore on a street of magnificent poplar trees. The year 2005
marked its 125th anniversary as a parish at the corner of Poplar Grove
and Prospect Streets in an area once known as Calverton.
Before World War II, wealthy residents contributed $180,000 for a
Romanesque sanctuary, a beauty accented with an altar of yellow,
Siena marble, and walls made of limestone, and terrazzo floors,
When the white flight of post-war suburbanization took hold,
St. Edward began losing its old parishioners to the county;
its pews began to fill with people of color who have kept the faith
alive and the doors open through decades of deepening poverty.
The parish runs a Head Start program in the 2800 block of West
Lafayette Street with the Transfiguration Catholic Community.

ST. PETER CLAVER, FREMONT AVENUE & PRESSTMAN STREET

*"As a kid, I wanted to be the president, a cowboy, a fireman. But really, I always wanted
to be a missionary and go to China. In the 7th grade, I had a nun who said:
'Forget about China, we need missionaries right here in the United States."*
Fr. Joseph F. Del Vecchio, S.S.J.

Josephite Father Joe Del Vecchio was ordained in 1972 at his home parish in Bay Shore, Long Island, N.Y.

An unapologetic Yankees fan in the heart of Birdland, Del Vecchio even found the mercy to absolve the truant Jeffrey Maher for skipping school in 1996 to see an Orioles-Yankees playoff game in the Bronx, where the kid interfered with a questionable home run that cost the Orioles the game.

"A kid after my own heart," laughed the 59-year-old priest, "he ditched school to go to a ballgame."

ST. PETER CLAVER / W. BALTIMORE

Established in 1888 for African-American Catholics, St. Peter Claver was named for the fabled Spanish Jesuit [1581-1654] who fought for and ministered to black slaves in the West Indies some two and a half centuries before the American Civil War. Today, 330 families make up the vibrant congregation at 1546 North Fremont Avenue. Parishioners work on a variety of outreach ministries to the poor along with the St. Pius V congregation and the nearby St. Gregory the Great community.

PAINTING OF ST. PETER CLAVER

Legend holds that Claver, while a young philosophy student
in Majorca early in the 17th century, was told by
a university doorman (St. Alphonsus Rodriguez)
of divine knowledge he'd received. Simply: the Jesuit novice
would find his life's calling by evangelizing Spanish conquests
in the Americas. Claver, the son of a Catalonian farmer,
landed in the Port of Cartagena, Colombia – the chief slave
market of the New World - in 1610. For the next 44 years,
until his death, Claver served as an apostle of African slaves,
feeding them, baptizing them, bringing succor as best he could.
Neither Claver nor the popes of that age were able
to suppress slavery. But the Spaniard devoted
his life to alleviating some its horror.

FATHER JOE DEL VECCHIO
photo by Kirsten Beckerman

The school at the church is no longer a parish school, strictly
speaking, but one maintained by the Archdiocese
with most of the 140 non-Catholic students in grades K-5.
During Lent, young people from the parish
spend a weekend at the church and fast for 24 hours.
"We try to educate them about hunger,
so they know what it is to feel hungry" said Del Vecchio.
"They raise at least $2400 from their fasts and we divide it
among Catholic Relief Services, Jonah House
and a couple of St. Vincent de Paul societies…"
There's an old adage that says no one quite gives charity
like those who have been helped by it themselves
– those who know the sting of want – and the Peter Claver
community is a fine example of this.
Summer Bible camp at the church campus costs
a dollar per week and many of those who attend are teenagers
who give out blankets to the homeless on downtown streets.
There is also a "shoe box project" in which
toiletries and other necessities are gift wrapped and given
to people in local shelters such as Martha's Table, a project
for homeless and otherwise needy women run by a Baptist
couple who have befriended St. Peter Claver.

A YANKEES FAN
photo credit: Jim Burger

Father Del Vecchio was first assigned to St. Peter Claver in the early 1980s, stayed for
three years and returned in the fall of 2000 after nearly 16 years in a poor Washington,
D.C., neighborhood.
At the top of his wish list for the parish and St. Pius V, for which he is also responsible:
"Money," he said, noting a considerable debt each parish owes the Archdiocese for this
and that and the other thing. "We need windows in the church, the bell tower needs
work… a new fence would be more attractive and make the grounds more secure.
Father Del Vecchio's voice trails off and then he laughs the laugh of one who knows
you can only do so much.
"Those," he says, "are just the highlights…"

LILLIAN HUMPHRIES
photo credit: Rosalia Scalia

"We don't have much, but we share what we have
with compassion and caring..." - Lillian Humphries

ST. PETER CLAVER PARISHIONERS

Photo: Jim Burger

Parishioners Bernadette Johnson, on left; Eva Randall
(middle); and Crystal Morris stand in front
of St. Peter Claver in West Baltimore.
Ms. Morris, an outreach worker for Baltimore City's
"Healthy Choice" parenting program, cooks weekday
dinners at the church rectory for Father Joe Del Vecchio
and his colleague, Fr. Henry Harper.
Not as fond of Italian food as his Pisano co-clergy,
the 80-year-old Harper runs a front door ministry
at St. Peter Claver, handing out soap, clothes and
sometimes advice to addicts who knock on the door.
Sometimes he will drive them to a clinic.
"I love cooking for the pastors, it means a lot to me,"
said Ms. Morris who also helps prepare the parish's annual
Lenten Fish Fry. "As a Catholic, I feel like I'm doing God's
work, cooking for my brothers and sisters."
Eva Russell graduated from the St. Frances Academy
in 1963. Now retired, the 65-year-old said her faith
took root years ago after the birth of her third child.
"I was sick and my husband was no count at all,"
she remembered while watching the funeral Mass
of fabled Baltimore sportscaster Chuck Thompson
at the Cathedral of Mary Our Queen on March 10, 2005.
"I told the Lord, 'If you get me up from here
I'll never bother you again-which was silly to say.
He got me up and I leaned on Him good after that.
My faith helps me through the hard times
and through the good times, too..."

Mervyn Johnson serves as sexton for St. Edwards. A convert from the Baptist Church, Johnson has been a Catholic for five years, embracing the faith once St. Edward's became the place where his faith came to rest.

Johnson is a man whose spirit glows in his faith. At St. Edward's, he organizes most of the children's programs, including two basketball programs. He helps the breakfast/lunch ladies do their shopping and is one of the many cogs that keep St. Edward's a bright spot in a neighborhood characterized, like so much of post-industrial Baltimore, by abandoned properties, homelessness, drug addiction and child abuse.

This is the little bit of the Third World in America to which the Rev. Sam Lupico asked to be assigned. As best anyone can tell, most parishioners tithe 10 percent of the income the world sends their way: 5 percent to St. Edward's and the other half to the charity of their choice.

"We try to make this an alternative place, a place where the evil of the world has no value," said Father Lupico, a man who walks the neighborhood without the shield of his priest's collar. "Our job is to accompany people on their journey without having to worry about adding up the numbers."

This is the sometimes reality of doing the Lord's work in a neighborhood on which most of the world has turned its back. During the 2004 Thanksgiving season, Fr. Sam was robbed by a man he'd been trying to help, a man well-known to the priest.

Stolen was the pastor's satchel containing his credit cards. While the police eventually recovered the property, they were assisted by a prostitute with a good heart. Seems the guy who stole the stuff was with the hooker after the theft. The woman noticed Fr. Sam's stuff and went to the church to warn him.

The good Reverend's response?

He found the thief – without getting the cops involved – and tried to talk it over. When he retires, he intends to remain at the church – a fixture, something to rely on – to continue helping out without taking a salary.

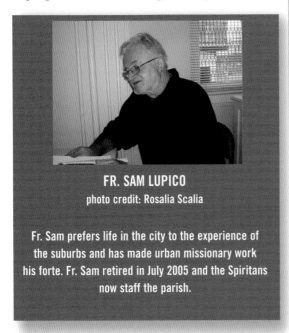

FR. SAM LUPICO
photo credit: Rosalia Scalia

Fr. Sam prefers life in the city to the experience of the suburbs and has made urban missionary work his forte. Fr. Sam retired in July 2005 and the Spiritans now staff the parish.

In 1881, Corpus Christi church – also known as the Jenkins Memorial for the legendary Baltimore family who financed it – was established at the corner of Mount Royal and Lafayette Avenues near the Maryland Institute College of Art in Bolton Hill.

CORPUS CHRISTI / BOLTON HILL

Founded in 1881 in Bolton Hill, Corpus Christi was one of the socially prominent "blue book" parishes through the Roaring 20s, as were the Basilica and St. Ignatius. The church came about through the munificence of the children of Mr. and Mrs. Thomas C. Jenkins in memory of their parents. The parish, under the leadership of its pastor, Fr. Richard J. Bozzelli, has declared itself, "an intentional community joined not by geography but by common vision... [we reach] out to one another, to our neighbors and to the world as we offer the hope of the living Christ..."

The year after Corpus Christi opened, Archbishop Gibbons initiated the cause of canonization for Mother Seton, which resulted in her being declared a saint more than 90 years later, in 1975.

MICHAEL ABROMAITIS AS YOUNG BOY

A young Mike Abromaitis making his First Communion at Corpus Christi. Abromaitis grew up to be an attorney with multiple law degrees, including Georgetown University School of Law. His late sister, Sr. Josanna Abromaitis, SSND, founded the Our Daily Bread soup kitchen, a service of Catholic Charities providing more than 250,000 hot meals annually to needy individuals and families. He and his wife, Loyola English professor Sue Abromaitis, have been members of the Cathedral of Mary Our Queen since the early 1970s. Over the years, children from Corpus Christi – which once had a parochial school through the eighth grade - represented a rich variety of Catholics from Bolton Hill, Reservoir Hill, and the south side of 23rd street.

ST. LEO THE GREAT

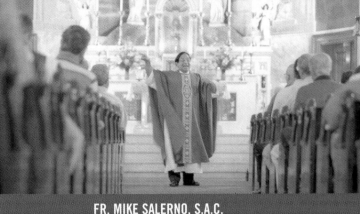

FR. MIKE SALERNO, S.A.C.
Photo: Kirsten Beckerman
The Rev. Michael Salerno, S.A.C., took over as pastor of St. Leo's in February of 1997 after the death of Father Pandola. A proud New Yorker whose accent gives him away the moment he speaks, "Fr. Mike" spices his sermons with funny, poignant stories of his childhood.
Salerno's stewardship has led to phenomenal growth in the old neighborhood church, with the pews packed each Sunday with Catholics and non-Catholics from as far away as Pennsylvania.
Fr. Mike's homilies inevitably end the same way: Is there someone important to whom you are estranged? Go home, call them up, tell them you love them, tell them you're sorry…Said one longtime resident who had switched parishes for a while and recently returned to St. Leo's: "He's breathed life into that place just by being honest with himself and everybody else…"

Willie Matricciani grew up on Exeter Street next door to the St. Leo rectory and as a young altar server would sometimes be awakened for morning Mass with a pounding from the other side of the wall. His is an example of a St. Leo's family that moved away but never left.

Willie, his wife Donna and their two children live in Harford County – like so many old East Baltimore families – but he drives downtown every Sunday to serve as an usher at 9:30 a.m. Mass.

[The family also attends Mass at St. Joseph in Fullerton from time to time.]

For years, Willie has donated time and material from his Fence Fair business – started by his parents in the early 1970s – for the parish's annual St. Gabriel and St. Anthony festivals.

"I can't describe the love that I have for that place, I get choked up when I think about it," said Mr. Matricciani, a member of one of the last classes to graduate from St. Leo's school in 1972 and a 1976 graduate of Mt. St. Joseph High School in Irvington.

"What a great place," he said. "I feel sorry that my children won't have the same experiences that I had here - that sense of oneness with a neighborhood."

Every year, each spring and again at the end of the summer, Willie puts up some 250 feet of fencing for the festivals, inserting red, white and green slats through the fence to make it look like an Italian flag.

"I feel some connection to the Lord, [that] he understands if I do good things, especially for a community that has given me so much," he said.

His grandfather on his mother's side, Dominic Pompa, and his father's uncle, John Matricciani, are credited with founding the St. Gabriel Society in Baltimore in December of 1929 along with a half-dozen or other founders. At recent festivals, Willie helped carry the banner.

"When I go back to the old neighborhood," said Willie, "it's like going back in the womb."

ST. LEO / LITTLE ITALY

Established the same year as Corpus Christi, at the corner of Stiles and Exeter Streets in one of Baltimore's oldest – and perhaps best known – ethnic neighborhoods just east of the Inner Harbor. The old parish school building is now a community and Italian culture center named in honor of former pastor, the Rev. Oreste "Rusty" Pandola, S.A.C., who died in January of 1997. At the Pandola Center, young people and adults can take classes in Italian, bread baking, watercolors and bocce ball.

WILLIE AND DONNA

photo: Kirsten Beckerman

The former Donna Ballisteri (left), graduated from
St. Patrick's parish school in Fells Point and
The Catholic High School of Baltimore. She and husband
Willie were married at St. Leo and are partners in the family's
fence business. Their daughter Lucia graduated from
Notre Dame Preparatory in 2003. Son Luigi, named for
Willie's father, attends Archbishop Curley High School.

photo: Kirsten Beckerman

The St. Leo rectory, which was renovated in part with a
donation from Willie and Donna Matricciani, bears a
plaque honoring Willie's parents, who lived next door for
many years. The former Angela Pompa died in 1988 and
her husband, Luigi Matricciani, passed away in 1995.

ST. ANTHONY OF PADUA / GARDENVILLE

Built in 1884 in what were then the rural sections of Northeast Baltimore, St. Anthony began as a mission of St. Joseph in Fullerton
and served German farmers who worked land in what became the neighborhood of Gardenville.
Over nearly 125 years, St. Anthony has grown to include two church buildings - the current one was dedicated in 1952 – a school, a
rectory with parish meeting rooms and a convent. In keeping with the name of the community it has served all those years,
Gardenville, St. Anthony tends a meditation garden open to all. In 1995, the parish was twinned with nearby Most Precious Blood in
Armistead Gardens to become one congregation served by a single pastoral staff.

ST. ANTHONY / MOST PRECIOUS BLOOD

Most Precious Blood was established
in 1948 to serve Armistead Gardens,
which was a planned community
of Baltimore City that took off in the years
just before and during World War II.
The first Mass was celebrated
by Father Joseph A. Graziani on August 1, 1948
at Fox Mansion, located at 4900 Wilbur Avenue.
Eleven years later, MPB relocated to
5010 Bowley's Lane.
When the parish school closed in 1988,
many of the students transferred
to St. Anthony's school.

Gary Adornato attended St. Anthony's grade school in the late 1960s, from first grade through 8th before moving on to Archbishop Curley High School, where he graduated in 1980. A media consultant, he is now a member of the Immaculate Heart of Mary parish.

"I still know many of the kids I met there. One of my first grade friends remains one of my closest friends to this day," said Mr. Adornato.

"The May Day festival always defined St. Anthony's for me. The school kids would attach tickets to hundreds of helium balloons and let them go and watch them until you could no longer see them in the sky.

"The tickets told whoever found them to call in for a prize and a prize went to the person's balloon that traveled the furthest... of course many of us couldn't resist breathing in the helium and talking in the funny voice it made."

Most Precious Blood began as the Catholic Church of Armistead Gardens a few years after World War II and served families connected to the then-booming defense industry.

The church hall is in the basement of the parish community center. The Herring Run Head Start program is on the second floor.

Together with St. Anthony, Most Precious Blood ministers to Northeast Baltimore through several outreach programs, including those that serve the homeless and the AIDS population.

St. Anthony also operates YANA – You Are Never Alone – a drop-in day shelter and advocacy/case management center for prostitutes in the City of Baltimore.

Both churches collect and donate clothes and other items used by the shelter as well as the "adopt-a-buddy" program for elderly parishioners.

MOTHER MARY LANGE

In late 2004, the Archdiocese of Baltimore approved a plan to combine the grade schools of St. Dominic on Harford Road and Shrine of the Little Flower on Belair Road with St. Anthony's.

The three schools, now housed at St. Anthony, have come together to form the Mother Mary Lange Catholic School, which opened under its new name for the 2005-2006 school year.

Sr. Rita Michelle Proctor, an Oblate Sister of Providence, was appointed the school's first principal.

In 1884, as Archbishop Gibbons began to plan one of the most important events of his young, promising career – the Third Plenary Council of Baltimore, which would serve as a model for subsequent councils around the world.

The Third Plenary Council (plenary meaning "attended by all qualified members," from the Latin *plenus* meaning "full") was held in Baltimore with Archbishop Gibbons at the helm from November 9 through December 7, 1884.

The bishops who assembled in Baltimore agreed that the parochial school would be "the bulwark for the preservation of the Faith" for future generations of American Catholics and made the building of such schools obligatory for parishes.

Other decrees of the Council included the edict that Catholics "who marry before a sectarian minister are excommunicated" and that "mixed marriages are not to be contracted unless promises are given that the Catholic party is in no danger of perversion, and will strive to convert the non-Catholic party."

The work was signed and approved by 14 archbishops, 61 bishops or their representatives, six abbots, and one general of a religious congregation who were in attendance.

The following year on the 7th of June, 1886, the red hat was conferred upon Baltimore's *wunderkind* archbishop. During the long and storied administration of Cardinal Gibbons, more than 80 churches were built in the Archdiocese of Baltimore.

One of the first to go up after the Third Plenary Council was St. Ambrose, which opened in Cresaptown, Allegany County in 1886.

Initially a mission of St. Patrick, Cumberland, the Capuchin Fathers of Ss. Peter & Paul were asked to staff the parish.

By the early 1950s, then pastor Fr. Hugh Rauwolf began a building fund to erect a brick church building, dedicated in 1957. St. Ambrose continued to grow along with

Allegany County, expanding with a rectory large enough to house a chapel for daily Mass, parish meetings, and day care.

As of 2004, St. Ambrose was planning a major renovation to the sanctuary and the addition of a vestibule leading to the nave of the church which currently counts more than 300 active families.

A variety of outreach projects includes the Samaritan program, which helps folks with everything from rides to doctor's appointments to help with household projects and the donation of medical supplies to a sister parish in Haiti.

The Baby Bottle Boomerang project asks people to fill baby bottles with loose change. Proceeds go to a local pregnancy counseling center.

As does virtually every parish in the Archdiocese, St. Ambrose of Western Maryland distributes Thanksgiving and Christmas baskets. It has provided items of support and comfort to American troops in Iraq.

Parishioners have also woven a peace quilt from scraps.

The year 1887 saw several new churches open in the Archdiocese, including the original Holy Rosary, west of Broadway in Fells Point.

Across the city line, Our Lady of Mount Carmel in Middle River would grow so large – more than 12,000 families at its peak in the decade after World War II – that two parishes would spring from it: Our Lady Queen of Peace and St. Clare.

ST. GREGORY THE GREAT / W. BALTIMORE

The parishioners of St. Gregory the Great built what was hailed as a gothic "mini-cathedral" when the sanctuary went up at the corner of N. Gilmor and Baker Streets 120 years ago.

Mass was celebrated there for the first time in 1894.

Though the Civil War had ended nearly 30 years earlier, the Church remained segregated and black Catholics who lived in and near St. Gregory's parish worshipped nearby at St. Peter Claver.

In the years immediately following the end of World War I, St. Gregory had more than 5,000 families. Not long after the Second World War – with changes in demographics affecting the entire Archdiocese, membership was down to a little more than 500 families.

Of those, nearly 90 percent were African-American.

Those numbers have more or less held on through the start of the 21st century, with some 310 devoted families supporting several ministries, including a Thursday night soup kitchen that feeds almost as many poor as there are parishioners.

The church building has been demolished, and since 1973 Mass has been celebrated on the second floor of the old parish school.

The center of Catholic worship in Middle River since the late 19th century, Our Lady of Mt. Carmel began with Masses celebrated in private homes as a mission of St. Joseph Church in Fullerton.

In 1893 a two-room church was built on Eastern Avenue and in 1904 Mount Carmel officially became a parish, growing steadily along with the greater Essex area.

The present church resembles one in El Paso, Texas, where Msgr. Nicholas Jaselli, who led the congregation in the World War I era, vacationed with his family and saw a sanctuary in honor of Our Lady of Mount Carmel that ministered to Tigria Indians.

"The beauty of the new church – its simplicity, its taste – caught the eye of everyone present," said the Catholic Review of the dedication in 1938.

Under Fr. Jaselli, who retired in 1949 and lived to be nearly 100, membership grew from about 100 families to more than 10,000 people.

Today, Monsignor Robert L. Hartnett – assisted by the Fr. Austin Murphy – leads the parish.

Volunteers participate in a number of outreach programs, including the Blue Army, a prayer group that petitions for the end of war as well as for the souls of sinners, and the Gabriel Project, which reaches out to women and families facing crisis pregnancies, as well as providing donations of food, clothing, furniture and, where necessary, money.

OUR LADY OF MOUNT CARMEL / MIDDLE RIVER

Catholic immigrants from Lithuania organized St. John's in 1887. In 1907, the congregation moved into a former Baptist church at Paca and Saratoga Streets, now the home of the fabled St. Jude Shrine, destination for pilgrims bringing hopeless causes to the saint of last resort.

With the permission of Cardinal James Gibbons, the Lithuanians moved from St. John's in 1917 to St. Alphonsus a bit south and closer to downtown.

By the beginning of the 1920s, St. John's was solidly Sicilian and being run by the Pallotine Fathers.

Although St. John's was closed as a parish in 1989, the Shrine offers daily Mass as well as perpetual Novena service, drawing people from all over downtown – including many employees of local hospitals - as well as suburban families descended from parishioners of days gone by, and pilgrims from around the nation.

Veteran Baltimore sportswriter, News American legend and local character John Steadman served as an usher until his death in 2001.

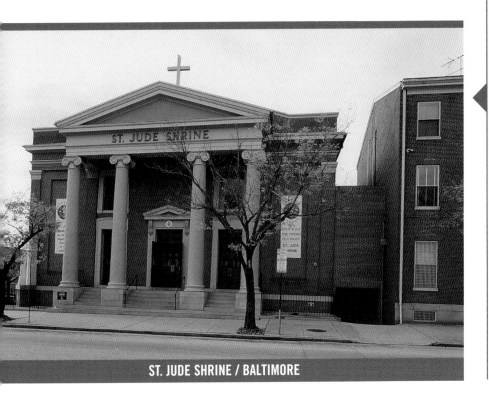

ST. JUDE SHRINE / BALTIMORE

THE MARY PORTERA STORY

Born Mary Josephine Cannatella in 1914, Mary Portera learned the catechism from the Mission Helper Sisters.

"And I started helping the sisters, you know how you do, dusting the church, something like that. I've been here ever since."

Ever since has lasted from the Roaring 20s to the 21st century; from the days of Calvin Coolidge to the death of Ronald Reagan and beyond.

Within the history of a parish that no longer exists, lies the story of St. Jude's Shrine over which Miss Mary has lavished love and labor as tens of thousands have made their way to the corner of Paca and Saratoga Streets every year.

"I've done everything," she says proudly, "except hear confession and say Mass."

When Mary was a little girl and her family lived on Pearl Street, the Lexington Market area was home to hundreds of Italians who worshipped at St. John's.

Their neighbors included the Renando family; the Libertos who made it to Baltimore from Mississippi, the Cammeratta family and Butler's Upholstery.

"That's where we grew up, around Baltimore and Pearl Streets," said Mary's Sister Josephine. "We'd go walking down Lexington Street to the Keith Theater.

You'd save your ticket from the movie and you could go upstairs and dance. They had another theater up the street, the Valencia and you could dance there too - it looked like they had little stars all over the ceiling."

In 1929, just a month or so before the great stock market crash St. John's opened a grade school.

"I went to school where St. Jude is now, I was in the first class to graduate from St. John the Baptist," said Josephine. "For us to be able to go to school there we had to clean the school and clean the church."

Josephine remembers Mary working especially hard, without complaint.

"She did practically everything, at first laundering

Mary Portera, a daughter of St. John the Baptist Roman Catholic Church, in the house she was born in at 638 Dover Street in the neighborhood where St. Mary's Seminary was founded and Saint Elizabeth Ann Seton began her work.

Said Portera of her childhood, "at Christmas, we didn't get many gifts. But I remember a little brass bed with a soldier doll in it and the doll alongside the bed was a nurse taking care of the wounded soldier."

the altar cloths with my mother. My mother loved to do those things and in many ways, Mary is a lot like my mother. Sometimes when you look at her, she looks like my mother."

■ ■ ■

The young Mary Cannatella was picked to be the angel of her First Holy Communion class and when Carmen Portera met her years later at a dance, he accepted a photo of her in that angelic role.

"You had it pinned to the wall of your house, didn't you?" said Mary during a New Year's Day interview at their downtown apartment in 2000.

"Yes I did," said Carmen, then 91 and not to see another birthday.

In those days, Carmen was an amateur prize fighter who ran with boys from the famed Dundee boxing family at the Belair Market. When he met Mary, she was a girl with many admirers who wasn't allowed to have boyfriends.

Carmen – a young man with a heart of gold and a world of patience - won out.

"I was better looking than the other guys!" he crowed. "I was selling fruit up Lexington Market and she used to come by there going to work. One day she asks if I want to go to a dance up St. John's."

"For a quarter!" laughed Mary. "The dances were a quarter."

"And I had the quarter," said Carmen. "So I went to the dance. I danced the first dance with her. And then I danced with everybody else because I couldn't find her. I found her upstairs with a bunch of little kids and she was crying."

"He danced with me once and disappeared," said Mary.

"So I grabbed her by the hand and took her back downstairs," said Carmen. "We danced the rest of the night and she asked me to walk her home. It was just a block away."

And they were together for the next 65 years.

"He gave me my engagement ring on the corner of Franklin and Paca Streets, in front of Koven's Furniture Store," said Mary.

And he gave her a wedding ring on the altar of St. Elizabeth's Church at East Baltimore Street and Lakewood Avenue on Easter Monday, April 22, 1935.

Her work – at home, at church and out in the city - continued unabated as the couple raised four children.

"Mom used to cater weddings, she'd do all of the cooking at home," said Joseph L. Portera, retired president of Local No. 176 of the National Association of Letter Carriers union and a former altar boy.

"She'd get those big bags of potatoes and peel them and make the slaw from scratch."

And she was always – always – doing something at church.

"It formed our whole family," said Joe. "If you couldn't find her, you knew where to look... it's something she's going to do as long as she has a breath in her."

■ ■ ■

Although Jude is known as the patron saint of hopeless causes, Mary and Carmen found themselves praying to him over time for help in everything.

"I wanted my children to have success in their lives, to make sure they went to school and go out in the world and do good," said Mary. "Some people criticize when you go to God through saints or the rosary, but you're still praying to God."

Mary's devotion to Jude, who, tradition holds, is pleased by public displays of gratitude for his intercession, can be seen in the gift shop Mary started during the war on a dining room table at the front of the church.

"We started with a little aisle of gifts in the vestibule," said Mary. "We sold the [Jude] medals and from the table we went up to a china closet with some religious articles and put it in the hallway of the rectory. From there we went into a cabinet in the little room where my office was and when we bought the house next door, we used the front room of it. It had been a jewelry place and they left the cabinets and we filled them up."

In the perfect reciprocity of prayer, Mary's life has been enriched by other people's devotion to the saint.

MARY & CARMEN PORTERA

For more than eight decades,
in the great tradition of "rectory ladies,"
Mary Portera is a Hall-of-Famer, having contributed
her time and energy – her heart and soul –
to the old St. John the Baptist parish
and then the Shrine that replaced it.
"Mary is more religious than me," said Carmen,
whose own devotion to St. John's and St. Jude
earned him the privilege of lying in state
in front of the altar when he passed on
to his reward in 2000 at the age of 91.

She found herself listening to strangers with problems no human could solve.

"I hear a lot of troubles, a lot of it is very sad. I've learned a lot about cancer," she said. "We prayed for them - Carmen would sit out in the church and pray for people when they had this or that - and when he got cancer, they prayed for him."

This has been Mary Portera's true vocation, the spiritual work wrapped inside the selfless and sometimes thankless job of cooking and cleaning.

"I'd be cooking in the rectory and if someone came in and needed help, I'd turn off the stove and go to them," she said. "That's when we lived up the street at 328 North Paca Street and I was always going back and forth between church and home.

"It worked out that I was here to help others when they came in with their troubles - talk to them, listen to them, try to console them," she said. "You don't pry, you listen. But it never occurred to me that I had a gift for listening. I was just doing my job as I felt it should be done."

And then, this mother of four, grandmother of seven and great-grandmother of four talks her way through an awkward moment.

"Sometimes I thought my life was nothing - no college, no fancy job with a title," she said. "But I was out in the world with people from all categories and when somebody needed a slice of bread, I could give it to them. I've had more friends than maybe I would have being a professional person.

"So it turns out that my life was good."

131

The building that would be St. John the Baptist Church and then become the St. Jude Shrine was built before the Civil War when Seventh Baptist Church built a church at Paca and Saratoga Streets in 1847.

A year into World War II, when so many people in the immediate neighborhood and across the city had loved ones fighting overseas, devotions to St. Jude began under the guidance of a priest named Fr. Henry J. Iannone, SAC.

As part of city-wide prayers for American servicemen, St. John's created a small shrine to St. Jude Thaddeus in an alcove off of the main sanctuary and a weekly Novena to Jude began in December of 1942.

The shrine consists of a marble statue of Jude and several mosaic panels, including one of the Blessed Mother.

"Father Henry gave a flag to everyone who had someone in the service. We kept a roll of honor," said Mary. "It was then I started praying regular to St. Jude."

The perpetual novena services in honor of St. Jude were officially started in October of 1941. The devotion to the patron saint of hopeless cases grew nationally in the 1950's through promotion by the Pallotines of the Immaculate Conception Province.

As the Italian families moved out of the city in the 1950's and 60's, the church moved toward its current status as the St. Jude Shrine, the nationwide center of devotion to the apostle.

In 1987, the Archdiocese sold the church to the Pallotines and the name was officially changed to St. Jude Shrine. In 1994, the old school building - closed since 1953 - was renovated into a visitors center and gift shop.

Today, pilgrims seeking hope come from around the world, and the Shrine welcomes some 75,000 each year. As well, there are liturgies, a half-dozen novena services, concerts, retreats, and extensive community outreach in a part of town that has been down on its luck from about the time St. John's closed its grade school in the early 1950s.

In 1887, Cardinal Gibbons gave his official blessing for the funding of Holy Rosary Church with the inaugural Mass celebrated on the Feast of the Immaculate Conception of the Blessed Virgin Mary. Services were held in an old Protestant Church at Eastern Avenue and Bethel Street, not far from the current parish buildings on Chester Street.

The parish was built to serve Polish Catholics living between Fells Point, Canton, and Patterson Park. During World War I, Holy Rosary sent 1200 volunteers to fight in what was known as Haller's Army for the freedom of *Polska*. When that freedom was won, money and care packages were sent with love and pride to the old country.

Today, the demographics of St. Casimir to the east of Holy Rosary in Canton are increasingly young and gentrified, making Holy Rosary the unrivaled anchor of Baltimore's Polish community.

Indeed, the parish website – www.holyrosarypl.org - invites visitors to browse in either English or Polish.

■ ■ ■

A renaissance and international notoriety came to the Holy Rosary after the 1995 healing of its pastor, the late Father Ronald P. Pytel, from congestive heart failure through the intercession of Sr. Faustina Kowalska, the Polish nun who received messages of Divine Mercy in visions of Jesus.

The pastor's heart was restored upon venerating a relic of St. Faustina at a healing service in the church while friends and parishioners prayed over him. As a result of the miracle, Sister Faustina was canonized on Divine Mercy Sunday in 2000.

Some 1,700 people showed up at Holy Rosary on April 7, 2002 for Divine Mercy Sunday. The Shrine itself is located on the spot where Cardinal Karol Wojtyla, who would become Pope John Paul II, prayed during a 1976 visit to Baltimore.

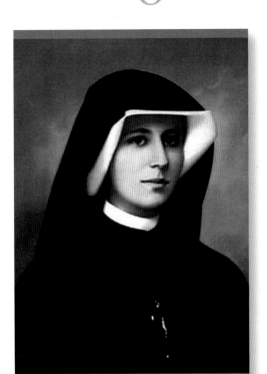

ST. FAUSTINA

The documented recovery from heart failure
through the intercession of the Blessed Faustina
in 1995 was the second miracle needed for
the Polish nun's canonization.
Born Helen Kowalska, she entered the
Congregation of the Sisters of Our Lady of Mercy
in Krakow as Sister Mary Faustina at 19.
In 1931, she received a vision of Jesus
that led to the Divine Mercy devotion.
The saint recorded in her diary that she saw
and spoke to Jesus, taking down His messages,
before dying of tuberculosis in 1938 at age 33.

HOLY ROSARY / FELLS POINT

Regular Masses in Polish, where you can often hear the faithful murmur: "Jezu, badz zemna." Or: "Jesus, be with me."
On Christmas Eve, "Oplatek" wafers are shared, as Poles have done for centuries.
Sacred white wafers, much like those used for Holy Communion,
are shared with each person present, with good wishes accompanying the exchange.
Those who have passed on to the next life are especially remembered.

133

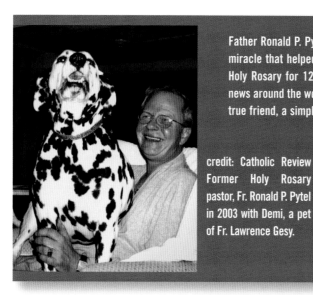

Father Ronald P. Pytel shown with Pope John Paul II after bearing witness to the miracle that helped canonize Faustina, saint of Divine Mercy. Pytel, who served Holy Rosary for 12 years, ultimately died of cancer in 2003. His passing made news around the world. The grandson of Polish immigrants, he was 56. "He was a true friend, a simple, honest, compassionate and caring person – a true priest," said Father Lawrence Gesy, an old friend and former pastor of congregations in Brunswick and Petersville.

credit: Catholic Review
Former Holy Rosary pastor, Fr. Ronald P. Pytel in 2003 with Demi, a pet of Fr. Lawrence Gesy.

"I think God chose him to be the instrument that led to Faustina becoming a saint so that His message of Divine Mercy will truly reach a world that needs it so desperately."

PAT GILNER

MARGUERITE PATRICIA GILNER

photo credit: Kirsten Beckerman

"Because of my Mom's illness, I attended St. Gertrude's Academy, a boarding school for girls on the Eastern Shore run by the Benedictine nuns," said Patricia Gilner, a cancer survivor who wears a small anchor on a necklace as a symbol of hope and gives others away to those still fighting the disease.

"At St. Gertrude's Academy, at the top of every page in school we put initials 'U I O G D' which in Latin stands for 'In all things may God be glorified.' It's the Benedictine motto."

"My years at the academy acquainted me with many of the Catholic religious customs and practices," said Miss Gilner. "We attended daily Mass and went to confession every Saturday evening following Benediction. There was something very spiritual about worshiping with all the young postulants, novices and junior sisters. The young sisters chanted the Divine Office in Latin and they sang like angels.

"As I look back, those years at Saint Gertrude's were nestled in an environment that was safe and wholesome. It was special seeing our parents on visiting Sundays and we always anticipated going home for the holidays and summer vacations.

The journey of faith that Marguerite "Pat" Gilner embarked upon at her birth in August of 1942 is one of those – so common in Baltimore - that encompasses enough Catholic institutions for two or three families.

A former School Sister of Notre Dame, Pat Gilner was born to Gerald Gilner and Marguerite Schab, members of the St. Martin's Parish on Fulton Avenue. They were married there, moved away to raise their family and returned there to be buried.

"As a young boy, my father was an altar server for Cardinal Gibbons at the Basilica and we had a signed formal portrait of the Cardinal in our living room," said Miss Gilner.

"When I taught at St. Mary's Seminary and University, a much larger image of the same portrait was on the back wall of the classroom where I was teaching. It brought back many memories."

Patricia and her sisters went to the old St. Mary's, Ilchester, in Howard County during their early years of schooling, but the family returned to St. Martin's in Baltimore every Sunday for Mass when she was growing up.

"During my grade years it was customary to go to Mass on the first Friday of each month. Because of the fasting rule, we could not eat or drink before leaving to get the bus to go to school. Mass was offered at the start of the school day. While we were all gathered in St. Mary's Church, which was above the four-room school house, we could smell the hot chocolate simmering on the stove. A religious brother from the Redemptorist novitiate up on the hill would prepare the hot chocolate and donuts for us to have after Mass.

"It was customary [then] for Catholic families to recite the rosary during the months of October [the month of the rosary] and May [the month of Mary] when I was in grade school. During Mary's months, our teacher (a Notre Dame de Namur sister from Trinity Convent on Ilchester Road) would give all of her students a turn to take a statue of Mary home for a night to encourage the praying of the rosary. The statue had a base that came off and a rosary was stored inside the statue.

"My parents would have summer parties around our swimming pool. And about 11:45 p.m. all the food and drinks would be put away because the Communion fast began at midnight.

"There was never a discussion about Sunday Mass. It was part of our Sunday routine. My mother went to church every Sunday until her final hospitalization on Christmas Eve, 1958. And it wasn't until years later that I realized Thanksgiving was not a Holy Day of Obligation.

"Every Friday was a meatless day and tuna fish with tomato soup was the Friday menu. Seldom did we deviate from it. The Friday ritual was easy to accommodate and accepted by family and friends alike. The rules for Lenten fast and abstinence were more confusing."

It was a time, Miss Gilner recalled, when priests and nuns and other religious leaders were often called on to help with moral dilemmas.

ST. MARK SCHOOL

"I remember priests blessing new houses, cars and religious articles. They made home visits when someone was sick and were called to homes and hospitals as loved ones were dying. When a family member was sick, an adult member would greet the priest with a lighted candle and silently lead the priest to the ill relative."

As a young woman, Pat Gilner took a religious pledge not to drink until she was 21. There was also a "Legion of Decency" that offered guidelines promoting modest and appropriate dress.

"There was a spiritual trust that I don't think the more educated people of today have," said Gilner. "My parents had this blind faith that if their girls went to Catholic schools and were taught by the good nuns, they would grow up to be good girls."

Influenced by the goodness of the sisters, Pat Gilner wanted to emulate their gentle spirit and chose to enter the School Sisters of Notre Dame after graduating from Seton High School.

"There was something impressive about seeing the sisters when I was a child, they always struck me as holy people – special people," she said, noting that her formative years in the convent affirmed this notion.

"This spiritual and religious training I received from the School Sisters of Notre Dame prepared me to accept life's challenges. I have no regrets, only a grateful heart. I believe I am privileged to have lived pre- and post- Vatican II. The mystery and wonder of a young child immersed in the traditions and customs of the Catholic Church created a sense of peace and security. The openness of Vatican II as a young woman gave me a different perspective on the role of the Catholic Church and my responsibility to live out those Christian values.

"Growing up, our world was very Catholic,'" she said. "We were educated in Catholic schools, socialized in Catholic circles and during high school our [part-time and volunteer] jobs were at Catholic institutions".

It was at St. Mary's, in the second grade, that Pat Gilner made her First Holy Communion.

ST. MARK / CATONSVILLE

"St. Mark's was the hub of social and spiritual life for us, everything from little league baseball to drama clubs and speech contests. It also produced a lot of vocations... they even awarded a religious medal when a woman gave birth to her 10th child."

"I remember the date, May 13, 1950 - the altar was decorated with roses in the form of an arch at the opening of the communion rail," said Miss Gilner, recalling that the children had been prepared for the day by practicing with military precision.

"Two by two we proceeded through the arch to the high altar and knelt in two's to receive Communion. Two eighth grade girls were dressed as angels and they held the white Communion cloth that went under our chin, to prevent any particles of the Host from dropping."

After the Mass, she said, the children went back to their classroom to receive religious articles as gifts from the sisters -green scapular, our prayer book and

our First Communion certificate. In the afternoon, the May Procession took place and then the family parties.

"My family celebrated our First Communion like no other celebration. All of the relatives came."

■ ■ ■

In 1957, Miss Gilner graduated eighth grade from St. Gertrude's Academy. The school closed two years later and the mid-19th century building that housed it has been demolished.

"Most of [the sites of] my childhood have been closed or torn down," said Miss Gilner. "After my mother's death in 1959 we moved to Catonsville and joined St. Mark's parish."

■ ■ ■

Built on land once frequented by Susquehanna Indians – and later given to Mary Carroll by her father Charles Carroll of Carrollton as part of her dowry when she married Richard Caton for whom the area is now named - St. Mark's traces its origins to 1888.

Always a vital parish, St. Mark's grew steadily and by 1908 was a parish with a chapel, rectory, convent and a school of about 165 children. At one point, it even housed a few bowling lanes, as did many buildings in Baltimore in years past.

Today, St. Mark's counts more than 2400 active families, among them volunteers at a variety of ministries. One of the more popular is God's Helping Hands, which aids people with transportation problems, as well as a bloodmobile.

■ ■ ■

Patricia Gilner especially remembers the Catholic Youth Organization events at St. Mark's.

"Father Bill Burke [now pastor of St. Francis of Assisi in Mayfield] was a young priest back then and shared the responsibilities of running the CYO with Father Thomas Donellan," she said. "Now teenagers go to the mall, but back then, CYO was where parents trusted their kids to be and knew they were being well supervised."

So pervasive was the church's role in the life of its flock, that Fr. Burke and Fr. Donellan were known to show up at the Varsity Drive-In on Route 40 after dances to check up on their young parishioners.

Pat Gilner graduated from Seton High School in 1961, one of 291 seniors. During her Seton days, she commuted to the North Charles Street campus on the No. 8 streetcar from Catonsville before transferring to the No. 3 bus in the city, an hour-and-a-half journey one way.

After high school came the convent and the seismic changes of the Second Vatican Council.

"It was a time of great grace in the Church but also a time of chaos as new emphases were placed on rituals, customs and religious practices," she said.

"The change initiated chaos and confusion. It also was the time when religious communities were faced with a grand exodus as young religious questioned their vocation and began considering lay ministries."

Although she eventually left the convent, Pat Gilner remains close to that time of her life. Several years ago, she organized a reunion of more than 30 former nuns who gathered at Villa Assumpta to visit with one another and to give back to the community that fostered their young adulthood.

Today, Pat Gilner remains connected with the Benedictine nuns and the School Sisters of Notre Dame. She served on the parish council of the Basilica throughout the 1990s and attends Mass at the Catholic Community of St. Francis Xavier in Hunt Valley.

She holds a graduate degree in pastoral counseling and psychology from Loyola College and a master's in adult education from The Johns Hopkins University.

Presently pursuing a master's degree at the George Washington University School of Medicine and Health Sciences, she serves as director of Palliative Care Services for St. Agnes HealthCare.

"It seems as though all of my life experiences have prepared me for this privilege," she says of her current duties. "I am so honored. I have lived a rich life and my experiences of growing up Catholic have given depth and breadth to the tapestry of my life."

ST. AGNES HOSPITAL / W. BALTIMORE

Credit: St. Agnes Hospital

In January 2006, St. Agnes Hospital announced a $160 million expansion and renovation, including a 192-bed new patient tower and a 500-car garage to be completed by 2011. The new inpatient tower will be built behind the current main hospital building.

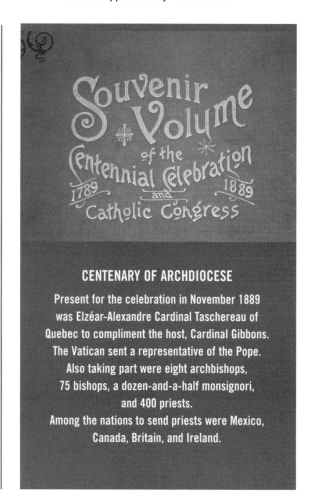

MSGR. JOSEPH S. LIZOR

ST. LUKE / EDGEMERE

St. Luke's was established in 1888 near the old Bethlehem
Steel company town of Sparrows Point. The current
church was built in 1962.
It serves approximately 750 families.

"My wish list?
I wish more people would
come to Mass..."

Father Joe Lizor has been pastor of
St. Luke's in the Edgemere area of eastern
Baltimore County for about the past seven
years. A native of Hagerstown, he was
ordained from St. Mary's Seminary in 1958
and spent 22 years as an Army chaplain.

Most of his flock, he said, are elderly
Bethlehem Steel pensioners and their
spouses, folks who filled the church when
the steel mill was booming after World
War II, on through the 1960s.

∎ ∎ ∎

In 1889, Baltimore celebrated the 100th
anniversary of the founding of the diocese
with a parade of men that numbered some
30,000 strong.

CENTENARY OF ARCHDIOCESE

Present for the celebration in November 1889
was Elzéar-Alexandre Cardinal Taschereau of
Quebec to compliment the host, Cardinal Gibbons.
The Vatican sent a representative of the Pope.
Also taking part were eight archbishops,
75 bishops, a dozen-and-a-half monsignori,
and 400 priests.
Among the nations to send priests were Mexico,
Canada, Britain, and Ireland.

ST. ATHANATIUS / CURTIS BAY

photo credit: Shawn Baron

A panel of the "painted glass" at the "new" St. Athanasius, which opened in 1958. Once dark and draped by heavy curtains, the sanctuary is now brilliant with color and light.

The images were transferred to glass from illustrations done by former pastor, the Rev. Timothy Klunk, who went on to serve as pastor at Our Lady of Victory parish.

Father Rob DiMattei, Jr., grew up in the Our Lady Queen of Peace parish in Middle River and there began to consider a life in the ministry.

"Growing up Catholic, I remember the happiness that was evident in the lives of most religious," he said. "Even in the midst of turbulent times, most seemed to be happy with their ministry and it was those who were most out-going and people oriented that I found most successful."

Fr. DiMattei, an East Baltimore native, was baptized at St. Wenceslaus and spent a couple of years at St. Elizabeth of Hungary parish school near Patterson Park before his family moved to Middle River.

"The influence of the Sisters of St. Joseph of Chestnut Hill and the diocesan priests that served [Our Lady Queen of Peace] made a lasting impression on me," he said.

"They often encouraged me to choose a life in service to others. They must have seen something in me early on that was worth challenging."

There are some things that a young person who is interested in the priesthood might anticipate: hearing difficult confessions, helping families bury loved ones or even getting dunked at the parish carnival.

And other parts of the job are not to be found in the catechism: like running a small business.

"The knowledge one needs to maintain an aging complex and the business sense you need is not something you get much training for," said Fr. DiMattei, whose charge includes the original St. Athanasius building, a small, brick church that has seen better days yet remains in the hearts of longtime parishioners.

"But overall, if one loves being with people," said DiMattei, who graduated from St. Mary's Seminary in 1991, "I believe that success is guaranteed and hurdles can be overcome."

Such parishioners include 74-year-old Mary Koppleman, who was baptized at Holy Cross but has been worshipping at St. Athanasius since she was a young woman.

Standing in the sanctuary near a shaft of brilliant, colored light from the new windows just before a Wednesday evening Novena service to St. Joseph the Worker, Mr. Koppleman points up the center aisle and says: "That altar is from our little church."

MR. FRED KONOPIK & FR. ROBERT DIMATTEI
photo credit: Shawn Baron

Father Robert DiMattei, pastor of St. Athanasius with Mr. Fred "Fritz" Konopik, who grew up in the parish during the Great Depression before marrying Betty McCormick from the St. Rose parish in Brooklyn Park. They later moved to Linthicum and joined St. Philip Neri.

"When you stood up here, you could see the coal pier down on the water with all the white lights lit up," said Mr. Konopik. "I grew up here in the 1930s when it was Polish and some Irish and a little bit of Czech."

1891 OLD ST. ATHANASIUS CHURCH
Photo: Shawn Baron

Father Rob says the bell in the old church — a touchstone for so many of Curtis Bay's older Catholics — still rings. On the pastor's long "to do" list, is the commissioning of an engineering study to see if the building where many of his parishioners were baptized, can be saved.
"There's a lot of devotion here," he said.
"They come because they want to be here."

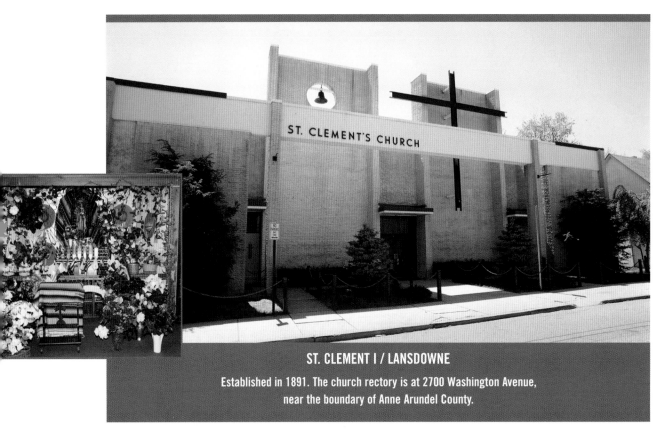

ST. CLEMENT I / LANSDOWNE

Established in 1891. The church rectory is at 2700 Washington Avenue,
near the boundary of Anne Arundel County.

ST. JOSEPH / MIDLAND

Established the same year as St. Clement--1891,
the parish of St. Joseph is located at 19925 Church Street-- just three miles from Lonaconing.
The town of Midland is rightly proud of the church and proclaims from its municipal website,
"The bells of St. Joe's and the chimes of Grace [United Methodist Church] ring out daily
from the hill at the edge of town where the churches sit side-by-side..."

MOTHER AND DAUGHTER

Connie Fletcher grew up across the street from St. Bernard's in the 1960s and thought it one of the most beautiful churches she had ever seen.

"Gray stone with two very pointed steeples on each side of the front," she remembers. "When I was about seven years old, one of the steeples was damanged and several very large construction trucks made their way down our quiet street.

"All of the families in the neighborhood came out to watch as both the steeples were removed. In my young mind," remembers Fletcher. "I found it unholy. They should have been repaired."

The inside of St. Bernard was just as breathtaking to the youngster.

"The back of the altar was round and had the most gorgeous stained glass windows... stained glass also lined each side of the church and the confessionals had heavy, velvet maroon drapes that softened the entrance. The altar rail was white marble and the statues appeared to be human."

At St. Bernard School, remembered Connie, her first grade teacher, Sr. Mary Elizabeth, R.S.M., was nothing less than "the sweetest woman I have ever known.

"You could say she was the perfect grandmother every little girl or boy would love to have... When I was sad, she would wrap her arms around me and I would lose myself in her long black habit with the big, jingly rosary... it gave me comfort and peace."

CONNIE & SARAH
Credit photo: Kirsten Beckerman

Connie Fletcher and daughter Sarah in front of St. Dominic School in Hamilton where Sarah attended Kindergarten. Connie was baptized at St. Bernard, where she also went to school and made her First Communion; and her daughter Sarah, a student at Notre Dame Preparatory School on Providence Road near Towson. Said Connie: "During times when I would find myself questioning life and death, I would always retreat to the quiet solitude of a pew at St. Bernard's..."

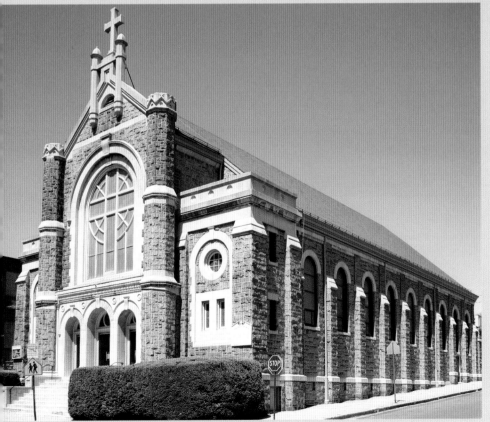

ST. BERNARD / BALTIMORE

In 1867, six churches were started or purchased for new congregations: St. Joseph in Sykesville; St. Ann at Tennallytown; the Church of the Immaculate Conception in Calvert County; St. Mary, Star of the Sea in South Baltimore; St. Thomas Aquinas in Hampden; and St. Bernard. St. Bernard's stood as a Catholic sanctuary at Gorsuch Ave. and Independence St. in Waverly for decades before becoming St. Bernard's Korean National Parish in 1989. It closed as a Roman Catholic church in 1997 when the Korean congregation moved to Woodlawn in Baltimore County and was sold to a Protestant denomination. The old St. Bernard convent at 949 Gorsuch Avenue has been redeveloped into the Marian House, which provides shelter, counseling, education and job programs for homeless women and their children. For more information on the Marian House, call: 410.467.4121.

There is a close connection between Brunswick's St. Francis of Assisi and St. Mary's nearby on Maryland Route 79. Together, they constitute a single parish serving about 400 families in Frederick County.

St. Mary's, Petersville, is the original Catholic Church in this part of Frederick County with nearly two centuries of history. In Brunswick, on the north bank of the Potomac River in southwestern Frederick County, St. Francis of Assisi was completed in 1894.

Before then, however, families from as far as the Pennsylvania border traveled to Petersville for Mass at St. Mary's as it was the only Catholic church in the Middletown Valley.

ST. FRANCIS OF ASSISI / BRUNSWICK

Established in 1893, St. Francis of Assisi stands at the corner of First Avenue and East B Street.

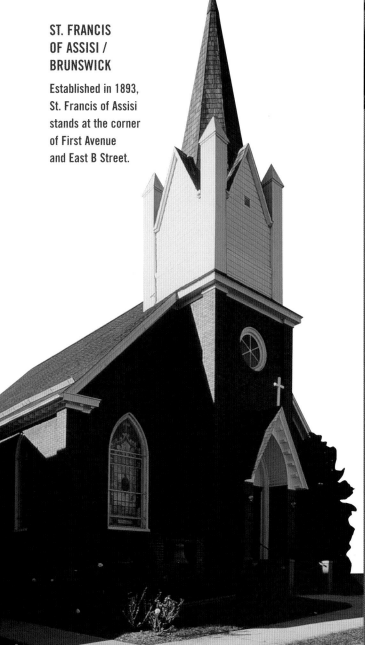

ST. MARY / PETERSVILLE

Established in 1826, St. Mary became a mission of St. Francis of Assisi in Brunswick in 1904 and in doing so, inspired this motto: "One Parish Family-Two Churches" Both churches house Masses for worship each Sunday.

In the early years of the valley settlement, Mass was offered in private homes by priests riding on horseback from Conewago near Hanover, Pa., to old Frederick Town. In those days – from just before the Revolution through 1796 - a mere two dozen priests served Catholics in what would soon be the fledgling United States of America.

When the Jesuits established St. John's in Frederick, priests visited the valley often. In 1825, a non-Catholic landowner donated property for a Catholic church where slaves could worship.

The present church was built in 1842 with bricks made and fired by slaves and was consecrated in 1845. In 1902, the parish started a school for "colored" children, which received aid from a annual and national collection for Indians and "Negroes". The school closed about eight years later.

Because the railroad was so strong in the area, the parish kept a priest's residence in Brunswick so that one was always nearby to administer last rites to those seriously injured in rail accidents.

ST. BENEDICT / S.W. BALTIMORE

Nancy Azzole grew up in the St. Benedict's parish, fell away from the Catholic faith and eventually moved out of Maryland. Some 50 years later, she began the journey back to the Church without knowing where it would lead.

"I've been searching for my roots," she said. "After a visit to Ireland, I knew that who I am is an Irish Catholic. That is who and what I need to be, so on a visit back home, I went to Mass at St. Benedict's where I'd grown up."

The memories, she said, were powerful, the people sincere and friendly.

"I decided to continue and went back a second time at Easter," she said. "This time I went to Communion. I was so glad, even if perhaps I wasn't exactly in a state of grace since it'd been more than 50 years since my last confession!

"But I came away with a feeling of peace and belonging – a wonderful sense of being home."

Now of Boca Raton, Florida, Mrs. Azzole was born Nancy Taylor shortly after World War II and grew up on Wilmington Avenue near Cardinal Gibbons High School. She was baptized at St. Benedict's, attended regularly as a child and made her First Holy Communion there.

"Even though all three of the kids in my family were baptized as infants, I was the only one who had the 'Catholic,' experience," she said. "My father is Catholic and my mother is not.

"As babies, we always had St. Christopher medals pinned to our undershirts, but I don't remember ever going to Mass until it was time to prepare for my First Communion. I remember that when I did go to Mass, it was always with a neighbor's family who had twins my age. They had a car, we didn't. I received Communion with the twins in 1954."

The physical beauty and spiritual power of St. Benedict made a big impression on the Mrs. Azzole, who remembers "a huge place with beautiful statues and high ceilings and dark benches, the wonderful smell of incense.

"It was magically beautiful at Christmas because the manger was set up in an alcove that had a deep, rich blue ceiling with twinkling stars."

Azzole recalled next to nothing about the catechism she learned in order to make her First Communion but everything about the dress she wore on the big day and the beauty of the annual May Day processions.

As far as confession went, "I made up sins so I'd having something to say. Mostly, I confessed to disobeying my parents or eating meat on Friday - and blaming my non-Catholic mother!"

And that was about it for many, many years.

"I believe it was during Confirmation classes that I became afraid to be a Catholic," she said, remembering a strange fusion of Cold War anxiety prompted by air raid drills and violently graphic stories the nuns told about martyrs of the faith.

"They also talked about how the Russians were persecuting Catholics and that if they were to invade the U.S. they would kill all of the Catholics in America," said Mrs. Azzole. "I became terrified and starting having 'stomach aches' every Sunday morning to avoid going to church.

"One day, two nuns visited our home to find out why I hadn't been attending church and my mother told them. They denied it and my parents gave me the option of going to the Protestant church with my friends and I chose to do that."

ST. BENEDICT

Established in 1893 on Wilkens Avenue, St. Benedict was built on a monastic tradition embracing Christian hospitality and community. The monks who first staffed the parish were Germans from the St. Vincent arch abbey in Latrobe, Pa. who were drawn to the area in the late 19th century to work at the now-closed 14 Holy Martyrs near the B&O roundhouse. The cornerstone of the present church was laid July 19, 1932 and the current pastor is the much beloved Rev. Paschal A. Morlino, O.S.B.

FIRST COMMUNION

"I left the Catholic Church when I was about nine. Much later, I really wanted to be part of a faith community so I decided to go back and explore the faith from an adult perspective."

But the St. Benedict experience proved to be indelible for Mrs. Azzole, "a greater impact on me than I would have suspected.

"I often find that my opinions and perspectives reflect a Catholic point of view. In the past few years, I have consciously tried to get more in touch with my Irish-Catholic roots and have begun attending Mass at least once a month. I am comforted by the rituals and enjoy being with a large group of people who have passed the faith on through generations."

It is that sense of "rightness," Mrs. Azzole said – one she is at a loss to describe or explain – that led her to pick up the lost thread of her childhood with RCIA – Rite of Christian Initiation of Adults - classes.

"Learning about the faith as an adult has taken away the fear factor from my youth and has given me an appreciation for what the faith gives – a road map for life," she said.

"It's not about breaking God's rules, but about how being guided by them can bring fullness to one's life. I keep being pleasantly surprised by how the Church has changed since Vatican II… how much more in tune I am with the Church than I would have guessed."

Nancy Azzole was confirmed in the Catholic faith on Holy Saturday, 2003 in her home parish in Boca Raton. She attends Mass at St. Benedict's whenever she is back in Baltimore visiting her family.

Cardinal Gibbons fights Anti-American sentiment Abroad

. . .

Anti-Catholic prejudice at Home

"Like all valuable commodities, truth is often counterfeited..."

- James Cardinal Gibbons

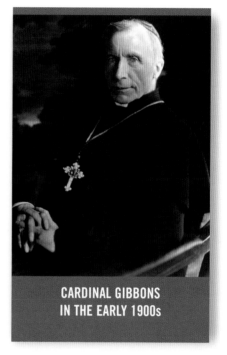

CARDINAL GIBBONS IN THE EARLY 1900s

Archbishop John Carroll was the vessel through which Baltimore became the anchor of Roman Catholicism in America.

Through the spirit, struggles and diplomacy of Cardinal Gibbons a century later in Baltimore, Catholicism found its American voice, however broken the English.

The challenge was not mere politics for Gibbons, who, as the archbishop of a port city second only to New York in the number of immigrants processed, helped shepherd thousands of Old World Catholics into American society through neighborhood parishes.

It was no small accomplishment for the newcomers or the bishop who fought for them.

Most of the battles within the American Catholic Church during the 19th century were all but resolved by the early years of the 20th century and the death of Pope Leo XIII. Cardinal Gibbons had been at the center of most of them.

The Knights of Labor union movement had fought and won the right to exist; the Catholic University was established and parochial schools were separate from the public school system.

The difficulties split the U.S. Catholic hierarchy-- rifts duly noted in Rome-- and Cardinal Gibbons of Mulberry Street emerged as unofficial spokesman for the Catholic Church in America.

One of the most prominent prelates in the nation, Cardinal Gibbons found himself cast as peacemaker in such quarrels time and time again.

Though fraught with a variety of meanings today, liberalism for an American Catholic in the early 20th century meant a strong appreciation of the United States government as a system under which Catholicism could bloom. More troubling to others, however, was the conviction that separation of church and state was best for both. It also included the desire for Catholic immigrants to be absorbed into the mainstream of a largely Protestant society which had founded the nation.

In 1887, Gibbons struck boldly when – upon elevation to Cardinal – he spoke in his titular church of Santa Maria in Trastevere, Italy with enthusiastic reverence for the land of his birth.

European eyes turned to the young and thriving Church in America as an example of a healthy relationship between church and state. Not everyone liked what they saw. Across Europe, and especially in France, the methods of American Catholicism were scrutinized, exalted, and demonized.

Gibbons stepped carefully. He continued to push the assimilation of Catholic immigrants into American society, maintained peace in the Church in America and was ever mindful of Rome's eyes on his back.

All the while, the Archdiocese in his backyard continued to boom.

Ilchester was the first home of St. Mary's College – originally called Mt. St. Clement - completed in 1868 and the Redemptorists who built the seminary served the nearby communities of Thistle and Gray's Mills as well as Ilchester. These villages would form the nucleus of Our Lady of Perpetual Help parish.

On September 14, 1879, the Redemptorists hung the portrait of Our Lady of Perpetual Help in the Ilchester chapel as part of their mission from Pope Pius IX to make the Blessed Mother – through the title Our Lady of Perpetual Help – known to the world.

Cardinal Gibbons officially established OLPH as a parish in February, 1893. Some folks continue to call the area St. Mary's because of its connection to the old college. A church cemetery opened in 1894. The parish has operated a series of parochial schools and in olden days, students sometimes arrived for class in horse-drawn sleighs.

In 1957, Archbishop Francis P. Keough [1947-1961] gave OLPH permission to build a one-story, four-room schoolhouse with a basement for a "temporary" church.

In 1968, a fire destroyed the church and school. Once again, OLPH took on new

OUR LADY OF PERPETUAL HELP / ELLICOTT CITY

The Redemptorist Order established Our Lady of Perpetual Help in 1893, about 30 years after its priests first set eyes on a rural farm near Ellicott City known as Ilchester, just a short train ride from the Order's former provincial residence – St. Alphonsus – in downtown Baltimore.
Today, the OLPH community is led by Msgr. Richard E. Smith, an archdiocesan priest appointed in 1996 after the Redemptorists withdrew from the parish. Ordained in 1966, Msgr. Smith has served throughout the Archdiocese, including as pastor of St. Clare's in Essex and Our Lady of Sorrows in Owensville.

construction, with a rectory and convent completed in 1978 and sights set on a new and permanent church. This effort, spearheaded by the Rev. Francis Nelson C.S.s.R., was completed in 1985.

Today, more than 1,600 families are listed in the parish registry, reflecting the development of Ellicott City and Howard County in the last 30 years.

At Our Lady of Perpetual Help – in the midst of so much activity, everything from a health ministry to a Catholic "formation ministry" encompassing all aspects of the Catechism-- a favorite spot is a garden devoted to Our Lady, known as the Fr. Albert Riesner Memorial Garden.

So touchy were the years leading up to the 20th century for Cardinal Gibbons that he was even criticized for recognizing the new American holiday of Thanksgiving. He was also praised for it. And so it went.

OUR LADY OF PERPETUAL HELP

Of all the stones thrown at the Church in America, the ugliest were hurled by the American Protective Association, the first major anti-Catholic movement in the United States since the dissolution of the Know Nothings.

Such problems echoed the so-called "Carmelite riots" in Baltimore in the early 1800s. Sometime around 1834, a Carmelite nun in Baltimore, Sr. Olivia Neale, suffered a mental breakdown and ran through the streets with tales of alleged mistreatment in the convent. This was a convenient excuse for anti-Catholic mobs to riot outside the convent doors in chaos that lasted for several days. Police were stationed outside the convent to protect the nuns and Sister Neale was transferred to a Catholic asylum known as Mount Hope.

By 1896, the APA had more than 2 million members. It was publishing false encyclicals bearing the name of the Pope and calling for Catholics to murder Protestants. The group's final assault, before it collapsed from within, was an attempt to influence the 1896 presidential election.

On the day the APA leadership was meeting in Washington, Cardinal Gibbons spoke out, asserting that the Catholic Church had never interfered in the politics of the United States. He then demanded the religion be treated fairly in the future.

The Republican party did not respond, but the Democratic party soon incorporated statements about universal religious freedom into their party platform.

■ ■ ■

Cardinal Gibbons' struggle to maintain unity within his Church and protect it at the same time was clearly taxing him. He was now in his early 80s and was visibly slowing down.

After surmounting the smear campaign of the APA, he told Archbishop Keane that he regarded "the attacks of Protestantism as mild compared with the unprincipled course of these so-called "Catholics" who could not accept the "Americanism" of the Church in the United States.

Passions on both sides – flamed by a poor translation of a biography of Paulist founder Isaac Hecker, circulating to great popularity and condemnation in France – led to heightened concern from the Vatican.

An encyclical from Pope Leo XIII - *"Longinqua Oceani"*- praised many aspects of American society but withheld complete approval, saying that complete division of church and state may not be the most favorable model for the church in every country.

Bickering continued until the Holy Father ordered silence on the issue in 1898.

Ss. Philip & James was named, in part, to honor Cardinal Gibbons, with the first church building ready in the spring of 1898 for the celebration of Easter Mass.

More than a hundred years later, the parish serves a wide and diverse population – university students, middle-class professionals from Charles Village, blue collar workers from nearby Remington and residents of Waverly to the east.

It is also a sanctuary for the homeless and has special ministries to victims of AIDS.

■ ■ ■

In time, the Vatican had wearied of the issue of "Americanism" and decided to settle the matter.

Despite a compelling letter by Gibbons to the Pope defending the Church in the New World – again, from severe criticism by other Catholics, this time a book by *Abbe* Charles Maignen - things appeared bleak for the course he was trying to chart for the Church in the United States, one that embraced both Rome and Washington.

In this light, the Pope composed an encyclical to end the controversy.

Released in January 1899, the *Testem Benevolentiae* was addressed specifically to the Archbishop of Baltimore. In sum, it was a condemnation of philosophies and policies associated with Americanism. For a month, Cardinal Gibbons remained silent before sending reply.

Ss. PHILIP & JAMES / HOMEWOOD

In 1897, ground was broken for Ss. Philip & James Church, a parish designed to serve what was then a suburban community near Wyman Park and the Homewood campus of The Johns Hopkins University. With a congregation estimated at more than 1,000 people, SS. Philip & James is led by Fr. William Au, pastor.

His response was cordial, yet candid about the disappointment with which he received the encyclical. Cardinal Gibbons asserted that the condemned doctrines were upheld by virtually all American Catholics and regretted that the heading of "Americanism" had been used to catalogue a wide range of misguided beliefs.

And then, considering the matter closed, he spoke no more of it and suffered a long spell of melancholy and depression.

Cardinal Gibbons' spirits were revived in 1902, the occasion of Pope Leo XIII's Silver Jubilee. In response to congratulations from the Cardinal, the Holy Father sent a letter to Baltimore.

It seems that with all of the unrest continuing to nettle Church and state in Europe, the aging pontiff found the Church in America a source of joy, an acknowledgement that validated Cardinal Gibbons' life work.

A year later, on July 20, Pope Leo died in Rome and Gibbons became the first American Cardinal to participate in the election of a pope.

Determined not to miss his chance, Cardinal Gibbons was at the ready in early July when news of the Pope's rapid decline reached Baltimore, dashing off with such haste that his accompanying conclavist left a half-written letter on his desk.

Cardinal Gibbons made it in time to participate in the election of Cardinal Giuseppe Sarto as Pope Pius X, the Bishop of Mantua who, fearing he was not worthy to be the Vicar of Christ, tearfully implored the Sacred College to pass him by. Maintaining that Bishop Sarto was the best choice by far, Cardinal Gibbons met with former Apostolic Delegate to the United States, Cardinal Francesco Satolli, asking his colleague to try to change Bishop Sarto's mind.

Bishop Sarto was then elected with 55 votes out of a possible 60. The coronation of the future saint took place on August 9, 1903.

At Cardinal Gibbons' request, the first audience given by the new Pope was to a group of American pilgrims. During the meeting, Pope Pius X would not allow Cardinal Gibbons to kiss his hand but embraced the Cardinal from Baltimore with a kiss on both cheeks.

ST. MARY / CUMBERLAND

Established in 1900, St. Mary's sits on East Oldtown Road in the south of Cumberland. Organizations include the Catholic Daughters of the Americas and Eucharistic Adoration. The pastor of St. Mary's is the Rev. Milton A. Hipsley.

148

OUR LADY OF THE FIELDS / MILLERSVILLE

When Our Lady of the Fields began in rural Anne Arundel County as a mission of St. Mary's in Annapolis back in 1891, not only was Mass celebrated in a private home but a piano served as the altar. A small chapel went up in 1902 and in 1908 a memorial chapel called St. Mary's, Millersville, was built near the present church on Cecil Avenue. Because of confusion with St. Mary's in Annapolis, the chapel was re-dedicated as Our Lady of the Fields. In 1945, a shrine honoring the Blessed Mother was built outside the chapel. After World War II, the chapel was renovated and the mission continued to grow. In 1965, it became a parish.

Since the late 1990s, two dozen or more members have traveled to Guymas, Mexico, to build houses and serve the poor. Others work with the homeless in Baltimore City, traveling to the Fallsway and Madison Street outside the Central Booking lock-up every Friday to distribute food and spend time with the poor.

During the winter months, Our Lady of the Fields participates in a program with other Anne Arundel County churches to shelter the homeless from the cold and feed them in the parish hall.

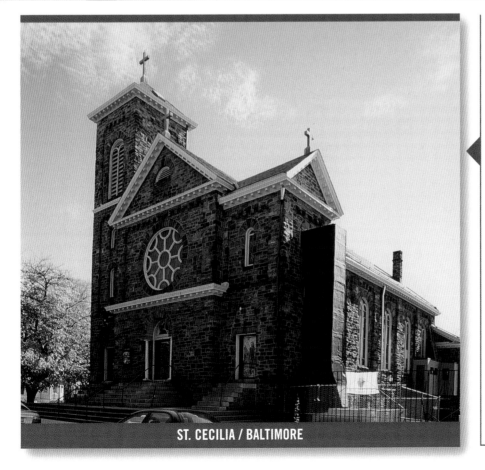

ST. CECILIA / BALTIMORE

Built at the corner of Hilton Street and Windsor Avenue in the Walbrook neighborhood by a predominantly Irish congregation, St. Cecilia was organized in 1902 and celebrated its first Mass in 1904. It stands on the site of an orphanage built for black children by the Josephite order with the financial help of the Jenkins family. Today, it is a sanctuary for more than 300 families. They praise the Savior through a gospel choir, youth choir, and a 12-member children's choir.

The St. Cecilia soup kitchen ministry feeds about 100 people a week each Thursday.

Grounded by the lay community, St. Cecilia aims to be "a moral force, to share the Word, and to respond to human needs and burdens," through outreach and spiritual celebration. The pastor is the Rev. Sylvester Peterka, C.M.

ST. CASIMIR

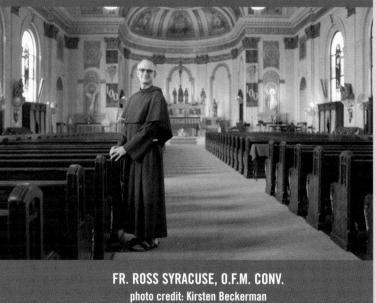

FR. ROSS SYRACUSE, O.F.M. CONV.
photo credit: Kirsten Beckerman

ST. CASIMIR / CANTON

St. Casimir was first organized in 1902. The current building, topped by a pair of golden cupolas that gleam over the southeast Baltimore waterfront, was completed in 1925.

The church began as a mission of St. Stanislaus in Fells Point when the Polish community along the Thames Street waterfront began expanding east into Canton and a priest from St. Stan's bought a tract of land on O'Donnell Street at Kenwood Avenue from the Canton Company.

Soon after, a two-story structure, made of red brick became the church and school building at a cost of $35,000. On November 9, 1902, the church was dedicated by Cardinal James Gibbons.

One of St. Casimir's first moves toward re-inventing itself from an old ethnic parish to one serving a new, upscale urban population was to address the Liturgy.

"Much time, energy, financial resources, etc. have been dedicated to making our Liturgies meaningful," said Fr. Ross Syracuse, pastor of the parish since 1998. "To the credit of the long-time parishioners, who realized it was up them to make things happen, there was a shift in attitude from 'Let's try to preserve the past' to 'What do we need to do to become more welcoming?' That was the key--welcoming."

At each Mass, Fr. Ross asks: "Who is here for the first time? Please raise your hand."

If he forgets to ask, someone in the pews reminds him. Afterward, parishioners try to greet the newcomers.

"We became a tithing parish five years ago, inviting the members of the faith community to think about the scripturally based practice of offering to God [through the parish and other charities] the first 10% of one's income," said Ross. "Many people have embraced tithing; that has promoted a real feel of belonging and ownership and has had a beneficial financial impact."

St. Casimir is under the care of the Rev. Ross Syracuse and the Conventual Franciscan Friars.

"When I first arrived here in 1997, Mass attendance was in a nose dive," said Fr. Ross, noting that the parish had been losing approximately 15 percent of its members a year for many years. "Something needed to be done."

Many of the new members, for the most part young adults, come from families without strong ethnic or cultural traditions, said Fr. Ross. When new parishioners embrace St. Casimir's, and the parish's strong appreciation for its Polish past and traditions, they find a rooted-ness unknown before.

"It has been gratifying and fulfilling to see everyone coming together," said Fr. Ross. "That's why we always refer to ourselves as a faith *community*."

FATHER TIMOTHY KULBICKI
Credit: St. Mary's Seminary & University Archives

Vice-rector of St. Mary's Seminary in Roland Park, Father Tim Kulbicki graduated from St. Casimir's parochial school in 1972 and Archbishop Curley High School in 1976. He holds a doctorate in ecclesiastical history from the Gregorian University in Rome, writing his dissertation on the arrival of the Franciscans in the United States. He has served at the St. Joseph Cupertino friary in Ellicott City and St. Clement in Rosedale.

The Rev. Timothy Kulbicki, who grew up on the north side of Patterson Park as a member of the St. Casimir congregation, wrote a history of the parish for its 100th anniversary in 2002.

He and his parents represent the community that made St. Casimir so vibrant for most of the 20th century.

"My parents were Polish Catholics to their roots," said Fr. Kulbicki, whose home was closer to St. Elizabeth's. "Every morning they drove me over to St. Casimir's for school or for serving Mass. I walked home alone through the park from the age of six."

Father Kulbicki, an historian, was asked what influence Catholic Baltimore may have had on the city as a whole and in answering cited the 1989 book "Public Catholicism," by David O'Brien.

"Genteel, colonial Catholicism [placed the faith in] an honored and vital part of Maryland and Baltimore history and culture," he said. "It's a contribution that respects Catholicism and has avoided the nastier anti-Catholicisms that marked America at many times and places."

Second to the culture established by the founders of the colony that grew from the St. Mary's settlement is the immigrant Catholic culture which Fr. Kulbicki – and so many of his fellow Baltimoreans in various ethnic neighborhoods around the city - was immersed in as part of St. Casimir.

The immigrant Catholic experience, he said, "did not much influence the wider secular culture. It was more interested in survival, scrambling for services, and holding onto its roots. Its children and grandchildren, however, have left a mark by trying to bridge the Catholic ethics they learned into local and national politics."

Obvious examples of this, said Fr. Kulbicki are Martin O'Malley, the current mayor of Baltimore who belongs to the St. Francis of Assisi parish near Herring Run Park and the D'Alessandro family, long connected to St. Leo in Little Italy and City Hall.

ST. CASIMIR HOUSE / CANTON
credit: Believe in Tomorrow Foundation

In October of 2004, the old St. Casimir convent across the street from the church was sold to the "Believe in Tomorrow" foundation to house children undergoing treatment at Johns Hopkins Hospital and their parents. Young patients undergoing a two-to-four month bone marrow transplant operation need to be within 15 minutes of the East Baltimore hospital.

The four rowhouses that comprised the old convent were sold for a reported $150,000 with the foundation spending nearly a million dollars in renovation.

ST. KATHARINE SCHOOL

Operating as the "Queen of Peace Inter-Parochial Schools," St. Katharine has been educating children in the neighborhood for more than 100 years.

The school has about 300 students – less than 10 percent of them Catholic - and an operating budget of about $2 million, much of it provided by the Archdiocese, according to principal Dr. Kirk Gaddy, a cradle Catholic who received his master's degree in education from Loyola College in Baltimore in 1989.

Dr. Gaddy had been principal of the St. Alphonsus school on Saratoga Street, which was closed in 2002.

"The evolution of the Catholic school principal in an urban center means you are the chief catechist, you play parental roles and you change light bulbs," said Dr. Gaddy. "We can't provide special education, but if a student is behind just two grades or less, we'll take you."

Dr. Gaddy works with two assistant principals. Sisters Margarita Musquera, an Oblate Sister of Providence who years ago taught Kirk Gaddy and his siblings, handles the middle school. Tracé Woodson supervises the elementary grades.

[One of Gaddy's brothers, a Redemptorist priest named Kenneth Gaddy, serves as vicar general of St. Croix in the Virgin Islands. A cousin is a nun. The family is not related to the late champion of Baltimore's poor and homeless, Bea Gaddy.]

"For an African American to be Catholic is a blessing," he said. "Our presence makes the Church stick to its [definition] of universality."

Dr. Gaddy's father, John, worked in the receiving department of Mercy Hospital and his mother, Beatrice, stayed home with the children. Money was scarce.

"But as poor as we were, we were considered the privileged boys at Eager and Preston streets because we went to Catholic school," said Dr. Gaddy.

"My thing is to give some of that back. Spirituality and education are the two most important things in black folks' lives if we're going to [transcend] our situation in America.

"There's not a black politician in Baltimore who can say the Catholic Church didn't build a bridge over troubled water for them or their constituents somewhere along the line."

ST. KATHARINE STUDENTS
Many students at the St. Katharine School attend on Cardinal Shehan Scholarships, according to school officials. The Shehan awards date to 1974, when a testimonial dinner in honor of Cardinal Shehan, who was retiring after 13 years of service, raised nearly $400,000. Scholarships in the Cardinal's name were launched with this start-up money. With other parochial tuition programs, it is supported by the Archdiocese in a variety of ways.

June 6, 1911 marked Cardinal Gibbons' golden jubilee as a priest and his silver jubilee as a cardinal. The celebration brought some 20,000 well-wishers to Baltimore: from ambassadors to laborers to holy men of various faiths. Official business in Washington nearly shut down because so many officials had left town for the event.

Both President William Howard Taft and former president Theodore Roosevelt, whom Cardinal Gibbons considered a friend, spoke in honor of the 76-year-old cardinal.

At the close of the ceremony at the Fifth Regiment Armory, Cardinal Gibbons told the crowd: "One merit I can truly claim regarding my civic life and that is an ardent love for my country and her political institutions.

"I consider the Republic of the United States one of the most precious heirlooms ever bestowed on man down the ages..."

ST. MARGARET / BEL AIR

Before the 2005 Christmas holiday, parishioners at St. Margaret were collecting material for a time capsule to be sealed after morning Mass on New Year's Eve. A Catholic school uniform, along with letters from children to the young people of the future, were some of the items being considered for the capsule.

St. Margaret, one of the largest parishes in the archdiocese, counts more than 5,200 families in its congregation. The Rev. Msgr. Michael Schleupner is pastor and Jane A. Dean is principal of the parish school.

153

On November 19, 1900, Fr J. Alphonse Frederick, the first pastor of St. Margaret Church, purchased three acres of land located on what was then Pennsylvania Avenue for $3,000, money inherited from his mother. In five years time, the property became the site of the Church of Saint Margaret - named for the third century martyr - with a cornerstone set in place on May 1, 1905.

Mass was first celebrated in the chapel on October 1, 1905 and is believed to be the first known celebration of the Catholic Eucharist in Bel Air. The original church was used for Mass until 1969, when the present sanctuary opened and blessed by Cardinal Shehan.

The altar of St. Margaret's is a single piece of marble in the shape of a table and weighing five tons. Within it is a relic of Pignatianus, a Roman martyr and contemporary of St. Margaret. The tabernacle of the Blessed Sacrament rests in the chapel at the back of the church.

The old church, now used for adult education, also houses the Archbishop William D. Borders Library, dedicated in the fall of 1995.

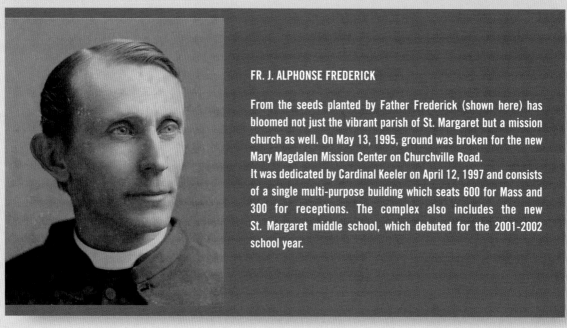

FR. J. ALPHONSE FREDERICK

From the seeds planted by Father Frederick (shown here) has bloomed not just the vibrant parish of St. Margaret but a mission church as well. On May 13, 1995, ground was broken for the new Mary Magdalen Mission Center on Churchville Road.

It was dedicated by Cardinal Keeler on April 12, 1997 and consists of a single multi-purpose building which seats 600 for Mass and 300 for receptions. The complex also includes the new St. Margaret middle school, which debuted for the 2001-2002 school year.

ST. DOMINIC / HAMILTON

When Marie Helene Driscoll Berger was just little Marie Driscoll making her Confirmation at St. Dominic parish, the nuns told the kids that God would give them whatever they wanted. Or so she remembers.

"After the ceremony we all went to the Chesapeake Restaurant for lunch and when I got home I went into the backyard, knelt down on the sidewalk and prayed for a pony," she said. "It didn't happen."

"I was very disappointed," said Marie, "but it never shook my faith."

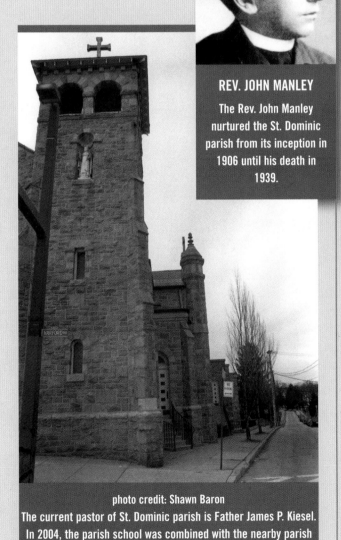

REV. JOHN MANLEY

The Rev. John Manley nurtured the St. Dominic parish from its inception in 1906 until his death in 1939.

photo credit: Shawn Baron
The current pastor of St. Dominic parish is Father James P. Kiesel. In 2004, the parish school was combined with the nearby parish schools of Shrine of the Little Flower and St. Anthony to create the Mother Mary Lange School.

St. Dominic parish at Harford Road and Gibbons Avenue in Hamilton has been a source of faith for Baltimoreans since 1906, when it was consecrated on the Feast of the Most Precious Blood.

When the speed limit along Harford Road was less than 15 mph, St. Dominic was a destination for Catholics from ethnic parishes from the old city neighborhoods, mostly German from St. James' and Irish from St. John's parishes as well as some Italian families.

Cardinal Gibbons sought to create a parish for the people in and around the growing areas of Carney, Hamilton, Lauraville and Parkville. The first pastor was the Irish-born Rev. John Manley, at the time chaplain of the Dominican Convent of the Perpetual Rosary in Irvington.

The first Mass inaugurating what would become St. Dominic was held in Hamilton Hall, which stood at the site of the old Hamilton branch of the Union Trust Company. Two hundred people showed up, yet Manley noted only $14.85 in the collection baskets.

Early on, as few as a half-dozen baptisms were recorded at St. Dominic, according to a speech given by Monsignor Joseph J. Leary, pastor of St. Mark's in Catonsville on the occasion of St. Dominic's Golden Jubilee in 1956.

By the peak years of the late 1950s and 1960s – before the move to the suburbs again pushed beyond the city line - more than 3,000 families belonged to St. Dominic.

In early May of 1907, Cardinal Gibbons presided over the laying of the cornerstone for the new church. Said Gibbons at the ceremony: "I think there are many, and some within the hearing of my voice, who will live to see the day when St. Dominic's will be within the limits of the City of Baltimore."

Newspapers reported "Hamilton's Greatest Day" with standing room only on streetcars ferrying people to the service.

Foreseeing the tremendous growth that was right around the corner for Baltimore's northeast corridor – the Harford County of its day - Manley also purchased land for what would become the St. Ursula parish.

Finishing touches were made to St. Dominic in June of 1911. Pews were installed along with a new organ that was subsidized by Andrew Carnegie and

BILL DRISCOLL & SISTERS

Bill Driscoll with sisters, Gail, on the left with photo of their parents - and Marie, oldest of the Driscoll siblings. Of the new generation, Marie says: "Our children are not nearly as Catholic as we were."

parishioners. And still the parish grew. In 1925, plans were approved to enlarge the sanctuary. At the time, just fewer than 500 children were registered in the parish school.

■ ■ ■

In 1958, when William Michael Driscoll was in the third grade, you could see entire families – a generation or two, uncles and cousins – in a single pew on any given Sunday at St. Dominic.

Same pew, every Sunday, an entire clan of Catholics from the neighborhood.

"We had one teacher for 65 kids in third grade and you could hear a pin drop," remembers Mr. Driscoll, a long time staff member for the Baltimore City Council.

Growing up in a family of six kids – Billy was the fourth in line with a "Little Christmas" birthday on Jan. 6, 1950 – Mr. Driscoll remembers his father as the one who took the kids to Mass.

"Always 10 o'clock Sunday Mass because 11 o'clock was High Mass and you'd be there for an hour and a half. My father was always involved in the Knights of Columbus and he was always an usher."

[The elder William Driscoll, a comptroller for the Rea Keech Buick and Tower Ford dealerships, died in 1999.]

"You'd see kids you knew in the neighborhood getting dragged in by their parents. As a little kid I remember the ladies in the pew in front of us wearing minks with the heads on them and we'd flick their noses and our father would see us and give us the 'silent arm clench.'

"He'd lean over and grab whoever the trouble maker was and give a squeeze, like a boa constrictor and then you'd shut up."

Bill remembers mouthing prayers that were incomprehensible to a young kid.

"We'd just whisper along with it," he laughed, "even though we didn't know what we were saying. As we got older, we got to go on our own and we went to a chapel Mass downstairs. The church was booming and they had to find more space."

Bill Driscoll's mother practiced her religious vocation at home, often calling on a multitude of saints for help.

"Recollections of Mom and church are very few. St. Anthony was her patron; he was the go-to guy, which is a very Irish thing. Or she would beseech, 'God in heaven, help me with these kids... Jesus, Mary and Joseph,' she'd call on all three."

Marie remembers her Mom – the former Grace Harkins, who also passed away in 1999, as a devotee of St. Jude, patron of hopeless causes.

"She had a few of those," said Gail.

BILL DRISCOLL

"Of course I remember the catechism," said Bill Driscoll, "But as I grew older, I sort of fell into this mass memory some Catholics have of a negative experience, which I now see was not the case. "I have come to believe that they were teaching me nothing but love and I wasn't listening."

ST. AMBROSE / PARK HEIGHTS

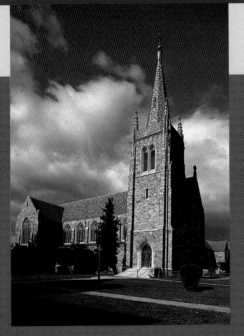

photo credit: Shawn Baron

Established in 1907 in the 4500 block of Park Heights Avenue near the old Avalon movie theater, St. Ambrose is comprised of African-American Catholics who pray in the cadences of Caribbean, Maryland and Carolina accents. The church is considered home and the parishioners family, including newly landed immigrants.

St. Ambrose supports a sister parish in the tiny West African nation of Burkina Faso and donated funds to build a chapel in honor of St. "Padre Pio" [1887-1968].

St. Ambrose runs a parish school and honors the sacrament of marriage with a Sweetheart Sunday held on or near Valentine's Day.

It's current pastor is the Rev. Paul Zaborowski, O.F.M. Cap.

KINDERGARTEN GRADUATION

Rosemary attended St. Ambrose School (holding hand of Sr. Madonna) through eighth grade graduation and went on to Seton High School, where she graduated in 1966.

"I lived next door to the Fleetway Cab Company and walked to school at St. Ambrose everyday. I walked past the kosher chicken store and the firehouse and watched the firemen throw their buckets of water out the window.

On May Day, I got to help carry the statue of the Blessed Mother. The girl who crowned her was the holiest one in our class. She went on to be a nun."

Rosemary says she didn't realize it at the time – back when the nuns were teaching her about the original American colonists and dressing them up in costumes from the period - but she was learning to love her Creator.

"I never had a fear of God and I learned to see Him in the wonder of the world and it has stayed with me," said Rosemary DiStefano, who works in corporate operations for Erickson Retirement Communities at Charlestown.

As an adult, Rosemary worked her way through the catechism a second time when she sponsored a convert to the faith.

"The most profound experience of revisiting the teachings of my youth was hearing my contemporaries describe their relationship to the faith with words like fear, punishing and anger.

"I had none of these feelings," she said. "My connection with God came from the strong relationship of neighborhood, church, school and a love of goodness and beauty that I could see in others. My love of books and learning was nurtured by the School Sisters of Notre Dame.

"How could you stand on the playground on the last day of school, so alone, but not afraid because of your faith in His protecting presence? How could you be on the beach and look out at the ocean, unable to understand where the horizon stopped and the water began – with no idea of what was beyond it - and not trust a loving God?"

FIRST COMMUNION

As Italian as freshly grated parmesan over homemade tomato sauce, Rosemary DiStefano is one of three children of Louis "Sam" DiStefano and the former Virginia DeMattia, who were married at St. Leo the Great in Little Italy on Oct. 22, 1945.

The couple raised their family at 4211 Reisterstown Road in a house that no longer exists.

157

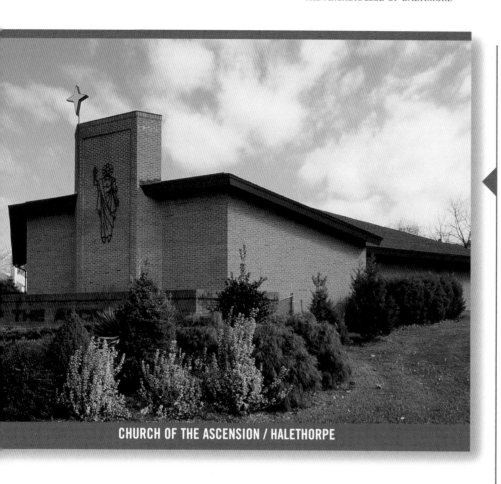

CHURCH OF THE ASCENSION / HALETHORPE

Established in 1913 in the southwestern Baltimore County community of Halethorpe, Ascension Church began as a mission of St. Clement in nearby Lansdowne.

The modern vestibule is enhanced by an indoor garden of seasonal flowers and a small pond with running water that calms and mesmerizes old and young alike. The garden is maintained by parishioner Emma McIntyre and her grandson Jason Gugliette in honor of McIntyre's late husband.

The original church was a small structure that held only 50 people and was fondly referred to as the "church on the hill."

Ascension Church grew along with the county and today counts more than 1,000 families in its registry. It operates an accredited middle school as well as a daycare program.

For almost 20 years, the pastor had been the Rev. Manuel Roman, Ph.D. Fr. Roman helped establish an evangelization committee that reaches out to those who have, in his words, "fallen away." The challenge in ministering to a modern congregation, says Fr. Roman, is finding enough young people to take over for aging leaders.

"It's hard," he said, "for men and women who work all day, then tend to their children's homework and to other household chores at night to attend church meetings."

NEW ALL SAINTS / LIBERTY HEIGHTS

All Saints, established in 1912 in Northwest Baltimore along Liberty Heights Avenue, merged in 1995 with Our Lady of Lourdes, which closed that year after 70 years of service. The resulting parish is called New All Saints. The parish currently counts 900 families with more than two dozen ministries of outreach, including support for the St. Vincent de Paul Society and a food pantry.

New All Saints is a member of Baltimoreans United in Leadership Development [BUILD], a coalition of social outreach organizations that helped bring a super-market to the area.

The parish middle school had an enrollment of 119 students for the 2005-06 school year. The leadership of the parish decided it would not be financially possible to re-open the school once the '05-'06 school year ended.

The pastor of New All Saints, the Rev. Donald Sterling, believes that a coalition of urban parishes, could do much to unify Baltimore. He would like to see them come together to discuss what they have in common and attract younger city residents to anchor the churches.

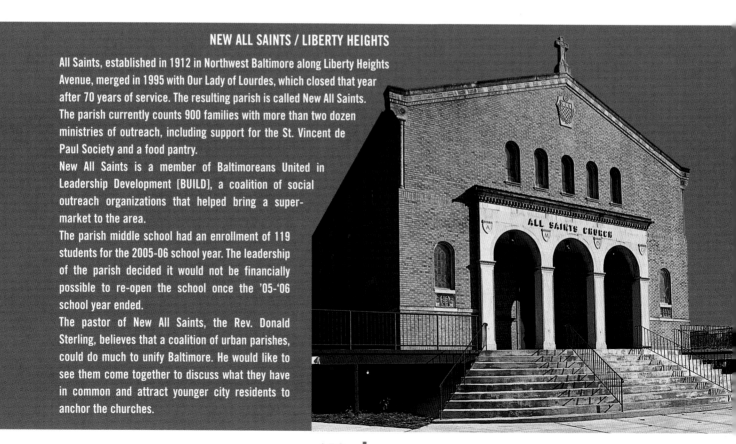

BLESSED SACRAMENT / N.E. BALTIMORE

An oasis of beauty and peace in yet another Baltimore neighborhood where these gifts are increasingly rare, Blessed Sacrament on Old York Road was organized in the Chestnut Hill/Willow Hill area of town in 1911 when it was largely farmland.

The church was dedicated in 1921, and the parish grew quickly, at one point celebrating 11 Masses every weekend to accommodate more than 1,000 families.

That number is down to a little more than 100 people today, with the parishioners' average age at 75 years. The church, however, remains vibrant with two choirs and an emphasis on multiculturalism in a rapidly changing neighborhood.

Parishioners include immigrants from Trinidad and Tobago, Jamaica, and Nigeria in addition to African-Americans and recent arrivals from Ireland and Poland.

Blessed Sacrament has re-invented itself to serve its current flock and those nearby. With other area churches in a coalition called GEDCO – the Govans Ecumenical Development Corporation - Blessed Sacrament has pioneered housing development for the elderly, the developmentally disabled, and the homeless.

The parish's former convent is now transitional housing for women whose lives have gone off track. Also with GEDCO, Blessed Sacrament has pioneered Epiphany House, a retirement community for low-to-moderate income seniors.

The parish shares a priest with St. Mary, Govans, a mile or so north on York Road. When a priest is unavailable, consecrated hosts are on hand for the pastoral administrator, Sr. Marie Mack, S.S.N.D., and other Eucharistic Ministers to distribute in a communion service.

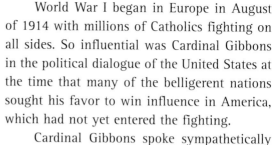

Established in Overlea in 1914,
St. Michael is a parish of nearly of
2,000 families. Among its many outreach
programs is "Spiritual Adoption,"
which hosts parish-wide baby showers for
the Baltimore Pregnancy Center as well
as sending volunteers to Project Rachel,
a diocesan ministry of reconciliation
and healing for men and women suffering
the trauma of abortion.
The St. Michael "Alpha Team" reaches out
to agnostics, a wide range
of the un-churched, and those seeking a basic
understanding of God.

ST. MICHAEL THE ARCHANGEL / OVERLEA

World War I began in Europe in August of 1914 with millions of Catholics fighting on all sides. So influential was Cardinal Gibbons in the political dialogue of the United States at the time that many of the belligerent nations sought his favor to win influence in America, which had not yet entered the fighting.

Cardinal Gibbons spoke sympathetically of no warring nation in public. However, he helped organize relief efforts for civilians in those countries, work that continued through the war's end.

When Germany's resumption of unrestricted submarine warfare led the United States to declare war in April 1916, Cardinal Gibbons told the nation: "it behooves every American citizen to do his duty, and to uphold the hands of the President and the Legislative department in the solemn obligations that confront us."

Also in April, bishops of the United States, led by Cardinal Gibbons, drafted a declaration of American Catholic loyalty along with a resolution aimed at speeding up the process of filling the quota of Catholic chaplains for the military. He also addressed soldiers at Ft. Meade in Anne Arundel County.

In Baltimore, a city with more immigrants from Germany than any other country, Cardinal Gibbons let it be known that the first and last U.S. soldiers to die in the Great War were German Catholics from East Baltimore.

The Pope himself was shielded by the Cardinal from Baltimore when a failed Vatican call for peace in 1917 was perceived by many to be pro-German.

THE HINKLES OF OLD ST. JOE'S ON LEE STREET

ST. JOSEPH, LEE STREET

Established in 1838, St. Joseph's parish was originally located at Howard and Barre Streets until 1915, when it was moved to 119 West Lee Street. The parish closed in 1962 and its records are kept at Holy Cross in Federal Hill.

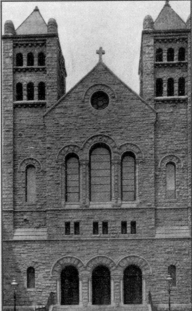

Mary Catherine Montgomery, 77, and her younger brother Michael Hinkle have strong memories of their mother, Margaret Gross Hinkle, as the hardworking woman who played the organ at old St. Joseph church on Lee Street.

"Mom went to church," said Mary Catherine, "and we went to church when she told us to. Her faith was inner. She never expressed the depth of it. She lived it."

These were hard times when a nickel was hard to come by.

"I worked at Murphy's 5 & 10 to pay my tuition. I also cleaned the row-house next to the church where the nuns lived and I hated it," remembered Montgomery. "We moved around South Baltimore a lot back then. The money Mom made playing the organ at church went to our rent. It was $17 a month and when they raised it to $21, we moved."

[Margaret Hinkle died in 1982 at age 78.]

In 1949, Mary Catherine was married at St. Joseph's to John Gilbert Montgomery, "our mothers knew each other before we were born."

The couple had a fairly typical Catholic home and, after the hardships of the 1930s and 1940s, carried the faith into the prosperity of their own, post-war family.

"Until one day I just said I wasn't going to church anymore," said Mary Catherine, who said didn't realize the extent of the world outside of Catholicism until she took college philosophy courses once her children were grown.

"I'd had eight kids and I was tired and disgusted. I asked myself: 'Who told us we had to have all these babies?' and my husband said, 'I'm not going to go anymore either.'"

And it went on like that for awhile until John Montgomery came to the end of his life.

"He was dying," remembers Mary Catherine, "and I asked him if he wanted a priest and he said, 'yes.' I said: 'Did you understand what I said?'

"And he said, 'Yes.'"

MIKE & MARY CATHERINE
Photo: Kirsten Beckerman

Mary Catherine Montgomery, born in 1927, shown with brother, Michael Hinkle.
"The old church is gone," said Mary Catherine Hinkle Montgomery, a star athlete with the Seton High School Class of 1945 and the first-born of seven.
"We lived in homes on both sides of the church. There were only eight kids in my eighth grade graduating class just before World War II. We came out of church one day and heard the news of Pearl Harbor. I wanted to be an Army nurse but my mother said no."

Michael Hinkle, 66, has a similar story of intense Catholicism in childhood, not to mention, he says, that with so many kids, by the time he got to take his bath in the same backyard tub as everybody else on Saturday nights, the water was almost like mud.

Michael's faith continued into adulthood pretty much as a residual of his youth and then stopped in the fall of 1990.

"I was going to church only for Communion, which I took as a prayer for family members," he said, describing his faith as a "seed" planted in him at birth that he didn't want to completely discard. "But I gave up."

For about the next decade, Michael stayed away from Mass. And then, sometime in 2002, he and his wife were visiting their daughter in Colorado and found out that the woman across the street, "only 42, a young girl," said Mike, had just lost her battle with cancer.

"I had this feeling of wanting to go to Mass," he said. "I did and it felt good."

ST. WILLIAM OF YORK / W. BALTIMORE

Established in the Ten Hills neighborhood just inside the city line along Baltimore National Pike, St. William of York was dedicated in 1914 as a memorial to William Lanahan, a prominent Baltimore businessman and philanthropist who had died two years before. Both Lanahan and his wife Catherine provided money to build the church. They are buried in separate tombs at the back of the nave. The current pastor is Fr. Martin H. Demek.

St. Rose of Lima Parish began as a mission of Curtis Bay's St. Athanasius Church in 1914. The school opened under the direction of the Dominican Sisters in 1926. The school was destroyed by fire in December of that year and a new school built the following year. The current church was built in the mid-1950s. When land was bought along the Patapsco River across from Fort McHenry by the Globe Shipbuilding Company of Baltimore - later known as Maryland Dry-dock Company – skilled Catholic shipbuilders arrived from Minnesota, Wisconsin and throughout the City of Baltimore to take good jobs. With the influx, Mass was often said in private homes, a business known as Helmstetters at 416 Patapsco Avenue and at the local Odd Fellows Hall. Helmstetters provided land for a small, unheated wooden church on the site of the present St. Rose of Lima Church. On cold winter mornings the water in the cruets for Mass would freeze.

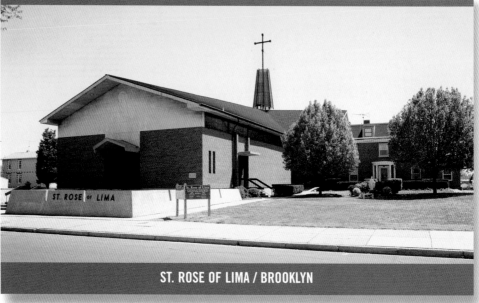

ST. ROSE OF LIMA / BROOKLYN

The Great War ended with the armistice of November 11, 1918. Cardinal Gibbons was now 84 and faltering. That year he blessed the opening of Bon Secours Hospital on West Baltimore Street, yet another gift to the people of Baltimore from the Jenkins family of bankers, silversmiths and shippers dating back to the late 17th century in Maryland.

The following year, Holy Trinity parish was established in the northern Anne Arundel county town of Glen Burnie.

In 1952, Holy Trinity broke ground for a church school. By the 1960s, having grown along with widespread suburban development, Holy Trinity had given birth to four spin-off parishes: St. Philip Neri in Linthicum, St. Bernadette in Severn, the Church of the Good Shepherd, and the Church of the Crucifixion, both nearby in Glen Burnie.

Noted as an astute businessman, Father Arthur Slade anticipated the population growth and purchased land for the new churches in advance.

Theresa Griiser, secretary of the Rosary Makers Guild at Holy Trinity, was born in 1916 and grew up in the parish. She has been a member for more than 80 years and her brother, Fred was among the first infants baptized there.

Griiser recalls visits from "the dear Mission Helpers who came down from Towson for vacation school or Sunday School" catechism classes.

She has fond memories of the days when Glen Burnie was mostly farm land, noting that her father's 15-acre property has been whittled away to half an acre.

"We're a tremendous parish," says Griiser, who watched Holy Trinity grow with the county. "The school occupies a good deal of our time and ambition now."

HOLY TRINITY / GLEN BURNIE

In 1919, St. Rose of Lima parish in Brooklyn began a mission among the farms and orchards of northern Anne Arundel County and named it Holy Trinity. Founded in Glen Burnie's Old Town Hall, the mission served the immediate area as well as nearby Linthicum and Ferndale, where African-Americans and Polish Catholics from East Baltimore often spent summers as migrant workers in the strawberry and bean fields. A congregation was quickly established, and construction of a sanctuary began on Baltimore & Annapolis Boulevard. Mass was held the following year with the entire church completed in 1931. The founding pastor, the Rev. Leonard J. Ripple, served until 1946. He was succeeded by Monsignor Arthur C. Slade, for whom the current school is named.

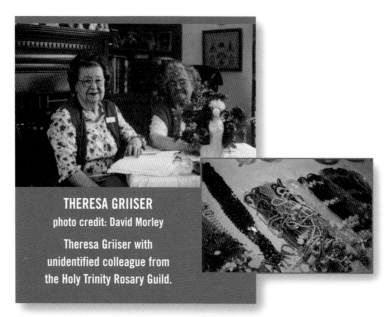

THERESA GRIISER
photo credit: David Morley

Theresa Griiser with
unidentified colleague from
the Holy Trinity Rosary Guild.

ST. JOAN OF ARC / ABERDEEN

In 1917, when the Sandy Hook testing facilities relocated to the newly-formed Aberdeen Proving Grounds, the area's Catholic population increased dramatically. Catholics in the area gathered at the Knights of Columbus' hut at the Proving Grounds for Mass, which was often celebrated by Catholic Army chaplains. The parish was created in 1920 and its first pastor was Father Francis Siggins, S.J. The hut would be expanded to accommodate the fledgling Catholic community until property could be purchased and a new church could be built. However, anti-Catholic bias in the Aberdeen area made this more difficult and required a mix of creativity and generosity. Thus, Mr. and Mrs. Frederick Hinder had to buy property on Law Street and donate it to the Archdiocese of Baltimore. And in the spring of 1963, the parish broke ground for a new rectory, convent and school/church facility, which are still in use today.

Toward the end of 1920, at the height of his popularity, Cardinal Gibbons began to succumb to his final illness. On December 5 he visited friends, the Shrivers in Union Mills to rest. In early January, sensing his end was near, he asked to return to Baltimore, to see his beloved Basilica one last time.

On March 24, 1921, the man whom Teddy Roosevelt called the most respected, venerated, and useful citizen of the United States, died.

At the request of the Cardinal, only a few were allowed to attend the final funeral rites.

Yet over 200,000 came to the wake, some 7,000 passing by the coffin per hour, according to reports at the time.

The Requiem Mass attracted a throng of notables – Catholic, diplomatic, and otherwise. As the service began on the afternoon of March 31, 1921, Maryland Governor Albert C. Ritchie ordered all activity in the state suspended for a full minute.

James Cardinal Gibbons, the ninth archbishop of Baltimore, is interred at the Basilica.

THE FUNERAL OF CARDINAL GIBBONS

At a requiem Mass for Cardinal Gibbons, Bishop Thomas J. Shahan said: "It was as a minister of Jesus Christ,
as an humble, unselfish and zealous priest, concerned chiefly about the divine and eternal interests
of his people and his country, that he went about his beloved city and state …guiding a society whose defects
and errors he well knew were rooted in spiritual ignorance rather than malice…"

Forty Years

From the Jazz Age to the Space Age The Era of Archbishops Curley & Keough 1921 to 1961

"I have not come to Baltimore to be the bishop of the Catholic rich..."

- *Archbishop Curley upon arrival in the Premier See*

The beginning of the Roaring 20s in Baltimore was marked by the arrival of a brusque, tough Irishman named Michael Curley who would lead the Archdiocese of Baltimore for the next quarter century.

Archbishop Curley served Baltimore through prosperity and Prohibition; the Great Depression and World War II. Toward the end of his life, he saw the beginning of seismic societal changes-- particularly the beginning of the middle-class exodus out of American cities-- coinciding with millions of GIs returning from war.

Though few knew it at the time, this exodus marked the beginning of the decline of the old neighborhood parishes-- most of them built around immigration and ethnic traditions--and the ascendance of big suburban churches with parking lots twice the size of the church.

ARCHBISHOP CURLEY

Born Oct. 12, 1879 in Athlone, Ireland, Michael Joseph Curley served as Archbishop of Baltimore from 1921 through his death at age 67 in 1947. He studied to be a missionary at the College of the Urban Propaganda in Rome and was ordained on March 19, 1904. Volunteering for duty in America, he was sent to the Diocese of St. Augustine in Florida. In the Sunshine State, he battled anti-Catholic bigotry as a pastor in Deland, a huge parish of some 7200 square miles. Father Curley proved so capable that he was named Bishop of St. Augustine by Pope Pius X in 1914. Seven years later he was appointed to succeed Cardinal James Gibbons. At 41, he was the youngest archbishop in America. A champion of education, he founded the first archdiocesan high schools and set aside scholarship funds to make secondary Catholic education available to young people who otherwise would not have had the opportunity. Michael Curley is perhaps the most underrated and unsung of all of Baltimore's archbishops.

Archbishop Curley was an outstanding-- some would say astounding-- orator. More than 50 years after his death, older Baltimoreans still recall the things that he said.

"He always said what was on his mind. More dangerously, he always wrote what was on his mind," said Father Michael Roach, a historian of the Church in America and an expert on Archbishop Curley.

"To one pastor who had driven his parish into debt on multiple occasions, he wrote, '...once again, Father, you show that you have the executive ability of a four-year-old girl.'"

"To another priest, he said 'I think instead of appointing you to a parish I should have consigned you for the rest of your life to Mount Hope [hospital for the mentally ill].'"

Archbishop Curley warned the hapless pastor that if he incurred another debt amounting to more than $20 he would be suspended.

He did, and he was.

The working people of Dundalk cleared the land, built the roads, and helped put the finishing touches on St. Rita's church, which also included a parish hall and a school, the last of which closed after the 2005-06 school year after nearly 80 years of service.

[So devoted were the families who founded St. Rita that they paid off the construction debt during the widespread unemployment and bankruptcies that followed the stock market crash of 1929.]

Although the number of registered parish families has been shrinking-- and Bethlehem Steel itself declared bankruptcy in 2001-- St. Rita's continues to provide guidance and comfort to the people of Dundalk.

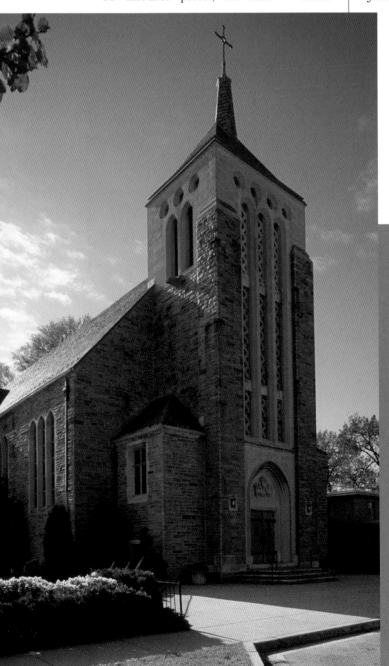

ST. RITA / DUNDALK

Established in 1922, St. Rita's was born out of the nearby steel mills and the persistence of the families who depended on blast furnaces and the Catholic faith to sustain them.

In June 1921 a group of Catholic men from Dundalk received permission from Archbishop Curley to build a new parish, an offshoot of St. Luke's in nearby North Point. While the families had Archbishop Curley's blessing, they lacked land and money.

At the time, Bethlehem Steel had a standing offer to donate one acre of land for any church that could be built in a year or less. The fledgling parish took the company up on its offer and with a loan from the Archdiocese, added a second acre.

Dedicated to Saint Rita Cascia, a 14th-century nun who endured a stigmata of the crown of thorns, the new church opened its doors on Thanksgiving Day, 1922.

CONSTRUCTION OF ST. MICHAEL'S SCHOOL / OVERLEA

As the Archbishop of Baltimore, Abp. Curley made the building of Catholic schools a priority. "Catholic education never had a better friend than Michael Curley," says Father Michael Roach. "He made it a rule that a pastor was first to build a school and only then, a church."

OUR LADY OF POMPEI / HIGHLANDTOWN
Capital of Baltimore's Second Little Italy

OUR LADY OF POMPEI / HIGHLANDTOWN

Established in 1924 at the corner of Claremont and Conkling Streets just off the Eastern Avenue shopping district in Highlandtown, "Pompei" got its start with the Rev. Luigi Scialdone, a former missionary who had served 17 years in China. For the first year, Fr. Scialdone celebrated Mass in the basement of nearby Sacred Heart of Jesus parish while Our Lady of Pompei was being built. The first child baptized was Palmieri Maria Grazia; the first wedding took place between Lorenzo Ruggiero and Rosaria Marino. Generations of children were educated there by the Sisters of St. Filipini, who arrived at the end of the Summer of 1928.

Pete Genovese, the son of a barber who kept a shop at 234 South Highland Avenue from the late 1940s through 1975, has a strange reaction when he hears a Gregorian chant. They remind him of the old-fashioned electric fans that used to cool Our Lady of Pompei during the dog days of his youth.

There was one at the front of each side aisle and they ran almost all summer long.

"They made a humming sound and gave accompaniment to the chanting of the priest, underscored the sermons and kissed the wet brow with just enough cool air to give hope of some comfort later on," said Mr. Genovese.

Pete Genovese has lived since 1970 in St. Louis, where he taught college English and writing. He returns to Baltimore regularly, sometimes just to visit and have pizza at Matthew's on the Avenue, but increasingly to attend funeral Masses at Pompei for his relatives.

His mother – christened Alfia and known as Freida – died in 2001. Pete the barber passed away in 1998.

"Mom was the religious one in the family," said Mr. Genovese. She kept all holy days and fasts, and went to novenas and benedictions. She never left the church without lighting at least one candle for the dead and never said a dead person's name without saying benedicala."

Which means: "bless them."

■ ■ ■

Today, Pompei continues to minister to immigrants and their families, reaching out to the latest wave – Latinos – with Masses in Spanish as well as Italian and English.

Parishioners participate in social justice outreach, supplying food for food baskets, regularly distributing food for the needy through Abbot Memorial Presbyterian Church a few blocks away at Bank Street and Highland Avenue, distributing gifts and food during the holidays, adopting needy families at Christmas, and other charity distributed through the Sons of Italy organization.

Parishioners have formed a Mystical Rose Prayer Group that meets weekly to pray the rosary on behalf of unborn children and for the end of abortion as well as for private intentions.

Other groups visit the parish's sick and home-bound, sing in the choir, and raise funds through old-fashioned stand-bys like Atlantic City and bingo.

In January of 2004, something new echoed the old at the school gymnasium: an indoor bocce court.

The unveiling and blessing of the court was attended by the regular players from Stiles Street in the St. Leo parish, a foursome from Delaware, the court's builder – neighbor Dominic Petrucci from Highland Avenue - and other fans of the old world game.

Organizers hailed it as the first regulation-size indoor court in Maryland.

Father Luigi Esposito, pastor since 1964, thought it a great idea, something that might help revitalize his often beleaguered patch of Highlandtown, which in 2004 saw the beloved Grand Theater razed by the Enoch Pratt Free Library.

PETE GENOVESE AND ANGELO DICARA

Photo credit: Rafael Alvarez

Pete Genovese (left) grew up in the Pompei parish and became a teacher, an author and a publisher. His most recent book is "*An Angel in the Street*" (Ramble House, 2005). With him is his uncle, World War II veteran Angelo DiCara, who starts each day in his Dundalk home by reciting the rosary while looking at photos of loved ones, both dead and alive.

In 1991, the Vincentian Fathers of the Neopolitan Province, who had served Pompei since 1928, decided they could no longer keep the commitment and withdrew.

Fr. Esposito was ready for the announcement and had earlier written his Superior General of the situation near the corner of Conkling & Claremont Streets: "The parish and the neighborhood are currently experiencing very difficult times. New realities are setting in: the polarization of the population which consists of two groups, the very young and the very old; the increased presence of transients...; [and] growing financial difficulties for the parish and the people..."

Father Lou wanted to stay with his congregation, even though his order was taking its energy else-

where, and asked Archbishop Keeler and his Superior General to allow him to move from the Vincentians to become a priest of the Archdiocese of Baltimore.

His petition was granted and he continues to this day, more than a decade after the sad news of 1991, a time when signs of hope are springing up around the old neighborhood.

Said Nunzio D'Alessio in his history of the parish: "We have committed ourselves through active involvement in the future of this small city neighborhood - Highlandtown.

"We love this city… we love this neighborhood. Just take a walk through its storied streets and one can experience the Old World charm of neighbors. From the woman making her morning walk to church as she has done for thirty years, to the man sitting with his comrades on the "stoop" discussing the days past…"

CURLEY & COOLIDGE

Archbishop Curley with President Calvin Coolidge at a Holy Name rally in Washington, D.C., 1924. "Under Archbishop Curley, there was a consolidation of a Catholic 'sense' in the country," says Cardinal William H. Keeler the 10th Archbishop of Baltimore. The Cardinal notes that today's Catholics tend to forget that their faith was not always a part of the American mainstream.

OUR LADY OF POMPEI SCHOOL

Our Lady of Pompei School reflected in the windows of the storefronts on Conkling Street. The first class of high school students – seven boys - graduated in 1963. The school closed in 2002. A thorough history of Our Lady of Pompei was written for the parish's Diamond Jubilee by Nunzio D'Alessio, a graduate of both the primary and secondary schools at Pompei and a parishioner since childhood.

ST. JOSEPH / ODENTON

Though formally established in 1924, the seeds of St. Joseph in Odenton go back to 1891
when the Millersville home of Mrs. Easby Smith was used to celebrate Mass. Land for a small church was donated
in 1902 by the Cecil family and the Woodward Memorial Chapel emerged. Two decades later, the Redemptorists
started a small church for the Catholics of the Odenton/Millersville area in mid-Anne Arundel County.
Original building materials came from discarded Army surplus at nearby Fort Meade.
By 1946, the number of registered families at St. Joseph was at about 200.
Thirty years later, St. Joseph was elevated from mission church to an independent parish.
Today, the church boasts more than 1,800 families and has a strong focus
on a health ministry that includes blood drives, flu shots, and health screenings.
It is one of 10 parishes in the Archdiocese of Baltimore named for the foster father of the Christ.

SACRED HEART OF MARY / GRACELAND PARK

Sacred Heart of Mary was established on Youngstown Avenue
near Dundalk in 1925, one of more than 50 churches and
chapels that got their start during the era of Archbishop Michael
Curley.

Sacred Heart's motto is: "We have been asked by God to service
these, His people and we will serve them as best we can until He
releases us from our task."

At its height, the parish counted more than 1,600 families on its
rolls, and an array of organizations included the Women's Polish
Alliance.

Among the young men who went on to seminary from Sacred
Heart is Archbishop Mitchell T. Rozanski, who in 2004 on the
Feast of St. Bartholomew was consecrated a bishop in the
Archdiocese of Baltimore.

During Archbishop Curley's tenure, the Catholic population of
the archdiocese increased from 276,200 to 429,517; the number
of churches and chapels went from 275 to 326; and parochial
schools increased from 97 with 31,802 students to 168, with 53,
027 students.

The number of diocesan priests jumped from 283 to 417, religious priests in diocesan work from 325 to 1,009, and religious
orders and congregations in the Baltimore area from 42 to 80.

SHRINE OF THE LITTLE FLOWER

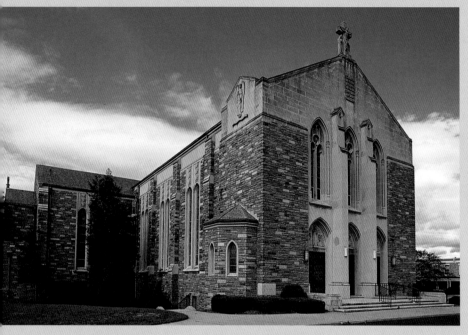

SHRINE OF THE LITTLE FLOWER / N.E. BALTIMORE

The Shrine of the Little Flower was established in 1926 along a stretch of Belair Road near Herring Run Park that was considered rural at the time.

Today, there are fewer than 800 families, less than the more than 1,000 families during the boom time of the 1950s and 1960s.

Led by Father Michael Orchik, the parish works hard to serve the needs of many Catholics and non-Catholics in a once solid middle-class but now increasingly impoverished area.

Working with the St. Vincent de Paul Society, "Little Flower" does extensive outreach, helping its neighbors with utility and medical bills, rent and transportation.

There is also an Evangelization Committee charged with "spreading the Word" through a variety of events, as well as support groups for expectant mothers and the deaf.

A strong devotion to the Blessed Mother is expressed in its Blue Army, an apostolate for spreading the message of Fatima through the Immaculate Heart of Mary. At the Little Flower Rosary Guild, volunteers make rosaries together.

ST. CLEMENT MARY HOFBAUER / ROSEDALE

Dedicated in 1925 on Chesaco Avenue in Rosedale. Their mission statement reads:
"We, the Church of St. Clement Mary Hofbauer in the Rosedale Neighborhood of the
Archdiocese of Baltimore,
are messengers of the Word of God. Through our celebration of the Eucharist and public
prayer, we live out the faith
that has been entrusted to us. That faith calls us to build up the Body of Christ present in
our neighborhood."

Father Thomas Jenkins Wheeler celebrated the first Mass in October of 1926 in a wooden chapel at the corner of Belair Road and Brendan Avenue, the original Little Flower.

A year later, congregants established a parish school. Groundbreaking for the current church building, built in the shape of a cross, took place in early summer, 1950.

Over the next ten years, the population of the Shrine exploded, from 5,900 to more than 12,000. Enrollment in the parish school [taught by the Sisters of St. Francis, who in 2005 celebrated 150 years as an order], of boys and girls in tan and brown uniforms neared 2,000 pupils in the Eisenhower era.

At the end of 2005, the last class of students received diplomas from the Shrine of the Little Flower, 27 graduates, joining alumni rolls that number more than 8,000.

The atmosphere of Little Flower school kids' being everywhere and something's always going on is what Joe and Dominic Cottone remember of the years when their grandparents lived at 2745 Pelham Avenue, within walking distance of the grand church.

■ ■ ■

Like many early twentieth century Italian families in Baltimore, the Cottone and Buscemi clans met through their work at the old Belair Market near St. Vincent de Paul church. One of Joe Cottone's grandfathers was a market

C. BUSCEMI & WIFE
Carmello Buscemi and his wife, Mary, shown at their 50th wedding anniversary, are the maternal grandparents of Joe Cottone, who served Mass in the 1950s and early 1960s at St. Anthony of Padua Church on Frankford Avenue. Carmello and Mary Buscemi belonged to Shrine of the Little Flower and naturally the family spent time there as well.

Joe Cottone's father, Sam, owned and operated Lippens Hall, a catering hall near the church, and, later, a restaurant known as Villa di Cottone.

"I remember big carnivals behind the school and funerals of relatives there," said Joe, a manager for the Baltimore Window Factory. "Both of my mother's parents had their funeral Masses at Little Flower. They're buried right up the road from there at Holy Redeemer cemetery. My Aunt Jennifer lived with them and she's buried next to them."

butcher, the other sold fruit and vegetables there.

Probably Joe's mother, Laura, who passed away in 2003, met his father, Santo "Sam" Cottone, who died in 1974, in the market. Sam, as a young man, served as an usher at St. Vincent de Paul.

"When they moved to Northeast Baltimore" before World War II, said Joe, "they were out in the country."

The best church food-- whether fried

LIPPENS HALL
It began as a dry cleaning business and then it was Lippens Hall, named for the man who owned the cleaners before changing over to catering when permanent press shirts stormed the market in the early 1960s.
Then it became a restaurant and eventually most of Baltimore came to know the building at Belair Road and Frankford Avenue as the Bo Brooks

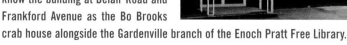

crab house alongside the Gardenville branch of the Enoch Pratt Free Library.
But before it was Bo's it was Villa di Cottone, site of countless wedding receptions, Knights of Columbus affairs, political gatherings, bingo games, crab feasts, and bull and oyster roasts.
"I helped Dad build it from the ground up," said Joe Cottone. "Mom helped out in the kitchen and was the hostess. Dad died in '74, part if of it from the stress of getting that place off the ground."

chicken at parish picnics, ravioli or sour beef and dumplings at wintertime dinners--is cooked and served by the parishioners.

Parish bazaars at St. Peter the Apostle in SoWeBo were famous for oyster fritters, sometimes known in Baltimore parlance as "flitters." A St. Pete's parishioner known as Big Betts bragged: "We might be poor, but we know how to eat."

Liz O'Neill, a former TV anchorwoman and a member of St. Louis parish in Clarksville, describes its 127-year-old classic bull roast. "Imagine a big, boisterous holiday dinner with all of your family members.

Multiply that by 10, add some great food and a good cause-- that's what I remember about the bull roasts I've attended."

And church carnivals, from Overlea to Oakland, brought people together, raised money for the parish, and provided teenagers with a place to hang out, perhaps even date, in an atmosphere acceptable to their parents.

Far south of the city, in the early years of Archbishop Curley, in the rural waterfront enclave of Severna Park, St. John the Evangelist began gathering parishioners.

■ ■ ■

ST. JOHN THE EVANGELIST / SEVERNA PARK
Originally housed in a one-room, wooden structure, St John's grew out of a 1927 mission effort of St. Mary's in Annapolis.
Today, with 3,300 families and 49 different community outreach programs operating out of a sanctuary built in 1964,
St. John's has something for everyone, including groups that support vocations, scouting troops,
and a home visit ministry that encourages members to bring the Eucharist to shut-ins.
The average age of a St. John's parishioner is 30-something, which means baptisms are happily running high.

ST. FRANCIS OF ASSISI / MAYFIELD

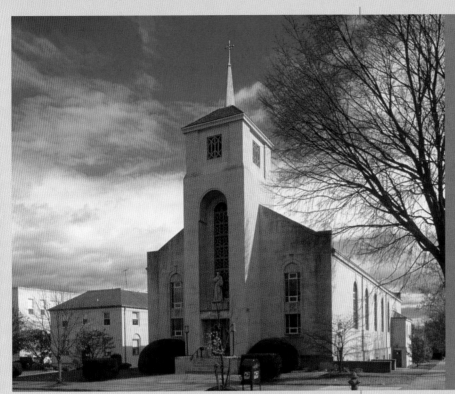

Established in 1927 on Harford Road and Pelham Avenue near Lake Montebello, St. Francis of Assisi church began in the school basement. Its first resident pastor, the Rev. William Neligan, arrived in 1934. The sanctuary used today was dedicated by Archbishop Francis P. Keough and the first SFA graduating class received their 8th grade diplomas on June 11, 1961.
Current parishioners of St. Francis of Assisi include the Mayor of Baltimore, Martin O'Malley and his family.
The parish is part of a coalition of Northeast Baltimore churches that helps struggling families faced with eviction and utility turn-off notices. In 2005, it launched an endowment campaign to benefit the parish school.
Since 1980, the pastor has been the Rev. Msgr. William F. Burke.

Secular heroes dominated the news in Baltimore in October of 1927, the year that the Baltimore & Ohio Railroad celebrated it centenary.

Charles Lindbergh, famed for his cross-Atlantic solo flight, gave a speech at old Baltimore Stadium. On October 9, the front page of the Sunday Sun told of hometown boy Babe Ruth leading the fabled '27 Yankees to a four-game sweep of the Pittsburgh Pirates in the World Series.

Dignitaries making their way to town from Philadelphia-- itself celebrating the 150th anniversary of the Continental Congress-- included 23 members of the Blackfoot Indian tribe. On Sunday, October 9, they attended a service at the Cathedral and were joined by 800 members of the Knights of Columbus.

Reporters described, "Archbishop Curley, in purple robes, on his throne, surrounded by a large body of priests, acolytes and choirboys, conducted a service which many described as the most impressive and gorgeous they had ever attended."

But the newspapermen missed a humble gathering that marked the beginning of what was destined to be an enduring institution: St. Francis of Assisi Church on the edge of Herring Run Park.

Not long after the turn of the century, farmland owned by the Erdman family began to be developed, as later farmland near St. Margaret's in Harford County was developed at the end of the twentieth century. Land records reveal that the anonymous donors of the property that became St. Francis of Assisi are the late Mr. and Mrs. Frank Novak, formerly of St. Wenceslaus.

SFA began as a mission of St. Dominic, a few blocks north on Harford Road, back when new houses on Walther Boulevard advertised for $6,700.

The celebrant of the first Mass in 1927 was Father John Forrest McGee, a Franciscan.

■ ■ ■

Tom Petr was 3-years-old in 1927 when his family – along with many other Czechs migrating out of St. Wenceslaus toward Northeast Baltimore – landed at St. Francis of Assisi.

Mayfield, the neighborhood that surrounds SFA, was developed by Frank Novak, and the builder's fellow Czechs moved there to support him and get a piece of the American Dream in the years before the Crash of '29. At the time, Norman Avenue was a stream emanating from Clifton Park.

"I went to school at St. Dominic's [but] my family became parishioners of St. Francis right away," said Petr, who was recruited to serve Mass at the new church. "We would be sent down to

St. Francis, and it was always good to get a funeral or a wedding there. The nuns would give us a nickel or dime to ride the No. 19 streetcar down Harford Road. We pocketed the money and walked down."

had to practice was before High Mass, and it was difficult because … we had to sing all different parts of the Mass in Latin." A pilgrimage to Rome in 1950, with visits to Lourdes and Fatima, attracted a large number of SFA members, among them an architect of the parish, John Eyring.

As trains and buses took the Baltimore pilgrims through Italy, France, Spain and Portugal, Eyring sketched outlines of churches great and small, inside and out. A year later, a final sketch of the new church for St. Francis of Assisi – similar to what Eyring had seen in Europe – was approved by Archbishop Keough.

Photo credit: ED MILLER
No. 19 Streetcar, ca. 1953, in service on Harford Road

ORIOLES MEMORABILIA
Photo Credit: Collection of Bill Driscoll
In April of 1954, with Baltimore giddy over the return of major league baseball with the move of the hapless St. Louis Browns to 33rd Street, construction of the St. Francis of Assisi church neared completion.

The major construction projects at SFA – a new sanctuary and a two-story school building just behind it - were launched in the early 1950s to accommodate the scores of World War II veterans who came home to marry and start families. Only then did the one-floor "basement" church grow.

"The parish has been so much a part of my life, I can't see myself ever leaving," said Gerald J. Curran, a long-time resident of nearby Lauraville. "I live in the house I grew up in, my parents moved there in 1942. My mother was the president of the Sodality, and my father was vice chairman of fund-raising," said Mr. Curran. "I'll never forget the carnival [because] that's where I met my wife Jeannette; she was working one of the stands."

■ ■ ■

After his Army discharge, artist Charles Devaud boarded with the Petr family in 1947 and joined St. Francis. Nearly 60 years later, the former Sun-papers illustrator remains a member of both the parish and the choir.

"I remember Mae Moran being the choir's director," said Mr. Devaud. "The only chance we

The Rev. Edward J.A. Nestor died of a heart attack near the end of April, 1954, and his funeral Mass was the first celebrated in the new, not quite yet finished sanctuary built to hold 450 people.

Though its cornerstone reads 1953, the church was dedicated on November 28, 1954. Archbishop Keough presided during the solemn High Mass along with the new pastor, Monsignor John J. Daly, a former director of Catholic Charities.

Debt for the new church was estimated at some $400,000, but there was no shortage of parishioners with skill, talent and generosity to offset the red ink. Anthony "Bud" Ebert donated plumbing work. Milton Thomas of Kentucky Avenue was a wizard with wood and pitched in on the paneling in the sacristy and Al DiGiacinto, who led the choir, was famous for the homemade sausage that graced many a church dinner.

Joseph Bonodio, who grew up to become "Father Joe," was a teenager when his family moved to Beverly Hills, Md. in 1954. A trombonist known for his spaghetti alla carbonara, Fr. Bonodio had served as an associate pastor at St. Francis of Assisi since 1990.

"You go into the priesthood to try to help people," said Bonodio, who now supervises the St. Charles Villa home for retired Sulpician priests. "You don't look for thank-yous – and not everything turns out to be a success-- but it's nice to hear that you helped someone." Asked if he ever dreamed of becoming a famous jazz trombone player, the former dance band member said: "I always wanted to be a priest...always."

Father Joseph Bonodio is one of many who grew up in the SFA parish to answer the call to religious vocation. Judy Waldt, who graduated from the parish school in 1971, joined the Mission Helpers of Sacred Heart. Her brothers continue to organize a charity golf tournament-- started by their dad-- that benefits the school.

"I have very fond, early memories of three priests," Father Bonodio said. "Monsignor Daly was the pastor, and there was Father [William] Dumps and Father [Patrick] Begley-- good priests who ran the parish well."

Among the constellation of beloved figures from St. Francis of Assisi, none shines brighter than a choir member turned music teacher named Geraldine Broccolino. Trained at the Peabody Conservatory, "Miss Geri" began to volunteer her time teaching music at SFA and soon organized a children's choir. Before long, there wasn't a holiday pageant untouched by her grace.

GERRI & NICK BROCCOLINO
Geraldine DeFina Broccolino, born into the Our Lady of Pompei parish in 1930, with her husband, retired attorney Nicholas Broccolino. Mrs. Broccolino graduated from Seton High School and attended the Peabody Conservatory's prep school, where she studied voice. The musical soul of St. Francis of Assisi, "Miss Geri" died on Dec. 1, 2000.

"The first time I ever saw Miss Geri was over at the rehabilitation center at Montebello State Hospital," says choir member Hedy Droski. "She was teaching music to the children who were in a special education program there... even then, the longest-standing member of the choir."

Another legendary family is the Buettner's, "Miss Reenie," her good-natured husband Jerry and their four daughters.

In the late 1980s, Reenie Buettner pondered the best way to prepare their youngest, Mary-- a stand-out athlete in the Mercy High School class of 2003-- for kindergarten. At the time, Reenie coached a basketball team that practiced in a gym at nearby St. Matthews United Church of Christ.

That's how the Mayfield Christian Preschool was launched in 1989, a joint ecumenical venture between the two congregations.

SFA SCHOOL GETS A 3RD FLOOR
Nearly 40 years later, a third floor was added to the school during a "Raise the Roof" campaign that netted nearly a million dollars in contributions, with a third coming from parish members and matching gifts. The doors to the third floor opened in the fall of 1997. On January 4, 1998, in the middle of winter, St. Francis of Assisi was blessed with a perfect, spring-like day for the official ribbon-cutting and dedication, presided over by Bishop P. Francis Murphy. "It was a dream that became a reality," says Carol Will, a member of the expansion campaign whose three daughters – Lauren, Stephanie and Bridgette – graduated from SFA and worked on the expansion campaign. "Sandy Budd and Vincent Quayle brought in the Abell Foundation. It was the first time in its history that it made a donation of that size to a non-public school."

Family membership at St. Francis of Assisi peaked at about 900 in the 1960s. Though that number has dipped below 600 families today, the parish remains vibrant.

An expansion of the school in the mid-1990s showed a commitment to Baltimore uncommon after decades of a declining city population.

"Our school is good and we're proud that people move into the neighborhood because of it. Some neighboring [Catholic] schools are closing and we're remaining open," notes Msgr. Burke. "In 1995, we added a third floor, and the people who supported that considered it an investment in both the school and the community."

A dyed-in-the-wool Baltimore native known to tell (sometimes) funny jokes about local customs in his sermons, Msgr. Burke was studying at old St. Mary's Seminary on Paca Street when finishing touches were being put on the new SFA church. As a young priest in the years that followed, he became a vocal proponent of the teachings of the Second Vatican Council.

He first served at St. Ann's Parish on 22nd Street during the riots that followed the 1968 assassination of Reverend Martin Luther King. Four years later, he became archdiocesan director of the Campaign for Human Development.

The average St. Francis parishioner has a significantly larger income than the city median, and Msgr. Burke remains committed to making the parish a beacon for poorer folks who have been moving to Northeast Baltimore over the past twenty years. Those changes have been racial, as well and the pastor is adamant that SFA be a place where all are welcome.

"The whole neighborhood changed around the church, but remained very stable with homeowners," said Msgr. Burke. "It works both ways, where the church is dependent on people who are active both at church and in the community and the community is dependent on a strong church."

During his work with the Human Development campaign, the monsignor came to respect the work of community activist Doris Mae Johnson, who in 1976 founded the Coldstream-Homestead-Montebello organization that serves neighborhoods directly to the south of SFA. "She was like Mother Earth," he says of Ms. Johnson, who joined SFA after converting to the faith in the early 1980s. At the same time, the parish started a pantry that distributed food to the needy.

"There's no other coordinated [spiritual] presence like the one that emanates from St. Francis," claims Monique Johnson, one of Doris' granddaughters. "Even though the church isn't located directly in the community, the parish is willing to do work in the community. "

THE MCMULLENS WITH MSGR. BILL BURKE
Photo credit: Kirsten Beckerman
(left to right) Baltimore Sun sportswriter Paul McMullen, whose history of St. Francis for the 75th anniversary of the parish in 2002 provided background for this profile; his son Donald McMullen, a member of the Class of 2006 at Archbishop Curley High School; daughter Kate, a student at Dickinson College; and Monsignor Bill Burke. McMullen's wife, Mary, was absent from this photo, taken in 2002, because she was working to keep pace with the family's tuition bills. A 1969 graduate of St. Rose of Lima parochial school in Brooklyn, Paul believes that tardiness may have saved his life. "Because my brother Kevin was perpetually late to school, we were driving past Club 4100 in February of 1967, late for Lenten services, when we heard that the church roof had caved in." A more humbling experience for the prize-winning sportswriter occurred in the first grade, Mr. McMullen said, "when Sr. Esperance asked me to not sing so loud in the choir loft, because I couldn't carry a tune..."

In the years before the stock market crash of 1929, mid-decade when Fitzgerald published *The Great Gatsby* and Joseph L. Wheeler was chosen to lead the Enoch Pratt Free Library into a new era, Archbishop Curley presided over the building of St. Mary's Seminary in Roland Park.

ST. MARY'S SEMINARY / ROLAND PARK

In the spring of 1925, the Sulpicians paid $176,000 for approximately 80 acres just south of what is now Northern Parkway. Baltimore Catholics responded to fund-raising appeals by digging deep, helping to defray a final cost of more than $2 million.

Construction lasted from 1925 to 1929 and served as a second campus for the seminary. The seminary is operated by the Sulpician Fathers, a French religious community founded in 1641 and dedicated to educating priests.

The history of Catholicism in Baltimore is near synonymous with the Sulpicians and St. Mary's was intended to serve as a national seminary. Soon, candidates began arriving in Baltimore from Europe and across the United States. A number of early Sulpicians were named bishops and played instrumental roles in building up the Church in such places as Kentucky, Louisiana, and, of course, Maryland.

Father John Francis Fenlon, eighth superior of St. Mary's Seminary in Baltimore, was in charge when the new school was needed.

"...The fathers of the seminary have no desire to erect a costly monument to art... neither do they wish to be responsible for ages to come for a building that will look like a factory or barracks."

Their hope was for a structure that would last for centuries. On November 16, 1927, Archbishop Curley turned the first shovel of dirt. Though not quite finished, the seminary opened two years later with a ceremony that attracted fifty archbishops from around the world, hundreds of priests, Maryland Governor Albert C. Ritchie, Mayor William F. Broening of Baltimore, Supreme Court Justice Pierce Butler and the French ambassador to Washington, D.C.

At the occasion, St. Mary's was again recognized as the mother seminary of the Church in the United States.

DR. TRICIA PYNE

In April 2002 the Associated Archives at St. Mary's Seminary and University opened. The program houses the archives of the Archdiocese of Baltimore, St. Mary's Seminary and University, and the U.S. Province of the Society of St. Sulpice. The new state-of-the-art facility was jointly funded by the three institutions. In bringing their archives together, they not only acknowledge the close relationship they have shared since the Archdiocese's founding in 1789, but have created one of the most important repositories of early U.S. Church history in the country. Dr. Tricia Pyne, the current director of the Associated Archives, is shown here in the reading room of the archives. The new building also houses the Rev. Raymond Brown, S.S. Center.

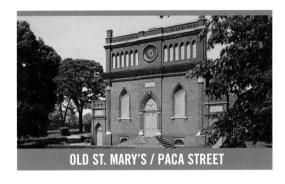

OLD ST. MARY'S / PACA STREET

The chapel of the original St. Mary's Seminary on Paca Street in downtown Baltimore. "The need for a new seminary is urgent and insistent," said Rev. Fenlon when plans were announced for a new seminary. "There are [now] 390 students in a building [made to hold] 260." The Paca Street location remained the seminary's school of philosophy until it was razed in 1975.

REV. RAYMOND BROWN

Rev. Raymond Brown, S.S. (1928-1998), was an alumnus of St. Mary's Seminary and a Sulpician. Recognized as one of the most influential Catholic biblical scholars of the twentieth century, he left his Johannine collection of 3,000 volumes to the seminary's library. He authored some 25 books on the Bible, including the *Death of the Messiah* (1994) and *An Introduction to the New Testament* (1997). He began his teaching career at St. Mary's and went on to serve on the faculties of Woodstock College, Union Theological Seminary, and St. Patrick's Seminary in Menlo Park.

A renowned author for his open-mindedness, Father Brown posited that Scripture may contain error in matters not pertaining to salvation, a relatively modern position when compared to traditional belief that Scripture is flawless that has since been repudiated.

Over time, through the tough years of the Depression, the sacrifice of the Second World War and the affluence that followed it – St. Bernardine became one of the largest parishes in the Archdiocese of Baltimore.

It became known as a place blessed with vocations. One of the first children baptized there was a girl named Barbara Catherine Wright, who grew up to become Sr. Mary St. Mel, IHM.

"Boys were always baptized first," said Sr. St. Mel, born in June of 1929 and one of seven children born to parents who had relocated from Illinois.

She would grow up to emulate the Immaculate Heart of Mary nuns who taught her at St. Bernardine, entering the convent after graduating from Western High School and teaching both primary and secondary grades.

SR. MARY ST. MEL
"As children, we all loved Archbishop Curley very much," said Sr. St. Mel, who was young Barbara Wright when she'd visit the archbishop downtown. "He would sit on the stone wall outside of the Basilica rectory and visit with us often."

ST. BERNARDINE / W. BALTIMORE
Built on the eve of the Great Depression between June of 1928 and 1929, St. Bernardine began as a largely Irish and German parish to serve the families buying row-houses on the suburban edge of West Baltimore at Edmondson Avenue and Mount Holly Street.

It met the needs of Catholics living between St. William of York and St. Edward.

Today, St. Bernardine is the largest African-American parish in the Archdiocese of Baltimore with more than 2,000 members, a liturgy that is both black and Catholic, and several dozen outreach ministries.

The parish opened a K-through-8 school in 1997 and recently displayed its continued vibrancy by hiring a full-time minister of community outreach.

Since 1975, the pastor has been Father Edward M. Miller.

ST. BERNARDINE

The Order assigned Wright the name St. Mel. At first, the young novitiate didn't think the obscure saint "was for real" but a trip to Ireland confirmed his status as the nephew of St. Patrick and Bishop of Armagh.

"I loved my life," says Sr. St. Mel, who at 76 is working as an administrator at a nursing home for IHM nuns in Scranton, Pa. "I thought everyone had a life like mine growing up."

The most recent ordination to come out of St. Bernardine was The Rev. Sidney Speaks, who became a Josephite in 1999. In 2003, parishioner Paul Barksdale was ordained a permanent deacon.

Mr. JAMES KEELTY, CARDINAL SHEHAN AND ARCHBISHOP KEOUGH

Nancy Byrnes Martel remembers the friendships she made growing up in the St. Bernardine parish after World War II.

To this day, she maintains a friendship with two of her old girlfriends from the parish grade school.

"There were high expectations in the school; the atmosphere was quite competitive, especially among the girls. Before school began in the morning, we attended scholarship classes to prepare for high school entrance exams," adds Mrs. Martel. "There were at least twenty scholarships won by the eighth graders in my class. Most of the girls I knew went on to college."

Relief from the academic arrived unannounced.

"We sang in the church choir, and we were glad to get out of class to sing at a funeral."

■ ■ ■

The transformation of the music and liturgy at St. Bernardine from the pre-Vatican II standards of its founding families to one that reflected the influx of African-Americans went a long way in healing the divide between old and new.

What the ethnic parishes of Baltimore generally enjoyed from inception-- a sense that this universal church was ready to meet their cultural needs, from the Bohemians who built St. Wenceslaus to the Vietnamese that today invigorate Our Lady of La Vang-- was hard won by African-Americans.

At Bernardine's, it began with Msgr. James Cronin in 1967. He knew before arriving that the place was in dire need of healing.

Msgr. Cronin had been assigned to the old St. Lawrence parish on Security Boulevard. On the

James S. Keelty, Jr., stands at the far right with Cardinal Shehan, then coadjutor of the Archdiocese, seated next to Archbishop Keough in 1961. Alongside of Archbishop Keough is former Baltimore Mayor Tommy D'Alessandro, Jr., along with others involved in that year's Catholic Charities campaign.
The namesake son of the man who built St. Bernardine's, Mr. Keelty headed the Catholic Charity Fund Appeal for several years during the 1950s, the same decade he served as president of the Baltimore Orioles baseball team.
"My grandfather, James Keelty, Sr., built the church because my aunt, Nora Bernardine Keelty, died of scarlet fever at age six," says Louise Keelty, an attorney.
A 1934 graduate of The Catholic University of America, Mr. Keelty, Jr. was honored by Pope Pius XII as a Knight of St. Gregory in 1958 and in 1965 was elevated to the rank of Commander in the Order by Pope Paul VI.
James S. Keelty, Jr. died in April of 2003 at 91. The family contracting firm built many of the row-houses in Baltimore City as well as more modern homes in Anne Arundel and Baltimore Counties.

ST. BERNARDINE CHOIR
The children's and adult choirs of St. Bernardine's are great sources of pride at the church; perhaps the aspect of this vibrant parish best known to the greater community.

"Each time I go there, I have to check the ceiling to see if it's still in place after the choir has sung," says Cardinal Keeler of the St. Bernardine gospel choir that sang for Pope John Paul II on his 1995 visit to Baltimore. "The power of the faithful is beautiful."

day he celebrated his twenty-fifth anniversary as a priest, Bishop Thomas J. Mardaga, later of the Diocese of Wilmington, lingered after the reception. The two were close friends. Bishop Mardaga asked for a private word.

"He smiled," recalls Msgr. Cronin, "and said that I had been selected to be pastor of St. Bernadine's. He sort of chuckled, indicating it would be a challenge and said: 'You've got quite a job ahead of you.'"

At that time, Eddie Edwards had been enduring the racial tensions at St. Bernardine's for about two years.

whose time was marked by the fight for civil rights.

"There was a great separation between the whites and the African-Americans," said Msgr. Cronin of the changes in the neighborhood, detailed in Edward Orser's 1994 book "*Blockbusting in Baltimore: The Edmondson Village Story.*"

"There were a lot of problems we had to encounter to make ourselves comfortable," recalls Mr. Edwards, saying that when he joined St. Bernardine in 1965 he could "count the number of black families on one hand."

photo credit: Joe Mooney

Monsignor James J. Cronin-- who in early 2005 celebrated the sixtieth anniversary of his ordination-- reminisces with his old friend, St. Bernardine parishioner Eddie Edwards. The meeting took place in late October of 2002 at St. Joseph parish in Fullerton, where "Father Jim" is in residence.
Said Mr. Edwards, "I just found out last Sunday that you're our only living ex-pastor." "What a thrill," quipped Msgr. Cronin, who served St. Bernardine from 1967 to 1970.

Edward Edwards was born to a West Indian family living near the Panama Canal the same year that St. Bernardine opened. Baptized as an infant in Panama in 1954 he landed in Baltimore, where his wife had family.

He has been a member of St. Bernardine since 1965 and was in the middle of the parish's somewhat abrupt transition from a white church to a black one during the tenure of Cardinal Lawrence Shehan,

"It was an old church and a lot of parishioners felt that blacks just weren't part of the tradition. But we couldn't stay away. The church was part of where we lived. I was determined that it would not make me not be a part of the parish."

This is what Msgr. Cronin inherited from his predecessor, the Rev. Louis Vaeth. A year later, riots following the assassination of the Rev. Martin Luther King, Jr. hit Baltimore.

"We stood on top of the school and could see the fires burning downtown," remembers Msgr. Cronin. "On the day of King's funeral there was a tremendous amount of looting in the area. After the funeral it was calm."

And the white families began leaving in droves, leaving their homes, their memories and, says Edwards, "St. Bernardine's too...

"We tried to establish awareness that St. Bernardine's was a warm community where everyone was welcome," says Msgr. Cronin, who marched in anti-blockbusting protests. "We made the liturgy more African-American and I hired a black cantor. Our vacation Bible school was intense, two months instead of just a couple of weeks. We brought in black leaders to help."

Through Msgr. Cronin, Eddie Edwards became an usher, made friends with an out-going white usher named Dan Heisey-- who made black families feel welcome-- and, with other African-Americans, joined the St. Bernardine's men's group.

"I believe I did all this through the spiritual guidance of Father Jim," said Edwards.

And then there was the White Coffee Pot story.

Edwards was making straws and cups at the Maryland Cup Corp. and, he "wasn't too fascinated with it."

Msgr. Cronin asked: "How would you like to go into another profession?" With a good word from the pastor, Ed Edwards got a job managing a family restaurant on Security Boulevard. After a year or so there, he joined up with Alan Katz, who'd launched the White Coffee Pot, Jr. chain in Baltimore, and liked it enough to leave the Maryland Cup Co.

"I wound up managing White Coffee Pots all over the city and it gave me a wonderful sense of a better future and I was always thankful to Father Jim [for the advice]. He was a priest in the true sense of the word."

Mr. Edwards stayed with the chain--which had locations in Randallstown and the corner of Erdman Avenue and Belair Road among others--until they closed their last store about twenty years ago.

He is also grateful for the chance that Cronin gave his oldest daughter, Gloria, to play the organ at church.

"Two of my children went to St. Bernadine's school, but we couldn't afford tuition for all six to go," comments Mr. Edwards. "My children are not as active Catholics as I hoped they would be. But it was important to raise them Catholic."

Most of all, Mr. Edwards is thankful for the work Msgr. Cronin did to remove the stones from the path of black Catholics making their way to worship at St. Bernardine.

"That's all part of my daily work," said Msgr. Cronin. "I'd rather work with people than plans and programs."

FR. EDWARD MILLER

As a child, the young Ed Miller attended his neighborhood parish, St. Joseph's Monastery in Irvington. When his family moved, he joined St. Ursula, graduating from the eighth grade there.

Father Miller studied at St. Charles Seminary in Catonsville for high school and the first two years of college. His last two years of college were at St. Mary's Seminary on Paca Street before studying theology at St. Mary's Seminary in Roland Park.

Says Father Miller of his long career as a white priest in a black congregation: "The Catholic Church has always tried to be a good neighbor. Though it had its faults-- such as the presence of racism-- it was also involved in the overall civil rights efforts in Baltimore [including] marches to desegregate the old Carlins Amusement Park and forbidding Catholic Schools to have their picnics there until blacks were admitted."

"Father Miller came to us determined that he was going to make St. Bernadine's the kind of church that it should be," notes Eddie Edwards. "And his sermons deal with what needs to be dealt with. He doesn't bite his tongue."

All are welcome at St. Bernardine and quite a few white families return now and again, especially for the annual "homecoming" Mass instituted by Fr. Miller.

Father Miller's predecessor, Msgr. Jim Cronin, calls him "one of the most beloved pastors in the Archdiocese.

"Ed Miller is the reason St. Bernardine's is what it is today... he's a white man with soul..."

183

HOLY FAMILY / DAVIDSONVILLE

Holy Family Church, in Davidsonville near Annapolis, began as a Marianist seminary in 1929 and celebrated its seventy-fifth anniversary in 2004 with a "the way things used to be" picnic. Ice cream sold for a nickel, old jalopies cruised the fairground; and some five hundred people turned out to celebrate the parish.

Holy Family is devoted to its sister church – St. Gregory the Great in Baltimore City. Each Christmas, the parish adopts more than one hundred St. Gregory families and provides holiday dinners with all the trimmings as well as toys and other goodies and staples.

Among its many activities is Lazarus Committee, formed to provide post-funeral fellowship and food for mourners.

The pastor is Rev. Joseph Barr.

FATHER JOE BARR

Joseph Barr was a young man with long hair and a beard in the hippie days of the Nixon Administration. He attended Hagerstown Community College, worked in the school library, and wrote for the school paper.

At the time, inmates from the state prison in Hagerstown were allowed to take courses at the college a year or two before their release. Through this program, Joe Barr became friends with the prison chaplain, the Rev. Kloman Riggie.

"He was the one who inspired me, by his ministry, to think of the priesthood instead of teaching," said Fr. Barr. "When I confided in him my aspiration to study for the priesthood I also revealed my fear. He convinced me that it was better to 'try' and 'leave' than to never have tried at all."

Father Barr received his degree in sacred theology from the Gregorian University in Rome and was ordained at St. Mary's in Hagerstown. He celebrated his first public Mass at Ss. Philip & James in Baltimore City, where he had served as a transitional deacon.

"Early that morning, Fr. Riggie arranged for me to have the Sunday Mass at Maryland Correctional Training Center," said Father Barr.

"When I complained about how early in the morning we had to be there he merely said, 'we have many security procedures to do.'

"After going through security and setting up for the Mass, Fr. Riggie said: 'Whoever has Mass hears confessions first. Here is your stole. There is the confessional.'

"I am forever grateful to that faithful priest. Fr. Riggie changed my life."

In 1939, the Archdiocese of Baltimore lost the territory that had launched the Maryland colony as a Catholic settlement with the landing of the *Ark and the Dove*.

The Archdiocese of Washington was created by Pope Pius XII to include historic St. Mary's County and St. Clement's Island as well as the rest of Southern Maryland that year, and in all, the Archdiocese consists of the District of Columbia, Calvert, Charles, Montgomery, Prince George's, and St. Mary's Counties.

In deference to Archbishop Curley, the Episcopal seat was left vacant and he served as administrator of the new archdiocese until his death in 1947, when Archbishop Patrick A. O'Boyle was named the first resident archbishop for Washington. He immediately began to desegregate Catholic schools and parishes, build new churches, and establish social service ministries. He was elevated to Cardinal in 1967 and retired in 1973.

In 1980, James A. Hickey, a native of Michigan, was appointed Archbishop of Washington. A champion of Catholic education and service to the poor, he was elevated to the College of Cardinals in 1988.

During Cardinal Hickey's tenure, the Archdiocese grew in diversity, with Mass celebrated in 25 languages, including Chinese, French, Korean, Polish, Portuguese, and Vietnamese.

ST. URSULA / PRIDE OF PARKVILLE

*"St. Ursula's had a parishioner who was a dentist who would come in and work
on the kids' teeth for free because a lot of families couldn't afford it.
My mother Bess and another woman assisted him.
The priests weren't concerned about how much money you put in the plate
but how you could assist the church. There were a lot of Italian
and German craftsmen in the parish and they donated a lot of their time and talent.
In our family it was required to help the church..."*

Tom Kilchenstein, baptized at St. Ursula in 1940

Bishop W. Francis Malooly, Vicar General and Western Vicar for 38 parishes and six missions between Howard and Garrett counties, was born in Parkville in 1944 and grew up in the St. Ursula Parish.

There, he was taught by the Sisters of Notre Dame de Namur, whose example influenced an early call to the priesthood.

"No one ever asked me about becoming a priest [but] the nuns, the school, and the great priests who were there--Fathers James Cronin and Tim Byrd--appeared to enjoy what they did," said Bishop Malooly. "That influenced my decision."

In 1970, Bishop Malooly was ordained a priest of the Archdiocese of Baltimore by his uncle, the late Bishop T. Austin Murphy. Before joining Cardinal Keeler's staff, Bishop Malooly's assignments included service at St. Joseph, Cockeysville; St. Anthony of Padua and the Monsignor O'Dwyer Retreat House in Sparks.

Bishop Malooly is impressed by the seriousness that young people in the 21st-century are bringing to their faith and predicts that religion will have a greater impact on American society in the future than today.

In 2005, St. Ursula counted more than 3,400 parishioners under the guidance of the Rev. Msgr. Thomas Baumgartner. As the church expands, so the pastor seeks to enlarge parish outreach.

Putting together a list of greeters to welcome newcomers to the church-- be they there for Mass or a wedding-- is something on Msgr. Baumgartner's to-do list.

"When people come to St. Ursula, they will know that it is a warm and friendly and welcoming church," he said.

St. Ursula began during the Great Depression as an overture to Catholics beyond the northeast city line who were tired of taking a trolley to St. Dominic in Hamilton that was said to lurch and sway like a camel. But to miss it would mean a long wait in fickle weather for the next one headed north to Parkville.

After giving the last blessing of Mass at St. Dominic, Father Manley would tell the Parkville contingent to make a run for the trolley stop, lest they miss it.

ST. URSULA / PARKVILLE

Formally established in 1937, St. Ursula began as a mission of St. Dominic in 1933. True to Archbishop Curley's edict, the school was built first, with Mass held in the basement until the present church came about in the early 1950s.

In the Summer of 1937, St. Dominic's pastor, the fabled Fr. John J. Manley, told the St. Ursula faithful: "Your new pastor will be with you next Sunday. You will like him... St. Dominic parish will watch with interest and affection, your growth as the most promising of the younger parishes..."

ST. URSULA MURAL

A panel from a disassembled Spanish altar in the Palencia region of northwest Spain shows St. Ursula being martyred by the King of the Huns. The most common legend surrounding the 4th-century saint from Cologne has the young virgin stalling the son of a pagan king for three years when he sought to take her as a bride.

She was then given ten young women of noble birth for companionship, and a thousand virgins accompanied each of the eleven as they sailed the seas. Finally returning to Cologne, they were riddled with arrows by armies faithful to the King of the Huns out of hatred for their Christian faith.

The killers are said to have been dispersed by angels. Ursula and her fellow martyrs were buried by the locals and a church built in their honor by a man of high-standing named Clematius.

According to the Catholic Encyclopedia, "This legend, with its countless variants and increasingly fabulous developments, would fill more than a hundred pages."

A more likely legend holds that Father Manley named the parish for his sister.

Land for the St. Ursula mission church was purchased by Father Manley the week of Valentine's Day in 1926; $6,500 worth of property owned by Abraham Niefeld on the west side of Harford Road near Mann Avenue.

Father John J. Russell, later a bishop of Richmond, Va., was named first pastor when St. Ursula became an independent parish.

Eager to make their new church a success, some 700 original parishioners went to work enlarging the existing hall to make room for crowds that showed up for bingo parties and chicken suppers.

At the beginning of the 1940 school year, 145 pupils attended the new school under the tutelage of the Sisters of Notre Dame de Namur. The sisters commuted from Ilchester until a convent was built the following year.

On All Saints Day 1954 the new church was dedicated by Archbishop Keough to accommodate a parish community closing in on 4,000 members. Thirteen years later, with plans for a new auditorium under way, Monsignor Sweeney succumbed to chronic heart problems. He had served St. Ursula for 22 years.

Cardinal Lawrence Shehan named the Rev. Myles McGowan, then pastor of St. Louis Church in Clarksville to take over a church that was now one of the largest in the archdiocese with 10,000 parishioners.

SR. JOAN
Photo credit: Kirsten Beckerman
Sr. Joan Kelly, S.N.D.,
with students at St. Ursula in 2002.
The school has a waiting list for enrollment.

By the summer of 1967, the parish had grown so large that it bought a dozen acres on Old Harford Road north of Joppa Road for an expansion mission. It would become St. Isaac Jogues.

In 1987, Monsignor McGowan retired as pastor of St. Ursula with the title pastor emeritus. At age 92 in 2005, he was still going strong at his residence at Mercy Ridge.

Monsignor Baumgartner became pastor the following year and remains in charge of a flock devoted to bereavement support, an AIDS ministry, Meals on Wheels and a project in which the elderly are picked up at their homes and driven to Mass.

One of Msgr. Baumgartner's major themes is the difference an individual can make in a world that can appear unmovable.

"People will learn how to change the world and bring about the kind of change that Jesus spoke about in his message by embracing discipleship," he said.

Photo credit: Mark Champion

Like many Catholics, whether they continue to practice the faith or not, Tom Kilchenstein's childhood is inextricably linked to the parish where he grew up.

His great-grandfather, John Adam Kilchenstein, started a general store called Parkville Supply and was deeply involved with the St. Dominic parish.

"I worked the store when I was a kid, I delivered groceries," said Tom, recalling days of building soap box derby racers. "And I remember when they laid the cornerstone for St. Ursula's in the early Fifties and it was an empty field. "I have pictures of the field and Fr. [William] Sweeney standing nearby with the holy water bucket."

As a boy, Sundays would begin early and last long for Tom, beginning with serving 6 a.m. Mass at St. Ursula.

"Then I'd go home and get my blind grandmother [Regina Jones] so she could play the organ at St. John's Lutheran across the street from St. Ursula. I'd sit through that service, bring Grandmom home and then we all got together to go to noon Mass at St. Ursula's as a family."

Though his father's side of the family has been involved with Catholic life in Baltimore for generations, Tom Kilchenstein's mother was the first Catholic in her family, converting to the faith and marrying his Dad at St. Dominic.

Late in her life, said Tom Kilchenstein, his Mom made a pilgrimage to Fatima and returned with a surplus of inexpensive rosaries blessed by the Pope.

"If anyone did a favor for her, she gave them a rosary," he said. "It was a big deal to get one of Bess's rosaries."

Today, Spanish-language Masses are celebrated at more than two dozen churches for the nearly quarter-of-a-million Hispanics living within its boundaries. Some additional 80,000 Catholics of African and Caribbean descent also belong to parishes there.

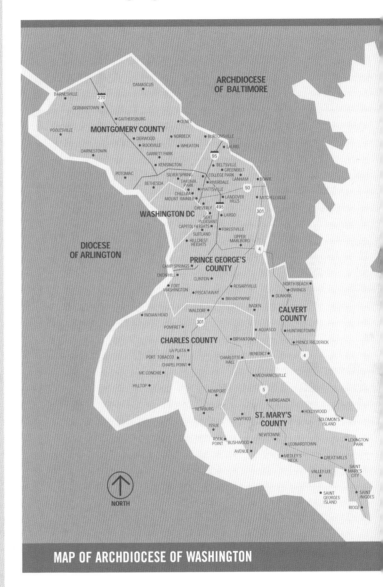

MAP OF ARCHDIOCESE OF WASHINGTON

Cardinal Theodore E. McCarrick was installed to lead the Archdiocese of Washington in January of 2001. A month later, he was made a cardinal. Cardinal McCarrick oversaw an area that is home to more than a half million Catholics as well as 115 schools in which more than 33,000 children are enrolled. In May of 2006, Cardinal McCarrick's resignation was accepted by Pope Benedict XVI and Donald W. Wuerl, Bishop of Pittsburgh, was installed as the sixth Archbishop of Washington on June 22.

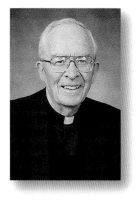

MSGR. MYLES MCGOWAN

Photo credit: Rosalia Scalia

Msgr. Myles Joseph McGowan, born in April of 1913 and believed to be the oldest priest in the Archdiocese of Baltimore, was recruited for the job while still in the seminary by a fellow Irishman, Archbishop Michael Curley.

Msgr. McGowan arrived in Baltimore from Ireland in 1939 after two years as a parish priest in Limerick. "When Archbishop Curley asked me if I wanted to come to Baltimore, I said 'yes'-- not knowing where it was even," he recalled from his former residence at Stella Maris.

Msgr. McGowan landed at St. Gregory the Great, where he spent many years. Of what he has seen come to pass in seven decades as a cleric, he said: "The changes have all been minor things. The important stuff is that [we are] the same Church Jesus Christ left us 2,000 years ago, the same faith."

That Archbishop Michael Curley would go toe-to-toe with anyone to defend himself and his convictions was well established before he landed in Baltimore. According to Father Roach, the Florida legislature passed a law during the time then-Bishop Curley resided there making it illegal for white people to teach in black schools. The move was widely viewed as an attack on the faith, since Catholic nuns were the only whites teaching what were then called "colored" schools.

Bishop Curley refused to remove the nuns or close the schools, forcing Florida officials into the embarrassing position of arresting religious women in order to uphold the law. Before the nuns were forcibly removed, police appealed to Archbishop Curley to make the nuns stop their work.

He is said to have replied: "Gentlemen, the law orders the arrest of these Sisters. It is your duty to carry out the mandate which your superiors have given you. The Sisters are in the school. They are teaching. No orders will be sent by me to stop them. The only way for you or the State to stop them is to arrest them... do your duty."

After the arrests, the nuns were released to their pastor, beginning a long and expensive legal battle which ultimately found the law unconstitutional. When letters of congra-tulations and admiration poured into Bishop Curley's office, he asked each person who took the time to applaud to contribute a dollar to help defray the cost of fighting the case.

Such is the bulwark faced by the Sun-papers editors in 1934 when they published a dispatch from an overseas stringer comparing Adolf Hitler to St. Ignatius Loyola. Before the fracas had been sorted out-- more or less behind the back of Archbishop Curley, who undoubtedly would have fought longer-- Baltimore Catholics were boycotting the paper and H.L. Mencken sailed into the fray.

In a history of *The Baltimore Sun* published on the paper's 150th anniversary in 1987, longtime editor Harold A. Williams noted a June 18, 1934 dispatch by S. Miles Bouton. A non-staff overseas stringer, Mr. Bouton had recently been expelled from Germany for stories the Third Reich found offensive.

Describing Der Fuehrer in the article that would incense Baltimoreans, Mr. Bouton wrote : "It has seemed to me at times that there is a kinship between him and Ignatius Loyola... one finds in both men the same complete faith in their missions, the same readiness and determination to exercise their power with utter ruthlessness and brutality to carry out that mission."

Holy Mackerel!

Irate letters began pouring in from Jesuits and lay people and plenty of others in between. *Sun* publisher Harry C. Black apolo-gized in a personal letter to the rector of Loyola College, Fr. Henri J. Wiesel, S.J., and Archbishop Curley was asked by the newspaper's management to smooth things over with the Catholic community.

Bad move.

Archbishop Curley, who had feuded with the *Sun* in the past, demanded a "complete" apology in print, not a small, standard cor-rection box on the inside of the front page. A week after the Mr. Bouton piece appeared, the Baltimore Catholic Review printed an open letter from Archbishop Curley on its front-page. In it, the archbishop denounced the column as "a gratuitous insult, not only to the Jesuit fathers... but also to every Catholic priest and every Catholic lay member..."

"We ask no favors of the *Sun*," he continued. "We demand justice. The organized Catholics of the archdiocese know exactly how to act."

The *Sun* balked and Archbishop Curley called for a boycott, making the appeal to the "Knights of Columbus... our organized groups of women, to our 80,000 Holy Name men of the Archdiocese, to our Polish, Bohemian, Lithuanian, and Italian organizations to tell *The Sun*, not by words, but by deeds that they resent the insult..."

Several thousand Catholics stopped buying the paper, and some advertising was lost, with the Baltimore Catholic Review saying the boycott also had the support of large numbers of Protestants and Jews.

The Baltimore Catholic Review kept up the attack, declaring in a series of front page notices that the memory of Cardinal Gibbons had been insulted and it was just as easy for Baltimoreans to have a Washington paper delivered as *The Sun*.

A break came when Archbishop Curley sailed for Ireland to visit his mother. Seeing an opening, The Sun scheduled a lunch with Bishop John M. McNamara, whom Archbishop Curley had appointed to keep up the fight. Present were H.L. Mencken, publisher Patterson, and editorial writer John W. Owens.

Mr. Mencken allowed how it would be impossible for *The Sun* to present its own case fairly while written in language that any priest of the Archdiocese could formally approve before publication. According to the Williams' book, Bishop McNamara suggested that *The Sun* make the most conciliatory statement possible and see what happens.

On July 19, 1934, *The Sun* released--but did not print itself-- a statement acknowledging that the words "ruthless" and "brutality" in the Bouton article "were badly chosen and are not in accord with the prevailing historical opinion."

Crafted by Mr. Owens, the statement blamed the error on a mid-level newsroom editor. The Catholic Review ran the statement on its front page with the headline: THE SUN APOLOGIZES.

Not quite. The newspaper explained, assigned blame, and expressed regret, but technically did not apologize. It would not be the last movement in *The Sun's* cautious dance with the hard-nosed archbishop.

For example, the paper inadvertently changed the archbishop's heritage from Irish to Polish. As grandly told by Father Roach, the slip occurred when Baltimore's large population of Polish Catholics held a convention and invited Archbishop Curley to be the guest of honor. *The Sun's* coverage of the event included a photo of the archbishop with a Polish dignitary. The picture's caption was not wide enough to include both names in one line and Archbishop Curley's name, along with the end of the Pole's last name, bumped down a line.

Thus, as can only happen in the daily miracle known as putting out a newspaper, the proud Irish cleric was identified as... Archbishop Michael J. Curleyiski!

All editions, including every copy from the presses, the mail room and the newsroom, were ordered destroyed in the fear that some wisenheimer might make a gift of one to the archbishop.

BLESSING CATHOLIC HIGH
Archbishop Curley blessing the cornerstone of The Catholic High School of Baltimore on Erdman Avenue in 1939.
Back then, the former Jean McGrail-- who grew up to be Sister Margaret Aloysius-- was one of the first young women enrolled at the school and part of the first graduating class in 1943.
Now 80, she has strong memories of visits from Archbishop Curley.
"He was a humble man... something about him was similar" to Pope John Paul II, said Sister Margaret, a Franciscan nursing administrator who volunteers daily at St. Francis Hospital in Wilmington, Delaware. "He made you feel special whenever he spoke to you."

First &
Forever
THE ARCHDIOCESE OF BALTIMORE

Connie Fay Stevenson was part of the Catholic High class of 1944. The big war was on, and she remembers gasoline rationing forcing the girls to walk to the prom in long gowns up Erdman Avenue.

A varsity basketball player, Stevenson remembered a ditty that girls from rival schools--usually the longer-established Seton--used to taunt Catholic High girls.

"I'm a raindrop, I'm a raindrop, I'm a raindrop from the sky/I'd rather be a raindrop than a drip from Catholic High..."

The friendships that Connie Stevenson made at Catholic High continue to sustain her. The Lunch Bunch, a group who met as teenagers, continues to meet together once a month some 60 years after leaving high school for the wider world. Now 78, Connie remains active at her beloved alma mater, planning reunions and other events.

Her daughter Fay graduated from

Catholic High in 1975, back in the last gasps of the mini-skirt. Fay remembers the nuns standing at the front door with a ruler to measure the distance between a student's knees and the hem of her skirt.

If it didn't measure up, the hem came down.

It is widely held that Archbishop Curley's most outstanding virtue was the way in which, despite his high station, he embraced the spirit of poverty.

According to Father Roach, Archbishop Curley kept his distance from the wealthy, making a point not to officiate at their weddings or permit them to maintain private chapels.

Father Roach tells the story of a reception that was held for Archbishop Curley soon after he arrived to be the new archbishop of Baltimore. At the affair, several women of aristocratic standing approached him and one

ST. VERONICA / CHERRY HILL

In 1945 the Josephite Fathers established St. Veronica in Cherry Hill near the line separating Baltimore City and Anne Arundel County to serve African-Americans returning from World War II and their families. Many of the church's founders, well into their golden years, continue to participate in church activities, including retired Deacon Willard Pinky, now 90. The parish population runs to about 230 families. Historically a poor parish, St. Veronica has never been able to launch a school. However, since 1969, the year man first walked on the moon, it has operated the largest Head Start program on the east coast. A parish thrift store operates six days a week. Those who can afford to pay give what they can and those who cannot are encouraged to take what they need.
Members of St. Veronica regularly bring the Eucharist to more than a dozen homebound parishioners and, once a month, Sunday Mass is celebrated with choreographed dances based on Scripture. The pastor is the Rev. Augustine Inwang, M.S.P.

ST. JANE FRANCES DE CHANTAL

Lori Pelesky is a lifelong member and, for the past decade, parish secretary at St. Jane Frances. "I enjoy working with everyone," she said.

In addition to numerous outreach activities in keeping with a parish their size, Ms. Pelesky said evangelization is a priority of the community.

To that end, the church's Disciples in Mission program helps guide parishioners through renewals of their interior faith as well as outreach to others in a way designed to transform society into a better place.

Before Lent, Ms. Pelesky said, the parish mounts a prayer campaign and training for leaders of small prayer groups. During Lent and the Passion season, faith sharing groups meet, during which there is time for individual reflection, and family activities.

There is also a Pentecost Novena and a parish reflection day in addition to bereavement support, a social justice committee and regular meetings of Alcoholics Anonymous and Al-Anon in addition to other church activities and athletics.

St. Jane Frances de Chantal [1572-1641] was the wife of the Baron de Chantal, who, in the early 17th century, was killed in a hunting accident. A widow at 28 with four children to care for, she took a vow of chastity as a way of protecting her children's property.

Once the future of her children was secured, she founded – along with St. Francis de Sales - the Congregation. The order labored to nurture the spiritual development of young women, widows, and others who may have lacked such desire on their own.

ST. JANE FRANCES DE CHANTAL / PASADENA

There are nearly 2,800 families belonging to St. Jane Frances de Chantal parish in the Riviera Beach area of Anne Arundel County. Founded about 1924, the parish started out celebrating Mass in a basement near the intersection of Old Annapolis Road and what later became Ritchie Highway.

During the summer of 1925, Mass was offered al fresco on a grassy lot near Riviera Drive and Church Road. It would not be so for long, as Anne Arundel County began to swell with transplants from South Baltimore and other city neighborhoods looking for a more pastoral life in the suburbs.

By 1946 there were 722 families and the beginnings of a parish school.

Twenty years later, that number had more than quadrupled.

of them said: "I hope you will find time to visit us at our country estate like Cardinal Gibbons did." They were greeted with the now legendary reply: "Ladies, I have not come to Baltimore to be the bishop for the Catholic rich.'"

Accordingly, his empathy for the poor--immigrant, African-American, and other--was deep and genuine. He encouraged ethnic Catholics to hang on to their language and native traditions, and he quietly pushed pastors to welcome blacks into otherwise all-white churches.

"Pay no heed to the calamity [and] howl that would inevitably follow a black man's receiving Communion in his church," he is quoted as saying. Treat them, he said, with "the kindness and gentleness of Christ."

Profound, but not especially politic in the Maryland of the mid-twentieth century, a state which witnessed its last known lynching in the Eastern Shore town of Princess Anne in 1933.

Taken with Archbishop Curley's other strong and not especially diplomatic traits, it made for a man never fully accepted by the Catholics whom he was assigned to lead. "He was an intelligent man with a tendency to be abrupt," said Monsignor McGowan, "but he was extremely gentle at other times."

To Archbishop Curley's dying day, despite leaving the Archdiocese stronger than he found it, the man from the Emerald Isle labored in the shadow of his mythic predecessor.

■ ■ ■

In 1946, parochial school kids in Baltimore and the rest of the country began receiving a treat in class when a Catholic comic book called *The Treasure Chest of Fun & Fact* began publication.

■ ■ ■

Archbishop Michael J. Curley died on May 16, 1947.

By that time, he'd given away everything he owned, almost all of it to poor parishes, except a single suit of clothes.

"They even had to go to Washington to get the special Sacramentary for bishops when he died," said Father Roach. "He'd given his away a few weeks earlier to a bishop from a poor missionary diocese."

[A Sacramentary is the book used by the priest at the altar for the prayers of the Mass. Its name comes from the fact that all of its contents center on the consecration of the Eucharist. First written by Pope St. Gelasius I in the 5th Century, it was revised and shortened by St. Gregory the Great, who followed Gelasius as pope about a hundred years later.]

FUNERAL OF ARCHBISHOP MICHAEL CURLEY

"If you're going to be honest, you can't paint Archbishop Curley as any kind of plaster saint," notes Father Roach. "He was too blunt and too much of a fighter to ever be canonized."

Indeed, he wasn't all that interested in being made a cardinal; according to Monsignor McGowan.

"He wasn't the kind of guy who cared."

CURLEY BOOK & COIN, ETC.
Photo credit: Ed Fishel
Archbishop Curley was welcomed to Baltimore with a dinner given
in his honor at the Belvedere Hotel on Dec. 13, 1921. Speakers included Maryland
Governor Albert C. Ritchie and Baltimore Mayor William F. Broening.
The reception was hosted by the Knights of Columbus, which made a gift to
Archbishop Curley of the medallion pictured with the program for the event.
The large black book in the photograph was produced by the Catholic Review,
published on the occasion of the Silver Sacerdotal Jubilee of His Grace.
It is titled *"Life of Archbishop Curley: Champion of Catholic Education."*
by Vincent de Paul Fitzpatrick.

Archbishop Francis Patrick Keough

FRANCIS P. KEOUGH

Francis Keough was not yet in grade school when he lost his father, his care falling to his mother, an older brother and a collection of friends and neighbors in working class New Britain, Conn., where he was born on Dec. 30, 1890.

Not unlike the grocer who influenced the young Cardinal Gibbons, a local businessman named Samuel Greenberg had great influence on the boy. Mr. Greenberg, however, saw a future in the Church for young Keough, not in commerce. He encouraged the altar boy to enter the seminary and while studying for the priesthood at St. Thomas in Bloomfield, Conn., young Francis Keough worked as a delivery boy, store clerk, and newsboy.

He also played for the seminary baseball team and was lauded by a coach who said: "When Frank Keough was in center field I had little worry about what would happen in right or left... the outfield seemed safe in his keeping."

In 1911, he sailed to France to enroll in the Sulpician seminary in Issy. When World War I erupted, he returned home to continue his studies at St. Bernard's Seminary in Rochester, N.Y.

Ordained at the Cathedral of St. Joseph in Hartford, Conn. on June 10, 1916, then-Father Keough was soon appointed assistant Chancellor for the Archdiocese of Hartford. In 1934 he became the fourth bishop of Providence, R.I.

Great changes swept over the United States and its old, colonial-era cities like Baltimore during the tenure of Archbishop Keough.

From his appointment as Archbishop of Baltimore in 1947 through his death in 1961, the country experienced years of post-war, middle-class prosperity that fueled the creation of "the suburbs" and a great exodus toward them.

In the years before the New Frontier of the Kennedy Administration, thousands of Catholic families and their Jewish and Protestant counterparts left their row house neighborhoods in Crab Town for the promise of a better life in a "single home" and a lawn to mow either on or beyond the city line.

From 1950 through 1960, the number of parishioners at St. Anthony of Padua in Gardenville soared from 3,100 to more than 12,000. Other booming parishes included Holy Trinity in Glen Burnie, St. Michael's in Overlea, Immaculate Conception in Towson, and St. Agnes in Catonsville.

ARCHBISHOP FRANCIS P. KEOUGH

The 11th Archbishop of Baltimore, Francis P. Keough served the *Premier See* from 1947 to 1961.

Archbishop Francis P. Keough arrived in Baltimore to take over the Archdiocese in 1947 following the death of Archbishop Curley. He was formally installed as the 11th archbishop of Baltimore in the Basilica of the Assumption on February 24, 1948.

During that time, according to Church records, the Catholic population of the Archdiocese grew to more than 403,000 people, an increase of fifty-two percent.

According to Cardinal Keeler, "He instituted the first big capital drives in the Archdiocese to [support] high schools and charitable institutions. He was our first modern fundraiser."

Archbishop Keough had a favorite story, one he told often, of a little girl with remarkable faith. The child had contracted a disease that nearly always proved fatal. Though an operation offered promise, hope was slim.

When the surgeon came to say that he needed to put her to sleep before he could operate, the girl said she had to say her prayers first, as she always did before bed.

She knelt, clasped her hands together and recited her prayers with the fervor of a believer. The operation failed and the girl died within hours.

The experience, however, left the doctor a changed man.

Although raised a Catholic, he'd not practiced his faith for 30 years. From that day on, the good doctor returned, said Archbishop Keough, "to the ways of grace."

ST. AGNES / CATONSVILLE

There were no Catholic churches in the area formerly known as Johnnycake in the early nineteenth century and the faithful would commute from there to Ellicott City or the City of Baltimore to attend Mass.

In 1852, a small group of Catholic laborers-- railroad men, ship builders and farmers among others-- began raising money for a church. It would be erected on an acre of land given to the Archdiocese for a dollar by a physician named Piggot.

The cornerstone of St. Agnes was laid in 1852 and the church was dedicated a year later. Today, with 1,420 families, St. Agnes anchors a number of outreach programs in the Catonsville area.

Programs range from a Mother's Day flower sale to benefit a pregnancy center to a Lenten "Soup & Stations" in which the faithful share a meal before reading the Stations of the Cross each Friday in Lent. Like virtually every parish within driving distance of downtown Baltimore, church volunteers make casseroles for Our Daily Bread.

The pastor is Father Carl Cummings.

HELEN DEGENHARD & FAMILY

Helen Degenhard, shown here with her husband Richard, and brother, the Rev. John J. Nissel, S.J.
"I love St. Agnes," said Mrs. Degenhard.
"I really feel it's the kind of place where one's faith grows..."
During Easter week of 2005-- and throughout the rest of the liturgical year--
St. Agnes welcomes the faithful to pray the Stations of the Cross.
Parish secretary Mary Kay Barrick gives some of the credit for increased attendance to the "soup
and stations" project. Each Friday at 6 p.m., upward of 150 people gather for soup and pizza
followed by meditation on the Passion of Our Lord.

Helen Degenhard joined St. Agnes as a 4ᵗʰ grader. Now 76-years-old, she has been a part of the church through virtually all of the major changes there.

Mrs. Degenhard landed in the St. Agnes parish as a youngster when her family moved to the area, on the edge of Kernan Hospital, from St. Benedict's on Wilkens Avenue.

"Out of the roots of that small school, a poor country school where Father Ignatius Fealy collected dimes and quarters for tuition, emerged a lot of leaders," said Mrs. Degenhard.

Two of those leaders were her brothers: Father John Joseph Nissel, SJ, and the Honorable J. Thomas Nissel, a retired Howard County Circuit Court judge who graduated from Loyola College in 1952.

"Back then we attended Mass at St. Lawrence [a mission of St. Agnes] in a hay barn on the hospital grounds," said Mrs. Degenhard, a graduate of Seton High

School. "The altar boys--including my two brothers-- would go outside and fill the water cruets from the spring outside."

While working for the old C & P Telephone Co. and taking night classes at Loyola College-- all the while living with her parents until she was 36-- Helen met Richard Degenhard.

"We were on a Catholic Student Mission Crusade Cruise that went from the harbor out to Fort McHenry" and were married a year later. The Degenhards still live in the house on Charing Cross where they settled after saying "I do" at St. Lawrence. Their children were raised in the St. Agnes parish, where Helen and Richard serve as Eucharistic Ministers and visit the elderly in nursing homes and shut-ins.

"Being active in the church has allowed us to see how God works through people and all the work being done to achieve the Kingdom of God," she said. "It allows us to contribute to that work in small ways."

■ ■ ■

As the suburbs boomed, families who once lived across the alley from one another in the old neighborhood now found themselves on opposite sides of a cul-de-sac. Today, the descendents of families who worshipped together at Our Lady of Pompei or Sacred Heart of Jesus in Highlandtown see one another at St. Margaret's in Bel Air.

■ ■ ■

In 1948, Baltimore saw the first protests over segregated tennis courts in Druid Hill Park, and an executive order by President Harry Truman ended segregation in the Armed Forces. It was also the year that Most Precious Blood parish was established on Bowley's Lane near Moravia Road and what would soon become the Harbor Tunnel Thruway.

Two parishes created at the beginning of Archbishop Keough's service-- St. Matthew's on Loch Raven Boulevard in 1948 and Immaculate Heart of Mary near Towson the following year-- now boast 800 and 2,800 families respectively.

MOST PRECIOUS BLOOD / ARMSTEAD GARDENS

Most Precious Blood was founded in 1948 at 5010 Bowley's Lane and began ministering to families who worked in the World War II defense industry. The multi-purpose building was dedicated in 1960. The first level includes office space, meeting rooms, and a space for worship. The Herring Run Head Start program is on the second level. In 1995, it was twinned with St. Anthony of Padua parish on Frankford Avenue.

IHM / BAYNESVILLE

Immaculate Heart of Mary was established on the eastern edge of Towson in 1948 on six acres of land donated by the Guidera family. It lists some 2,800 families with a parochial school population of about 600 students. Religious education for non-IHM school students serves another 200 or so children, and other ministries serve people of all ages. Immaculate Heart of Mary has a prayer chain for special intentions, a Respect Life committee and a thriving sports program, particularly in soccer. The pastor is Father Michael W. Carrion.

FATHER MUTH & MARY JANE VAETH
"Our 11 a.m. Mass is packed every Sunday," said longtime St. Matthew's parishioner Mary Jane Vaeth, shown here with pastor, Father Joseph Muth. "Father Joe goes out on a limb for people and they reach out to him because of it."
Mrs. Vaeth, a 1944 graduate of The Catholic High School, grew up in the St. Bernard's parish in Waverly and educated all of her children at St. Matthew's. Some of them were married there.
It nettled Mrs. Vaeth when the neighborhoods around St. Matthew's became integrated and she saw white neighbors-- many of them Catholic-- move away.
"I felt," she said, "that they were not acting very Christian."

ST. MATTHEW / NORTHWOOD

The corner of Loch Raven Boulevard and Woodbourne Avenue was thick woods in 1949 when Archbishop Keough authorized Father Charles H. Yingling to launch a new parish there. A house at 4800 Loch Raven Boulevard served as a temporary rectory for a parish that already had a population of 4,000. The St. Matthew parish school opened in 1951 with 571 children and a permanent rectory was built in 1958.
Only then did plans for a sanctuary envisioned by Father Yingling in 1949 begin to take shape.
St. Matthew's dedicated its current church building in 1964. Two years later, in the thick of the civil rights movement championed in Baltimore by Cardinal Shehan, it was among the first Baltimore churches to form a social action committee.
Today, the church has a vibrant outreach to immigrants and has formed a board to aid new arrivals to the United States. Parishioners hold blood drives, comfort the bereaved and staff a trauma committee.

ABP. KEOUGH AT STELLA MARIS GROUNDBREAKING

The Stella Maris project began when the Cathedral
Foundation, founded by Archbishop Curley in 1936
as an educational non-profit body, donated 116 acres
of land near Pot Spring Road to Archbishop Keough.
The archbishop-- seeking a retirement home for
Baltimore area Catholics-- broke ground for
Stella Maris in 1950. The facility opened three years
later under the aegis of the Sisters of Mercy.
It focuses on the comprehensive health and housing
needs of the elderly, the sick, the injured, and the dying.
George H. Schott, a retired barber, arrived shortly
after Stella Maris opened.
"The priest, the doctor, the sisters were ready
to come at any hour. Daily Mass is only one floor away,"
said Mr. Schott. "Who could ask for more?"

IDELLA NICHOLS
Idella Nichols, a retired educator
and school librarian, has lived at Stella Maris
for a decade. The 85-year-old has made a world
of new friends there while staying in touch
with loved ones from her former life.
"My favorite game is the crossword puzzle,"
Mrs. Nichols said. "They put a huge crossword
puzzle on a blackboard and then the moderator
calls on all of us who think we know the answers."
She is also grateful for the weekly visitor
who helps her write letters to friends.
"I have multiple sclerosis and lost the use of
my right hand. The volunteer comes and writes
my letters for me. I can dictate well, but not write,"
she said. "I still keep in touch with people
from my church [Sharp Street
Memorial United Methodist Church]
and members of my high school graduating class,
Frederick Douglass High, class of 1937!"

About the time that Idella Nichols and
her colleagues were pioneering the presence
of libraries in Baltimore City public schools, a
mission in Hagerstown called St. Joseph was
becoming a full-fledged parish.

ST. JOSEPH / HAGERSTOWN

Initially a Western Maryland mission church, St. Joseph formally became a parish in 1951. Before then, Catholics were called to worship by an old railroad bell, and Mass was celebrated in the rectory and a volunteer fire company hall in the town of Halfway.

Today, some 500 families call the parish home, with good food flavoring nearly every church event, from weddings to yard sales. In recent years, about one family a week has been joining the parish.

There are weekly donations to the Williamsport Food Bank, and during the Christmas holiday, parish women make and sell home-made candles. The sale of home-made peanut butter and chocolate Easter eggs has helped pay the church mortgage.

OUR LADY OF FATIMA / S.E. BALTIMORE

Located in the 6400 block of East Pratt Street on the far eastern edge of Highlandtown, Our Lady of Fatima began in a storefront and was formally established in 1951. The pastor is Father Kevin Milton, C.Ss.R., who is assisted by longtime resident of Fatima, Father Richard Poetzel, C.Ss.R.

FATHER RICHARD POETZEL

Father Richard Poetzel grew up in the Sacred Heart of Jesus parish not far from Our Lady of Fatima, where he would spend many years after serving as a priest in New York for several decades.

"My birthday is November 1," he said. "I never had to go to school on my birthday because it's a holy day of obligation, and Catholic school was always closed on that day."

When Richard Poetzel was just a kid in kindergarten at Sacred Heart, "the nuns started asking who in the crowded classrooms of boys and girls wanted to grow up to be a priest or a nun."

Early on, he remembers, nearly every hand in the room went up.

"They'd ask this question of all the classes through all the grades and as the children got older, fewer and fewer hands went up," Father Poetzel recalled.

But his was among the few that never wavered and went on to become a Redemptorist. Having spent the bulk of his career as a parish priest, Father Poetzel is most concerned about low attendance at Mass among contemporary Catholics.

"[Many] people see no need to attend anymore, something that [seems to have]

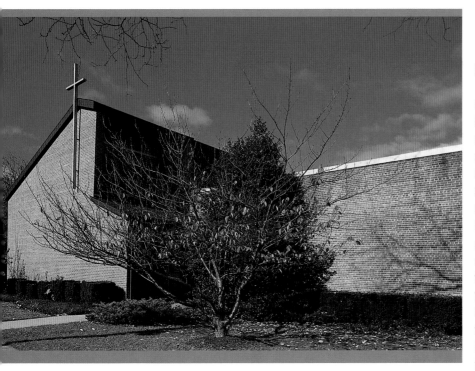

OUR LADY OF VICTORY / ARBUTUS

Located at 4414 Wilkens Avenue, Our Lady of Victory is rich in tradition. Its eleven hundred parishioners raise money for a variety of good causes, including Southwest Emergency Services. In 2005, families held a baby shower to collect items for the Catonsville Pregnancy Center, a program that aids pregnant women in crisis. At other times, suds and sponges fly as parish car washes support the youth ministry's outreach projects or a Saturday morning's sleep is forgone to feed the hungry. A men's Catholic Fellowship meets twice a month and there are currently about 21 "Prayer Warriors" at Our Lady of Victory whose devotions are committed to the needs of others. The pastor, Father Timothy B. Klunk, is an accomplished artist who designed the new stained glass windows at his previous parish, St. Athanasius in Curtis Bay.

developed over the last three years," he said. "We may be one of the only churches that still have the First Saturday devotion to Our Lady of Fatima."

In Baltimore, 1952 was the year that Hutzler's Department Store followed its customers out of the city and opened a new store at the corner of Dulaney Valley and Joppa Roads in Towson.

The Baltimore Evening Sun reported that the store's design served a single purpose: to meet the needs of the suburban automobile age with one of the store's main entrances opening directly onto a 1,000 car parking lot.

That same year Our Lady of Victory began as a small congregation in the old St. Mary's Industrial School across from St. Agnes Hospital. The first order of business was getting volunteers to help move pews from the school's huge third floor chapel to a first floor dining room that would be transformed into a fledgling church. The following year Our Lady Queen of Peace was established.

Legend has it that during the early days of Our Lady Queen of Peace, slot machines-- ubiquitous in Maryland at the time-- were used to raise money for the parish. One day,

the cops showed up and hauled the one-armed bandits away. A single machine remains as a testament to excess and reform in the early 1950s.

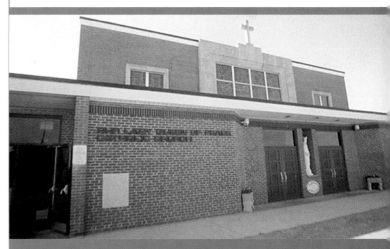

OUR LADY QUEEN OF PEACE / MIDDLE RIVER

Established in 1953, Our Lady Queen of Peace in Middle River has about 1,300 families. According to Father Jason Worley, pastor, the parish is still growing. Classic Baltimoreans-- hard working and generous-- the people of "Queen of Peace" reach out to their brethren in a number of ways. This includes donations to the Franciscan Center and "Giving Trees" that provide food and clothing to local families in need during holidays. Said Fr. Worley, "Challenges never change, just the faces."

Also from that era: the formalization of the St. Augustine parish in Williamsport.

In 1954, at the direction of Archbishop Keough, the first attempt was made to microfilm the Sacramental registers of all the parishes in the Archdiocese of Baltimore, amounting to a Catholic Hall of Records for the port city and surrounding area.

The second effort, begun in 1977, was made by the Maryland State Archives. A majority of parishes participated the first time around, and less than half took part in the State's effort. Copies of the registers microfilmed by the state are available to researchers at the Maryland State Archives in Annapolis, the Maryland Historical Society in Baltimore, and the Associated Archives at St. Mary's Seminary and University.

Sacramental registers microfilmed by the archdiocese are available only at the Associated Archives at St. Mary's Seminary and University in Roland Park.

ST. AUGUSTINE / WILLIAMSPORT

Formally established by Fr. Henry Myers of Hagerstown when he purchased the old Williamsport Methodist Church for $1,000, St. Augustine's was dedicated in 1856. Because the congregation was small, it was impossible to support a resident priest and the church became a mission of St. Mary's in Hagerstown. In 1953, Archbishop Keough changed that and named Fr. Linus Robinson pastor.

Today, 250 active families call St. Augustine home. They send volunteers to Shepherd's Table, the local food bank, and regularly visit nursing homes in the area.

RYBCZYNSKI FAMILY

"I have heard people say they have resentment toward their parents for not raising them with any kind of religious belief," said Julie Kline Rybczynski, shown here with husband David and daughter Ella.

Mrs. Rybczynski helps adults prepare to receive sacraments at St. Clare parish in Essex. She was baptized at St. Dominic's, made her First Holy Communion at St. Thomas More, and married at St. Casimir in Canton.

"I think it's detrimental to a child to be raised without a belief structure," she said. "A child needs more than to just be taken to church and enrolled in a Catholic school... they need to see their parents actively living out their faith... the foundation for faith is so important [because] we never know when tragedy will hit.

"When it does, the only thing we have to lean on is faith..."

THE CATHEDRAL OF MARY OUR QUEEN

". . . will ever stand as a monument to Archbishop Keough . . ."
Cardinal Lawrence Shehan, inaugural sermon as Archbishop of Baltimore, 1961

Groundbreaking for Baltimore's "new" cathedral took place on an October afternoon in 1954 through the generosity of fabled Baltimore department store magnate Thomas O'Neill.

"On this land a great new cathedral, the new Mother Church of this ancient See will rise to the glory of God and the honor of our heavenly Mother," said Archbishop Francis P. Keough at the ceremony.

Of the Irish-born O'Neill, whose 1912 Last Will and Testament left the bulk of his fortune to Cardinal Gibbons for "the erecting of a Cathedral Church in the City of Baltimore," Archbishop Keough said, "well knowing he would never see with earthly eyes the results of his magnificent generosity, he gave his great fortune to the One who gave him earthly life and the promise of eternal life."

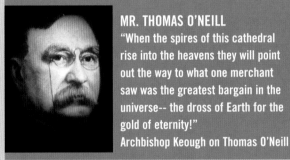

MR. THOMAS O'NEILL
"When the spires of this cathedral rise into the heavens they will point out the way to what one merchant saw was the greatest bargain in the universe-- the dross of Earth for the gold of eternity!"
Archbishop Keough on Thomas O'Neill

It was also in early October of '54 that Pope Pius XII released a letter to the world entitled *Ad Caeli Reginam*.

In it, the pontiff stated, "...by our apostolic power, decree and institute the Feast of Mary as Queen to be celebrated throughout the entire world every year on May 31."

The pope's proclamation influenced the name of the new cathedral and on the first celebration of the Feast of Mary Our Queen-May 31, 1955-- Archbishop Keough led the laying of the new building's cornerstone.

On Oct. 15, 1959, nearly five years to the day of groundbreaking, Baltimore's Cathedral of Mary Our Queen was consecrated by Auxiliary Bishop Jerome D. Sebastian. The ceremony was heavily influenced by Old Testament scripture and included elaborate rituals dating back to the early years of the Church.

The Cathedral of Mary Our Queen is both the "Bishop's Church" of the Archdiocese of Baltimore and a community parish for Catholics in North Baltimore and beyond.

In 2002, the City Paper interviewed a dozen or so local folks, asking what it was like to work on Christmas. Father John A. Williamson, associate pastor of the Cathedral said, "counting Christmas Eve, we have seven masses [and] you just kind of go with it. Midnight Mass is my favorite because [of the] solemnity and I find it to be the most moving," he said. "Exactly at midnight, when the bells start ringing and the procession starts, you know it's officially Christmas."

As the "Bishop's Church," the Cathedral is the scene of major events in the Archdiocese.

A year after it opened, in 1960, Cardinal Giovanni Montini of Milan, later to become Pope Paul VI, visited the cathedral. In the autumn of 1995, His Holiness Pope John Paul II prayed and spoke there.

"The challenge facing you, dear friends, is to increase people's awareness of the importance for society of religious freedom; to defend that freedom against those who would take religion out of the public domain and establish secularism as America's official faith," said the Holy Father in the Cathedral's vast sanctuary.

"And it is vitally necessary, for the very survival of the American experience, to transmit to the next generation the precious legacy of religious freedom and the convictions which sustain it."

It was an encore appearance at The Cathedral of Mary Our Queen for the Pope, who first toured Baltimore in 1976 as Cardinal Karol Cardinal Wojtyla, Archbishop of Krakow. At the time, he was in the United States for the Eucharistic Congress.

THE CATHEDRAL SCHOOL

The Cathedral School has its roots in Saint Joseph's Metropolitan School, established near the Basilica in downtown Baltimore in the 19th century. Archbishop Spalding requested that the School Sisters of Notre Dame staff the school and renamed it The Cathedral School. It attracted students from throughout the metropolitan area. In the late 1950s, as the Cathedral of Mary Our Queen was about to open, plans were made to relocate it to the grounds of the new cathedral on Charles Street. It opened there in 1960.

CATHEDRAL MAUSOLEUM

Five people are entombed in the Cathedral mausoleum: Cardinal Lawrence Shehan; Archbishop Francis Keough; Auxiliary Bishop Jerome Sebastian; Auxiliary Bishop T. Austin Murphy, and Auxiliary Bishop P. Francis Murphy.

O'NEILL STAINED GLASS

This stained glass panel of Thomas O'Neill is one of several in the Cathedral's Memorial Chapel honoring Catholic laymen. Also shown, along with saints and martyrs, is the merchant's store during the Great Baltimore Fire. A panel devoted to St. Francis of Assisi is fitted above the entrance to the chapel, a reminder that both saint and benefactor were cloth merchants and the sons of cloth merchants.

INSIDE THE CATHEDRAL

The Cathedral of Mary Our Queen parish provides more than 80 different ministries-- both sacramental and outreach-- to its members and others. Religious education is offered to more than 700 youngsters in the parish school and to those who attend Sunday School.

The Cathedral congregation is comprised of more than 1,600 families and since 1984 has been led by Msgr. Robert A. Armstrong, rector.

ST. CLARE / ESSEX

Established on Myrth Avenue in 1956, St. Clare's in Essex was built by a group of loyal Catholics
who saw the need for another parish in eastern Baltimore County. At first, the one building
on site housed an eight-room school and a basement church.
The first decade of the new millennium, 50 years after St. Clare opened its doors,
has brought new challenges and adventures. In 2001, St. Clare began a friendship
with a Haitian parish in the town of Desarmes. As well as forwarding prayers and money,
St. Clare has sent church members to their Haitian sister parish of St. Francis,
carrying gifts of love and religious articles.
The parish of nearly 1,500 families is administered by Deacon Kevin Bagley,
with Father Gregory Ferri assigned to attend to the parish's sacramental life.
The parish school registers approximately 300 students a year.

The first Mass at St. Clare took place on July 15, 1956 with the Rev. Albert T. Stallings celebrating. The school opened in September, and a month later, Archbishop Keough officially dedicated the parish. That same year, the estate of Alex. Brown was razed near the corner of Liberty Heights Avenue and Gwynns Falls Parkway to make way for the Mondawmin Shopping Center and the B&O

Railroad discontinued train No. 523-- "The Marylander"-- for passenger service between Washington and New York.

In 1957, the Cold War space race began when the Soviet Union launched Sputnik I, a basketball-sized satellite that orbited the Earth in about an hour and 40 minutes.

And development began for a parish dedicated to St. Pius X in the Rodgers Forge area.

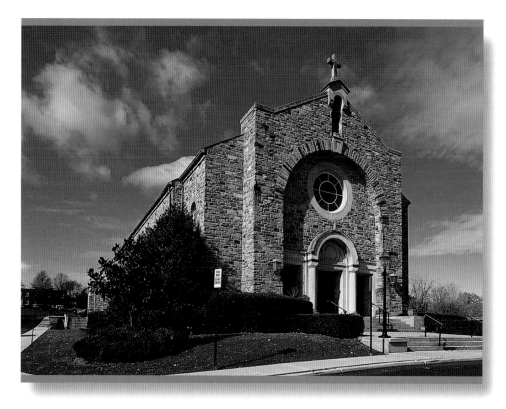

ST. PIUS X / RODGERS FORGE

Once the site of St. Vincent's Orphanage, St. Pius X was completed in 1958 and dedicated to the pope of the same name, who had been canonized in 1954.

About 1,230 families call St. Pius home, with nearly a dozen new ushers added in recent years to meet the growth. The Pastoral Life Director is Mrs. Carol J. Pacione, whose husband Mark directs the Archdiocese's Division of Youth and Young Adult Ministry.

"The hardest part [of running a parish] is the multiplex of tasks and keeping everything straight," comments Mrs. Pacione, adding that with six priests celebrating Mass each weekend, the schedule for Masses has not changed despite the absence of a full-time pastor for more than two years.

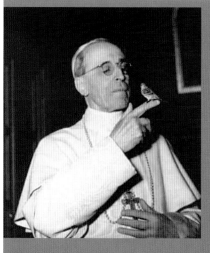

POPE PIUS XII

Pope Pius XII died on October 9, 1958. Of the Harlem Globetrotters basketball team, who gave the pontiff a private exhibition in 1952, he said: "My how clever these men are. If I had not seen it with my own eyes, I would not have believed it could be done."

Upon the death of Pius XII a half-dozen years later, President Eisenhower said of the man he knew personally: "An informed and articulate foe of tyranny, he was a sympathetic friend and benefactor to those who were oppressed, and his helping hand was always quick to aid the unfortunate victims of war… he kept peace with a rapidly changing universe, yet never lost sight of mankind's eternal destiny."

In Baltimore, Archbishop Keough commented that "even the heartless guns of war" paused to note the Holy Father's passing.

ARCHBISHOP KEOUGH & POPE JOHN XXIII

Baltimore's Archbishop Keough with Pope John XXIII. The former Cardinal Angelo Giuseppe Roncalli ascended the Throne of Peter on Oct. 28, 1958 upon the death of Pope Pius XII. At the time, Msgr. Arthur F. Valenzano of St. John's in Westminster was a 4th grader at St. Michael's in Frostburg. "I remember Pius the 12th because he looked so austere," notes Msgr. Valenzano. "To a child, John the 23rd looked like a welcoming grandfather that you could crawl up on his lap and give him a hug. John the 23rd reached out his arms to the world," adds Msgr. Valenzano. "He opened the window to let in fresh air and made the Church respond to a changing world."

JB HOWARD

"I look at pictures of my Baptism and there's the Baptismal font that's still there," said Mr. Howard, a Baltimore attorney shown outside the Cathedral on his wedding day in 1998.

"I remember walking out of the church when I got married and seeing the font out of the corner of my eye. It was an emotional thing to be in the same place for sacraments you only receive once."

The Cathedral of Mary Our Queen—which took nearly a half-dozen years of care and labor as well as $12.5 million to complete, opened in 1959.

Not long afterward, J.B. Howard Jr., a descendent of the Catholic Revolutionary War hero John Eager Howard, was baptized there. Years later, he would be married there as well.

CATHEDRAL OF MARY OUR QUEEN

One of the largest churches in the United States, it can seat 1,900 and is used annually for graduation ceremonies for high schools in the Archdiocese. The myriad of details involved in erecting the magnificent building were closely supervised by Archbishop Keough.

ST. JEROME / S.W. BALTIMORE

The St. Jerome cornerstone was set at Scott and Hamburg Streets
near Camden Yards on September 26, 1887 by Cardinal Gibbons.
The church thrived until the 1960s when its parishioners began leaving the city or dying.
In 1995, St. Jerome was united with the nearby parishes of St. Martin and St. Peter the Apostle.
In 1997, the Capuchins took over, and the parishes became the Transfiguration Catholic Community.
Mass is held at the St. Jerome church each Sunday at 8:45 a.m. followed by Sunday school.
The old parish school is used during the week for Head Start programs.
Poor neighborhoods such as those served by Transfiguration are ones "that most needs
the presence and the hope that the Church can offer," said former pastor, Father John Harvey, O.F.M. Cap.
"I see us trying to follow the lead of the Good Shepherd who said:
'It is not the healthy that need a physician but rather the sick and those most in need.'"

As old and new began blooming in the suburbs during Archbishop Keough's tenure, old limbs on the archdiocesan tree began to droop and fall in the city. One example is St. Jerome on the southwest side of downtown.

∎ ∎ ∎

By the beginning of the 1960s, St. John the Evangelist [est. 1853] at Valley and Eager Streets near the Maryland Penitentiary had fewer than 500 members. St. Katharine of Siena [est. 1902] went from a peak of 8,000 members to less than 1,000 and St. Paul's [est. 1888] lost 90 percent of its congregation, shrinking from a population of 6,000 to 600.

All three parishes merged with their Catholic neighbors and closed their doors forever.

∎ ∎ ∎

Toward the end of his life, Archbishop Keough moved into the Stella Maris complex that he had helped to build. His assistant was a newly ordained priest, then-Father Robert Bozel, who had been assigned to St. Edward's parish. Now 83, Monsignor Bozel lives at Stella Maris in the Mercy Ridge community there.

Born in the Pigtown neighborhood not far from St. Jerome, an area known to by-gone residents as "the Lumberyard", Robert Bozel moved to the St. Dominic parish in Hamilton with his family at age 4. By grammar school, he knew he wanted to be a priest. Almost immediately after realizing that dream, he was summoned to help Archbishop Keough with his day-to-day duties.

For the most part, this consisted of ministering to residents of Stella Maris. But there were unforeseen duties as well, such as filling in as the archbishop's driver on short notice.

"I don't know what happened to his driver, but after he was gone, I took on that role for two or three months until a new one could be hired," said Msgr. Bozel, who worked

for Abp. Keough in the last six years of the archbishop's life. "He was scared to death to be in a car, from the moment he sat in the backseat to the moment he got out.

"And he was very quiet in the car. I think maybe he was praying the whole way!"

After the archbishop's death on Dec. 8, 1961, Father Bozel continued the work that had become paramount during his mentor's tenure: grooming new parishes for a growing and mobile population.

Father Bozel was assigned to a number of parishes before landing at Holy Trinity in Glen Burnie. There, he and a staff of priests worked to open mission churches for a booming Catholic population in Anne Arundel County. The goal, he notes, was to "open new churches in the area where people were already gathered and worshiping in store fronts or in public school halls."

With Archbishop Keough's death, the care of the Premier See was left to Cardinal Lawrence Shehan, who served through a time of social turbulence unseen in the nation since the Civil War.

NOTRE DAME PREPARATORY SCHOOL / HAMPTON

CREDIT: NOTRE DAME PREPARATORY SCHOOL In 1960, Notre Dame Preparatory School moved from the College of Notre Dame campus on North Charles Street to a new complex in the Hampton area of Baltimore County.

First & *Forever*

THE ARCHDIOCESE OF BALTIMORE

CHAPTER **8**

Cardinal Lawrence Shehan

Vatican II & Civil Rights in Baltimore

> *"...our Christian faith imposes upon us all a special duty of both justice and charity toward all men, no matter what may be their racial and social origin."*
>
> *- Cardinal Lawrence Shehan*

So beloved was Cardinal Lawrence Shehan that when he died on August 26, 1984, certain church leaders wanted to carry his casket by hand from the Basilica of the Assumption, where he had lain in state, to his funeral Mass at the Cathedral of Mary Our Queen. The idea was for teams of men to take turns on the nearly eight-mile route.

"He would have been so embarrassed by such a procession, which would have taken three hours to get up to North Charles Street that he would have gotten up and walked himself," says Fr. Richard Lawrence, the St. Vincent de Paul pastor who knew well the unassuming cardinal.

Cardinal Shehan was a small, wiry man, just a few inches above five feet tall. Though some thought him frail, he walked with quick, purposeful steps, never stood on rank or ceremony, and led some 400,000 Catholics in the Archdiocese of Baltimore from 1961 to 1974 with exceptional ability, grace, humility, and good humor.

Remembers Fr. Lawrence: "At a dinner, he once said, 'everyone wants to know how I get things done. Well, I am a small man and people always think I need help getting things done. So I let them....' "

CARDINAL LAWRENCE SHEHAN

Baltimore's Cardinal Lawrence Shehan attended St. Charles Seminary in Catonsville and St. Mary's in Roland Park before continuing his studies at the Pontifical North American College in Rome. He was ordained a priest at the Lateran Seminary on Dec. 22, 1922, a year after the death of Cardinal Gibbons. The future cardinal was installed as the twelfth Archbishop of Baltimore in September of 1961 and was made a cardinal by Pope Paul VI on February 22, 1965. His motto comes from first Corinthians: "All things [be done] in charity..." One of the true giants of the Second Vatican Council, Cardinal Shehan died in 1984 at Mercy Hospital in Baltimore.

Young Lawrence was the son of Thomas Patrick Shehan and the former Anastasia Dames Schofield. His paternal grandfather, a dairyman named Daniel, hailed from Limerick and met his wife, Mary Kelly of Galway, on the boat that brought them to America.

Cardinal Shehan's mother was a distant relative of Augustus Dames, who fought in the battle of North Point as a member of Pinckney's militia that helped save the nation during the War of 1812. For all of these legacies, however, the child born in the last years of the nineteenth century was most truly a son of St. Ann's parish of East 22nd Street and Greenmount Avenue.

As children, his parents watched St. Ann's church rise from the estate of sea captain William Kennedy and later named their son after a favorite priest there: Fr. Lawrence McNamara.

Lawrence Joseph Shehan was born on March 18, 1898 in a Greenmount Avenue house decorated in a Baltimore style typical of the time and still visible, though rare, in some neighborhoods. Made of brick, the house was painted a deep, brownish red with white lines added to resemble mortar between the brick.

Lawrence was often quizzed by his father, who worked in the tailor supply business. The first and most important subject was always the Baltimore Catechism and afterward came spelling and arithmetic. "The best thing that [my parents] did to promote our religious education and development was to provide a home life built upon their firm religious and moral convictions," wrote the cardinal in his autobiography, *A Blessing of Years*, published in 1982 by the University of Notre Dame Press.

Cardinal Shehan was one of six children. His brother, Daniel became a dentist and his beloved sister, Mary, worked with the federal government and regularly took dinner with her brother until her death. He had three other siblings: Tom, Brooke, and Bill. Lawrence's youth included tennis in Clifton Park and trolley rides to the shore at Point Breeze near Broening Highway.

While he enjoyed sports, and would play baseball in the seminary, Lawrence knew before the 8th grade that he would become a priest, becoming the first St. Ann's student to be ordained.

"Quite suddenly," he wrote in his memoir, "when I entered the seventh grade, a great change occurred within me. I suppose the basic cause was that my mind had been slowly, almost imperceptibly, maturing. But, also, a new and excellent teacher, Sister Euthemia, appeared on the scene. She was to be my teacher for the next two years.

"During that school year... another important event took place that had a deepening effect on my religious thought and life. As I passed my 12th birthday I became eligible to receive the Holy Eucharist for the first time. This was the spring of 1910, and Pope Pius X's decree on the early reception of the Eucharist was not to appear until August.

"I was therefore a member of the last group that was required by Church discipline to wait until after my twelfth birthday. In preparation for that, I chose as my confessor and spiritual guide Father Bart Hartwell, who also was to have a real influence on me then and in the future."

■ ■ ■

In his more than 50 years as a priest, Cardinal Shehan marked numerous achievements. He earned his doctorate in theology from the Urbana University in Rome, directed Catholic Charities in Washington throughout World War II, at the same time serving as a parish priest at St. Patrick's in the nation's capital.

Cardinal Shehan played baseball in his seminary days.

THE FUTURE CARDINAL

Though he briefly doubted his calling-- and worthiness-- while at the St. Charles Minor Seminary in Catonsville, Cardinal Shehan's rise to prominence was swift. In 1939, he was made a monsignor and in early 1945, he was made a "domestic prelate," or honorary member of the papal household. By November 1945 he was appointed Auxiliary Bishop of Baltimore and Washington, installed as Co-adjutor Archbishop on September 28, 1961 and named Archbishop of Baltimore on December 8, 1961—the same day Archbishop Keough passed away.

From the end of World War II through 1953 he served as pastor of Ss. Philip & James near the Homewood campus of Johns Hopkins University. In 1953, he became the first bishop of Bridgeport, Conn. In 1964, he became the head of the U.S. Bishops' Commission for Ecumenical Affairs.

And from 1969 through his early retirement in 1975, Cardinal Shehan held the position of President of the Permanent Committee for Eucharistic Congresses.

CARDINAL GIBBONS SCHOOL

In 1961, the Cathedral Foundation gave $500,000 to the fledgling Cardinal Gibbons High School to help cover building and equipment costs. The school, which now operates a middle school as well as grades 9-12, opened for the 1962-63 school year.
In 2006, Brother Kevin Strong, F.S.C., served his third year as president of the Cardinal Gibbons School, famous as the site of the old St. Mary's Industrial School at Wilkens and Caton Avenues. Being absorbed into the worldwide network of LaSallian schools several years ago gave Gibbons "a real shot in the arm," says Brother Kevin, who spends much if his time fundraising. From a peak of about 1,200 students in the late 1960s, enrollment fell in the mid-1990s to less than 30 seniors. Today's total enrollment stands at about 500, Brother Kevin notes, with each year's freshman class growing.

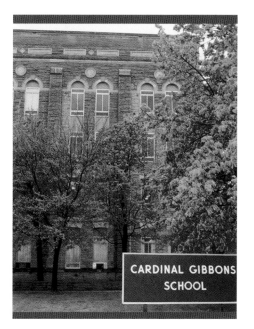

CARDINAL GIBBONS SCHOOL

But the two areas for which Cardinal Shehan will long and best be remembered are his deep involvement with the decrees of the Second Vatican Council, the historic Council called by Pope John XXIII on October 11, 1962 and completed by Pope Paul VI, on Dec. 8, 1965; and his passion for the African-American civil rights movement, which numerous white Catholics in Baltimore strongly opposed.

Of basic civil liberties for all, Cardinal Shehan said that attempts at "mere justice," were not enough and argued forcefully for genuine love of neighbor.

Responsibilities occurred during a time in which more than forty-six million Americans were Catholic. At the same time hundreds of U.S. priests and nuns departed from religious life in the turn-the-world-upside-down epoch that was the 1960s.

POPE JOHN XXIII
OPENING VATICAN II

The Second Vatican Council was the first major overhaul of the Church and its customs since the Council of Trent addressed the charges of Martin Luther in 1545. Famously, Pope John XXIII described his call as a desire to: "…throw open the windows of the Church so that we can see out and the people can see in."

ARCHBISHOP CURLEY HIGH SCHOOL

Archbishop Curley High School was founded on Sinclair Lane in Northeast Baltimore
in the spring of 1960 under the leadership and direction of Archbishop Francis P. Keough.
Attached to the central structure are wings which house the chapel, auditorium, gymnasium,
student dining room, library and the Friary residence of the Franciscan Friars at Archbishop Curley.
Named in honor of Archbishop Michael Curley, the school is the first archdiocesan high school
in Baltimore established for the education of young men.
It opened in the spring of 1961 to a class of 420 freshmen.
It was dedicated on April 17, 1962, by Cardinal Lawrence Shehan.
In December of 1969, after extensive renovation,
the Lawrence Cardinal Shehan Library and Multi-Media Instructional Center was dedicated,
the first building in the Archdiocese of Baltimore to be dedicated to Cardinal Shehan.
Since its first graduating class in June, 1965,
Archbishop Curley has graduated more than 5,000 young men.
Fr. Michael Martin, OFMC, a 1979 graduate of the school,
is president of Archbishop Curley High School. The principal is Mr. Barry Brownlee.

From September 18, 1961, when Cardinal Shehan was installed as Baltimore's archbishop, until the following fall when he traveled to Rome for the opening of Vatican II, several important events occurred in Crabtown.

A pair of Catholic high schools were launched: Archbishop Curley opened for the 1961-62 school year at 3701 Sinclair Lane near Herring Run Park, and money was earmarked for a high school at the old St. Mary's Industrial School in the southwest Baltimore named in honor of Cardinal Gibbons.

■ ■ ■

Now 75, Br. Kevin is a native of Cumberland and a 1949 graduate of its LaSalle High

TYLER & BRYAN SMITH

"My Catholic education allows me to stay on the right track," says Bryan. "It teaches me kindness, to be generous." His brother Tyler, set to graduate with the Gibbons class of 2006, enjoys the small school atmosphere where everyone knows your name, "If I earn a B in public school it would only be a C at Gibbons," comments Tyler. "And you think twice about doing something that might disappoint your teachers - it would be the same as hurting your family."

School that later merged with other area Catholic schools to become Bishop Walsh School. He entered religious life within a week of graduating high school and, he says, has "loved every minute of it."

Part of Br. Kevin's joy comes from seeing kids like Bryan Smith, a 9th grader from the nearby Our Lady of Victory parish, prosper. Bryan's father, who attended public schools and died unexpectedly at age 39, had vowed that his children would receive a Catholic education. Left to raise two boys-- Tyler and Bryan-- on her own, Victoria Ingram Smith is carrying out her late husband's wishes. Tyler, now 17, attended Our Lady of Victory from kindergarten through 8th grade graduation-- where Mrs. Smith was a class mother-- and Bryan did the same, starting at OLOV in pre-K. Both boys are now at Cardinal Gibbons School.

The early 1960s also saw the opening of St. Thomas More at 6806 McClean Boulevard near Perring Parkway. In the late 1950s, with the suburbs booming, the neighborhoods east of Towson were growing so fast that existing parishes were overwhelmed. Anticipating this, a dozen acres of land were purchased on McClean Boulevard in 1959 for a new

CARDINAL SHELAN WITH POPE JOHN XXIII

Cardinal Shehan stands with Pope John XXIII during the Second Vatican Council. Contrary to appearances, Vatican II did not simply arrive on its own, out of nowhere. Its reforms were built upon changes of thought working within the church for at least the previous hundred years.

Catholic church along with a school, rectory, and convent for a yet-to-be-named parish.

The new pastor, the Rev. Thomas Kelly, held meetings with volunteers in a rented space at the Hamilton Park Shopping Center. Using reverse telephone books – "criss-cross" directories favored by door-to-door salesmen and newspaper rewrite men – they called resident after resident to identify potential parishioners.

The first Mass was celebrated in September of 1962, about the same time that a team of Sisters of St. Joseph of Chestnut Hill arrived to teach the catechism.

On June 3, 1963, one of the twentieth century's great prophets of change, the humble and beloved Pope John XXIII-- the kind of man who took it upon himself to visit sick children and petty criminals-- died of cancer in Rome after four-and-half years on the Throne of St. Peter.

ST. THOMAS MORE / N.E. BALTIMORE
Outreach at St. Thomas More includes support for the nearby Harford Road Pregnancy Center. Each Mother's Day, parishioners sell silk roses and donate what they've made to the center. Disposable diapers and used maternity clothes are also donated.
The parish now counts about 500 families on their rolls, many of them senior citizens who help make up a Resurrection Choir that sings at funerals. The pastor is Fr. Brian A. Zielinski, O Praem.

Of the groundbreaking events in his tenure, like his personal welcome to the Vatican of a representative of Soviet leader Nikita Khrushchev, John XXIII said: "It can be a disappointment or a mysterious thread of Providence that I do not have the right to break off."

"In spite of his recent illness, he manifested the hope that he would live to see the Council through to a happy ending," said Cardinal Shehan upon the pope's death. "Although his papacy had lasted but a brief five years, it seems certain that he will go down in history as one of the truly great popes. I can think of no pope who has left a deeper imprint on the Church, with the possible exception of Pope Leo 'the Great.'

■ ■ ■

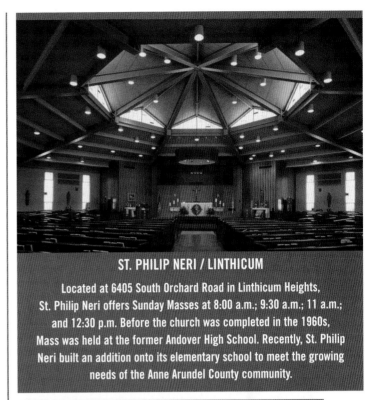

ST. PHILIP NERI / LINTHICUM

Located at 6405 South Orchard Road in Linthicum Heights, St. Philip Neri offers Sunday Masses at 8:00 a.m.; 9:30 a.m.; 11 a.m.; and 12:30 p.m. Before the church was completed in the 1960s, Mass was held at the former Andover High School. Recently, St. Philip Neri built an addition onto its elementary school to meet the growing needs of the Anne Arundel County community.

CHURCH OF THE HOLY SPIRIT / JOPPA

Founded in 1963, the Church of the Holy Spirit stands at 540 Joppa Farm Road in Harford County. The pastor is the Rev. Joseph C. Simmons and Lurine Kunschman serves as director of religious education.

Between 1962 and 1965, Cardinal Shehan participated in all four sessions of the Second Vatican Council in Rome. He and his successor, the future Cardinal Keeler-- then a priest attached to the bishop of Harrisburg, Pa., -- crossed the Atlantic on the same ship for the council meetings.

In all, sixteen documents were published from the Second Vatican Council: four Constitutions, three Declarations, and nine Decrees. According to Ed Wall, editor-in-chief of the Catholic Review at the time, the paper was the first in the United States to publish the entire translated texts of all Vatican II documents.

The achievement, said Mr. Wall, is due to the perseverance of Thomas N. Lorsung, then a young reporter/photographer at the Review.

"I took great pride in the Catholic Review being the first to publish those documents," comments Mr. Lorsung. "It was a tremendous experience, exciting to be part of what was happening in Rome. It was the great personal presence of [Pope] John XXIII that created the symbolism for the new openness. My faith was already deep at the time, but it was certainly enhanced" by the events of Vatican II.

THOMAS LORSUNG

Tom Lorsung joined the staff of the Catholic Review in Baltimore in 1963 and stayed until 1969. In 1972, he went to work for the Catholic News Service in Washington, from which he retired as editor-in-chief in 2003. Now 67, he is a member of St. John the Evangelist parish near his home in Columbia, MD.

"I'm still a faithful Catholic," said Mr. Lorsung. "I stand behind the Church throughout its various problems because it's a divine institution and divine guidance carries people a long way."

Sitting on the Secretariat for Christian Unity-- and later establishing the first commission on the same subject in the United States-- Cardinal Shehan was intimately involved with Council documents on Ecumenism, especially the statements regarding the Jewish people and religious liberty.

From the document *Nostra Aetate*, roughly translated as "our time," the Council declared: "Since the spiritual patrimony common to Christians and Jews is thus so great, this sacred synod wants to foster and recommend that mutual understanding and respect which is the fruit, above all, of biblical and theological studies as well as of fraternal dialogues."

Toward this ideal, Cardinal Shehan addressed the Brotherhood Convocation at Baltimore's Chizuk Amuno temple in 1965, the first time that an Archbishop of Baltimore had spoken under the auspices of a synagogue. In December of that year, the National Conference of Christians and Jews presented him with its highest honor, the "National Brotherhood Award."

It marked the beginning of a modern journey between Catholics and Jews that led Pope John Paul II to pray at the Wailing Wall in Jerusalem in 2000 and weep while visiting Yad Vashem, Israel's Holocaust memorial.

In a letter to Cardinal William H. Keeler expressing condolences after John Paul II's death in 2005, Marc Terrill, president of the Associated Jewish Community Federation of Baltimore, wrote that the Polish pope "did everything in his power to promote friendship and understanding with the Jewish people."

"Only two Americans were on the [religious liberty] committee at Vatican II," notes Fr. Lawrence of St. Vincent de Paul. "Cardinal Shehan and Cardinal [Francis Joseph] Spellman of New York-- giants of their generation."

■ ■ ■

Pope John XXIII was succeeded by the former Archbishop of Milan, Giovanni Cardinal Montini who became Pope Paul VI after his election on June 21, 1963. He immediately announced that bishops would meet for the second phase of the Council in late September of that year to resume work.

During his early months as the new pontiff, Pope Paul VI named Cardinal Shehan to the Secretariat for the Promotion of Christian Unity. The work continues today with results like a May 2005 statement from the Anglican-Roman Catholic International Commission on the Blessed Mother called "Mary: Grace and Hope in Christ." The Commission is the official instrument of dialogue between the Catholic Church and the Churches of the Anglican Communion, first called for in 1966 by Pope Paul VI and Archbishop Michael Ramsey of Canterbury.

Its statement known as "the Seattle Statement," outlines the significant degree of agreement about Mary already achieved and focuses on the remaining differences, particularly the Catholic dogmas of Mary's Immaculate Conception and her Assumption, which Anglican authority does not believe are sufficiently supported by Scripture.

CARDINAL SHEHAN & CIVIL RIGHTS

*The duty of justice and charity... must guide us in our personal relationships -- within our block,
our neighborhood, our community; in our social and fraternal organizations;
in the business we may conduct; in the labor unions to which we may belong;
at work and at play; in all the circumstances of everyday life.*
- Cardinal Shehan's letter on Racial Justice

CHAMPION OF CIVIL RIGHTS

Protests like the one in this photograph were common during Cardinal Shehan's tenure in the turbulent '60s. When protestors picketed the Church during the era of racial integration in Baltimore, Cardinal Shehan invited them to talk and argued in his quiet, persuasive way, that there was room for everybody in the Catholic faith.

It was an amazing moment, remembers Tom Lorsung, the sight of three Catholic priests at a protest to de-segregate Gwynn Oak Park on July 4, 1963. Not something, he adds, that one was likely to see in his native Wisconsin. (The priests, Monsignor Austin Healy, Father Joseph Connolly, and Father Henry Offer, a Josephite, would be arrested and taken to the Baltimore County Police Station in Woodlawn).

Tom Lorsung was a young reporter for the Catholic Review at the time, so new on the job that he had to borrow someone else's press credentials to cover Cardinal Shehan's participation in the historic March on Washington for Jobs and Freedom led by the Rev. Martin Luther King, Jr. on August 28, 1963. Cardinal Shehan pointed out that such actions were particularly appropriate in the centennial years of the Emancipation Proclamation.

"Here in our own State," he wrote in his landmark letter on racial justice, "recent experience has shown that much-- very much-- remains to be done; that grave wrongs still need to be righted.

"...As Catholics, we have an even higher and more sacred duty to all those who are 'of the household of the faith.' In his Epistle to the Galatians (3:28), St. Paul tells us: 'You are all children of God through faith in Jesus Christ ...there is neither Jew nor Greek; there is neither slave nor freedman'-- and today St. Paul would certainly have added: 'There is neither black nor white; neither brown nor yellow'-- for you are all one in Christ..."

"That letter," remembers the Cardinal's secretary, Betty Sweeney, "was a bombshell... he fought a good battle. He was always astonished that people would react the way they did to the various things he had done, including helping to bring about the changes from Vatican II, which involved educating the clergy as well. He once said of the difficulties the laity had in adjusting to the changes, 'Don't they know the changes are hard for me too?'"

■ ■ ■

On March 1, 1963, *Baltimore Evening Sun* reporter Jerome Kelly-- a former altar boy at St. Ann's and longtime newspaperman before his death in 2005-- filed a story about Cardinal Shehan's work in fulfilling the Gospel of St. Paul:

"Archbishop Shehan today officially banned all practices of racial discrimination in Catholic schools, churches, social organizations and charitable institutions in the Baltimore Archdiocese," he wrote, adding a quote from the Cardinal which said that Catholics "have been all too slow in the correction of our shortcomings... we have a special obligation to place ourselves in the forefront" of efforts to end "injustices and discrimination which still remain."

Responding to the Cardinal's edict, the *Baltimore Afro-American* wrote: "...Catholic businessmen trying to gauge what is prudent in hiring and upgrading colored employees may be guided by the Catholic Church's example..."

Some forty years ago, the prospect of sudden racial integration was a tough and bitter pill for many within the white Catholic community, and some argued that integration not be applied across-the-board, as Cardinal Shehan argued, until new schools and other institutions were built.

On March 15, 1963, the Catholic Review reported on the ban of racial discrimination by Cardinal Shehan.

"This act of bold religious courage is a historic turning point in Baltimore's struggle against prejudice... old prejudices do not die easily, and we do not expect this action to change Baltimore overnight. But it nonetheless leaves no room for doubt as to where the Catholic Church stands on one of the great issues of our time.

"It is especially fitting that such a stand should be made in Maryland which was founded by Catholics as a haven of religious freedom."

The Cardinal then made an unequivocal endorsement of the state's public accommodations law, adding strong criticism of Catholic legislators who opposed it.

While the Cardinal's legal authority held sway within the Archdiocese of Baltimore, he had to rely on moral power on January 13, 1966 when he spoke in favor of the "Open Housing Bill" before a Thursday night meeting of the Baltimore City Council. The turn-out was huge, an estimated 2,000 people, and the meeting was moved from City Hall to a larger room across the plaza to the War Memorial Building.

The Cardinal was invited to speak by the president of the City Council, Thomas D'Alessandro III, son of the legendary Italian-Catholic mayor "Old Tommy" D'Alessandro.

Before the hearing, the Cardinal's brother, Daniel, received an anonymous call from a man who said that if the Cardinal testified in favor of the bill, he would be shot.

Knowing that the Cardinal would be undeterred, Daniel Shehan did not tell him of the call but instead reported it to the archdiocesan attorney, Francis X. Gallagher, and the police.

No one mentioned the threat to the Cardinal, who, wearing a simple Roman collar, was the first witness to be called. In the audience was a prominent rabbi as well as bishops of the Episcopal and Methodist churches. Before he'd read the first sentence of his statement, booing and heckling began.

The loud jeering from the segregationists, hundreds of Catholics among them, continued for two minutes, according to newspaper reports. "We immediately began clapping as loudly as we could to drown out the noise from the opposite side," notes Betty Sweeney. The Cardinal maintained his composure as police removed the hecklers.

"He simply stood there with a benign expression on his face and waited until the hullabaloo died down before he read his statement."

As for the persuasiveness of moral argument, the open housing bill failed to pass the Baltimore City Council. Apartheid would remain legal in Baltimore until the United States Congress enacted legislation forbidding discrimination in all public places of the nation.

CHARLES TILDON AND CARDINAL SHEHAN

Charles Tildon, named by Cardinal Shehan as the first chair of the Archdiocesan Urban Commission, formed in 1966, was the first layman appointed to head a major archdiocesan post.

"At that time, blacks suffered much prejudice even within the church," recalls Mr. Tildon, 78, who grew up worshipping with his family at Saint Pius V, an historically African American church.

"I remember coming home from college one year and my mother asking me if I had 'made Easter.' I told her I had not and she told me to go up to Immaculate Conception, three blocks away from our house, to go to confession so that I could go to Communion on Easter.

"I went and stood in the line for confession on the Blessed Mother side of the church, only to be told then by the priest,

'Boy, don't you know that colored people can't go to confession on the Blessed Mother side? You have to move to the Saint Joseph side of the church'.

"There was a long line of white people on the Blessed Mother side, and the black people on the Saint Joseph side had to wait until the white people on the Blessed Mother side were finished..."

Cardinal Shehan stood at the vanguard of change. His courage helped spare future generations the humiliation that Charles Tildon and other black Catholics endured on both sides of the Church doors.

The Archdiocesan Urban Commission first worked to identify problems-- race relations, community development, the situation within prisons and homeless shelters-- and then labored, as a way of making the Church more relevant to a troubled city in a troubled nation, to solve them.

One of the commission's expressed goals was addressing discrimination within the Archdiocese itself. Father Offer served as executive director.

"Before my appointment to the commission, I had been a passive Catholic, but I was active in the Civil Rights movement outside the church," notes Mr. Tildon, a high school biology teacher who retired as president of Baltimore City Community College.

"I became a very active Catholic after that appointment."

Under Charles Tildon, the commission asked the Cardinal for $100,000 to fund various projects and received it. "That is big money now," says Mr. Tildon. "But it was bigger money then."

The budget was used to study access to health care and treatments of blacks in Catholic hospitals. "The findings resulted in a number of changes in the way Catholic hospitals operated," said Mr. Tildon. "One nun in particular, who was resistant to the changes the Cardinal instituted as a result of the study, received a phone call from the Cardinal and after that she experienced a change of heart."

The money also funded a number of community organizations. The commission gave small grants to various nascent neighborhood groups such as the South East Community Organization (SECO), Harbel in the northeast part of the city and social justice work like the Saint Ambrose Housing Aid Center.

Dr. Beverly A. Carroll was a twenty-four-year-old secretary in 1966 when she joined the Urban Commission. Today, she is executive director of the Secretariat for African-American Catholics at the United States Conference of Bishops in Washington.

"Charles Tildon opened a lot of doors for black

ANDY WAGNER

For the past decade, 71-year-old Andy Wagner has driven from his Annapolis home to Baltimore three times a week to volunteer at the St. Ambrose Housing Aid Center. He works in "D &D."

"Default and delinquent," describes Mr. Wagner, retired from the marketing department of Exxon. "We help people who are behind on their mortgages and work with lenders to come up with a plan that will enable the people to save their houses."

Mr. Wagner, an Ignatius Lay Volunteer, finds much of what he does with St. Ambrose unsettling.

"I do not enjoy seeing people in dire straits," he says of the work which brings him satisfaction.

"I used to volunteer on boards and other kinds of organizations but I really wanted to do more hands-on work," says Mr. Wagner. "St. Ambrose does what the gospels say to do, working with people who need help and that's what I like about it."

The St. Ambrose Housing Aid Center has its roots in community protests and lawsuits against blockbusting real estate tactics and unfair mortgage practices of the late 1960s. Early on, its pro-bono attorneys included Larry Gibson, who would go on to guide the political career of former Baltimore Mayor Kurt Schmoke, and Ron Shapiro, who became a super sports agent for the likes of Cal Ripken, Jr.

St. Ambrose was formally organized in 1972 by Vinnie Quayle to assist first-time homebuyers. Located at 321 East 25th Street in Charles Village, it has helped more than 5,000 families find their way to the settlement table to become homeowners.

It has added other services such as a home-sharing program that matches people living alone who need extra income with compatible housemates who need an affordable place to live.

"I served on the board of [the archdiocesan group] called Project Equality with Charles Tildon," notes Mr. Quayle. "He was relentless in his determination to make positive change. Wherever you went in those days, you heard his name."

Catholics," says Dr. Carroll. "After he was appointed to the commission, people began thinking that they too can make a difference."

"He's the kind of person," adds Dr. Carroll of Mr. Tildon, who was named a Papal Knight of the Order of St. Gregory the Great, "...who brought people together who normally would not want to be in the same room with each other."

A BEATLE SEEKS MERCY

GEORGE HARRISON
Born February 25, 1943 in Liverpool, England; died November 29, 2001 in Los Angeles.
"I was thrilled to see George in the hallway during a chemistry test," recalls Fran Dukehart, a Mercy alumnus. "I remember the scene like a movie. It was a challenge to stay calm instead of screaming and yelling."

Phyllis Herz Procheska was sitting in her shorthand class at Mercy High School at the beginning of the 1964 school year, mad at herself for letting her boyfriend-- a mere boy-- talk her out of going to see the Beatles at the Baltimore Civic Center on September 13.

Her mind wandering, Phyllis stared out the classroom door and saw an apparition.

A Beatle walking the halls of Mercy High School? Impossible!

"It was the day after their Baltimore concert and I saw him walking down the hall," remembered Mrs. Procheska, who'd graduated from St. Mary's, Govans and was a member of Mercy's second graduating class.

"I asked the teacher if I could be excused to go to the ladies room and go to the office and when I went into the office there he was…"

There he was: the quiet Beatle, George Harrison, born a Catholic before turning to Eastern religion and mysticism, touring an American high school.

"I don't know how I got the nerve," said Mrs. Procheska, "but I just had to find out if it was him, so I just did it."

And so she became one of a handful of folks at Mercy on that Monday, and perhaps the only student, to meet Harrison, scoring an autograph that today she can't find.

Typically, Paul McCartney was young Phyllis's favorite Beatle - "he was the cutest," she said – and though the 17-year-old found herself in awe of Harrison, she was not shy in his presence.

"Sr. Michelle was in the office with us and she told me to stay where I was until he left the building so I wouldn't cause a riot in an all-girls school," remembers Mrs. Procheska. "She knew what I'd done and I saw her smile."

Sr. Michelle was Sr. Michelle Carroll, the principal. She claims not to have known much about rock and roll. "I knew vaguely that the Beatles were an English group," she said [but was savvy enough to know there'd be bedlam if word got out].

"I was in my early 40s in 1964 and there were always crazes that girls" were susceptible to, she says of her teaching career. "But I can't recall any nearly as strong as this one. It was a different magnitude."

Just how did George Harrison wind up at a Catholic girls high school on Northern Parkway?

"I got a call from a manager or an agent, a very professional call," says Sr. Carroll, now living in Atlanta. "This person said the Beatles had a short period of time [in Baltimore] and really wanted to know what schools in the United States were like and could one of them come over."

At the time, Mercy was just four years old and considered state-of-the-art for girls' secondary education in the Catholic tradition. The classrooms were new and spacious with plenty of storage room with an up-to-date science lab for chemistry and biology. Tuition was approximately $100 a year.

"I didn't have any real time to respond," Sr. Carroll said, "but it seemed like a professional request to know more about secondary education in the United States. I said I'd be glad to have a visit."

Harrison arrived in the company of a handler connected to the tour. The guitarist, then twenty-one and a disciple of rockabilly great Carl Perkins, was given a tour of the gym and the cafeteria, where a meeting of parents was taking place. During the walk-around, Phyllis Procheska, then of East Lake Avenue and now of Hydes, looked up and slipped out.

Later, she spilled the news to classmates. "I passed a note to my friend, Mary Johnson," she said [but no one believed her].

No one ever does.

An announcement before the end of the school day confirmed it and a girl offered to buy the brown sweater she wore that day. George, apparently, had brushed against it. Mrs. Procheska declined.

Harrison returned to the then-new Holiday Inn on Lombard Street, which featured a space-age revolving rooftop restaurant. The band then flew on to Pittsburgh. The following year they played old Griffith Stadium in Washington, and the year after that, 1966, they stopped touring.

"He was just a very courteous young man," says Sr. Carroll of the Beatle. "I think he stayed less than half-an-hour," recalls the Sister of Mercy, who was in full habit at the time. "We wound up in the front lobby near the office. The man who was with him expressed thanks and whisked him away. Some girls had seen him drink from the fountain, and when school was out girls lined up to get a drink."

Just after Thanksgiving, 2001 that same water fountain bore a sign of mourning at the death from cancer of the fifty-eight-year-old George Harrison on November 29th. By then, Sr. Carol Wheeler was principal at Mercy.

"I was an English teacher here at the time, a young nun in my 20s. We liked the Beatles; God knows we liked them, but I was a bit old for Beatle mania," says Sister Wheeler. "I happened not to be teaching that period and was asked to stand at the edge of the lobby to see if two men came up the front steps."

Sr. Wheeler's job was to alert Sr. Carroll. "We didn't know which Beatle would arrive, only that one was coming," she said [so she did not get to meet Harrison].

"I think a phys-ed class recognized him when [Harrison] stood on a balcony in the gym and Sr. Carroll quietly whisked him out," she said.

Some 37 years later, Sr. Wheeler led a new generation of students in prayer for the soul of George Harrison.

"It was nothing like it was for the girls at the time" of the British Invasion, adds Sr. Carroll. "But one of the kids put up a sign over the water fountain outside of my office that said: 'George Harrison drank here...'"

According to Sr. Carroll, Harrison did drink out of the front lobby water fountain at Mercy on the day of his visit more than forty years ago. But as with so much that becomes myth, it wasn't the one standing there at the time of his death.

The original had worn out some years before and had been replaced.

Yesterday and today: Sr. Michelle Carroll as she looked as principal of Mercy High School in 1964 and as she appeared in 2003.

ELEVATION TO CARDINAL

Of his elevation to Cardinal in 1965, Cardinal Shehan wrote: "My immediate reaction was stunned silence and utter amazement. I could not understand why this honor was being bestowed upon me. Here I was already 67 years old... not conscious of any diminution of such powers as had been given to me but in my judgment of men generally, passed the prime of my life."

Adds his former secretary, Betty Sweeney: "When [the Cardinal] heard the rumors that he was going to be named to the See of Baltimore, he wrote to the Apostolic Delegate in D.C., Archbishop Edigio Vagnozzi, and presented very forcibly (he thought) his unworthiness for such an honor: his unprepossessing appearance, slight stature, lack of either a forceful speaking voice, etc... He later showed me the letter which had obviously not been effective."

To make this point even more pointed, remembers Miss Sweeney with a laugh, the Cardinal-to-be added: "And I don't sing well either."

On Dec. 8, 1965, Pope Paul VI closed the Second Vatican Council with the words: "Ite in Pace!" "As I looked back over the years that had elapsed since Pope John XXIII had announced the opening of the Council, down to this, its solemn closing," wrote Cardinal Shehan in his memoir. "I was deeply conscious of the fact that I had not only lived through, but also had been a part-- a very small part-- of the four most significant years of the Church's modern history."

On the first day of 1966, Pope Paul VI sent a message to the leaders of the United States, the Soviet Union, the People's Republic of China, and the government of North Vietnam imploring them to end the war in Southeast Asia. His September 15 encyclical, *Christi Matri Rosarii*--- Rosaries to the Mother of Christ-- urged Catholics to say the rosary for peace during the month of October.

That year, the Baltimore Orioles won their first World Series of the modern era; a blizzard dumped twenty inches of snow over central Maryland; and the tugboat men along the South Broadway waterfront, members of the Seafarers International Union, went on strike for six months for better wages and a guaranteed work week.

It was also the year that the congregation of St. Ann in Hagerstown began celebrating Mass at their sanctuary on Oak Hill Avenue.

ST. ANN / HAGERSTOWN

Entering its fortieth year in 2006, St. Ann's emerged from St. Mary's in downtown Hagerstown and boasts a diverse congregation of longtime residents and commuters from the Washington metro area. Other communicants travel from Pennsylvania and West Virginia.

At the beginning of the summer of 2005, Bishop Francis Malooly, Western Vicar for the Archdiocese, broke ground for an expanded parish center at St. Ann. The two-story brick addition will provide four new multi-purpose rooms and was scheduled for completion in early 2006. Future plans call for a choir loft above the main entrance to the sanctuary and a new pipe organ.

With nearly 1,300 families, St. Ann's offers a wide range of outreach activities, including an annual blood drive, food for a local cold weather shelter, and a collection of Christmas gifts for area poor children.

Of special pride to the members at St. Ann's is its relationship with sister parishes in Kentucky and Haiti.

"The challenge of a priest today is to help a community articulate a mission of evangelization," said the Rev. Richard Murphy, pastor. "Ministries [must be] provided for parishioners and for those beyond the boundaries of the parish."

In 1967, in the middle of Mary's month of May, Pope Paul VI traveled to Fatima in Portugal to warn that the world was threatened when moral progress failed to keep up with advances in science and technology. The pontiff's visit marked the fiftieth anniversary of the apparition of the Blessed Mother to three young Portuguese children. The sole survivor, Sister Lucia Dos Santos, sixty years old at the time, kissed the pope's ring in her first public appearance in two decades. It was also the first time a pope had met privately with the Carmelite Lucia, who died at her convent in Coimbra, Portugal on Feb. 13, 2005 at age 97.

When she was 10 in 1917, Sr. Lucia and her younger cousins, Francisco and Jacinta, were visited by the Blessed Mother three times. Soon after, Lucia revealed Mary's message: predictions of World War II, the rise of atheistic Communism in Russia and the urgent need of believers to pray the Rosary for world peace. A third message was kept secret by a succession of Holy Fathers until May of 2000 when Pope John Paul II revealed the text of the vision.

In it, said Pope John Paul II, were references to a "bishop dressed in white," who was shot while struggling toward the Cross. The pope concluded that the vision, over six decades before the fact, predicted the failed attempt on his life in 1981.

■ ■ ■

When Ed Wall was editor of the Baltimore Catholic Review, now simply the Catholic Review, he dined often with Cardinal Shehan in the archbishop's private residence alongside of the Basilica. "The rule," remembers Wall, "was to enjoy the food, read the newspapers and discuss no business until the table was cleared of dishes and silverware bearing the seal of the great James Cardinal Gibbons."

One morning, Mr. Wall was needed in the Catholic Review print shop, where hot lead type and rolling presses added to the humid nightmare that is Baltimore in summer. Dressed in shorts and a t-shirt for his work-

day, Wall skipped morning Mass that day because he didn't think he was dressed appropriately to assist the Eucharist.

When Cardinal Shehan saw Mr. Wall later, he asked where he'd been and the editor explained. "Ed," answered the Cardinal with dismay, "everyone is always properly dressed for Mass."

ED WALL w/CARDINAL SHEHAN

Ed Wall, former Catholic Review editor, on the job with Cardinal Shehan.

The 1960s, said Mr. Wall, "Were not easy times. The Cardinal was under frequent attack by the extremely committed on both extremes, left and right.

"It was a fast-changing world for Catholics [and] by the time Vatican II adjourned it was clear that Cardinal Shehan's goal of 'every Catholic child in a Catholic school' was not going to happen. His [vision for a] preparatory seminary was not going to be built and although the [archdiocese was] granted a license for a television system, it wouldn't be used.

"It was suddenly post-Council time. Catholics were stretching their minds, serving on brand-new parish councils, celebrating Mass in English, and proclaiming a new ecumenism by singing hymns that had belonged to Protestants.

And then, 1968.

A year of assassinations, riots, and mass arson in cities across America; the audacity of the Tet Offensive in Vietnam, in which every major city and town in the south was attacked, affirming the tenacity of the Communists; along with vast protests against the war.

It was the year in which both Robert Kennedy, running for president as a U.S.

OUR LADY OF HOPE / DUNDALK

Founded at 1727 Lynch Road in Dundalk in 1967, Our Lady of Hope merged its school in 1991
with St. Luke's parish school in Edgemere. The main school is located at Our Lady of Hope
and serves grades K-through-8. Pre-kindergarten classes are held at the St. Luke campus
on North Point Road in Edgemere. Staffing is done by the School Sisters of Notre Dame
with Sr. Irene Pryle serving as principal. The pastor of Our Lady of Hope is Fr. John "Jack" B. Ward.

ST. JOHN THE EVANGELIST / COLUMBIA

Founded along with visionary planner James Rouse's experimental Howard County town of Columbia in 1967, St. John's is part of the Interfaith Center at Wilde Lake and also Oakland Mills. The pastor is Fr. Richard Tillman.

He grew up in Immaculate Conception parish in Towson and entered the old St. Mary's Seminary on Paca Street.

He was ordained in 1965 at the Cathedral of Mary Our Queen. "There was no built-in cultural heritage dictating the way church should be done in this new city of Columbia, with this new-fangled concept of sharing faith between Protestants, Catholics and Jews," said Father Tillman to the Catholic Review upon the fortieth anniversary of his ordination in 2005.

Since then, the St. John's congregation has grown to nearly 3,000 families.

"We're a very diverse parish," notes Father Tillman. "If you come to Mass here and take a look at the people participating in the sacraments, they're African, Filipino, Vietnamese, Chinese, Hispanic and from Eastern European countries. I think they span the spectrum, and I hope they do feel welcome here."

Senator from New York, and the Rev. Martin Luther King were murdered. In November, Richard Nixon was elected president.

After the death of Dr. King in Memphis, Cardinal Shehan flew to Montgomery, Alabama for the civil rights leader's funeral and also defended the right of priests and nuns to take part in demonstrations for civil rights. That same year, "folk Mass" spread throughout the Church with guitars and songs borrowed from Protestant hymnals, and six new parishes opened in the Archdiocese of Baltimore.

Cardinal Shehan openly opposed the Vietnam War and arranged for priests arrested (including the Berrigan brothers) in anti-war protests to have attorneys.

"It's ironic," comments Betty Sweeney. "Cardinal Shehan's family coat of arms is a dove, a symbol of peace, and he received all kinds of threatening phone calls, hate mail, and hostility for his stances on the war, civil rights and fair housing."

CATONSVILLE NINE

CREDIT: BALTIMORE COUNTY PUBLIC LIBRARY

On May 17, 1968, the Berrigan brothers – Philip, then a Josephite priest and his brother Daniel, a Jesuit, along with seven others, were arrested after breaking into a Catonsville draft board, removing records, and setting them on fire on the parking lot outside before reporters and other witnesses. Known as the "Catonsville Nine," the group was convicted and sentenced to prison. The protest became the centerpiece of the strongest action of radical Catholic politics since the Depression-era socialist activities of Dorothy Day, founder of the Catholic Worker movement.

"Every day before he left the office, [the Cardinal] stopped by my desk and thanked me for all I had done that day," notes Mary Elizabeth "Betty" Sweeney, Cardinal Shehan's long-time secretary. "He was easy to work for and easy to talk to. When he asked me to come to work for him he apologized that there was no retirement plan but he was working hard to implement one."

"How can you say a Cardinal is lovable," reminisces Miss Sweeney, "except to say he was lovable."

Lovable, devoted and persistent.

"Many priests felt they could not support the Church's stance on birth control as outlined in *Humanae Vitae*," continues Sweeney. "Cardinal Shehan met with each one of them individually and discussed the Church's position, getting them to agree to present [Rome's] position even if they did not personally support it.

"Many men ended up leaving the priesthood over that issue and it pained the Cardinal greatly to lose a priest for he loved the priesthood so."

BETTY SWEENEY AND CARDINAL SHEHAN

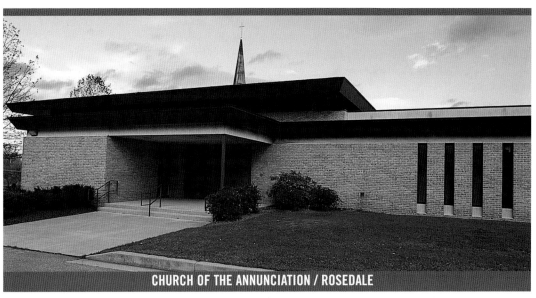

CHURCH OF THE ANNUNCIATION / ROSEDALE

The Church of the Annunciation serves the Rosedale area from 5212 McCormick Avenue.
In Thanksgiving, 2005, the parish register listed 917 families.
Social justice work concentrates on programs like Sarah's Hope,
a daytime resource for the homeless at 9100 Franklin Square Drive near Rossville Boulevard,
to which Annunciation members take food once a month. Parishioners also collect money and school supplies
for the St. Joseph Indian School on a reservation in South Dakota.
The pastor is the Rev. William P. Foley; Kathy L. Brotzman heads the religious education program.

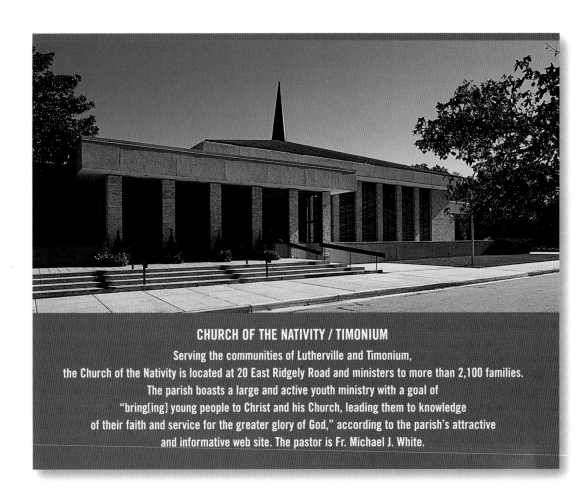

CHURCH OF THE NATIVITY / TIMONIUM

Serving the communities of Lutherville and Timonium,
the Church of the Nativity is located at 20 East Ridgely Road and ministers to more than 2,100 families.
The parish boasts a large and active youth ministry with a goal of
"bring[ing] young people to Christ and his Church, leading them to knowledge
of their faith and service for the greater glory of God," according to the parish's attractive
and informative web site. The pastor is Fr. Michael J. White.

RESURRECTION OF OUR LORD / LAUREL
Resurrection of Our Lord in Laurel is located at 8400 Brock Bridge Road near the Howard County and Anne Arundel County lines. The pastor is the Rev. John Wielebski.

As Anne Arundel County and Baltimore County burgeoned in population in the 1950s and 1960s, so Harford County has experienced enormous growth. Reflecting that, St. Mark's in Fallston has almost 1,800 families as members.

A beloved tradition at the parish is the long-running fundraiser known as Winter Wonders, an arts and crafts fair held each December. The event allows children to buy inexpensive Christmas gifts, play games, and have their photograph taken with St. Nick. Grown-ups enjoy hot holiday drinks and home-baked goodies in the Tea Room.

The parish's youth group dresses up as the Holy Family, and parishioners can have their photos taken by the manger.

The pastor of St. Mark's is Fr. Edward B. Hemler.

ST. MARK / FALLSTON
Established in 1887 as a Harford County mission of St. John the Evangelist in nearby Hydes,
St. Mark's became a parish in 1968. Ground was broken for a new church in 1989, which opened in September of 1990.

ST. ISAAC JOGUES / CARNEY

Established in 1968, St. Isaac Jogues is located at 9215 Old Harford Road in the Carney section of Baltimore County. The pastor is Fr. H. Martin Hammond. In recent years, one of the more important events at St. Isaac Jogues took place in 2004 with the "Choose Life High School Social Action Day" that attracted students from around the Archdiocese.

Of particular interest was a presentation and discussion of the archdiocese's "Project Rachel" program, an outreach to women and men, whoever they might be, hurting emotionally and spiritually in the wake of an abortion. [Those in need of counseling offered by Project Rachel are urged to call 1.800.286.4224.]

ST. ISAAC JOGUES

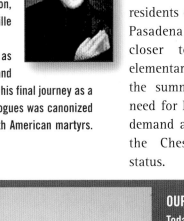

St. Isaac Jogues was a French missionary and professor of literature born in Orleans on January 10, 1607. A Jesuit believed to be the first Roman Catholic priest on Manhattan Island, St. Isaac Jogues was martyred in 1646 at Ossernenon, in what is now the town of Auriesville near Albany. Auriesville is home to the National Shrine of Our Lady of Martyrs.

Regarded by the Mohawk and their fellow Indians as a sorcerer-- and the cause of their blighted crops and widespread disease-- he was captured by the Iroquois on his final journey as a missionary in upstate New York and decapitated. Isaac Jogues was canonized by Pope Pius XI on June 29, 1930, with seven other North American martyrs. Their collective feast day is October 19.

In the summer of 1968, the Rev. Thomas J. Fannon, pastor of St. Jane Frances de Chantal parish in Riviera Beach began offering residents of the Lake Shore area of Pasadena warm-weather Masses closer to home in a local elementary school. By the end of the summer of 1975, there was need for Mass year-round to meet demand and in 1980 Our Lady of the Chesapeake earned parish status.

OUR LADY OF CHESAPEAKE

Today, Our Lady of the Chesapeake counts more than 1,500 families as members. There are more than 50 Eucharistic ministers, 30 lectors and liturgical readers and 25 musicians providing support at Mass. Outreach includes the Elizabeth Ministry to expectant mothers and those with newborn children.

The pastor is the Rev. Brian M. Rafferty.

In the summer of 1969, Pope Paul VI visited Uganda to bless the new altar at the shrine of the Namugongo martyrs, more than 30 African saints burned to death between 1885 and 1887 for refusing to renounce their Christian faith. Paul VI became the first pope to visit the African continent.

In 1970, newspapers in Baltimore, led by unionized pressmen, went on strike for ten weeks and a swath of aging go-go saloons along "the Block" on East Baltimore Street near the Fallsway were torn down to make way for a new city police headquarters.

Also in 1970, Pope Paul VI published a decree that relaxed the rules for marriage between Catholics and non-Catholics while in the world at large, President Richard Nixon signed a Constitutional amendment giving 18-year-olds the right to vote and the Beatles announced they were calling it quits after nearly a decade at the top of the pops.

One of the first things the parishioners of the Church of the Good Shepherd wanted for their community was a religion center, and in 1973 volunteers began working to build one. A year later, on March 10, 1974, their effort was destroyed by arson. The next morning, volunteers returned to the rubble and began again. Ground breaking for a sanctuary took place in 1975, with nearly 100 volunteers laboring for almost two years. The first Mass in the new church was celebrated in the autumn of 1977, and today

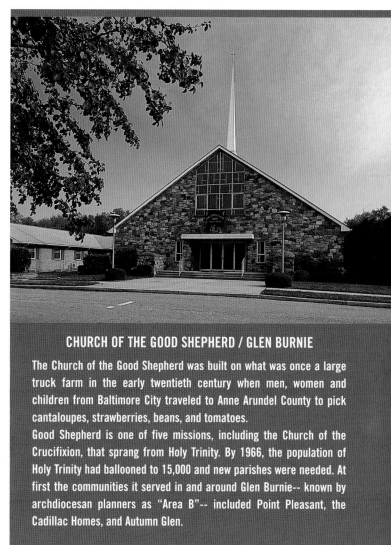

CHURCH OF THE GOOD SHEPHERD / GLEN BURNIE

The Church of the Good Shepherd was built on what was once a large truck farm in the early twentieth century when men, women and children from Baltimore City traveled to Anne Arundel County to pick cantaloupes, strawberries, beans, and tomatoes.

Good Shepherd is one of five missions, including the Church of the Crucifixion, that sprang from Holy Trinity. By 1966, the population of Holy Trinity had ballooned to 15,000 and new parishes were needed. At first the communities it served in and around Glen Burnie-- known by archdiocesan planners as "Area B"-- included Point Pleasant, the Cadillac Homes, and Autumn Glen.

the Church of the Good Shepherd is home to nearly 500 families.

RELAY CATHOLIC COMMUNITY, INC.

In 1972, the Catholic Community at Relay was established on the principles of peace and justice that evolved from an Ecumenical Campus Ministry. The congregation is led by the laity, attracting about two hundred and fifty worshippers.

South West Emergency Services [SWES] was founded in the basement of the Community church, as a clothing closet and a food pantry. It is now housed in a building and cares for the needs of people in the 21227 zip code with everything from utility cut-off notices to prescription medicine.

The first floor of the house on the congregation's property is used as a shelter in conjunction with Associated Catholic Charities Fresh Start Program. The old village of Relay, near both Halethorpe and Arbutus, was named because, once upon a time, stagecoaches changed horses there.

ST. BERNADETTE / SEVERN

Located on Stevenson Road in Severn, St. Bernadette – like the Church of the Crucifixion and the Church of the Good Shepherd – got its start in the late 1960s. Masses were held at the Archbishop Martin Spalding H.S. auditorium and would continue to be celebrated there through 1979 when the current sanctuary was completed.

Pioneering members of St. Bernadette include George Donadoni, a long-time lector at Holy Trinity before helping get the new parish off the ground, and Fr. Edwin Mylin, an early pastor.

In 1976, Fr. Joseph M. Connolly, a civil rights activist known for his sharp intellect, took over at St. Bernadette. The current pastor, the Rev. Domenic L. Cieri, arrived in 1992 and is known to all as "Father Nick." He serves some 1,200 families.

A project in which St. Bernadette takes particular pride is the Fause Center, alongside the state Motor Vehicle Administration on Ritchie Highway. Named for James Fause, a longtime parishioner, the center is a homeless shelter and transitional living community providing stability and various skill training for homeless men.

Mr. Fause, who worked to make the center a reality for years, died before his dream was realized in 1999.

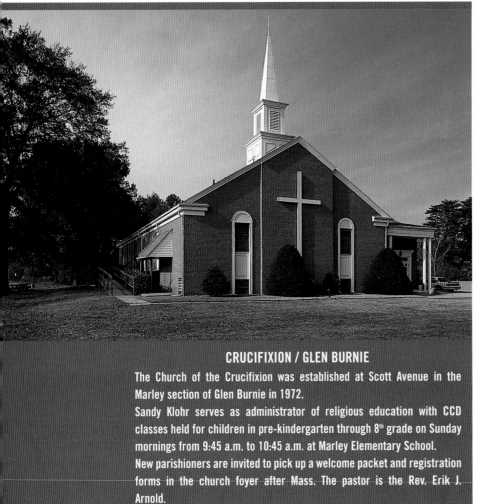

CRUCIFIXION / GLEN BURNIE

The Church of the Crucifixion was established at Scott Avenue in the Marley section of Glen Burnie in 1972.

Sandy Klohr serves as administrator of religious education with CCD classes held for children in pre-kindergarten through 8th grade on Sunday mornings from 9:45 a.m. to 10:45 a.m. at Marley Elementary School.

New parishioners are invited to pick up a welcome packet and registration forms in the church foyer after Mass. The pastor is the Rev. Erik J. Arnold.

In January of 1973, Pope Paul VI received Prime Minister Golda Meir of Israel at the Vatican as Catholics worldwide gradually, though not without reluctance in many sectors, came to accept the changes brought about by Vatican II. In her visit, she paid tribute to the work of Pope Pius XII on behalf of the Jewish people.

Cardinal Shehan, in one of his last official roles before retiring the following year, was appointed by Pope Paul VI as the "papal legate" to the fortieth Eucharistic Congress in Melbourne, Australia, held in February of 1973.

According to Fr. Richard Lawrence, no one had informed the Cardinal that he would be viewed as the Pope himself wherever he went during the event.

"He was sitting on the plane next to his colleagues when the flight attendant, near the end of the first leg of the flight asked him to come to the front," recalls Father Lawrence. "He shrugged and agreed, turning to his colleagues wondering why. They realized he had no idea what was to come and they didn't have time to brief him."

When the door of the airplane opened, Cardinal Shehan was greeted with the same pomp and circumstance as any head of state, with a full rendition of the Vatican anthem, the Australian national anthem, the red carpet, and a state dinner.

The next day, Cardinal Shehan and his entourage were flown to Melbourne on Australia's equivalent of Air Force One.

■ ■ ■

On April 2, 1974, at age 76, Cardinal Shehan resigned his See and retired. In June, he was replaced by Archbishop William Donald Borders.

Cardinal Shehan died a decade after his retirement. His galero hangs in the sanctuary of the Cathedral of Mary Our Queen almost directly above his tomb. It is an old tradition of the Church to hang the red hat of a deceased cardinal in the sanctuary of his

cathedral. Legend holds that when the hat falls to the ground, the cardinal's soul has entered heaven. "It's only a legend," explains a secretary at the Cathedral, noting that Cardinal Shehan's hat-- at times the subject of homilies-- continues to hang in place.

THE GRANDFATHERLY CARDINAL
The countenance of Baltimore's twelfth archbishop struck many who knew him as grandfatherly. He celebrated daily Mass at the Basilica as well as 8 a.m. Sunday Mass and heard confessions on Saturday afternoons. He had a taste for roast leg of lamb and a distinct handwriting style that crept up to, or slightly beyond, the right hand edge of the paper. For all of his forward-thinking work - "The Cardinal's instincts were far more liberal than those of any other cardinal I have known," said Ed Wall.

Archbishop William D. Borders

"I will listen that I may serve..."

- Archbishop Borders

In 1936, as the Spanish Civil War began to spread across the Iberian Peninsula, William Donald Borders left seminary in his native Indiana for Notre Dame Seminary in New Orleans. He was ordained in the Crescent City at St. Louis Cathedral on May 18, 1940 and assigned to a parish in Baton Rouge.

In 1943, Archbishop Borders enlisted in the United States Army Chaplain Corps, serving with the 91st Infantry Division in Africa and Italy. Upon his discharge in 1946, he'd attained the rank of major.

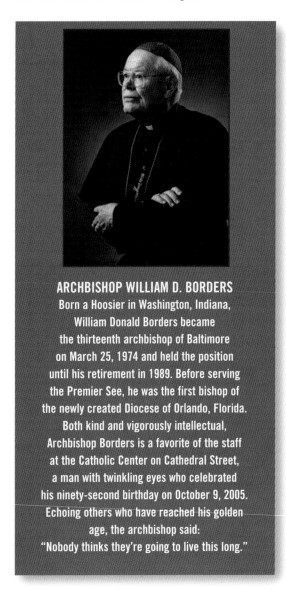

ARCHBISHOP WILLIAM D. BORDERS
Born a Hoosier in Washington, Indiana,
William Donald Borders became
the thirteenth archbishop of Baltimore
on March 25, 1974 and held the position
until his retirement in 1989. Before serving
the Premier See, he was the first bishop of
the newly created Diocese of Orlando, Florida.
Both kind and vigorously intellectual,
Archbishop Borders is a favorite of the staff
at the Catholic Center on Cathedral Street,
a man with twinkling eyes who celebrated
his ninety-second birthday on October 9, 2005.
Echoing others who have reached his golden
age, the archbishop said:
"Nobody thinks they're going to live this long."

Serving as a military chaplain is challenging under any circumstances. But the experience of offering sustenance and counsel to combat soldiers on the front lines of World War II, says Archbishop Borders, was far too complicated for easy analysis.

After the war, Archbishop Borders enrolled at the University of Notre Dame in South Bend, Indiana, received a master's degree in education in 1947, and became associate pastor at Our Lady of Lourdes in New Orleans.

Next, he spent many years as chaplain at the main campus of Louisiana State University in Baton Rouge, and in 1963 was made monsignor. On May 2, 1968, Pope Paul VI named him Bishop of the new diocese of Orlando.

After six years in Orlando, where he ushered in the changes dictated by the decrees of the Second Vatican Council, he was named to succeed Cardinal Shehan as head of the Archdiocese of Baltimore. Here, he divided the Archdiocese into three vicariates and appointed three auxiliary Bishops over them. On most matters, these vicars were authorized to act in the name of the archbishop.

THE FUTURE ARCHBISHOP MAKES AN UNEXPECTED DELIVERY
BY DAVID MORLEY

In times of war, strange things happen.

Like a man of God delivering a baby in an Italian cave in the Apennine Mountains.

It was 1944 after crossing the Arno River, and things were looking up for the Allies. Archbishop Borders, then thirty, traveled at night, often with the medics to administer anointings in an emergency. The group looked for a place to set up a first-aid post.

"We moved at night because we were pretty vulnerable," he recalls, noting that he and three others split up to find a safe spot. "A medical sergeant and I came across an excellent cave where we'd be pretty safe from any artillery."

Inside, the two heard the echoes of what sounded like whimpering. Father Borders' strong flashlight helped led him deeper into the cave, where he found "a young girl about 16 years of age ...terribly frightened."

She was also in labor. The medical sergeant took off in search of the Army doctor while chaplain Borders tried to comfort the girl.

"I was trying to convince her I was a priest, but she didn't believe me," he said, saying he feared she'd give birth before the medics arrived. "You cannot give a complete analysis of what it's like to be a military chaplain."

Finally the doctor arrived and in about three minutes, so did the baby, a boy.

When Fr. Borders performed the sacrament of Baptism, the young mother finally believed he was what he claimed to be: a Catholic priest.

Pearl Harbor brought the young priest into the military. Thousands upon thousands of men were lining up to enlist after the Japanese sneak attack and more were being drafted. The future archbishop's call was something more than patriotic – he felt called to take Catholicism to the front lines.

"There was a need. My joining was a response to that need."

Six months after signing up, he was assigned to the 362nd Infantry Regiment of the 91st Infantry Division. They started in Northern Africa and marched into Italy and "climbing the boot" by way of the Apennines.

"You didn't have a set place for counseling the soldiers. They'd contact you and you'd maybe take a walk or maybe go in the jeep to counsel them."

He often celebrated Mass on the hood of a Jeep & comments that the large number of attendees could be the result of a hunger for hope or the fact of death's being close at hand.

While serving as a war chaplain in Italy, word came that Pope Pius XII had invited clerics from the frontlines to meet with him at the Vatican. "I'd never been in Rome when I hear that the Pope would like to hear reports from chaplains, and so I went and had an interview with him," remembered Archbishop Borders. Most striking, he said, was the impression of the Holy Father as a fellow human being - a kind, intelligent man burdened with all the responsibilities and weariness of the times.

There was common ground, the archbishop said, and "It was very evident that Pope Pius [XII] was completely worn out because of the pressure of the office and the strain of the war."

On Christmas Eve, 1944, another regiment relieved the 362nd for the day, and the veterans pulled back from the line about a dozen or so miles.

He describes the ruined building: "We came across an old [bombed-out] church and the windows were blown out. But we decided we were going to have midnight Mass on Christmas, and so I started with the sacrament of reconciliation in the afternoon and stopped at about six to take a break and have a sandwich."

During the day, infantrymen swept and cleaned; they blacked out the windows and chopped down trees to decorate the sanctuary. Battery-powered headlights from Army trucks lit the church. By 11:30 p.m., the building had been transformed.

"That," the Archbishop says, "was the most memorable midnight Mass of my life."

Since the war, as his career developed, Archbishop Borders has seen the world change. He has no doubt that the Church will remain, and perhaps increase, as a vital force in society--but not without work.

"It's got to be people who are really dedicated and those who really practice the religion," he says, noting that he's not the ultimate authority on such things.

"You need to speak to the Holy Spirit," he said.

233

Many of Archbishop Borders' accomplishments were internal, unseen by most of the public. He initiated a Department of Pastoral Planning and Management, an Office of Fund Development to carry out an effective stewardship program, and a strong evange-- lization effort to reach the un-churched of the Archdiocese.

At the national level, he served as a member of the Bishops' Committee on Moral Values and was chairman of the ad hoc Committee of Bishops and Catholic College Presidents.

CHURCH OF THE RESURRECTION / ELLICOTT CITY

Located at 3175 Paulskirk Drive in Ellicott City, the Church of the Resurrection was founded in 1974. Adoration of the Blessed Sacrament at the parish is held each Monday from 9:30 a.m. – immediately after morning Mass – until 7 p.m.

The pastor is the Rev. Msgr. James O. McGovern.

"...spreading the Good News has changed since those early days when the message was given orally then written and compiled into book form," says Msgr. McGovern on the parish Internet site. "Long gone are the quill pens and monastic scriptoriums. However the message of Jesus is timeless and perhaps more important for the world to hear than in any other time in our human history..."

OUR LADY OF GRACE / PARKTON

The roots of Our Lady of Grace in the Parkton section of Baltimore County grow from the St. Joseph congregation in Texas, Md. In the late 1960s, parishioners at St. Joseph petitioned the pastor for a mission for Catholics living in the upper reaches of the county. Initially called the Hereford Mission, it opened in the auditorium of Hereford High School in the fall of 1968, attracting more than 350 people and expanding almost immediately. Religious education was started for elementary and high school students, and a Ladies Guild was created to lead fundraising efforts.

In the spring of 1977, construction began on a 6,400 square-foot community building with a sanctuary that held four-hundred for the celebration of Mass. Today with more than 1,300 families, Our Lady of Grace participates in a number of outreach ministries, including a special effort with sister church Saint Cecilia in Baltimore City.

At St. Cecilia, the Catholics from Parkton volunteer in a soup kitchen and adopt school children each September, providing them with school supplies. School books are also given to children at St. Veronica parish school in Cherry Hill.

The pastor is Msgr. Nicholas Amato. Sr. Helen Wiegmann, S.S.J. is the school principal.

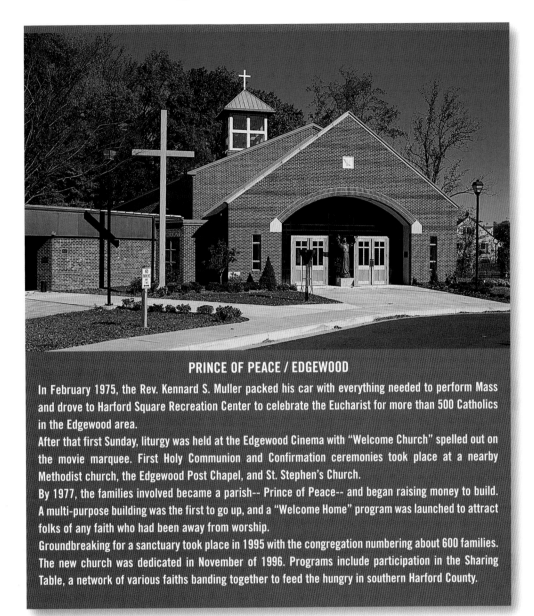

PRINCE OF PEACE / EDGEWOOD

In February 1975, the Rev. Kennard S. Muller packed his car with everything needed to perform Mass and drove to Harford Square Recreation Center to celebrate the Eucharist for more than 500 Catholics in the Edgewood area.

After that first Sunday, liturgy was held at the Edgewood Cinema with "Welcome Church" spelled out on the movie marquee. First Holy Communion and Confirmation ceremonies took place at a nearby Methodist church, the Edgewood Post Chapel, and St. Stephen's Church.

By 1977, the families involved became a parish-- Prince of Peace-- and began raising money to build. A multi-purpose building was the first to go up, and a "Welcome Home" program was launched to attract folks of any faith who had been away from worship.

Groundbreaking for a sanctuary took place in 1995 with the congregation numbering about 600 families. The new church was dedicated in November of 1996. Programs include participation in the Sharing Table, a network of various faiths banding together to feed the hungry in southern Harford County.

Known for his scholarship in the field of ethics, Archbishop Borders has written extensively about the ways in which ambition and humility have an impact on our lives.

"The greatest difficulty that we have in this journey... is coping with problems and pressures often spurred by personal ambition, which is a terrible sin of pride," he writes. "We need to understand how grace and revelation work, together in personal growth through the virtue of humility. A humble person judges himself in relation to God, and in that process understands that separated from God, life has little meaning and purpose.

"Humility," he continues, "is not just an ideal, which remains static, but an attitude and insight that pervades every decision and action of human relations... the gifts and virtues of faith and charity, united with humility, enable a person to live in the real world that belongs to God."

When Archbishop Borders arrived in Baltimore in 1974, there was a slight drop in enrollment in Catholic high schools nationwide from the year before, although the number was almost a million. In May of 1974, Pope Paul VI addressed the United Nations on the issue of apartheid while criticizing violence as a response to discrimination. The pontiff also used the forum to condemn discrimination against "all who live at the margin of society and are without voice."

The Rev. Frank Callahan, the recently retired, longtime pastor of St. Margaret parish in Bel Air, was part of what was known in the early 1970s as the "Priests Senate" within the

Archdiocese of Baltimore, a group that helped recommend Archbishop Borders for his job here.

"He was well-versed in the [decrees] of the Second Vatican Council," says Father Callahan, 68, who grew up in the St. Bernardine parish. "His big thing was collegiality – bringing pastors and parish councils to work together, even though they sometimes clashed."

Archbishop Borders, Father Callahan said, was not shy about removing priests who did not see the relationship between pastor and parish council as a partnership.

"He believed that the laity deserved a very strong role in parish policy and encouraged them to participate in [planning], which was a new thing back then," adds Father Callahan. "Now planning is not an especially spirited activity, but it's important."

In 1975, Baltimore mayor William Donald Schaefer won an easy re-election over Republican Claudette M. Chandler, by a more than 5-to-1 margin. Also that year, the city's first African-American school board president, Roland Patterson, was fired by the board for deliberately lowering academic standards while failing to deal with rising school violence.

This was also the year, on September 14th, of Mother Elizabeth Ann Bayley Seton's canonization. Less noticed by local Catholics was the canonization that fall of Archbishop Oliver Plunkett, a seventeenth-century Irish prelate executed in 1681 by Great Britain on charges of treason.

Before the end of 1976, Archbishop Borders declared St. Elizabeth Ann Seton congregation, formerly a mission church, a parish.

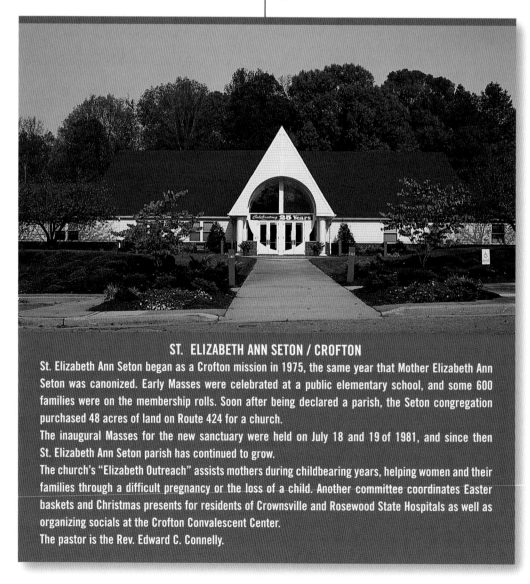

ST. ELIZABETH ANN SETON / CROFTON

St. Elizabeth Ann Seton began as a Crofton mission in 1975, the same year that Mother Elizabeth Ann Seton was canonized. Early Masses were celebrated at a public elementary school, and some 600 families were on the membership rolls. Soon after being declared a parish, the Seton congregation purchased 48 acres of land on Route 424 for a church.

The inaugural Masses for the new sanctuary were held on July 18 and 19 of 1981, and since then St. Elizabeth Ann Seton parish has continued to grow.

The church's "Elizabeth Outreach" assists mothers during childbearing years, helping women and their families through a difficult pregnancy or the loss of a child. Another committee coordinates Easter baskets and Christmas presents for residents of Crownsville and Rosewood State Hospitals as well as organizing socials at the Crofton Convalescent Center.

The pastor is the Rev. Edward C. Connelly.

OUR LADY OF PERPETUAL HELP / EDGEWATER

In 1976, Our Lady of Perpetual Help opened in Edgewater in Anne Arundel County. In a December, 2005 message to parishioners, former pastor Fr. Frank Brauer wrote:

"Perhaps part of our Christmas preparation might consist in looking more closely at the goodness we have brought into our world. To whom or what has the Lord called us to be present?

How have we become the face of love and kindness for others... God has put us into the lives of certain others so that we could show them the face of Christ. May we have the strength and perseverance we need to continue to bring kindness and comfort..."

It was the Year of Three Popes.

In less than three months of 1978, the Catholic Church mourned the deaths of two popes and elected a third who became the first non-Italian in more than four hundred and fifty years.

On August 6, the fifteen-year-reign of Pope Paul VI ended with a heart attack. He was succeeded on August 26 by Cardinal Albino Luciani, who took the name Pope John Paul I. A month later, the pope known for his friendliness and humility, was found dead in bed at his Vatican apartment. John Paul I's tenure is one of the shortest papal reigns in history.

■ ■ ■

The following year, Pope John Paul II launched his on-the-road papacy with visits to Poland, Turkey, Mexico, Ireland, and the United States. Wherever the new Pope traveled, the crowds were huge, and he reaffirmed Church doctrine and tradition while being entertained by native culture the world over.

In Puebla, Mexico - where he attended the Third General Assembly of Latin American Bishops – he flatly rejected the use of violence as a response to the region's many dictators and their policies.

"It is not permissible," said the Pope, "to kill in order to impose a solution."

Also in 1979, the Archdiocese of Baltimore formally established St. Michael of Poplar Springs as a parish. Its history dates to the decade following the American Civil War.

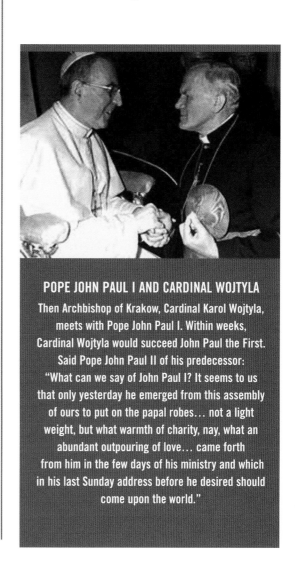

POPE JOHN PAUL I AND CARDINAL WOJTYLA

Then Archbishop of Krakow, Cardinal Karol Wojtyla, meets with Pope John Paul I. Within weeks, Cardinal Wojtyla would succeed John Paul the First. Said Pope John Paul II of his predecessor:

"What can we say of John Paul I? It seems to us that only yesterday he emerged from this assembly of ours to put on the papal robes... not a light weight, but what warmth of charity, nay, what an abundant outpouring of love... came forth from him in the few days of his ministry and which in his last Sunday address before he desired should come upon the world."

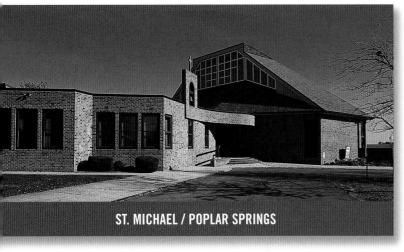

ST. MICHAEL / POPLAR SPRINGS

Back in 1879, a non-Catholic property owner near Mt. Airy named Lilbourne Kuhn gave permission for a young priest to celebrate Mass at his house. The priest did not return the following Sunday, but Mr. Kuhn had advertised in Mt. Airy and Woodbine that Mass would again be held at his home. That week, about 20 people showed, and Mr. Kuhn contacted a local bishop to tell him of the dilemma: a flock of faithful with no shepherd to lead them. Soon, Rev. Charles Ferrari, S.J., arrived, baptizing the Kuhn family, who then donated their property for a church and cemetery. By 1882, St. Michael was a mission church of St. Joseph in Sykesville. Today's structure was built in the 1980s and attracts believers who participate in a wide range of outreach ministries including the "Food Cellar" that donates groceries to anyone in need throughout the year. The church website proudly announces that pastoral visitors at St. Michael call on the sick, the homebound, and those in area nursing homes with an emphasis on friendliness and spirituality. Pastoral visitors also send cards from the parish community to those on the visitation list on religious holidays and their birthdays. The pastor at St. Michael is the Rev. Michael J. Ruane.

Pope John Paul II continued his globe-trotting in 1980, visiting a half-dozen African nations-- including celebrating Mass before a million and a half people in Zaire-- as well as appearing before huge crowds in West Germany, Brazil, and France. President Valery Giscard d'Estaing noted that the Pope's visit to France was the first visit by a pontiff to the country of the apparitions at Lourdes in more than 165 years.

According to Vatican statistics, more than 81,000 Americans became Catholics in 1980, for a total of nearly 50 million Catholics in the United States.

During his papacy, Pope John Paul II had more meetings than any of his predecessors. More than 17,600,000 pilgrims participated in the General Audiences held on Wednesdays and the millions of faithful he met during pastoral visits in Italy and throughout the world.

■ ■ ■

A world which had pretty much seen it all, where it seemed that nothing retained the power to shock, had to reconsider its fatigue on May 13, 1981 when Pope John Paul II was shot by an assassin before a crowd of 10,000 pilgrims in St. Peter's Square. A convicted murderer from Turkey was arrested in the attack, which sent the Pope into surgery for more than five hours to repair intestinal damage, By the fall of 1981, after a few return hospital visits to treat infections, John Paul II, then 61, was deemed fit for duty and returned to his public ministry with vigor.

1981 SHOOTING OF POPE JOHN PAUL II
credit: Catholic News Service

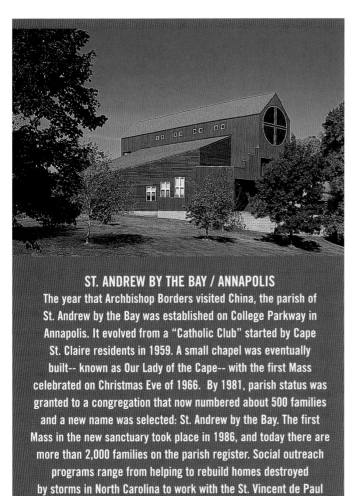

ST. ANDREW BY THE BAY / ANNAPOLIS
The year that Archbishop Borders visited China, the parish of St. Andrew by the Bay was established on College Parkway in Annapolis. It evolved from a "Catholic Club" started by Cape St. Claire residents in 1959. A small chapel was eventually built-- known as Our Lady of the Cape-- with the first Mass celebrated on Christmas Eve of 1966. By 1981, parish status was granted to a congregation that now numbered about 500 families and a new name was selected: St. Andrew by the Bay. The first Mass in the new sanctuary took place in 1986, and today there are more than 2,000 families on the parish register. Social outreach programs range from helping to rebuild homes destroyed by storms in North Carolina to work with the St. Vincent de Paul Society. The pastor is Fr. Stephen D. Gosnell.

ST. TIMOTHY / WALKERSVILLE

Located on a 12-acre campus at 8651 Biggs Ford Road, St. Timothy began as an experiment to see if there were enough "active Catholics" in the Walkersville/Woodsboro area to establish a faith community.
Most of the early families that arrived at a small, rented chapel came from the St. John parish in Frederick while others were members of St. Peter in Libertytown or Our Lady of Mt. Carmel in Thurmont.
Archbishop Borders appointed Fr. Paul Whitthauer to launch the mission; the first Mass was celebrated on July 27, 1980.
Formal plans to build a church were made public in 1992, with groundbreaking taking place in 1995. The new sanctuary opened two years later, and today some 900 families worship at St. Timothy.
Twice a year, the parish organizes "giving tree" events with all donations going to underprivileged children from the Walkersville area: when school begins and at Christmas.
Members of St. Timothy are stalwart supporters of the local Habitat for Humanity project, which is located about a half-mile from the church. The pastor is Father Andrew D. Aaron.

In, one of the most poignant photos of the 20th century, TIME magazine ran a cover showing the Holy Father counseling his would-be assassin in prison two days after Christmas, 1983. The pair spoke privately for more than an hour.

"I spoke to him as a brother whom I have pardoned and who has my complete trust," the Holy Father said.

■ ■ ■

In the fall of 1981, in company with other leading Catholic educators, Archbishop Borders made a three-week tour of the People's Republic of China to investigate the possibilities for an exchange of cultural and educational programs between that nation and the United States.

In 1983, the Baltimore Orioles won the World Series for the third time in their history, and – as of 2006 – the last time. Polish labor leader Lech Walesa, the Solidarity leader, was awarded the Nobel Peace Prize. And Walesa's fellow countryman, Pope John Paul II signed a revised code of Catholic canon law, which took effect in November of 1983.

The new document replaced a 1917 code governing all aspects of Church life and incorporated changes made at the Second Vatican Council. While reducing the number of offenses necessary for excommunication, the 1983 code stood firm on traditional laws concerning marriage and divorce.

CATHOLIC COMMUNITY OF ST. FRANCIS XAVIER / HUNT VALLEY

The Catholic Community of St. Francis Xavier began as a "Mass station" in 1986 in response to overcrowding at St. Joseph in Texas, Md.
It was launched as a mission in 1988 by a small group of disciples guided by Father Thomas Donellan,
priest in residence. Since then, the community has grown to include more than 1,000 families in and around northern Baltimore County.
The intensely pro-life parish offers a range of social action programs, including ministries to the unborn, the elderly, the sick,
and the poor. The Catholic Community of St. Francis Xavier became a parish in 1992. The pastor is Fr. Francis Brauer.

JUDI KEYS

From typing up weekly bulletins for Sunday Mass to chief cook and bottle washer at the Catholic Community of St. Francis Xavier, Judi Keys has just about done it all in the many years she has worshipped there.

A Methodist who entered the Catholic Church after marrying Marion Keys some 40 years ago, Judi did not expect her life to be transformed when she began putting together the Sunday bulletin in the days when St. Francis met in a hotel ballroom. But slowly and surely it did.

In time, Judi returned to school to earn a bachelor's degree and from there moved on to St. Mary's Seminary in Roland Park for a master's degree in theology "which comes in handy," she said, "now that I am in charge of adult formation classes."

Says Mrs. Keys, simply: "I really love the Catholic Church."

When it became a mission in 1989, the Catholic Community of St. Francis Xavier operated out of an office on the lower level of the O'Dwyer Youth Retreat House in Sparks. By the beginning of 1990 Mass was offered at the Sherwood Episcopal Church. The following month, 27 acres along Cuba Road were purchased to build a church. The capital campaign was launched in March of 1995, and the first Mass in the new St. Francis Xavier sanctuary was celebrated on January 17, 1998.

The building was formally dedicated by Cardinal Keeler on April 26, 1998.

In the primary elections in the fall of 1987, former Baltimore City state's attorney Kurt Schmoke beat former City Council president Clarence "Du" Burns to become the first African-American elected mayor of Baltimore in 193 years.

In January of 2003, Mr. Burns was eulogized at the Cathedral of Mary Our Queen

ST. FRANCIS OF ASSISI / FULTON

The first liturgy of the new faith community-- in time to be known as St. Francis of Assisi of Fulton-- was celebrated on Dec. 10, 1988. Then, as now, the focus of the faithful was community service.

In addition to visits to the homebound and those in the hospital, the St. Francis community reaches out to those who are physically fit in an effort to help maintain health. Parish groups monitor blood pressure, distribute first-aid kits, and have established a lending library of health-related materials and literature. There is also an annual Lenten blood drive.

St. Francis was a founding member of Churches Concerned for the Homeless, today known as Congregations Concerned for the Homeless. The organization assists the needy with housing, childcare, and education while insisting that participants attend job counseling, parenting, and financial counseling classes in a campaign for self-sufficiency.

The pastor is Fr. Dennis P. Diehl, formerly active in television work, locally and nationally.

by a new mayor, Martin O'Malley, who said of his predecessor: "...he believed a man should scatter and not hoard. He believed that the mark of a true leader is not so much someone who surrounds himself with the greatest and most talented people but someone who surrounds himself with ordinary people and makes them believe that they have great talent and can do great things..."

Archbishop William Donald Borders submitted his resignation to Pope John Paul II on his 75th birthday, almost twenty years ago. What is so joyful about the archbishop's longevity, said one priest who helped bring him to Baltimore, is that he often said he wouldn't live to be sixty-five, much less ninety-two.

"He was hesitant at first because he'd had a heart attack," remembers Father Callahan,

As the decades have proved, that hesitancy has been shown to be needless.

A MAN OF PRAYER
CREDIT: RICK LIPPENHOLZ PHOTOGRAPHY
Archbishop Borders prays at the Cathedral of Mary Our Queen during the Mass to celebrate Cardinal Keeler's 50 years of priesthood. Archbishop Borders, though retired, continues to keep office hours at the Catholic Center and celebrates Mass for the residents of Mercy Ridge.

The Man Who Brought the Pope

to Baltimore Cardinal William H. Keeler 1989 to the present

"Do the work of an evangelist..."

- *Cardinal William H. Keeler*

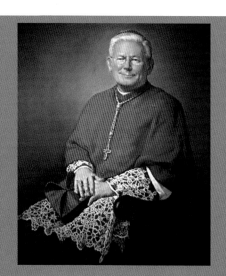

CARDINAL WILLIAM H. KEELER
Painted by the internationally known Baltimore artist and sculptor Joseph Sheppard, this portrait of Cardinal William H. Keeler, the 14th archbishop of Baltimore, hangs in the archbishop's residence next to the Basilica of the Assumption.
Cardinal William H. Keeler was appointed Archbishop of Baltimore by Pope John Paul II in April of 1989, and was formally installed atop the nation's oldest See on May 23 of that year at the Cathedral of Mary Our Queen.
Only the third Cardinal in the history of the Archdiocese, Cardinal Keeler received the fabled red hat from Pope John Paul II at the Vatican on November 28, 1994.

ardinal Keeler took his motto from a letter of St. Paul, whose message rang especially strong for him during the Second Vatican Council, which he attended as a young priest from the Diocese of Harrisburg, Pa.

The call to evangelization, to do the hard and often difficult work it demands, is a message the Cardinal heard loud and often during the reign of Pope John Paul II.

"I think Pope John Paul II gave evangelization such a major emphasis during his years because it was emphasized so much during the Second Vatican Council," the Cardinal said.

In a wide-ranging interview with Catholic Review editor Daniel Medinger for a special edition honoring his 2005 golden jubilee, Cardinal Keeler said that celebrating daily Mass and preaching the Word of God were his greatest joys. These are also part of the legacy of Vatican II, he said, noting that during Council sessions he "listened to the debates about the importance of preaching".

"I came," he said, "to a kind of personal evolution in recognizing how important, how precious, God's Word is and the sacramental qualities it has when it's properly proclaimed."

Some may see the work of an evangelist only in the direct preaching of the Gospel of Jesus Christ. But the work has taken many other forms during Cardinal Keeler's long and vigorous tenure as head of the Archdiocese of Baltimore.

Among the programs launched since Cardinal Keeler arrived after the retirement of Archbishop William D. Borders include the RENEW spiritual sessions held in private homes by and for the laity; The Emmaus program to foster priestly spirituality, with support groups still meeting; Partners in Excellence, in which corporations, foundations and citizens donate money - more than $1.4 million in 2005 - to help pay tuitions for low-income students in Baltimore City; and the annual Lenten Appeal for a constellation of ministries.

Cardinal Keeler's time in Baltimore has been marked by staunch, unwavering support for the pro-life movement. From 1998 through 2001, he served as chair for the United States Conference of Catholic Bishops Committee on Pro-Life activities and was re-elected to head that group in late 2003.

He is known for sensitivity toward those contemplating a vocation, hosting regular "discernment" suppers at his home while encouraging those contemplating a vocation to talk it over with someone they trust.

[By the fall of 2004, there were 251 Archdiocesan priests in the Baltimore area, 62 of them retired. The overall figure does not include active priests from various religious communities at work in the Archdiocese of Baltimore.]

Cardinal Keeler also showed both candor and courage in getting out ahead of the news during the church sex scandal that began to break across the nation in 2000. In a May 14, 2002 press conference, the Cardinal said that the Archdiocese of Baltimore has "...since '84, been reporting [abuse] cases to the civil authorities if there is a crime involved, if there is something criminal to be pursued, their investi-

gation is the one that we count on to turn up details."

In September of 2002, Cardinal Keeler released the names of some 50 priests and religious brothers credibly accused of sexual abuse or misconduct going back more than half-a-century, a move that angered some priests. [Note that only those living or, if deceased, who had confessed when questioned about abusing minors, were named.]

"The truth is going to come out one way or another," the Cardinal said at the time. "We may as well face the issue clearly and cleanly."

On this issue, and others, those close to Cardinal Keeler say that he shares at least one quality often associated with former Maryland Governor William Donald Schaefer: a no-nonsense discipline about getting things done.

As Archbishop Daniel Pilarczyk of Cincinnati said of Cardinal Keeler's tenure as president of the National Conference of Catholic Bishops: "There was no messing around."

And in the autumn of 1995, Cardinal Keeler welcomed Pope John Paul II to the Premier See on the shores of the Patapsco River.

CARDINAL KEELER AND POPE JOHN PAUL II AT CAMDEN YARDS

CNS file photo, Karen Callaway

"It is well to remember how remarkably [Pope John Paul II] renews for our day the role of Peter in the Church ...here in Baltimore, he prayed and spoke with marvelous effect, commending the great good of local efforts, especially in our Catholic schools..."
Cardinal Keeler, Oct. 16, 2003

Cardinal William H. Keeler was born a Texan on March 4, 1931 in San Antonio and moved to the Pennsylvania town of Lebanon on Quitapahilla Creek as a young boy. There, he attended parochial school and graduated from Lebanon Catholic High School before entering the St. Charles Seminary in the Overbrook section of Philadelphia.

While William was still a young boy, a local priest proclaimed the child would himself grow up to become a priest. The older man had apparently said the same to another boy, who did not fulfill the hunch. But in 1955, then 24-years-old, Cardinal Keeler was ordained after receiving a Licentiate in Sacred Theology from the Pontifical Gregorian University in Rome. In 1961, he was awarded a doctorate in Canon Law from the same university.

NEWLY-ORDAINED FATHER KEELER
"We moved to Philadelphia from Texas when I was 5 or 6 and to Lebanon [Pa.] after I finished the fifth grade," recalled Cardinal Keeler, who said he was aware that Baltimore was the first diocese in the United States from a very early age. "My grandfather's family on my father's side lived in Baltimore for a while, in St. Martin's parish."

In the early 1960s, providence determined that the future Cardinal would have a front row seat to the most historic Catholic council of the 20th century: Vatican II.

"I count it as one of the great graces of my life even though it happened quite accidentally," Cardinal Keeler told the Catholic Review. "I had made arrangements for Bishop George Leech of Harrisburg and another bishop to stay in Rome. Then the bishop who was supposed to [accompany Bishop George L. Leech] died suddenly."

Young Father Keeler would go instead. Once there, he was appointed special advisor to the Council by Pope John XXIII, who had called for the Council.

"That," the Cardinal recalled, "opened a whole new chapter for me."

As secretary to Bishop Leech, he took detailed notes on all speeches and was assigned to the press panel, where he and others struggled to explain to an old school corps of war and political correspondents the inner workings of an ancient faith.

"I saw how those on the press panel didn't answer the questions that were asked by the reporters but instead answered those that the reporters should have asked but didn't have enough wit to do so," said the Cardinal. "The reporters weren't necessarily at fault because they... were not at home talking about spiritual things like liturgy, scripture and theology."

■ ■ ■

In 1979, Cardinal Keeler was ordained Auxiliary Bishop of the Diocese of Harrisburg, Pa., less than a hundred miles from Baltimore. In 1982, he became bishop of that diocese, where since 1956 he'd held a wide range of jobs, including chancellor and a stint he likes to joke about as a school bus driver.

In Harrisburg Cardinal Keeler began a ministry reaching out to men and women in turmoil after going through an abortion. It was called Project Rachel and he brought the program with him to Baltimore when he took the reins of the Archdiocese of Baltimore on April 11, 1989.

BISHOP LEECH AND BISHOP-ELECT KEELER

Bishop Leech and the newly-appointed Bishop Keeler, in 1979 at St. Anne's Home in Columbia, PA, where Bishop Leech was recovering from an illness.

The year that Cardinal Keeler arrived in Baltimore, the Archdiocese established a parish in the Middletown area just west of Frederick near Interstate-70 known as Holy Family Catholic Community.

POPE JOHN PAUL II ABOVE WORLD YOUTH DAY IN DENVER
photo credit: Cardinal William H. Keeler

Cardinal Keeler, an accomplished photographer who captured many compelling images while traveling with Pope John Paul II, is president of the American Division Catholic Near East Welfare Association, and Chair of the Black and Native American Missions Board. He serves on the Boards of The Catholic University of America; the Basilica of the National Shrine of the Immaculate Conception in Washington, D.C.; and Mount St. Mary's University in Emmitsburg.

The Cardinal is chairman of the board of Catholic Charities, the largest non-governmental agency providing assistance to the needy of Maryland. While he maintains that technology has eclipsed his pursuit of photography, his interests include art exhibits and reading history.

HOLY FAMILY CATHOLIC COMMUNITY / MIDDLETOWN

Holy Family Catholic Community in Middletown began when a small band of modern-day pilgrims gathered in the summer of 1985 to organize a mission church. The first Mass was on the Feast of the Epiphany in 1986 in Middletown High School's auditorium.

By May of 1986, there were plans to build a church, with all of the attendant fundraising and feasibility studies. Groundbreaking took place in August of 1995 with a dedication ceremony two years later.

Currently 640 families strong, the church conducts a Helping Hands Project every Christmas during which they adopt about 20 families. The pastor is Fr. J. Kevin Farmer.

Pressure on the Catholic Church from Soviet-backed governments in Eastern Europe began to ease in 1990. During that year, diplomatic ties were formed between the Vatican and Hungary, Czechoslovakia and Bulgaria.

In February of 1990, ground was broken in Poland for the "Center for Information, Dialogue, Education and Prayer" at the site of the former Nazi death camps in Auschwitz. In early December, the first Canadian-born saint – Marguerite d'Youville, 18th-century founder of the Sisters of Charity of Montreal, commonly known as the "Grey Nuns" – was canonized.

By the following year, Communism was discarded as impotent and unwanted in what quickly became known as the former Soviet Union. During the stunning, virtually bloodless changing of the guard, Pope John Paul II contacted Soviet President Mikhail Gorbachev to say he was praying for his safety. The Vatican then quickly appointed ten bishops for the Ukraine.

In one of 1991's major encyclicals, Pope John Paul II encouraged Catholics to share their faith in parts of the world where Christianity was weak and wavering.

In 1992, the year a new universal catechism was issued for the first time since the Tridentine Catechism of 1566, Cardinal Keeler was elected President of the National Conference of Catholic Bishops (NCCB) and the United States Catholic Conference. He served in both roles through 1995.

As part of his work with the NCCB, Cardinal Keeler built on a reputation for effectively building interfaith bonds. He is particularly noted for his work in furthering Catholic-Jewish dialogue and serves as moderator of Catholic-Jewish relations for the USCCB, stating that the strong and frequent declarations by Pope John Paul II for reconciliation between Christians and Jews had made him "personally aware" of the need.

In 1986, the Holy Father was welcomed at the Great Synagogue of Rome, the first time a pope had entered a Jewish house of worship since the days of Peter's reign. The next year, Pope John Paul II invited Cardinal Keeler along with other members of the International Liaison Committee of Catholics and Jews to his summer home at Castel Gandolfo. There, the pontiff spoke of his first-hand experiences with anti-Semitism in his native Poland by the Nazis. Before the war, there was a vibrant Jewish community in his childhood village, he said, along with many Jewish children who were his friends. When he returned after the war, all of the Jews were gone.

When John Paul II visited the United States in 1987, it was Cardinal Keeler, still in his role as the Bishop of Harrisburg, who arranged for the Holy Father's meetings in Miami with Jewish leaders as well as visits with Protestant 2nd orthodox authorities in Columbia, S.C. On the Los Angeles leg of that tour, the Cardinal also organized the first interfaith ceremony in the United States involving Jews, Muslims, Hindus, and Buddhists.

RABBI MITCHELL WOHLBERG
In the early 1990s Rabbi Wohlberg and Cardinal Keeler were honored in a Baltimore ceremony by the Shaarei Vedek hospital of Jerusalem.

"A Cardinal who lends his support to a Jewish hospital in Jerusalem!" the rabbi enthused.

"That is a lifetime's achievement for the Jewish people, and its been made possible because of a Cardinal Keeler - not just a prince of the Church, but to a prince of a man who has helped change the course of Christian-Jewish relations."

Through his friendship with the Cardinal, Rabbi Wohlberg - who grew up in post-World War II Brooklyn, N.Y. fearing that Christians might kidnap him and force him to convert - had the privilege of meeting with Pope John Paul II shortly before the pontiff's death.

"Intellectualism is not what [Cardinal Keeler] is about - the heart is the issue. He is somebody that can be called on at any time," said the rabbi, illustrating his point with a personal story.

"When my wife Sherry had a knee replacement at St. Joseph Hospital he came to visit her. That means so much more to me than any proclamation. If he ever has to go to Sinai [Hospital], I'll make sure he's taken care of."

Each year, Cardinal Keeler holds a retreat for members of major faiths in the conference center at St. Mary's Seminary in Roland Park. His open relationship with other families of belief was illustrated in the days after the September 11th, 2001 terror attacks against America when he held a prayer service at the Basilica at which Muslims, Jews, and all denominations of Christians participated.

Along with the National Council of Synagogues, Cardinal Keeler helped draft a response to the attacks. In part, the letter read: "We note with sorrow that some have seized on these events to suggest the futility of inter-religious conversations. We, on the contrary, see in recent events a reminder of the urgency of dialogue in order to foster mutual under-standing and respect."

Earl El-Amin, a Muslim imam who estimates there are about 45,000 followers of Islam in the Baltimore area, has worked closely with Cardinal Keeler. Their efforts have been on behalf of Islamic-Catholic issues to Muslim refugees around the globe and social issues like the spread of pornography.

"We've also worked on landmine issues in Sri Lanka and places like Angola," said Mr. El-Amin. "[The Cardinal has helped] on any topics in the Baltimore area or the world [that are] an affront to religious people."

"I consider him a friend," said Mr. El-Amin, who with Cardinal Keeler has tried to address the high rate of homicide in the Baltimore area. Abroad, their attention turned to victims of the Asian tsunami – in which local Muslims sent money through Catholic Relief Services.

■ ■ ■

"We [also] held a joint prayer vigil for the people in Darfur," said Mr. El-Amin, noting that the Islamic population in the Baltimore area in-cludes African-Americans like himself, some Africans, a significant number of Pakistanis, Arabs from various homelands as well as believers from Indonesia and Malaysia.

The prayer vigil for the Sudan, hosted by the Cardinal and Catholic Relief Services, was held at the Basilica September 21, 2004. There,

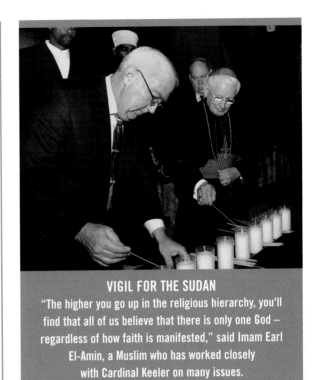

VIGIL FOR THE SUDAN
"The higher you go up in the religious hierarchy, you'll find that all of us believe that there is only one God – regardless of how faith is manifested," said Imam Earl El-Amin, a Muslim who has worked closely with Cardinal Keeler on many issues.

CRS president Ken Hackett calling the situation "the greatest humanitarian crisis facing the world today."

Also present were Jewish and Muslim leaders as well as representatives of the Ethiopian Orthodox church while the choir of St. Gregory the Great sang: "Let us fall down on our knees and pray... it is time to serve the Lord..."

Several months prior to the vigil, at the 19th World Youth Day in Rome, a teenager from the Sudan had asked Cardinal Keeler why the western world had done so little to deter the nightmare that had befallen his country. In that moment, the Cardinal decided he would begin speaking of the crisis "in every setting at my disposal."

Once, when Pope John Paul II was asked why he is so fond of young people, why he took so much time to speak with them, he said: "Because they listen."

■ ■ ■

In 1992, Cardinal Keeler initiated the Lenten Appeal, a campaign of giving through special Mass collections that in a little more than a decade has raised nearly $45 million for local Catholic education as well as help for the poor and other ministries of corporal acts of mercy.

CATHOLIC RELIEF SERVICES

CRS uses the teachings of the Gospel of Jesus Christ – and enormous amounts of love and labor and intellect - to alleviate human suffering, promote development and foster charity and justice throughout the world.

Founded in 1943 by the Catholic Bishops of the United States, CRS began by resettling European war refugees during World War II. Its mission remains focused on the poor overseas.

Operating on five continents and more than 90 countries, CRS has a parallel mission in the land of plenty: to educate the American people about their moral responsibility to the rest of the world.

Headquartered in Baltimore, Catholic Relief Services and the Archdiocese of Baltimore function as good next-door neighbors. After the organization's move to Baltimore, former Auxiliary Bishop John H. Ricard, SSJ served on the CRS Board of Directors and was chairman from 1996-to-2001.

One of the largest partnerships between the organizations is Operation Rice Bowl, the CRS Lenten program built upon prayer, fasting and giving.

In the wake of the Asian tsunami of 2004, CRS collected more than $3.8 million from parishioners in the Archdiocese of Baltimore.

"One of the enduring legacies of the earthquake and tsunami is the sense of foreboding - a palpable fear and trauma - it has left among the people," wrote Hackett in a March 2005 travel blog from Sumatra Island after a second earthquake hit Indonesia.

"As I write this, the sun has not yet risen. We don't yet know the extent of the damage caused by this latest earthquake. But we do know that a wave of fear has been unleashed, as if the residents along the ruined coastal communities are reliving the tsunami again."

CATHOLIC RELIEF SERVICES IN SUDAN
credit: Catholic Relief Services

CRS President Ken Hackett visiting a Sudanese refugee camp in Darfur in August of 2004. Hackett arrived with Bishop John Ricard and the Rev. Mike Perry of the U.S. Conference of Catholic Bishops to assess humanitarian and security conditions. At the time, more than 1.2 million people were facing threats of violence, hunger and disease.

In 1994, Roman Catholic bishops from Africa were welcomed at the Vatican for a month-long meeting – a "Special Assembly for Africa of the Synod of Bishops" called by Pope John Paul II - about the religious and social needs of Church members on the continent. By the early 21st century, Catholicism was growing at a faster rate in Africa than anywhere on the planet. Archbishop Keeler was named a member of the Synod for Africa by Pope John Paul II.

[There are an estimated 700 million people in Africa, with about 200 million of them practicing local and tribal religions. According to Vatican records, there were 2 million African converts to Catholicism in 1900. Nearly a hundred years later, that number had grown to more than 90 million.]

In the summer of 1994, Cardinal Keeler was appointed to the Pontifical Council for Promoting Christian Unity and by Thanksgiving of that year was assigned to work with the Congregation for the Oriental Churches. On Thanksgiving Day 1994, the 14th Archbishop of Baltimore was elevated to cardinal by Pope John Paul II.

[The Congregation for the Oriental Churches was established by Pope Pius IX in 1862 to work with Catholic churches in the East to insure their traditions were protected while keeping them sensitive to the canonical discipline of the larger Catholic Church.]

■ ■ ■

In 1995, the Vatican Congregation for the Doctrine of the Faith, under Cardinal Joseph Ratzinger of Germany, upheld Pope John Paul II's affirmation of Church teaching against the ordination of women. In 1995, the Holy Father visited the United States for the fourth time since his election in 1978. Organized around John Paul II's address to the United Nations during celebrations of the organization's 50th anniversary, the tour would include his first visit to Baltimore as pope.

■ ■ ■

Three days after addressing the United Nations, Pope John Paul II was welcomed to Baltimore by Cardinal Keeler and a huge

credit: Catholic News Service
Pope John Paul II and Cuban President Fidel
Castro in Cuba in 1998

crowd from all faiths and walks of life when he arrived at Camden Yards to celebrate Mass.

At the October 8, 1995 stadium service, which included participants from every parish in the Archdiocese of Baltimore, Communion was served to an estimated 50,000 people. The chalice used by Pope John Paul II to consecrate the wine was given to Baltimore Archbishop Ambrose Maréchal in 1821 by Pope Pius VII.

■ ■ ■

On November 19, 1996 in Rome, John Paul II received Cuban president Fidel Castro, who by degrees had been declaring his Communist nation no longer atheist but secular. During the visit, the pope promised to visit Cuba, which he did in January of 1998, celebrating Mass before more than 100,000 people at the Plaza of the Revolution in Havana. Among those present, according to the New York Times, was the Colombian Nobel-winning author Gabriel Garcia Marquez, author of *"A Hundred Years of Solitude,"* and a longtime friend of the Cuban president.

HOMILY OF HIS HOLINESS POPE JOHN PAUL II DURING MASS AT CAMDEN YARDS

Dear Brothers and Sisters in Christ,

Each day, the Church begins the Liturgy of the Hours with the Psalm which we have just prayed together: "Come, let us sing joyfully to the Lord" (Ps 95:1). In that call, ringing down the centuries and echoing across the face of the globe, the Psalmist summons the People of God to sing the praises of the Lord and to bear great witness to the marvelous things God has done for us. Priests, women and men Religious, and increasing numbers of lay people daily recite the Liturgy of the Hours, giving rise to a powerful mobilization of praise to God - officium laudis - to God who, through his Word, created the world and all that is in it: "In his hands are the depths of the earth, and the tops of the mountains are his. His is the sea, for he has made it, and the dry land, which his hands have formed" (Ps 95:4-5).

Not only are we God's creatures. In his infinite mercy, God has chosen us as his beloved people: "For he is our God, and we are the people he shepherds, the flock he guides" (Ps 95:7). He chose us in Christ, the Good Shepherd, who gave his life for his sheep and who calls us to the banquet of his Body and Blood, the Holy Eucharist which we are celebrating together this morning.

The Psalmist's call to hear the Lord's voice has particular significance for us as we celebrate this Mass in Baltimore. Maryland was the birthplace of the Church in colonial America. More than three hundred and sixty years ago, a small band of Catholics came to the New World to build a home where they could "sing joyfully to the Lord" (Ps 95:1) in freedom. They established a colony whose hallmark was religious tolerance, which would later become one of the cultural cornerstones of American democracy.

credit: Catholic News Service

Baltimore is the senior Metropolitan See in the United States. Its first Bishop, John Carroll, stands out as a model who can still inspire the Church in America today. Here were held the great Provincial and Plenary Councils which guided the Church's expansion as waves of immigrants came to these shores in search of a better life. Here in Baltimore, in 1884, the Bishops of the United States authorized the "Baltimore Catechism", which formed the faith of tens of millions of Catholics for decades. In Baltimore, the country's Catholic school system began under the leadership of Saint Elizabeth Ann

**PRAYING AT THE BASILICA OF
THE ASSUMPTION**
credit: CNS, Michael Okoniewski

OCTOBER 8, 1995

Seton. The first Seminary in the United States was established here, under the protection of the Virgin Mother of God, as was America's first Catholic College for women. Since those heroic beginnings, men and women of every race and social class have built the Catholic community we see in America today, a great spiritual movement of witness, of apostolate, of good works, of Catholic institutions and organizations.

With warm affection therefore I greet your Archbishop, Cardinal Keeler, and thank him for his sensitive leadership in this local Church and his work on behalf of the Bishops' Conference. With esteem I greet the other Cardinals and Bishops present here in great numbers, the priests, deacons and seminarians, the women and men Religious, and all God's people, the "living stones" (1 Pet 2:5) whom the Spirit uses to build up the Body of Christ. I gladly greet the members of the various Christian Churches and Ecclesial Communities. I assure them of the Catholic Church's ardent desire to celebrate the Jubilee of the Year 2000 as a great occasion to move closer to overcoming the divisions of the Second Millennium (cf. Tertio Millennio Adveniente, 34). I thank the civil authorities who have wished to share this sacred moment with us.

Our celebration today speaks to us not only of the past. The Eucharist always makes present anew the saving mystery of Christ's Death and Resurrection, and points to the future definitive fulfillment of God's plan of salvation. Two years ago, at Denver, I was deeply impressed by the vitality of America's young people as they bore enthusiastic witness to their love of Christ, and showed that they were not afraid of the demands of the Gospel. Today, I offer this Mass for a

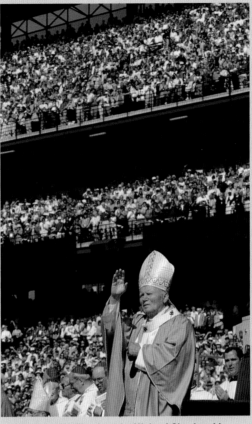

credit: CNS file photo by Michael Okoniewski

strengthening of that vitality and Christian courage at every level of the Church in the United States: among the laity, among the priests and Religious, among my brother Bishops. The whole Church is preparing for the Third Christian Millennium. The challenge of the great Jubilee of the Year 2000 is the new evangelization: a deepening of faith and a vigorous response to the Christian vocation to holiness and service. This is what the Successor of Peter has come to Baltimore to urge upon each one of you: the courage to bear witness to the Gospel of our Redemption.

In today's Gospel reading, the Apostles ask Jesus: "Increase our faith" (Lk 17:5). This must be our constant prayer. Faith is always demanding, because faith leads us beyond ourselves. It leads us directly to God. Faith also imparts a vision of life's purpose and stimulates us to action. The Gospel of Jesus Christ is not a private opinion, a remote spiritual ideal, or a mere program for personal growth. The Gospel is the power which can transform the world! The Gospel is no abstraction: it is the living person of Jesus Christ, the Word of God, the reflection of the Father's glory (cf. Heb 1:2), the Incarnate Son who reveals the deepest meaning of our humanity and the noble destiny to which the whole human family is called (cf. Gaudium et Spes, 22). Christ has commanded us to let the light of the Gospel shine forth in our service to society. How can we profess faith in God's word, and then refuse to let it inspire and direct our thinking, our activity, our decisions, and our responsibilities towards one another?

In America, Christian faith has found expression in an impressive array of witnesses and achieve-

ments. We must recall with gratitude the inspiring work of education carried out in countless families, schools and universities, and all the healing and consolation imparted in hospitals and hospices and shelters. We must give thanks for the practical living out of God's call in devoted service to others, in commitment to social justice, in responsible involvement in political life, in a wide variety of charitable and social organizations, and in the growth of ecumenical and inter-religious understanding and cooperation. In a more global context, we should thank God for the great generosity of American Catholics whose support of the foreign missions has greatly contributed to the spiritual and material well-being of their brothers and sisters in other lands.

The Church in the United States has sent brave missionary men and women out to the nations, and not a few of them have borne the ultimate witness to the ancient truth that the blood of martyrs is the seed of Christianity. In my visits to Catholic communities around the world I often meet American missionaries, lay, Religious and priests. I wish to make an appeal to young Catholics to consider the missionary vocation. I know that the "spirit of Denver" is alive in many young hearts. Christ needs many more committed men and women to take that "spirit" to the four corners of the world.

CREDIT: CNS file photo by Nancy Wiechec

Today though, some Catholics are tempted to discouragement or disillusionment, like the Prophet Habakkuk in the First Reading. They are tempted to cry out to the Lord in a different way: why does God not intervene when violence threatens his people; why does God let us see ruin and misery; why does God permit evil? Like the Prophet Habakkuk, and like the thirsty Israelites in the desert at Meribah and Massah, our trust can falter; we can lose patience with God. In the drama of history, we can find our dependence upon God burdensome rather than liberating. We too can "harden our hearts".

And yet the Prophet gives us an answer to our impatience: "If God delays, wait for him; he will surely come, he will not be late" (cf. Hab 2:3). A Polish proverb expresses the same conviction in another way: "God takes his time, but he is just". Our waiting for God is never in vain.

Every moment is our opportunity to model ourselves on Jesus Christ - to allow the power of the Gospel to transform our personal lives and our service to others, according to the spirit of the Beatitudes. "Bear your share of the hardship which the gospel entails," writes Paul to Timothy in today's Second Reading (2 Tim 1:8). This is no idle exhortation to endurance. No, it is an invitation to enter more deeply into the Christian vocation which belongs to us all by Baptism. There is no evil to be faced that Christ does not face with us. There is no enemy that Christ has not already conquered. There is no cross to bear that Christ has not already borne for us, and does not now bear with us. And on the far side of every cross we find the newness of life in the Holy Spirit, that new life which will reach its fulfillment in the resurrection. This is our faith. This is our witness before the world.

Dear Brothers and Sisters in Christ: openness to the Lord - a willingness to let the Lord transform our lives - should produce a renewed spiritual and missionary vitality among American Catholics. Jesus Christ is the answer to the question posed by every human life, and the love of Christ compels us to share that great good news with everyone. We believe that the Death and Resurrection of Christ reveal the true meaning of human existence; therefore nothing that is genuinely human fails to find an echo in our hearts. Christ died for all, so we must be at the service of all. "The Spirit God has given us is no cowardly spirit... Therefore, never be ashamed of your testimony to our Lord" (2 Tim 1:7-

8). Thus wrote Saint Paul to Timothy, almost two thousand years ago; thus speaks the Church to American Catholics today.

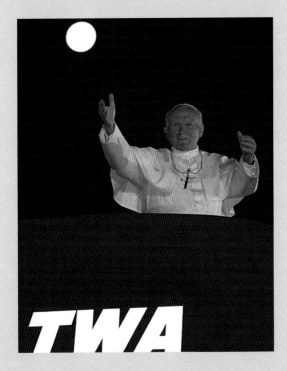

credit: Catholic News Service

Christian witness takes different forms at different moments in the life of a nation. Sometimes, witnessing to Christ will mean drawing out of a culture the full meaning of its noblest intentions, a fullness that is revealed in Christ. At other times, witnessing to Christ means challenging that culture, especially when the truth about the human person is under assault. America has always wanted to be a land of the free. Today, the challenge facing America is to find freedom's fulfillment in the truth: the truth that is intrinsic to human life created in God's image and likeness, the truth that is written on the human heart, the truth that can be known by reason and can therefore form the basis of a profound and universal dialogue among people about the direction they must give to their lives and their activities.

One hundred thirty years ago, President Abraham Lincoln asked whether a nation "conceived in liberty and dedicated to the proposition that all men are created equal" could "long endure."

President Lincoln's question is no less a question for the present generation of Americans. Democracy cannot be sustained without a shared commitment to certain moral truths about the human person and human community. The basic question before a democratic society is: "How ought we to live

together?" In seeking an answer to this question, can society exclude moral truth and moral reasoning? Can the Biblical wisdom which played such a formative part in the very founding of your country be excluded from that debate? Would not doing so mean that America's founding documents no longer have any defining content, but are only the formal dressing of changing opinion? Would not doing so mean that tens of millions of Americans could no longer offer the contribution of their deepest convictions to the formation of public policy? Surely it is important for America that the moral truths which make freedom possible should be passed on to each new generation. Every generation of Americans needs to know that freedom consists not in doing what we like, but in having the right to do what we ought.

How appropriate is Saint Paul's charge to Timothy! "Guard the rich deposit of faith with the help of the Holy Spirit who dwells within us" (2 Tim 1:14). That charge speaks to parents and teachers; it speaks in a special and urgent way to you, my brother Bishops, Successors of the Apostles. Christ asks us to guard the truth because, as he promised us: "You will know the truth and the truth will make you free" (Jn 8:32). Depositum custodi!

We must guard the truth that is the condition of authentic freedom, the truth that allows freedom to be fulfilled in goodness. We must guard the deposit of divine truth handed down to us in the Church, especially in view of the challenges posed by a materialistic culture and by a permissive mentality that reduces freedom to license. But we Bishops must do more than guard this truth. We must proclaim it, in season and out of season; we must celebrate it with God's people, in the sacraments; we must live it in charity and service; we must bear public witness to the truth that is Jesus Christ.

Catholics of America! Always be guided by the truth - by the truth about God who created and redeemed us, and by the truth about the human person, made in the image and likeness of God and destined for a glorious fulfillment in the Kingdom to come. Always be convincing witnesses to the truth. "Stir into a flame the gift of God" that has been bestowed upon you in baptism. Light your nation - light the world - with the power of that flame!

Amen.

Later, with Castro standing next to him, John Paul II said: "In our day, no nation can live in isolation. The Cuban people, therefore, cannot be denied the contacts with other peoples necessary for economic, social and cultural development, especially when the imposed isolation strikes the population indiscriminately, making it ever more difficult for the weakest to enjoy the bare essentials of decent living... food, health and education."

And then, quoting the Cuban patriot and poet Jose Marti [1853-1895], the Holy Father said: "Every people needs to be religious... an irreligious people will die, because nothing in it encourages virtue."

■ ■ ■

HENRY & GINGER BAHR

Henry and Ginger Bahr have raised four children – from left to right, Beth, Lindsay, Alexandra and Chris - in the faith and are active in various marriage preparation classes at St. Margaret. "We really believe that the family and marriage are an important part of community," said Mrs. Bahr. "There is a lot going against marriage these days. The church is an important support for it."

Henry Bahr and his wife Ginger have served as sacristans at St. Mary Magdalen for about six years. Mr. Bahr, a longtime parishioner at St. Margaret, enjoys the intimacy of St. Mary Magdalen. Every other Sunday, the couple prepares everything needed for Mass at St. Mary Magdalen, which, despite the heavy development of Harford County, still has the feel of a country church.

"It helps me spiritually and it helps me feel like part of the community and not someone who just comes for Mass and leaves," said Mr. Bahr. "I like helping people. If they ask a question and I don't know the answer, I try to find out for them."

Ginger Palermo Bahr is a cradle Catholic born in Worchester, Massachusetts. For the past 16 years, she has taught kindergarten and first grade at St. Margaret's parish school. At St. Mary Magdalen services, she said, "My students come and look for me. I believe I am teaching the future church."

ST. MARY MAGDALEN / BEL AIR

Established in 1997 as a mission of St. Margaret parish in Bel Air – a church so large that it held
14 Christmas Masses over the holiday and needed the aid of State Troopers to direct traffic –
St. Mary Magdalen is located about two miles from St. Margaret.
The church office operates out of the St. Margaret campus at 141 Hickory Avenue.

ST. GABRIEL / WOODLAWN

About the time that the Korean Martyrs congregation moved to the St. Lawrence address, the parish of St. Gabriel in Woodlawn was formed by combining the former congregation of St. Lawrence in Dickeyville and the Shrine of Our Lady of Perpetual Help, which was established as a country chapel in the village of Woodlawn in 1936. Both the St. Lawrence parish and the one at the Shrine of Our Lady of Perpetual Help, closed with special Liturgies and ceremonies on the First Sunday of Advent on November 30, 1997. Afterward, St. Gabriel – named for the archangel – was selected by ballots cast by parishioners to be the name of the new congregation. St. Gabriel Roman Catholic Church is a diverse congregation of more than 800 families serving Woodlawn and western Baltimore County. Its seven-acre campus includes the John Paul Regional Catholic Elementary school. The pastor is Msgr. Thomas L. Phillips.

In 1997, the Baltimore congregation of Korean Catholics moved from old St. Bernard's church in Waverly to the former St. Lawrence parish in Woodlawn. Known as Holy Korean Martyrs, the church honors the souls of some 20,000 Catholics and priests killed by the Korean government in a systematic persecution lasting from the late 18th century through the 1860s. Pope John Paul II beatified 103 of the martyrs in 1984.

HOLY KOREAN MARTYRS / WOODLAWN
There are currently about 450 families registered at the Holy Korean Martyrs parish. The pastor is the Rev. Joseph Kim.

OUR LADY OF LA VANG / DUNDALK

Credit: Catholic Review

Established in 2000, the Our Lady of La Vang congregation, the first Vietnamese parish in Baltimore, began with a little more than 130 families in Middle River. In 2006, with more than 300 families, the faithful worship in a sanctuary at 335 Sollers Point Road in Dundalk.

The parish is named in honor of the appearances by Our Blessed Mother near the former royal city of Hue, Vietnam in 1798. In the great tradition of immigrant churches in Baltimore, Our Lady of La Vang offers English classes for its members and others in the Vietnamese community.

ST. KATHARINE DREXEL / FREDERICK

Established in 2000 as a mission of St. John, Frederick, it became an Independent Mission in 2003. St. Katharine serves nearly 600 families and is undergoing an extensive capital campaign to pay for a new church. They share the 27-acre site with St. John Regional Catholic School. The pastor is Father Keith Boisvert.

BISHOP FRANCIS P. MURPHY

BISHOP FRANCIS P. MURPHY

The Most Rev. P. Francis Murphy was born in Cumberland in 1933 and went to St. Mary's School there. He graduated from the St. Charles high school seminary in Catonsville, earned a bachelor's degree from St. Mary's Seminary in Roland Park and then a degree in Sacred Theology from the Pontifical Gregorian University in Rome. Bishop Murphy was ordained in Rome in 1958. He died on Sept. 2, 1999.

"To listen to God speaking in Human Voices ..."
- **Episcopal motto of Bishop P. Francis Murphy**

Joyce Seng (right) and Annabel Hardin work the Bishop Murphy Memorial Rosary Garden at St. Ignatius in Ijamsville.
The garden is between the church and parish center at St. Ignatius, which has grown from about 250 families to more than 1,000 in less than five years.
"My Catholic faith is my life," said Mrs. Seng, "My husband and I have always made decisions small and large with our faith at the center ... those of us who were privileged to know Bishop Murphy loved and admired him."

Bishop Frank Murphy was known and loved as a warm-hearted man who labored for social justice and promoted the role of women in the Church. He strongly supported nuclear disarmament and campaigned on behalf of the poor and disabled.

After his ordination in Italy, Father Murphy returned to Baltimore and served as an associate pastor at St. Bernardine. He returned to Rome in 1961 and often said that his favorite memory from that time was being in St. Peter's Square on October 11, 1963 for the opening of the Second Vatican Council.

Two years later, he was appointed Papal Chamberlain with the title of Very Reverend Monsignor and took the position of Priest Secretary to Cardinal Lawrence Shehan, who played a crucial role at the Second Vatican Council.

In Baltimore, Bishop Murphy helped Cardinal Shehan implement the changes that Vatican II brought, particularly on issues relating to race and interfaith affairs.

Bishop Murphy was named Titular Bishop of Tacarata by Pope Paul VI in 1976. The honor coincided with his appointment as auxiliary bishop of the Archdiocese of Baltimore.

In 1986, he co-chaired the ninth Jewish/Christian workshop, which led to the creation of the Baltimore Institute for Christian/Jewish studies.

Bishop Frank Murphy served the Archdiocese of Baltimore as its western vicar. In that role, he ministered to Catholics in Howard, Carroll, Frederick, Washington, Allegany, and Garrett counties and co-founded Interfaith Housing of Western Maryland, which serves the rural poor.

After Bishop Murphy lost his battle against cancer in 1999, St. Ignatius Loyola of Ijamsville began a garden in his memory fashioned on the rosary.

The garden consists of five Japanese snowball trees, each representing a mystery of the rosary. A pair of horseshoe-shaped flower beds, consisting of hostas, marigolds and geraniums among others, surround each tree.

"The garden is designed to move you from mystery to mystery, a place where you can be outside in nature, but still away from it all, where you can meditate or pray the rosary," said Joyce Seng, a member of St. Ignatius who tends the garden.

The garden was the idea of parishioner Annabel Harden, who saw it as a devotion to the Blessed Mother. After Bishop Murphy's death, Mrs. Seng suggested that it be dedicated to the bishop, a beloved visitor to the parish.

In such a place, thought Mrs. Seng, people would be able to hear God speak-- as Bishop Murphy believed. He does-- through one another.

The garden, where the St. Ignatius parish time capsule was buried on Sept. 15, 2000, has taken shape slowly.

A recent First Communion class planted one of the flowers beds, with three of ten completed so far. Three stone benches are also in place. When the project is finished, a dedication service will be held.

Contributions are always welcome, said Mrs. Seng, "Gardens," she said, "are never done."

The halfway mark of a century and the last year of a century are traditionally celebrated in the Church as Jubilee years in which the faithful are encouraged to make pilgrimage to Rome. As 1999 drew to a close, the media hyped it as Y2K. In the Church, the dawn of Christendom's third millennium was hailed as "Jubilee 2000," a year in which to focus on forgiveness and reconciliation.

In response, an estimated 30 million people made their way to Rome in 2000 for a variety of jubilee activities throughout the year. Pope John Paul II launched the celebration with a symbolic opening of the Holy Door at St. Peter's Basilica – a practice dating to the year 1500 - on Christmas Eve, 1999. The ritual echoes the opening of the human heart to the Word of God.

On March 12, the Pope celebrated a Mass in which he asked forgiveness for the sins that Christians had made in the preceding millennia. In June of 2000, the Holy Father invited 200 of Rome's poor and homeless to share a meal with him. The following month more than 1,000 bikers filled St. Peter's Square with the roar of their engines during a special Jubilee service for motorcyclists. The Jubilee ended on January 6, 2001 with Mass at St. Peter's Basilica and the closing of the Holy Door.

FATHER PIOTR KONCZ
A refugee priest from Russia, the Rev. Piotr Koncz established St. Stanislaus church in 1879. He directed the building of the original sanctuary and parish school. He died in 1886.

"We went to church every morning before school and the girls had to keep their heads covered," said Kathy Garayoa Marks of her Catholic childhood.

"I always knew that when I had children I would send them to a Catholic school," said Marks, who graduated from Seton High School in 1973. "If you are educated Catholic, [chances are] your children will be.

"Catholic schools go the extra mile," she said. "In a public school, class rings are just handed out. When my son received his ring at Archbishop Curley it was performed in a beautiful ceremony with a Mass.

"...and of course, Catholic schools are able to teach religion, which I believe is essential."

Richard Marks graduated from Our Lady of Fatima before attending Archbishop Curley High School, where he finished his junior year in 2006 and was a member of the National Honor Society as well as a Franciscan scholar.

Like her brother, Rachel Marks received an 8th grade diploma from Our Lady of Fatima near the city-county line between Highlandtown and Dundalk. In 2006, she was a student at John Carroll High School, which sits on an 87-acre campus in Bel Air, Harford County.

ST. STANISLAUS KOSTKA

ST. STANISLAUS KOSTKA / FELLS POINT

St. Stanislaus Kostka parish began in 1879 in a rented row house on South Bond Street. The church was launched by the Rev. Piotr Koncz and the St. Stanislaus Kostka Benevolent Society for the hundreds of Polish Catholics in the old seamen's village.

A chapel on Ann Street was completed in 1881, and the sanctuary was completed eight years later.

The first Polish Roman Catholic parish in the Archdiocese, St. Stanislaus was closed in 2000 in the face of gentrification of the Fells Point area, and dwindling numbers of registered parishioners.

"We had an upper and lower church," said Ray Weber, who owned the funeral parlor across the street. "There were so many people that two Masses would take place at the same time.

Nearby St. Caimir welcomed parishioners from St. Stanislaus, with whom they shared a pastor in Fr. Ross Syracuse, O.F.M. Conv.

Father Conrad Miller, a Franciscan priest sometimes known as "Father Connie," was born into the old neighborhood dominated by St. Stanislaus near the beginning of the First World War.

The priest's mother, Barbara Bialek, had emigrated from Poland and his father, Martin Miller, spent his youth in Woodstock, Maryland. The couple met at St. Patrick's on South Broadway, where his mother worked as a parish housekeeper. Smitten, Mr. Miller proposed in Patterson Park.

"I grew up on Wolfe Street between Gough and Bank, there were six of us," remembered Father Conrad, born in the spring of 1914. "We only had Franciscans for teachers, priests and nuns. I'm the only one [of six siblings] who became religious."

The family lost several sons in World War II. "For the sake of my mother, I didn't want to add any more sorrow to the family," said Father Miller, and instead of joining the military he joined the seminary.

KOLEDA RITUAL

The Rev. Richard Philiposki of Holy Rosary parish blesses the Essex shore home on Muddy Gut Creek of Edward and Eleanor Rybczynski in early 2006. The custom is pronounced koh-len-dah.

The symbols, made with a piece of blessed chalk above a doorway, represent the date of the New Year and the initials of the Three Kings - Caspar, Melchior and Balthazar. The inscription also stands for "Christus Mansionem Benedicat," meaning: "Christ, bless this home."

Longtime residents of South Patterson Park Avenue before their move several years ago, Edward and Eleanor attend Mass at both Holy Rosary, where they were married and all of their ten children were baptized, and Our Lady of Mount Carmel, which is closer to their current home.

FR. CONRAD MILLER

After graduating from St. Francis high school seminary in Athol Springs, N.Y. — "it was a seminary for students from poor families and I was one of those," said Fr. Miller — the young man — entered the Franciscan Order at St. Joseph Cupertino Novitiate in Ellicott City.

From there, "I spent the next 35 years living out of a suitcase."

From the Cupertino novitiate, he went for further study at St. Hyacinth Seminary in Granby, Mass., and from there to Rome, where Father Miller was ordained in 1938. In pre-war fascist Italy he saw Benito Mussolini, the arrogant Il Duce, give speeches and on a trip to Poland, not yet invaded by Nazi Germany, he met St. Maximillian Kolbe.

A Polish priest murdered at Auschwitz, Father Kolbe traded his life for that of a fellow prisoner, Franciszek Gajowniczek, who begged for mercy because he had a wife and children. It's for Maximillian Kolbe that the former St. Casimir parish school, which merged with the St. Stanislaus and St. Leo grade schools in 1975, is named.

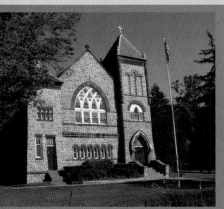

SHRINE OF ST. ANTHONY / ELLICOTT CITY
Credit: Franciscan Friars Archives

Father Miller returned to the United States before the bombing of Pearl Harbor and served in various parishes in upstate New York as well as Montreal. After the war, he began a preaching ministry that led him to parishes, missions and retreats along the Atlantic coast. Beginning in 1960, he served in parishes in Padua and Assisi, Italy as well as St. Peter's in Rome.

In 1976, Father Miller returned to the Ellicott City friary where he'd taken his vows and resumed preaching the gospel. He later moved to the Immaculate Heart of Mary Friary at Archbishop Curley High School and remained there until moving into Stella Maris in 1999 at age 85.

Although he needed a wheelchair to get around in his last few years, Father Miller spent his time at the hospice visiting other residents and helping the chaplain meet the spiritual needs of people throughout the complex.

Known for his special love of Christmas, he was known to decorate anything and everything for the holiday. Father Connie Miller died at Stella Maris in early September of 2005, some four months before what would have been his 91st Christmas.

Throughout 2002, the Holy See collected information from every diocese in the world for a 2,000 page yearbook that was eventually presented to Pope John Paul II in early 2004. According to the document, there were more than 1.07 billion Catholics in the world at the time - about 17 percent of the population of the Earth – for an increase of some 11 million over 2001. Half of those people lived in the Americas with a little more than a quarter located in Europe.

FUNERAL OF JOHNNY UNITAS
CREDIT: CATHOLIC REVIEW

A member of St. Joseph in Texas, Md. as well as the pro football Hall of Fame, mythic Baltimore Colts quarterback Johnny Unitas died of a heart attack on September 11, 2002 at age 69.

Later that week, more than 2,000 people arrived at the Cathedral of Mary Our Queen to say farewell to the man who put the National Football League on the map with the Baltimore Colts' 1958 championship victory over the New York Giants. Pallbearers for the great No. 19 were all six of his sons.

"We remember the cheers that rang out from 33rd Street, celebrating a man in black high-top shoes," said Cardinal William Keeler at the funeral Mass. "He humbly and generously dealt with everyone, whether a grandson beginning to play football or a fan seeking an autograph.

"He led and he touched others by his integrity and loyalty."

By 2002, the sexual abuse scandal within the U.S. Catholic Church had broken across the country with the discovery of widespread abuse within the Archdiocese of Boston. It was a time of sadness and outrage in which the Archdiocese of Baltimore was not spared, a period which Cardinal Keeler termed, "by far, the most difficult" of his tenure.

EXCERPTS OF A LETTER FROM CARDINAL KEELER TO THE PEOPLE OF THE ARCHDIOCESE OF BALTIMORE

September 25, 2002

Dear Friend in Christ,

In recent months, you have read, heard and seen much about the crisis in our Church regarding child sexual abuse. I want to take this opportunity, at a time when our Archdiocese is charting a new course on this disturbing issue, to write to you directly.

I, along with my fellow bishops in the Archdiocese of Baltimore, have worked to address this crime and sin since my arrival in 1989. We have strived to be diligent in removing all priests and others in the employ of the Church credibly accused of abuse. And we have reported all allegations to the appropriate civil authorities.

However, the simple, painful truth is that the Church did not go far enough to protect children from sexual abuse. After much reflection and prayer – and following a thorough review of our records, going back decades – I have decided that we must be more open and transparent in our efforts to eradicate this evil within our Church. Therefore, we are making public an accounting of priests and religious men who have served in the Archdiocese and have been credibly accused of child sexual abuse. We also are releasing an accounting of the funds expended as a result of this issue. This is part of the transparency and openness called for in the Charter for the Protection of Children and Young People approved by the U.S. bishops in Dallas.

My fellow bishops and I must respond to the violence already visited on our children by saying we are sorry. At times, we have let our fears of scandal override the need for the kind of openness that helps prevent abuse. In the past, we sometimes have responded to victims and their families as adversaries, not as suffering members of the Church. I am deeply sorry for the harm done to children entrusted to our care.

As a result, the Catholic Church in the United States has been experiencing a crisis of trust – a crisis brought on by horrible and criminal actions, and by inaction and secrecy. Our faith calls upon us as believers to forgive. But we leaders of the Church must earn forgiveness and rebuild trust by being resolute, consistent, open and accountable in our actions. We make an absolute commitment:

To protect children;
To reach out to victim-survivors of abuse;
To ensure that there is no place in ministry in our Church for those who harm children; and
To commit to the truth, reaching out to victim-survivors and preventing future abuse, with:
• Public disclosure of priests and others credibly accused of child sexual abuse,
• Public disclosure of amounts paid in counseling assistance and to settle lawsuits, and
• Public disclosure of costs associated with priests removed from ministry due to abuse.

I realize that releasing decades of information on one day may be overwhelming and disturbing to many among the faithful. I understand that transparency must be an ongoing process. Our accounting is based on what we know today, and may change based on information that comes to light in the months and years ahead. I pledge that if and when we learn more, we will report more. We will not make public any information concerning victims. However, I share the concern of some that this release of information, while intended to bring healing, could cause pain to some victims who fear that disclosing their abusers' names may bring them unwelcome attention.

Recognizing each of these realities, I have come to the conclusion that public disclosure is the right thing to do. Ultimately, there is nothing to be gained by secrecy except the avoidance of scandal. And rather than shrinking from facing this scandal – which, too often, has allowed it to continue – we must address it with humble contrition, righteous anger and public outrage. Telling the truth cannot be wrong.

I pray our actions will:
• Help provide survivors with the strength to come forward, knowing they are not alone and their Church values and believes them – so we may apologize and offer assistance.
• Help protect children by rooting out and preventing this evil – making clear that the Church will not tolerate child sexual abuse, and shining a purifying and healing light where darkness has allowed abuse to continue.
• Help remove suspicion from the priests who serve and guide our parishes and our people. They are the heart and soul of our Church, and we have no reason to believe that any among them has committed the crime of child sexual abuse.

The Church, like all institutions comprised of flawed human beings, will encounter people who do bad things. The opportunity to rise above betrayal, and continue to do good in the name of Jesus, lies in how an institution responds. If Judas' betrayal had not been confronted – and if the other 11 had not carried on in servant leadership, the Church and its centuries of good works might not exist. We each must answer evil with personal acts of holiness. While taking responsibility for the betrayal of priests who abused children – and serving those they harmed – we must rededicate ourselves to the mission and faith served by the remaining 11 apostles.

In times of scandal and drift, leaders and saints rise to renew the Church. During the years following the Reformation, one such leader, St. Francis de Sales, stepped forward to help reclaim the Church from corruption and sin. He described the scandals of his day as "the spiritual equivalent of murder." That phrase rings especially true today, in considering the harm done to children when a person they – and their parents – trust completely, abuses their trust and their faith.

Survivors of abuse, who summon the courage to testify about the damage done to their lives and their hearts, are leaders helping to renew the Church today. The priests who serve selflessly and protect consistently the souls entrusted to our care, are leaders renewing the Church today. And the many people – including clergy, religious and laity – living our mission of service to others, are leaders renewing our Church today.

We bishops have a responsibility to recommit ourselves to loving and serving the faithful. I humbly ask forgiveness for my mistakes. Please pray for me so that I may better serve.

Now, is a pivotal time for our Church. Now is the time to answer scandal with witness, service and holiness, rededicating ourselves to embody Christ on earth. We must come together, rather than turn away, in response to this terrible problem, restoring trust at every level within our Catholic community. I pray that from this pain the Church will emerge, purified and more holy. Now, please God, we must lead and we must serve.

The Archdiocese remains committed to the protection of children and has established a hotline for people to call if they suspect clergy or other church personnel of committing abuse. The number is 1-866-417-7469.

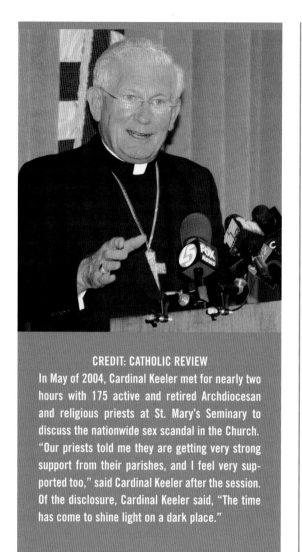

In May of 2004, Cardinal Keeler met for nearly two hours with 175 active and retired Archdiocesan and religious priests at St. Mary's Seminary to discuss the nationwide sex scandal in the Church. "Our priests told me they are getting very strong support from their parishes, and I feel very supported too," said Cardinal Keeler after the session. Of the disclosure, Cardinal Keeler said, "The time has come to shine light on a dark place."

At 14, young Richard Wojciechowski knew he wanted to be a priest. "I was involved in the church from early on and the priests and nuns made a deep impression on me," he said. "I knew that this is what I wanted to do with my life."

Though retired, Fr. Wojciechowski continues to celebrate Mass at the St. Clare parish in Essex. His faith tells him that in the future there will be more kids, like he once was who will seek ordination.

"This isn't the first time that the church faced dwindling numbers of priests," he said. "The church has been around for 2000 years and has faced everything before... vocations will come back."

Late in the summer of 2003, the Archdiocese announced the closing of Christ the King parish in the Turner's Station section of Dundalk. The final Mass at the Sollers Point road sanctuary was held August 31, 2003.

Father Richard Wojciechowski, who grew up on Gough Street, served Christ the King as its last pastor.

■ ■ ■

After attending Holy Rosary Elementary School, the East Baltimore youngster entered the St. Charles high school seminary in Catonsville and from there went to St. Mary's in Roland Park.

A priest for more than four decades, Fr. Wojciechowski has served his entire career in the Baltimore area with three assignments at Holy Rosary along with periods at St. Rita's

in Dundalk, St. Stephen's in Bradshaw, Church of the Annunciation in Rosedale, and Sacred Heart of Mary in Dundalk. A quarter-century ago, he was sent to Christ the King and remained there until it closed.

"It was a racially mixed parish and a different experience for me because of that. I enjoyed the people there very much but the parish was changing as people moved away.

"Those who stayed were older," Fr. Wojciechowski said, "but they worked very hard to keep their church open. But it was so close to St. Rita's that the Archdiocese felt that one church could see to the needs of both areas."

■ ■ ■

In November of 2003, Cardinal Keeler offered a funeral Mass at St. Clement in Rosedale for Fr. John P. Barbernitz, a Vietnam veteran and former pastor of Our Lady of Good Counsel and St. Alphonsus.

Father Barbernitz, a Highlandtown native who attended the parish school at St. Clement, served nearly a quarter-century of his career as an Army chaplain, completing two tours in Vietnam while earning a Legion of Merit award among other decorations.

In a Catholic Review interview at the time of his death, the priest's sister, Patricia Barbernitz of St. John parish in Columbia, said: "He had a special decoration for the number of hours he spent in a helicopter going to have Mass in the field... he believed that if there were any boys ready to come to Mass, they deserved to have Mass available to them."

■ ■ ■

The year 2004 was one of many anniversaries in the Archdiocese of Baltimore, including the 140th anniversary of St. Joseph Medical Center in Towson, founded in East Baltimore by three nuns from Philadelphia as St. Joseph's German Hospital in a couple of adjoining row houses on Caroline Street. Those houses, some of the earliest built in the city, were crumbling by the 1960s and St. Joseph moved to Towson in 1965. Today, the medical center is known for the largest open heart surgery program in Maryland.

In November of 2004, members of the Xaverian Brothers celebrated the 150th anniversary of their arrival in the United States from Belgium by renewing their vows at St. Ignatius Loyola church in downtown Baltimore. Earlier that fall, the Catholic High School of Baltimore on Edison Highway celebrated 65 years of Franciscan education, with more than 11,000 young women getting diplomas since 1939.

In the spring of 2004, clear, 12-foot tall glass windows - duplications of the originals designed by Benjamin Latrobe - began taking the place of nine stained glass panels installed at the Basilica of the Assumption. Removal of the stained glass, installed in the 1940s, is part of the overall restoration of the early 19th century structure on Cathedral Street, which continued into the early months of 2006.

RENDERING OF NEW ST. LOUIS / CLARKSVILLE
The parish encompasses the estate of Charles Carroll, cousin of Bishop John Carroll,
first Catholic bishop in the United States and initiator of the first cathedral.
Dedication of the new church was to take place in April 2006.

ST. PETER / LIBERTYTOWN
In early June of 2004, fire destroyed the 133-year-old Libertytown sanctuary of St. Peter the Apostle in a four-alarm blaze that is believed to have been ignited by workmen repairing the church steeple.

The fire and the effort to put it out — commanding 22 fire companies from three counties - destroyed all of the church's stained-glass windows and other objects that had survived for generations.

New construction planned by the 1,900 member congregation will result in an $8.4 million church that echoes the traditional appearance of the old sanctuary in a much larger space. The old church seated 300 people and the new one, with groundbreaking expected around Easter of 2006, is designed for more than 800.

A new daily Mass chapel will be a replica of the one that burned and the new church steeple will also look like the original, which was considered a landmark by the people of Libertytown.

"We had a solid gold cross at the top that we had put there in place of the old one," said Kate Palmisiano, a Eucharistic minister who publishes the St. Peter newsletter. "And now it's gone."

HOLY APOSTLES / GAMBRILLS

Holy Apostles in the Gambrills section of Anne Arundel County was made a parish in 2004 after five years as an independent mission.

More than 375 families belong to Holy Apostles and nearly 500 students are enrolled in the inter-parish school, which draws children from Odenton, Gambrills, Crofton, Millersville, Edgewater and Davidsonville.

The change in status means Holy Apostles is recognized canonically as a separate parish community, entitled to its own pastor.

"This is a wonderful, dynamic community - youthful, vigorous and committed to serving others. We hope to continue building up the Body of Christ and serving the Lord with joy in the years to come," said Fr. Michael Callaghan, the founding pastor. Fr. Jeff Dauses was appointed pastor in 2005.

On July 1, 2004, the former Tri-Parish Catholic Community of St. Jerome, St. Martin, and St. Peter the Apostle in West Baltimore became a single parish known as the Transfiguration Catholic Community. Together, the three historic parishes represent Baltimore Catholicism going back more than 150 years.

■ ■ ■

On August 6, 2004, Archbishop Borders celebrated noon Mass at St. Alphonsus in downtown Baltimore, on the Feast of the Transfiguration.

"The importance is that of the original Transfiguration, the tremendous help it gave Peter, James and John," the archbishop explained after Mass. "They had been close to Christ for three years and when Christ told them he was going to die, Peter especially couldn't accept it and for that reason and because of the fact that they were going to be shaken from every experience they'd had with Christ – He clearly indicated it was a divine act of Love – he reached back to Moses and Elijah, who had been dead for centuries, an insight into the eternal presence of Christ. All they had to do [afterward] was reflect back on

TRANSFIGURATION CATHOLIC COMMUNITY / WEST BALTIMORE

Mass is celebrated at each of the three churches that make up the Transfiguration Catholic Community: St. Jerome at Scott and Hamburg Streets; St. Martin at 31 North Fulton Avenue and St. Peter the Apostle at Poppleton Street near the Hollins Street Market.

In all, more than 900 families comprise the new parish. The change from "Tri-Parish Catholic Community" to "Transfiguration Catholic Community" was formally made on August 29, 2004 when Cardinal Keeler celebrated Mass at St. Martin and the congregation marched through the streets with a banner proclaiming the new name. The day ended with a barbecue in the parking lot of St. Jerome.

TRANSFIGURATION OF CHRIST
Artist: Raphael [1483-1521]
The final work of Raphael's short life, the masterpiece
that is *"The Transfiguration of the Christ"*
is an altarpiece that was left unfinished at his death.
Completed by an assistant, it hangs
in the Vatican museum.

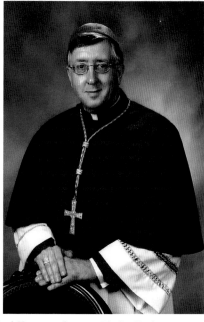

CREDIT: F. PAUL GALEONE PHOTOGRAPHERS
On August 24, 2004, Msgr. Mitchell T. Rozanski, then 46, was consecrated as a bishop at the Cathedral of Mary our Queen with Cardinal Keeler performing the ancient rite. Prior to his appointment, Bishop Rozanski, had been pastor of St. John the Evangelist in Severna Park.

The first reading, chosen by Bishop Rozanski, detailed the doubts of the prophet Jeremiah, who complained he was too young to answer the call of God. Expressing this sentiment later the new bishop said: "It is certainly an experience that I never thought would happen in my lifetime. I thank his Eminence for his trust and confidence..."

the Transfiguration for their strength... it was another evidence of the love and power of God. There are so many things we cannot control but we're never alone, regardless of what happens."

Archbishop Borders said that he ranks the Feast of the Transfiguration closely behind Easter and Christmas as one of the most important days in the Christian calendar.

In October of 2004, St. Philip Neri parish in Linthicum completed about $80,000 in renovations on the school's first floor, which was made into a new library, computer lab, rooms for art and music as well as permanent daycare. The library boasts a collection of some 10,000 books, about a third of them new. The space was made available when the parish erected a new building – named for longtime pastor, the Msgr. Francis X. Zorbach - housing a gym, cafeteria, and auditorium in 2002.

In early December, Fr. James P. Farmer, a former Baltimore City public defender who earned a law degree from Catholic University, celebrated the 25th anniversary of his ordination at St. Thomas Aquinas in Hampden. That same week, a walking cane once owned by Cardinal James Gibbons was given to Cardinal Keeler by a woman whose late husband found it in a Hampden antique store.

A walking cane once owned by Cardinal James Gibbons was donated to the Archdiocese of Baltimore by Birdie Jones whose late husband Harold Jones obtained it from a shopkeeper in Hampden several years ago. Mr. Jones, expressed his wish that Cardinal William H. Keeler be given the cane. Cardinal Keeler visited Mrs. Jones at her home, where she presented him with the cane. Cardinal Gibbons served as Archbishop of Baltimore from 1844-1921.

An inscription appears on the gold handle and reads as follows, "His Eminence James Cardinal Gibbons 1861-1886-1911 from the School of the Immaculate Conception, Towson, Maryland." The dates refer to his ordination to the priesthood, his elevation to the College of Cardinals and the 50th anniversary of his ordination to the priesthood.

SR. DOROTHY STANG

Credit: Sisters of Notre Dame de Namur

About a year after Sister Dorothy Stang's murder, a Brazilian jury convicted a pair of hired assassins in her death. A pair of ranch owners and a third man said to have orchestrated the shooting were awaiting trial in early 2006.

Witnesses said that when Sr. Dorothy realized she was about to be murdered, she pulled a Bible from her pocket and began to read the beatitudes.

"Blessed are the poor in spirit for theirs is the kingdom of heaven; blessed are those who hunger and thirst for justice, for they shall be satisfied; blessed are the peacemakers, for they shall be called children of God..."

The gunmen were said to have listened to her in silence before they opened fire.

During the week of St. Patrick's feast day in 2005, a small group of grim and determined nuns – colleagues of a fellow Sister of Notre Dame de Namur murdered in Brazil - stood witness to the martyrdom of 73-year-old Sr. Dorothy Stang at St. Ursula parish in Parkville.

Sister Dorothy was killed on Feb. 12, 2005 by hired thugs along a dirt road in Anapu, Para for trying to protect farmland from wealthy ranchers seeking to throw off the peasants who sustained themselves on it. In 2003, Sr. Dorothy sat for a long oral history with her old friend and colleague from Baltimore, Sr. Barbara Ann English, S.N.D., founder of the Julie Community Center at Washington and Lombard Streets in East Baltimore.

[Sr. Bobbie and Sr. Dorothy had founded their order's mission in Coroata, Brazil in the 1960s.]

"I have learned that faith sustains you," said Sr. Dorothy, "I have also learned that three things are difficult: as a woman, to be taken seriously in the struggle for land reform; to stay faithful to believing that these small groups of poor farmers will prevail in organizing and carrying their own agenda forward; and to have the courage to give your life in the struggle for change."

The memorial, which functioned as a lecture on the plight of poor in rural Brazil, drew several dozen people to St. Ursula, including Roberto Abdenur, the Brazilian ambassador to the United States.

Said Sister Bobbie of the work that cost Sr. Dorothy her life: "We've got to keep her issues alive... Doing things that impinge on the wealthy and powerful anywhere brings repercussions" she says.

JUST A FEW OF THE GOOD SISTERS OF BALTIMORE

"God is not solitude, but perfect communion. For this reason the human person, the image of God, realizes himself or herself in love, which is a sincere gift of self . "
Pope Benedict XVI, May 22, 2005

Each year, the Archdiocese of Baltimore passes the basket for the Retirement Fund for Religious, a collection for those who have served long and well before taking their rest.

In 2005, there are an estimated 40,000 Catholic religious in the United States over the age of 70. The appeal to help them was established in 1987 by the National Religious Retirement Office of the United States Conference of Catholic Bishops.

The Baltimore area campaign has been directed by Sr. Rosalie Murphy, S.N.D., Cardinal Keeler's delegate for those in religious life. In an interview with the Catholic Review in 2004, Sr. Rosalie likened the situation to that of the elderly throughout the United States.

"I parallel this collection with what is going on with Social Security," she said. "In years past, the giving base was larger than the receiving base. But now that earning base has been critically reduced, and there are more people who need benefits.

"...The numbers of retired religious have increased, and they are living longer and need more care while the pool of active religious has dwindled in number."

There was a day, not unlike those captured by Norman Rockwell, when physicians would tend to the religious virtually free of charge, said Sr. Rosalie; not-so-distant times when parishioners regularly donated food to religious communities and parish priests gave out Christmas bonuses.

"This is no longer happening on a large scale," said Sr. Rosalie, noting that whatever salaries the priests, brothers and nuns may make from teaching or nursing or other jobs is put into a common fund for the good of all.

SR. ROSALIE MURPHY, S.N.D.

Sister Rosalie Murphy was named by Archbishop Borders to be the first director of the Diocesan Office of Collegial Services.

In 1990, Sr. Rosalie was awarded the Pro Ecclesia et Pontifice Medal. Established by Pope Leo XIII in 1888 upon the Golden Jubilee of his priestly ordination, the medal honors those who have given significant service to the Church.

"Vatican II called on each religious order to go back to its roots and look at its origin to see if it was being faithful to the original charism of its founder," said Sr. Rosalie, still working for the Archdiocese at age 81. "The orders began to see that they were needed in different places, especially serving the poor, and not just schools and hospitals."

ORIGINAL LITTLE SISTERS CONVENT

The Congregation of the Little Sisters of the Poor was founded in 1839 in France and arrived in Baltimore, along with three other American cities, in the first years after the Civil War.

The quintet of sisters who arrived in Baltimore began with a pair of small houses on Calvert Street. The next year they moved into a new building on Valley Street, not far from St. John the Evangelist near the Maryland Penitentiary, from which they served the poor and elderly of Baltimore for the next 100 years. The building no longer exists.

In the mid-1960s, just a few years before the 1968 riots that claimed much of their old neighborhood in the 10th Ward, the Little Sisters of the Poor moved to their current home in Catonsville, dedicated to the patronage of St. Martin of Tours. The name was selected to honor Archbishop Martin Spalding, who presided over the Premier See when the congregation landed from Brittany, France in 1868.

The Little Sisters, who today number more than 3,000 members serving the elderly poor in thirty-one countries, moved to Maiden Choice Lane in Catonsville on May 25, 1969. Their mission is to bear witness to respect for life and the compassionate love and mercy of God.

At one time, they clip-clopped through the streets of Baltimore in a horse-drawn "begging wagon." Today, they drive a van, going forth as always under the guiding words of their founder, the Blessed Jeanne Jugan: "Never forget that the poor are our Lord..."

■ ■ ■

In 1964, Sr. Mary Elizabeth Gintling of the Little Sisters of the Poor, then 50-years-old, had the strong notion that she was not pursuing her true call. At the time, "Sister Mae" had been a Catholic nun for more than 20 years.

The beckoning of another road began to take hold when she visited the Cathedral of St. Peter in Chains in Cincinnati. There, Sister Mae encountered a painting of the French priest, Blessed Charles de Foucauld, living a quiet Christian witness among Muslim poor in the Saharan desert.

Details of the painting escaped her. But upon seeing de Foucauld, of whom she knew virtually nothing, Sister Mae was changed. She remembered thinking: "Why am I a Little Sister of the Poor when that's who I should belong to?"

Thus began the second major journey in the life of Sister Mae Gintling

"For some reason," she said, "I felt that I belonged to this family of Charles de Foucauld..."

■ ■ ■

"In seeking the true and the good, our contemporaries tend to prefer authentic and modest witnesses, symbols of the salvation of the human family.

That was the intuition which guided Charles de Foucauld, a great man of God, who sought to show the Gospel in a hidden, laborious way...

...in the silence which God signifies his presence as if it were a gentle breeze."
- Pope John Paul II

CHARLES DE FOUCAULD

Charles de Foucauld was a bon vivant and French Army officer born into status in Strasbourg in 1858. An agnostic, de Foucauld began his military service in Algeria in his early twenties and by 1883 was working to map oases in remote parts of Morocco.

There, while observing how Muslims lived their faith, the young officer began making a daily prayer: "My God, if you exist, let me come to know you." By 1883, he'd been transformed into a believer. A few years later he joined a Trappist monastery but soon moved to Palestine to live as a hermit.

Ordained in 1901 at age 43, de Foucauld was now back in Algeria, living the life of a lone missionary among poor, nomadic Muslims. His desire was to live with those, "the furthest removed the most abandoned" from the rest of the world.

De Foucauld was murdered by Arab bandits in an anti-French uprising on Dec. 1, 1916. His goodness, it seems, had created friendly feelings toward the hated colonizers.

Followers of de Foucauld began forming communities in Algeria in the early 1930s, calling themselves Little Brothers and Little Sisters of Jesus. They lived and worked shoulder-to-shoulder with the poor, with no overt attempts to proselytize or debate theology. Their purpose was to live simply among others as Christians.

In 1999, the Ignatius Press of Fort Collins, Colo. published a biography - Charles de Foucauld — by Jean-Jacques Antier. Virtually unknown during his lifetime. The hermit priest was beatified in Rome on November 13, 2005.

Sister Mae's call, as she understood it, was to create "a little City of God" within the harsher confines of the American city. She embarked on this ideal a year after her epiphany at the Cathedral in Cincinnati.

"Having left the Little Sisters of the Poor, where for twenty-one years she provided nursing and other medical care for the elderly, Sister Mae launched Joseph House, named for the protector of the Holy Family, in a donated row house at 2009 McCulloh Street in West Baltimore".

The project attracted lay and religious helpers from all walks of life, including seminarians; college students; dropouts; conscientious objectors to the war in Vietnam and anyone else looking to alleviate hardship in the world. No one, either those seeking help or those seeking to help, was turned away.

Before long, there was a Montessori pre-school, a soup kitchen, literacy training for adults, marriage counseling, home nursing care, and an ex-offender program in addition to emergency social services.

In 1974, Sr. Gintling met Patricia Guidera, a woman some thirty years her junior, a nurse's aide, and former Daughter of Charity who'd been volunteering at Joseph House. The pair shared a yearning to begin a vowed religious community that would minister to the poor.

Using the example of Charles de Foucauld as a guide, they embarked upon the founding of the Little Sisters of Jesus and Mary, initially made up of women who had left religious communities but remained committed to relieving the sufferings of the poor.

Their stated mission is to live by the ideals of simplicity, poverty, love for the poor, love of Jesus in the Eucharist, charity to all, and faithfulness to the Gospel and to the Church.

Seeking permission for the fledgling endeavor, they approached Bishop F. Joseph Gossman, then the urban vicar of Baltimore during the transition between Cardinal Shehan's retirement and the arrival of Archbishop Borders. The nuns told Bishop Gossman their community would serve the poor and promote social justice in a religious and contemplative spirit and the bishop gave his blessing.

After Sister Mae left the Little Sisters of the Poor, she often traveled to Berryville, Va., to make retreat at the Trappist monastery there. It was in Berryville on July 7, 1974 that Sister Mae and Sister Guidera received their habits in a simple ceremony at Holy Cross Abbey in the monastery. That date is now known as Foundation Day.

SR. M.E. GINTLING

Mary Elizabeth Gintling was born in Philadelphia in 1914 and moved to Baltimore a short time later, living in a house her father built in the steel town of Sparrows Point.

She graduated from St. Ann's parish school on East 22nd Street and in 1934 received her high school diploma from Sparrows Point High School. At the beginning of World War II, Sister Mae completed nursing studies at Mercy Hospital and worked as a public health nurse before taking vows in 1943 with the Little Sisters of the Poor. In twenty-one years with the order, she worked in nursing homes in Baltimore, Cleveland, Detroit, Louisville, Ky., and Manhattan, at times supervising the pharmacy in those locations.

In 1989, she received the Lumen Christi Award from the Catholic Extension Home Mission Society for her lifelong service to the poor. That same year, the Maryland State Senate named her a Woman of Honor.

Sister Mae – lovingly known to her fellow sisters as Mother Goose, a cheerful woman who always had a few dog biscuits in her pocket for the odd pooch that might cross her path - died at age 89 on Oct. 27, 2004 in Salisbury. She is buried there in Parsons Cemetery.

In 1978, the Little Sisters and Joseph House moved to the Eastern Shore of Maryland. They first settled in Ocean City, where their Joseph House by the Sea gift shop continues to operate; and soon moved to a hundred-year-old house in Salisbury. Both locations are part of the Diocese of Wilmington. There, the ministry began to focus on the rural poor, who are often overlooked in their poverty.

The first new postulant entered the Little Sisters' community in 1979 and in 1984 the Joseph House Center opened in an old Campbell's Soup warehouse. Refurbished with the help of local volunteers, the center offers a wide range of services. Two years later, the Bishop of Wilmington, the Most Rev. Robert Mulvee, approved the constitution of the Little Sisters of Jesus and Mary.

In 1996, the St. Joseph Cloister was established in Princess Anne as a place of quiet reflection and prayer for the Little Sisters. Five years later, a novitiate for the order also opened in the Somerset County town of Princess Anne.

■ ■ ■

In 1972, a bit worn down by her work, Sister Mae was unsure about the future of Joseph House. In October of that year, she met with Blessed Mother Teresa of Calcutta, founder of the Missionaries of Charity. Known for her work among the poorest of the poor, Mother Teresa was then in the

MOTHER TERESA IN BALTIMORE

Blessed Mother Teresa of Calcutta made three visits to Baltimore (and one to Emmitsburg) in her life beginning with a talk delivered in 1975 at the College of Notre Dame during the North Charles Street school's celebration of International Women's Year.

On her two following visits to Baltimore, she drew thousands of admirers from all faiths. The founder of the Missionaries of Charity first visited the Premier See in August of 1992 to visit her sisters' new hospice for AIDS patients, the Gift of Hope, in the former St. Wenceslaus convent at Collington and Ashland Avenues.

In late May of 1996, Mother Teresa returned to Baltimore. At the Basilica of the National Shrine of the Assumption of the Blessed Virgin Mary, she accepted the renewal vows of thirty-five of her sisters at a Mass celebrated by Cardinal Keeler. On her 1992 visit to celebrate the opening of the Gift of Hope, Mother Teresa emphasized at a Mass at St. Wenceslaus that the hospice was available to anyone. "Any man, woman or child feeling unloved with nowhere to go is welcome to come here," she said. "I have no gold or silver to give you but I'm giving you my sisters."

United States to visit one of her institute's convents in the Bronx, New York.

Was it possible, Sister Mae asked the older nun that the Missionaries of Charity might take over operation of Joseph House, then still on McCulloh Street? Mother Teresa declined but suggested that for the enterprise to be a success there needed to be a community of sisters working together under a vow of obedience to a superior.

The response rang true in Sister Mae's heart and it wasn't too much longer that she met Pat Guidera and the move toward a vowed community of religious women gained momentum.

At the Gift of Hope on North Collington Avenue, a half-dozen nuns in the simple white saris edged with blue that are the habits of the Missionaries of Charity tend to the poorest of the poor along with men dying from AIDS and other afflictions. They are helped by a handful of volunteers, including some of the area's best doctors and nurses from nearby Johns Hopkins Hospital.

They minister to the least of society's brothers and sisters, extending kindness to those whom the world has not been so very kind.

"We take care of people who come to us from prisons, from Johns Hopkins. Some are homeless and have no one, but they are all sick," said the Italian-born Sister Pietra, the convent's superior. "We nurse them back to health by giving them basic care, and we love them... some get strong enough to go out for short periods. Some get strong enough to leave, but many die."

Once loved and cared for, however, once treated with dignity for perhaps the first time in their life, the afflicted find their way to something that would surely have eluded them otherwise: a peaceful death among friends.

MISSIONARIES OF CHARITY IN BALTIMORE
Members of the Missionaries of Charity outside the Basilica of the Assumption in Baltimore during the visit of Pope John Paul II in 1995.
"Some people have never known love," said Sister Pietra, M.C. "Sometimes they don't know how to react when someone shows them love...everyone is made in the image of God...none of these transformations would be possible without him."

James was one of the first.

A medical parolee from prison suffering from the end stages of AIDS, James was brought to the Gift of Hope weak and in chains.

The sisters cleaned him and put him to bed; made sure he received his medicine and fed him. Eventually, James became well enough to spend short times away from the residence. Before long, he was back on drugs and the sisters were forced to ask him to leave.

But they couldn't forget him and soon went looking for him, learning that he had family in a nearby housing project.

While praying the rosary, two of the Missionaries of Charity and a volunteer went to the high rise building to look for James without a clue as to which of the scores of apartments he might be in. They took the elevator to the top and began working their way down, knocking on every door.

"We got onto the elevator which smelled of alcohol and urine. The apartment building, the hallways, the elevator, everything was filthy," said Sister Pietra. "When the elevator doors closed and it rose, the lights inside blinked off."

Door after door, no one apparently knew of James. Soon, the sisters began asking for him by name and on the seventh floor, they found him weak and on a couch. They asked if he was ready to go home and James said he was. Except, he said, that he owed his nephew $20. The volunteer accompanying the nuns paid the debt and James returned to the Gift of Hope.

There, he gave up drugs for good, was baptized, received Communion regularly and agreed to go to the hospital when necessary. In that last year of his life, he preached to his family about the mistakes he had made.

On his deathbed, surrounded by the Sisters who could not abandon him, he described in vivid detail the approach of the Lord Jesus coming for him.

He died about a year after that and when he did, "His face was relaxed and peaceful," said Sister Pietra. "His last words were, 'He's coming for me now.' "

■ ■ ■

And then there is the story of the Jewish liquor store mogul and the nun who loved him.

Because of the devotion they had for one another, the late Benny Rubin, a big-time spirits merchant in the glory days of downtown Baltimore and Sr. Mary Joannene of the School Sisters of Notre Dame – an endowment of some $1 million is available to send Baltimore area women to college.

"Benny was my father's very, very good friend," remembers the former Grace Merendino, whose dad was a wholesale liquor salesman who sold to Mr. Rubin's store. "I think I was the daughter he never had."

Sr. Mary Joannene, now 83, lives at her community's Villa Assumpta residence at 6401 North Charles Street. She still drives, is adamant that she has been helped on the road by angels and regularly receives middle-aged visitors who come by to thank her for the education and kindness they received from her in their schooling.

After Mr. Rubin died of prostate cancer at age 84 in 1987, the Associated Jewish Community Federation of Baltimore learned that a Jew who had never made his bar mitzvah had left almost $800,000 to endow scholarships for deserving women from all backgrounds.

Mr. Rubin's will dictated that if the Associated wanted the money, Sister Joannene, his best friend for more than a quarter-century, had to be on the board that gave the cash away.

She was the one who sat with him under a tree at the Inner Harbor on sunny afternoons, who cleaned his house when he was sick and decorated it at Christmas; she the gentle soul who held his hand and prayed for him as he died.

And Benny was the guy with the deep tan and white hair who loved the way the convent cook made short ribs, the sport who drove golf balls on the grounds of Notre Dame Preparatory while waiting for Sister Joannene to finish up so they could get some dinner.

"Everybody thinks I had something to do with Benny leaving that money," said Sr. Joannene, who taught world cultures at NDP from 1969 until her retirement. "Benny was a millionaire in the liquor business, but I didn't know what he was going to do. All I know is that he was interested in children, and he saw me so many times correcting papers."

The nun's hunch is that "this whole thing is [about] his great love of his mother. They were poor, and he was always working to take money home to Mama. I guess he didn't want other women to have to work as hard as his mother did."

At board meetings of the scholarship fund, Sister Joannene has been known to tell a room full of Jewish men and women: "I fell in love with a Jewish man, and his name is Jesus, and I thank you all for Him..."

For many years, Benny Rubin was the owner of People's Liquors at Howard and Fayette streets; a 12-hour-a-day, six-day-a-week working man who liked steak for breakfast, a glass of beer to wash it down and was known to make book on wagers before the end of Prohibition gave him new opportunity.

Mr. Rubin was a brusque, tough business man from the old school, a sport who hid a compassionate heart under a barrel chest; a character who could have come out of Damon Runyon's Corona as easily as he emerged every morning from his mother's boarding house near Greene Street to take on the world.

"His scholarship is a tribute to every Jewish mother," said Sister Joannene. "He [landed in America] a greenhorn who knew he had to fight his way through. But he always talked about Miss Irma, his third-grade teacher who hugged him when he was catching on to English."

After graduating from Poly, surviving the Depression and hustling to put together a nest egg, Mr. Rubin opened People's Liquors in 1933 and ran it for the next forty years. Margaret, his Polish Catholic wife, worked the cash register. The couple had no children.

Mr. Rubin's empathetic side, rarely shown to his business associates, was a big part of his relationship with Sister Joannene, a kid from Blessed Sacrament parish in Govans who entered the convent at 16. He had a close friendship with the girl's father, a Sicilian immigrant named Frank Merendino who sold whiskey for Standard Distillers.

"I had heard of Benny for many years before I knew him, and he had seen many pictures of me before we met," says Sister Joannene. "When daddy died in 1958, Benny kind of took his place."

As Sister Joannene moved from assignment to assignment - from orphanages in Philadelphia to high schools in New York and New Jersey - Benny stayed in touch.

"He loved the nuns, and wherever I was stationed, he was very generous. He'd say, 'Are the penguins ready for a party?' and throw us crab and shrimp feasts," remembered Sister Joannene. "He couldn't understand how we didn't have kids of our own but could have so much love for others."

She remained dear to Mr. Rubin until his dying day and more than once tried to make chicken soup the way his mother did. By the summer of 1987, Benny's time was running out. By the 21st of September, it was up.

"That day I sat down beside his bed at 5 p.m. and held his hand until ten when he died," said Sr. Joannene. "I sat there reciting the second part of the Hail Mary: 'Holy Mary, mother of God, pray for us sinners, now and at the hour of our death. Amen.'"

Credit: Notre Dame Prep.
Sr. Mary Joannene Merendino, S.S.N.D., during her teaching days at Notre Dame Preparatory School.

A week after Easter Sunday, on April 2, 2005, Pope John Paul II died in Rome. He was mourned for six days and buried in a funeral Mass beamed around the world via television. The Mass was celebrated by Cardinal Ratzinger.

"None of us can ever forget how, in that last Easter Sunday of his life, the Holy Father, marked by suffering, came once more to the window of the Apostolic Palace and one last time gave his blessing," eulogized the Cardinal. "We can be sure that our beloved pope is standing today at the window of the Father's house, that he sees us and blesses us..."

All week long, hundreds of John Paul II's fellow Poles among the millions of pilgrims who journeyed to Rome held signs proclaiming: "Santo Subito."

"Make him a saint now!"

"We lost our great father," said Diane Wisniewski during a memorial Mass celebrated at Holy Rosary Church in Canton by Cardinal Keeler. "I'm so sad that God took him from us."

The novemdiales – the nine days of official mourning – led to the conclave of cardinals that would elect Pope John Paul II's successor.

Asked how the world's cardinals would replace a man with the superstar status of John Paul, Cardinal Keeler said: "You get another person who's extremely intelligent, a great linguist...

"The best way to get continuity is to find someone who has the intellectual and spiritual capacity" the job demands.

That person would be Cardinal Joseph Ratzinger, the onetime Archbishop of Munich who from 1981 until he became Pope Benedict XVI and served Pope John Paul II as Prefect for the Congregation of the Doctrine of the Faith.

DEATH OF JOHN PAUL II

POPE REMEMBERED AT HOLY ROSARY
CREDIT: THE CATHOLIC REVIEW
A Mass in honor of the late Pope John Paul II was celebrated by Cardinal Keeler at Holy Rosary parish in Fells Point, where the late Holy Father visited in 1976 as Cardinal Wojtyla.
Concelebrating with Cardinal Keeler is Fr. Richard Philiposki, S. Ch., pastor, Holy Rosary.
Fr. Robert Jaskot, Chancellor, Archdiocese of Baltimore, is Master of Ceremonies.

Cardinal Keeler celebrates Mass in honor of the 200th anniversary of the Grotto at Mount St. Mary's Seminary & University on April 3, 2005. The Cardinal was informed shortly after the Mass that Pope John Paul II had died. Pictured with the Cardinal, from L to R: Monsignor William Parent, Executive Director for Catholic Identity & Mission; Fr. Jack Lombardi, Chaplain of the Grotto; Msgr. Stephen Rohlfs, Seminary Rector; Fr. Raymond Harris, Director of Pastoral Field Education at the Seminary.
Credit: Mount St. Mary's Seminary & University

FUNERAL OF JOHN PAUL II

CREDIT: CATHOLIC NEWS SERVICE
Pope John Paul II died in Rome on April 2, 2005 after reigning over the Roman Catholic Church for 26 years.
His funeral prompted an outpouring of grief, reverence and affection not seen in recent memory.
Up to the very end, said Cardinal William H. Keeler, the second archbishop of Baltimore to participate
in the election of a pope, there was hope that the Holy Father
would hang on for another day, another appearance, another tour,
said he Cardinal: "He'd fooled us so many times."

Of the services for one of the most beloved people in the world, Cardinal Keeler said: "I felt like the whole world was in with us… I don't think a single crowd has been assembled of such size for a funeral."

The last time Cardinal Keeler saw John Paul II was January 14, 2005 on a visit to the Vatican to attend a meeting on Christian unity. Landing in Rome, the Cardinal learned that a funeral was about to take place for his colleague from Belgium, 76-year-old Cardinal Jan Schotte.

The Pope presided over a funeral Mass for Cardinal Schotte in St. Peter's Basilica and lauded the deceased as a "man of peace," before greeting family members and other mourners. "On the Pope's way out I stood nearby as his chair went by, he certainly saw me, we didn't really speak [but] I got a nod," said Cardinal Keeler.

Asked if he'd ever had the chance to tell John Paul II what he meant to him, the Cardinal said he often brought the Pope tidings of love from Baltimore.

ELECTION OF POPE BENEDICT XVI

"...the Church is alive. And the Church is young. She holds within herself the future of the world and therefore shows each of us the way towards the future."
- Pope Benedict XVI in his inaugural address as Supreme Pontiff

CREDIT: CATHOLIC NEWS SERVICE
Pope Benedict XVI in prayer before the tomb containing the body of Pope Benedict XV. Explaining his choice of name upon his elevation as the 265th bishop of Rome, the former Cardinal Ratzinger said: "I wanted to... bind myself to the venerated Pope Benedict XV who guided the church in a troubled period because of the First World War.
"He was a courageous and authentic prophet of peace and worked with valiant courage... first to prevent the drama of war and then to limit its nefarious consequences."

Eleven American cardinals took part in the election of Pope Benedict XVI to lead the world's 1.1 billion Roman Catholics. Cardinal William H. Keeler of Baltimore was one of them.

[Along with Cardinal Gibbons, Keeler is the only Baltimore bishop to participate in the election of a pope.]

On April 17, 2005 in Rome, Cardinal Keeler offered Mass for the people of Baltimore. The conclave began the following day and the man they chose to be pope was the dean of the 115-member College of Cardinals.

Pope Benedict XVI, age 77 upon his elevation, is the son of a German policeman; an accomplished pianist with a fondness for Mozart; a scholar and author who considers his personal library a kingdom of sorts. Perceived as a somewhat lonely figure, the new pope is noted for his ability to listen whether or not he agrees with whom he is speaking.

"He reminds me of my mother, a school teacher" said Cardinal Keeler, "very sweet and clear."

As the newly installed pope, Benedict XVI was driven around St. Peter's Square as loudspeakers played Bach's Tocata and Fugue in D minor for organ. One of his first decisions was to drop the traditional three-tiered crown from the papal coat of arms and replace it with a pointed miter.

In his first homily, delivered to a crowd estimated at more than a quarter-of-a-million people, the new pope said: "The human race, every one of us, is the sheep lost in the desert which no longer knows the way... the son of God will not let this happen; he can not abandon humanity in so wretched a condition."

CREDIT: CATHOLIC NEWS SERVICE
"The pope is not a prophet," said Pope Benedict XVI several weeks after he took the throne of Peter.
"He is infallible in very rare circumstances, as we all know."

CREDIT: RICHARD LIPPENHOLZ,
PHOTOGRAPHY
The golden jubilee of Cardinal Keeler's ordination as a priest was celebrated on October 5, 2005 with more than 1,200 people in attendance at the Cathedral on North Charles Street. The crowd included fellow cardinals, bishops, priests, deacons, seminarians, religious and laity. It was also the cardinal's 25th anniversary as a bishop of the Roman Catholic Church.
After Communion was served, Cardinal Keeler told those gathered:
"I thank the Lord for my years of ministry, and I thank you for helping me celebrate the Lord's gift of the priesthood."

Back in Baltimore after the conclave, Cardinal Keeler observed the 50th anniversary of his July 1955 ordination in a fall ceremony at the Cathedral of Mary Our Queen. The following month, in late August, he ordained Monsignor Denis J. Madden the 15th auxiliary bishop of the Archdiocese of Baltimore, naming him urban vicar. A former priest-in-residence at St. Martin of Tours in West Baltimore [now part of the Transfiguration Catholic Community], the 66-year-old Madden was the first American priest named bishop in May by Pope Benedict XVI.

In the aftermath of the near Biblical flood that nearly washed New Orleans off the map when Hurricane Katrina hit the Crescent City in late August of 2005, Cardinal Keeler asked every parish in the Archdiocese to pass the basket for immediate relief and long-term rehabilitation in the Gulf Coast.

The Cardinal also encouraged local Catholics to pray for all the people of the Southern United States including the Diocese of Biloxi, where 20 percent of Catholic churches and one third of Catholic schools were destroyed.

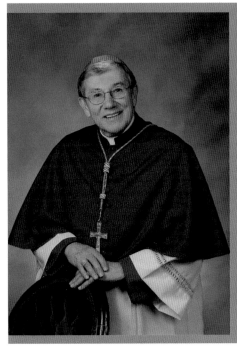

CREDIT:
F. PAUL GALEONE PHOTOGRAPHERS
A member of the Archdiocese of Baltimore since 1974, Bishop Madden is a native of Carbondale, Pennsylvania originally ordained as a Benedictine in 1967 before becoming an archdiocesan priest in 1974. He holds a doctoral degree from the University of Notre Dame in South Bend, Ind., and has used that training to work in the field of peace and reconciliation.
During his ordination at the Cathedral of Mary Our Queen, Bishop Madden said: "I will fulfill this office humbly and with great devotion."

As the people of New Orleans and southern Mississippi began to find new schools for their children, some of them landing in the Baltimore area, a new principal took the helm of Towson Catholic High School, the 84-year-old co-educational school at 114 Ware Avenue.

Susan Banks, who grew up in the Shrine of the Little Flower parish, said the small enrollment of about 300 total students allows Towson Catholic to function like a family, one in which she invited the entire school to her house for a Christmas party in 2005.

Beyond setting academic standards, the goal of the former principal at Holy Family parish school in Randallstown is to inspire students to sincere community service.

"They have so much. I think they can do more to give back to the community," said Mrs. Banks, who holds a master's degree in education from Loyola College in Maryland.

In 2005, teenagers at Towson Catholic collected funds for victims of Hurricane Katrina. When the school's bin for donated clothing was set on fire by vandals, students re-doubled their commitment to gathering up a large amount of sweaters and winter coats as well as food for the St. Vincent de Paul Christmas drive in just two weeks.

Another of Mrs. Banks' goals is to spread the word about the great value of an education at Towson Catholic.

At age 82, Ann "Nancy" Perrin is one of the more active members of Immaculate Conception in Towson, a proud Irishwoman with parental roots in Galway and a childhood spent at St. Brigid parish in Canton.

According to a 2004 Catholic Review profile written by Stefani Manowski, Mrs. Perrin's faith reveals "God [as the] center of everything...

"God is first, and then you do whatever else you have to do," she said, recalling lessons learned before she knew the catechism. "We would come downstairs in the morning, and if we dared to put on the radio, my mother would say, 'Have you said your morning prayers?'"

Mrs. Perrin graduated from Eastern High School on 33rd Street, now a campus of the Johns Hopkins Medical Center, and retired in 1989 as a credit manager for Becton Dickinson, a healthcare company headquartered in Franklin Lakes, N.J.

At age 42, the former Nancy Flaherty married Norman J. Perrin, the widowed father of an assistant pastor at St. Brigid whom she met at a church social. She was widowed in 1988 and her stepson, Fr. Norman J. Perrin, Jr., passed away in 1991.

TOWSON CATHOLIC HIGH SCHOOL
Towson Catholic began in 1922 as a parish school for the Church of the Immaculate Conception. More than 90 percent of the school's graduates go on to college after high school. Parent volunteers at Towson Catholic work in the school library and take an active part in fund-raising. The school's Campus Ministry is associated with the Archdiocesan Division of Youth and Young Adult Ministry.

For more than a dozen years now, Mrs. Perrin has volunteered at Good Samaritan Hospital as an advocate for patients. In 2004, she received a lifetime award by the Ladies Ancient Order of Hibernians, an Irish heritage organization.

■ ■ ■

When it was time to baptize the infant Nancy, the pastor at St. Brigid told her parents that "Nancy" or "Nan" – the Gaelic name for Ann – was not acceptable. Her mother reluctantly agreed for the purposes of the baptismal record but called her Nancy from the start.

Growing up in Canton in the 1930s with two brothers and a sister, the youngster learned that the neighborhood was an extended family where everyone looked after one another.

"When my mother couldn't find my brother John in Patterson Park, she knew to look for him at the rectory because he was always there doing something for the priests," Mrs. Perrin said.

Of those two brothers, John entered the seminary at St. Charles but left to marry. And her oldest brother, William J. Flaherty, was killed at age 23 in World War II.

"My parents survived but they never got over his death," she said. "My mother would always say that if he had to die at age 23, she was glad that he died serving his country."

When her sister, the late Margaret Flaherty Doyle, left home to marry, Nancy stayed to take care of her mother and father. Her mom died first and soon after her dad had a stroke and became paralyzed. To keep the house afloat, Nancy, now in her 30s, went to work.

After getting sick, her father would spend a lot of time at the local barbershop "I say he walked but he dragged his leg there," said Mrs. Perrin – to shoot the breeze with the men waiting for a haircut. If for some reason he missed a day, the barber would come to the house to make sure everything was okay.

When Mrs. Perrin went to work, a neighbor named Mrs. Duffy showed up every morning to cook breakfast for her father, continuing the ritual for nearly a decade until Mr. Perrin died.

IMMACULATE CONCEPTION / TOWSON

On December 8, 2005—the Feast of the Immaculate Conception—the Towson parish rededicated its newly renovated church with a Mass celebrated by Cardinal Keeler. The pastor is Msgr. F. Dennis Tinder.

A NEW BEGINNING

CREDIT: CATHOLIC REVIEW

On September 29, 2005, a quartet of Baltimore mayors - current Mayor Martin O'Malley along with his predecessors Kurt Schmoke, William Donald Schaefer and Thomas J. D'Alessandro III — joined Cardinal Keeler in breaking ground for a new Catholic Charities multi-purpose center built around an expanded Our Daily Bread meal room at Fallsway and East Madison Street.

Also in the autumn of 2005, ground was broken near Fallsway and Madison Street in downtown Baltimore for the new home of the Our Daily Bread soup kitchen, which has stood alongside of the Basilica on Cathedral Street since the beginning of the Reagan era in 1981.

To be known as the Our Daily Bread Employment Center, the three-story, $14 million, 52,000 square foot complex will be the first of its kind, according to Catholic Charities Executive director Harold A. Smith.

As always, guests to Our Daily Bread will receives a hot meal, part of some 250,000 plates of food Catholic Charities annually serves to the poor in Baltimore. In one way

or another, Catholic Charities serves some 160,000 people a year, asking nothing in return.

At the Our Daily Bread Center, said Mr. Smith, "We'll also offer many alternatives to life on the streets: the help to get ready to apply for a job, training and support to keep that job, and the other services they may need until they can rely on themselves."

To make that happen, the following existing programs will join Our Daily Bread in the new building: the Christopher Place Employment Academy; St. Jude's Employment Center, and the Samaritan Center for emergency services.

"She never wanted anything," said Mrs. Perrin. "I tried to give her a token of my appreciation and she started to cry. She refused, saying, 'I know you'd do the same for me.'"

"That Is how it was in Canton," she said.

■ ■ ■

Pope Benedict XVI issued his first encyclical, on January 25, 2006. Its subject: love.

"In a world where the name of God is sometimes associated with vengeance or even a duty of hatred and violence, this message is both timely and significant," the pope wrote. "For this reason, I wish in my first encyclical to speak of the love which God lavishes on us and which we in turn must share with others."

Titled *Deus Caritas Est* – "God is Love" – the letter to all Catholics and the world at large won wide praise for its lyrical understanding of human nature. Previously known as Pope John Paul II's defender of Church doctrine, the 78-year-old pope revealed himself to be a sympathetic poet.

"Love is indeed 'ecstasy,' " he wrote. "Not in the sense of a moment of intoxication, but rather as a journey, an ongoing exodus out of the closed inward-looking self towards its liberation through self-giving, and thus toward authentic self-discovery and indeed the discovery of God."

At times, the pope said, the Church has viewed sexuality as negative, writing: "Nowadays Christianity of the past is often criticized as having been opposed to the body; and it is quite true that tendencies of this sort have always existed.

"Yet the contemporary way of exalting the body is also deceptive. Eros, reduced to pure 'sex,' has become a commodity, a mere 'thing' to be bought or sold."

Rather, said the pope, erotic love between a married man and woman is actually the centerpiece of God's plan and sex should mature in a way that creates an attitude that is "less and less concerned with itself [and] increasingly seeks the happiness of the other."

Ultimately, he argued, such joy leads to a greater concern with charity and justice outside of the home.

The path leads from eros, he preached, to agape.

While gentle in approach, there was no wavering in the encyclical, however, from teachings which the pope has so vigorously defended throughout his career.

■ ■ ■

About the time of the pope's encyclical, which also included a long second section on charity begun by Pope John Paul II, Cardinal Keeler announced that Pope Benedict XVI would not be visiting Baltimore in 2006 as he had hoped.

The Cardinal had wished to have the pope, whom he has known for many years, present at the dedication of the newly renovated Basilica. Papal scheduling demands made that impossible and the new hope was for a 2007 visit by the pontiff to see the Our Daily Bread complex nearing completion.

"Most likely," said the Cardinal, "he will be able to come next year."

Gratias Agere

In the time it took me to write this sitting-around-the-kitchen-table history of the Archdiocese of Baltimore, I could have earned a divinity degree. Not that I've ever wanted one.

I got the call from Cardinal Keeler, via my Loyola College English professor, Dr. Carol "Sue" Abromaitis, over the summer of 2001. The last of the manuscript was turned in as the Orioles began spring training for the 2006 season.

In between?

Everything from washing dishes on ships at sea to flying to Strasbourg to apaiser the project's long-suffering French publisher to writing dumb scripts about poker for Hollywood.

I also signed a rider to the original contract saying that if I turned everything in

by June of 2004 a bonus would kick in. I'd been raised with the carrot-and-the-stick and, in what would become one of many sincere yet broken promises, assured everyone that the deadline shouldn't be a problem.

Hah!

By 2004, I'd only made it up to the end of the Civil War, when St. Lawrence in Jessup and St. Francis de Sales in Abingdon joined the Archdiocese and Cardinal Shehan was not yet born.

Onward I marched through 370 years of history armed with an old composition book and a single question: "Did you grow up Catholic?"

That's all it took for the puzzle to begin falling into place as one person after another told stories of relatives and playgrounds and neighbors and bull roasts, inevitably ending with: "You should talk to so-and-so."

And then they'd make a phone call on my behalf and so-and-so would offer emeralds like this one from Cornelius "Reds" Driscoll: "We lived between poverty and death."

What Reds meant was that his old 10th Ward neighborhood around St. John the Evangelist in E. Baltimore was book-ended by the convent for the Little Sisters of the Poor on one side and Greenmount Cemetery on the other.

Margaret Crogan recalled the old Tip Top Restaurant near the corner of Greenmount Avenue and Presstman Street and remembered leaving the movies reluctantly on a Saturday evening to "make a Novena where we prayed for a happy death..."

Was this book a Catholic story told through a Baltimore filter or a Baltimore story told through a Catholic filter?

Didn't matter. I couldn't lose with my magic question and its corollary - "What does it mean to be Catholic? – as they led me from Baptisms to marriages and, inevitably, the obituary page.

Which is where I encountered Dominic Guzzo, a 92-year-old steelworker who died at St. Agnes Hospital on May 14, 2005.

Born in a coal mining region of West Virginia, Mr. Guzzo moved to Baltimore in his early 20s and found steady work as a Bethlehem Steel sheet metal mechanic at Sparrows Point. He lived in a Highlandtown rowhouse and regularly took Communion at Our Lady of Pompei.

This was the kind of life I'd known about forever. My grandfather, Rafael Alvarez spent nearly 40 years down the Point as a shipyard machinist and lived off of Eastern Avenue on Macon Street from the middle of the Great Depression until his death in 1990.

And though he'd turned his back on the Catholic Church over its partnership with the fascist Franco during the Spanish Civil War, he momentarily renounced one passion for another to marry my Italian grandmother at Our Lady of Pompei during the Roaring 20s.

The part that captivated me about Dominic Guzzo was what he had done with the gift of his retirement. Where my grandfather led a fairly solitary life outside of the family after becoming a widower in 1976, Mr. Guzzo went around giving haircuts to shut-ins and driving his elderly neighbors to doctor appointments.

This is what Cardinal Keeler's Jewish friends would call a mitzvah.

And that is what it means to be Catholic.

■ ■ ■

It took so long to finish this project that time has overtaken some of the information. A few of the young people pictured among the many black-and-white portraits commissioned from Kirsten Beckerman are young men and women now. Some of the older folks have joined Dominic Guzzo on the other side and it is possible that the priest who gave the homily at your parish last week is not the one listed in the book as your pastor (though we tried to catch those).

Please forgive and please know that before the manuscript went to press it was read, in turn, by Dr. Abromaitis, who clocked me for some of the same mistakes I was making 30 years ago in her Victorian literature class, and Fr. Michael J. Roach, who teaches Church history to seminarians; and Cardinal Keeler, who proved not only an excellent historian (no surprise there), but a strict grammarian as well.

Among the many people deserving thanks are my son Jake [Mt. St. Joseph High School, 2001], who spent a month researching the chapter on Cardinal Gibbons at the New York Public Library for what amounted to minimum wage; my daughter Sofia [St. Francis of Assisi grade school, 1999], who early in the game keyboarded basic information on dozens of parishes; and my colleague Rosalia Scalia, who was never too busy to set aside her own writing to make many a last-minute phone call.

I am grateful to Ray Kempisty, the first of several archdiocesan communications directors whom the project would outlast and the man who, having read my work for the The Sun on Baltimore's Orthodox Jews in the 1990s, recommended me to Cardinal Keeler.

Sean Caine, who took over PR for the Archdiocese in December of 2003, committed to seeing the book through to publication despite numerous delays, blown deadlines and a full plate of other work at the Catholic Center. Caine also proofed the text and tracked down many of the archival photos with the help of Tricia Pyne of the Associated Archives at St. Mary's Seminary and University.

A thousand pardons and many thanks to publisher Christian Riehl, for showing me the delights of Strasbourg and, for five long years, displaying the patience of Job, even if it was only French charm.

■ ■ ■

Most of all, I am thankful to my mother, Gloria Alvarez, for taking me and my brother to Mass when we were kids. It has served me well.

Rafael Alvarez
Ash Wednesday 2006
Los Angeles

ABOUT THE AUTHOR

Rafael Alvarez graduated from St. Philip Neri parochial school in Linthicum in 1972.

In 1976, he graduated from Mt. St. Joseph High School in Irvington during the Xaverian landmark's centennial year. Four years later, he earned a degree in English from Loyola College in Maryland.

Alvarez is currently producing a documentary film on the rosary. Anyone who wishes to support or participate in the project – titled "The Great Rosary Giveaway" – should send an e-mail to: rosary@alvarezfiction.com

The author's mother, Gloria Theresa Jones, of 2729 Dillon Street, in her old Canton neighborhood at the beginning of the Second World War.
Gloria's mother, Anna, skinned tomatoes and snipped green beans in waterfront canning factories and her father, Willie, worked at the National Brewery. She graduated from St. Casimir School a year after victory over Japan and in 1953 was married at the church to Manuel R. Alvarez.
Polish through-and-through despite her maiden and married names, Mrs. Alvarez claims to have made so many indulgences in her youth that her soul had been cleansed for this lifetime and, hopefully, the next.

Index